PRAISE FOR *Murdered by Capitalism*:
A San Francisco Chronicle Book of the Year
NPR *TALK OF THE NATION* SUMMER PICK

"A ripsnorting and honorable account of an outlaw tradition in American politics which too seldom gets past the bouncers at the gateways of our national narrative."

Thomas Pynchon

"A hilarious way to learn the true down-home history of the American Left's heroic past. Bravo to John Ross!"

Lawrence Ferlinghetti

"Ross is a prodigiously gifted stylist and storyteller."

David Kipen, *San Francisco Chronicle*

"True and dubious, colorful and carrying, Ross prose breaks like a wave, a great booming salute to radicalism that is, for all its missteps, still an inspiring force. A candent, mordant tribute to left-wing America."

Kirkus Reviews (Starred)

"[Ross is a] sixty-six-year-old Huck Finn/Holden Caulfield/Dennis the Menace/Weatherman wannabe and subversive journalist who is no happier than he was in any decade of the old one. But he is in no more danger of selling out than he is of finding a buyer . . . *Murdered by Capitalism* reports what happened to both Americas, North and South, after Hugh Thomas and John Demos stopped looking, after Joan Didion left El Salvador, after NAFTA opened like an operetta to an audience of globo-cops. And Ross, a vestigial Wobbly who's been on the losing side of every cause since the Spanish Civil War, is as close as we've got to a Lapu Lapu."

John Leonard, *Harper's*

Also by John Ross

Rebellion from the Roots: Indian Uprising in Chiapas (1995)
In Focus Mexico: A Guide to the People, Politics and Culture (1996)
We Came to Play! Writings on Basketball
(editor, with Q. R. Hand, Jr.) (1996)
The Annexation of Mexico: From the Aztecs to the IMF (1998)
Tonatiuh's People: A Novel of the Mexican Cataclysm (1999)
The War Against Oblivion: Zapatista Chronicles (2002)
*Murdered by Capitalism: A Memoir of 150 Years of Life & Death on the
American Left* (2004)

Anthologized In:
Nuclear California (1984)
Third World Ha Ha Ha (1995)
The Zapatista Reader (2002)
Puro Border (2003)
Shock and Awe (2003)

Poetry Chapbooks:
Jam (1974)
12 Songs of Love and Ecocide (1977)
The Psoriacis of Heartbreak (1979)
The Daily Planet (1981)
Running Out of Coastlines (1983)
Heading South (1986)
Whose Bones (1990)
Jazzmexico (1996)
Against Amnesia (2002)

¡ZAPATISTAS!

Making Another World Possible
Chronicles of Resistance 2000–2006

John Ross

NATION BOOKS
NEW YORK
www.nationbooks.org

¡Zapatistas!:
Making Another World Possible
Chronicles of Resistance: 2000–2006

Published by
Nation Books
An Imprint of Avalon Publishing Group, Inc.
245 West 17th St., 11th Floor
New York, NY 10011

AVALON
publishing group incorporated

Library of Congress Cataloging-in-Publication Data is available.

ISBN-10: 1-56025-874-8
ISBN-13: 978-1-56025-874-2

9 8 7 6 5 4 3 2 1

Maps reprinted courtesy of Common Courage Press

Book design by *Ivelisse Robles Marrero*

Printed in the United States of America
Distributed by Publishers Group West

Table of Contents

To those who have always resisted
and to those who always will. To us.

"Entonces el rebelde en vez de angustiarse busca otros caminos para
que otro mundo sea posible."
    —Sign on the kitchen door of the Caracol That Speaks for All
during the Red Alert 2005

("Instead of anguishing, the rebel looks for other roads to make
another world possible.")

"Be a Zapatista where you are."
                              — Subcomandante Marcos, February 1994

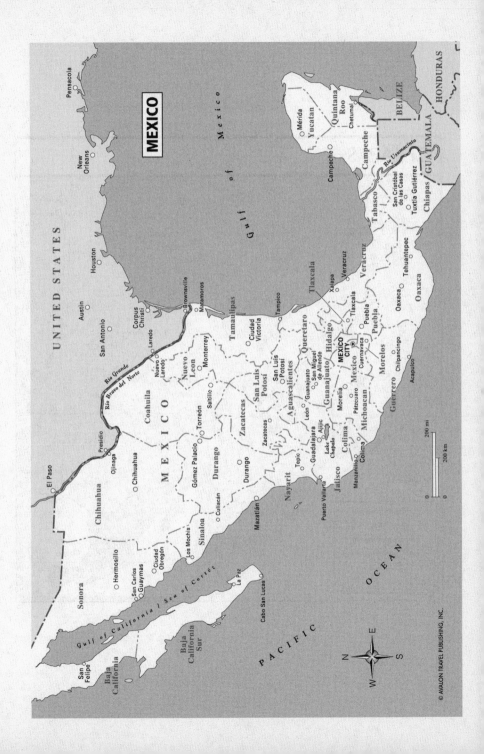

CHIAPAS

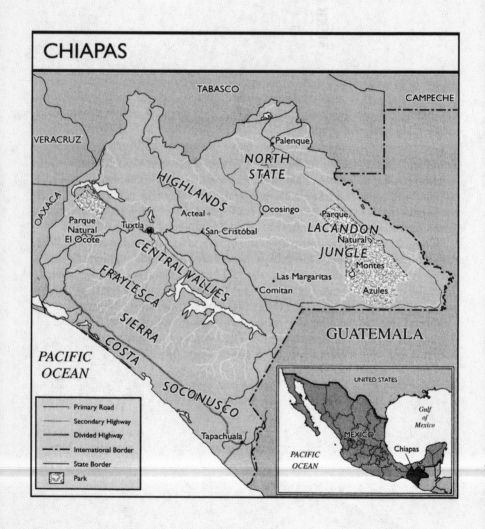

TABASCO

CAMPECHE

VERACRUZ

Palenque

NORTH STATE

HIGHLANDS

OAXACA

Parque Natural El Ocote

Tuxtla

Acteal ○

Ocosingo

San Cristóbal

Parque

LACANDON

Natural

JUNGLE

CENTRAL VALLIES

Montes

FRAYLESCA

Las Margaritas

Azules

SIERRA

Comitan

PACIFIC OCEAN

COSTA

GUATEMALA

SOCONUSCO

Tapachuala

Primary Road

Secondary Highway

Divided Highway

International Border

State Border

Park

UNITED STATES

Gulf of Mexico

MEXICO

PACIFIC OCEAN

Chiapas

Chiapas Municipalities

1. ACACOYAGUA
2. ACALA
3. ACAPETAHUA
4. ALTAMIRANO
5. AMATAN
6. AMATENANGO DE LA FRONTERA
7. AMATENANGO DEL VALLE
8. ANGEL ALBINO CORZO
9. ARRIAGA
10. BEJUCAL DE OCAMPO
11. BELUVISTA
12. BERRIOZABAL
13. BOCHIL
14. BOSQUE. EL
15. CACAHOATAN
16. CATAWA
17. CHALCHIHUITAN
18. CHAMULA
19. CHANAL
20. CKWULTENANGO
21. CHENALHO
22. CHWA DE CORZO
23. CHWILU
24. CHICOASEN
25. CHICOMUSELO
26. CHILON
27. CINTAWA
28. COAPILLA
29. COMITAN DE DOMINGUEZ
30. CONCORDIA, LA
31. COPAINALA
32. ESCUINTLA
33. FRANCI SCO LEON
34. FRONTERA COMALAPA
35. F RONTERA HIDALGO
36. GRANDEZA' LA
37. HUEHUETAN
38. HUITIUPAN
39. HUIXTAN
40. HUIXTLA
41. INDEPENDENCIA, LA
42. IXHUATAN
43. IXTACOMITAN
44. IXTAPA
45. IXTAPANG^IOYA
46. JIQUIPILAS
47. JITOTOL
48. JUAREZ
49. LARRAINZAR
50. LIBERTAD, LA
51. MAPASTE PEC
52. MARGARITAS. LAS
53. MAZAPA DE MADERO
54. MAZATAN
55. METAPA
56. MITONTIC
57. MOTOZINTLA
58. NICOLAS RUIZ
59. OCOSINGO
60. OCOTEPEC
61. OCOSOCOAUTLA DE ESPINOSA
62. OSTUACAN
63. OSUMACINTA
64. OXCHUC
65. PALENOUE
66. PANTELHO
67. PANTEPEC
68. PICHUCALCO
69. PIJIJAPAN
70. PORVENIR, EL
71. PUEBLO NUEVO SOLISTAHUACAN
72. RAYON
73. REFORMA
74. ROSAS, LAS
75. SABANILLA
76. SALTO DE AGUA
77. SAN CRISTOBAL DE LAS CASAS
78. SAN FERNANDO
79. SAN JUAN CANCUC
80. SAN LUCAS
81. SILTEPEC
82. SIMOJOVEL
83. SITALA
84. SOCOLTENANGO
85. SOLOSUCHWA
86. SOYALO
87. SUCHWA
88. SUCHIATE
89. SUNUAPA
90. TAPACHULA
91. TAPALAPA
92. TAPILULA
93. TECPATAN
94. TENEJAPA
95. TEOPISCA
96. TILA
97. TONALA
96. TOTOWA
99. TRINITARIA, LA
100. TUMBALA
101. TUXTLA CHICO
102. TUXTLA GUTIERREZ
103. TUZANTAN
104. TZIMOL
105. UNION JUAREZ
108. VENUSTIANO CARRANZA
107. VILLA COMALTITLAN
106. VILLA CORZO
109. VILLAFLORES
110. YAJALON
111. ZINACANTAN

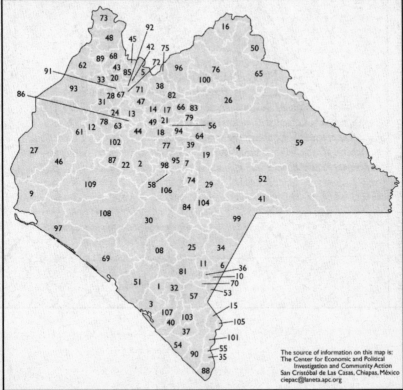

The source of information on this map is:
The Center for Economic and Political
Investigation and Community Action
San Cristóbal de Las Casas, Chiapas, México
ciepac@laneta.apc.org

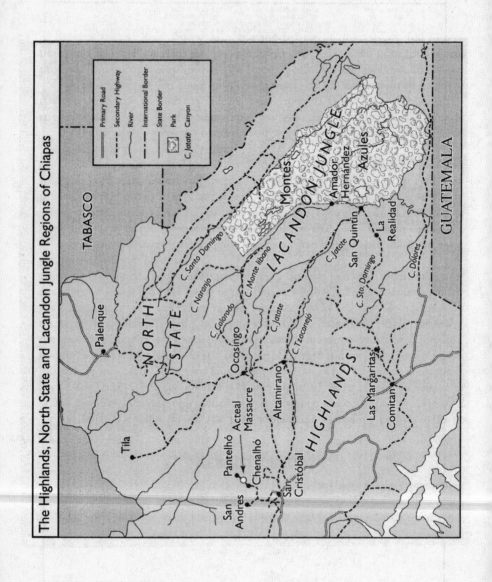

The Highlands, North State and Lacandon Jungle Regions of Chiapas

Legend:
- Primary Road
- Secondary Highway
- River
- International Border
- State Border
- Park
- C. Jatate Canyon

TABASCO

GUATEMALA

NORTH STATE

HIGHLANDS

LACANDON JUNGLE

Montes Azules

Palenque

Tila

San Andres

Pantelhó

Acteal Massacre

Chenalhó

San Cristóbal

Altamirano

Ocosingo

C. Santo Domingo

C. Naranjo

C. Colorado

C. Monte líbano

C. Jatate

C. Tzaconejó

C. Jatate

C. Sto. Domingo

C. Dólores

San Quintín

La Realidad

Amador Hernández

Las Margaritas

Comitan

Zapatisa Caracoles and Autonomous Muncipalities

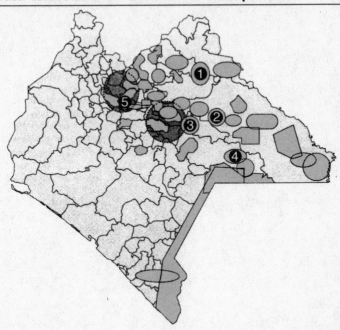

1
Name: Caracol That Speaks for All
Region: North
Junta de Buen Gobierno: New Seed That Will Fructify
Meeting at: Roberto Barrios
Autonomías: La Paz, Del Trabajo, Ak'abal Na, Francisco Villa 2, Benito Juárez, Rubén Jaramillo, Del Campesino, La Dignidad, Vicente Guerrero

2
Name: Resistance Until the New Dawn
Region: Tzeltal jungle
Junta de Buen Gobierno: Road of the Future
Meeting at: La Garrucha
Autonomías: Francisco Villa 1, Francisco Gómez, Ricardo Flores Magón, San Manuel

3
Name: Whirlwind of Our Words
Region: Altamirano area
Junta de Buen Gobierno: Heart of the Rainbow of Hope
Meeting at: Ejido Morelia
Autonomías: 17 de Noviembre, Ernesto "Ché" Guevara, Genaro Vázquez, Las Montañas, Lucio Cabañas, Miguel Hidalgo, Olga Isabel, Primero de Enero, San José en Rebeldía

4
Name: Mother of Caracoles–Sea of Our Dreams
Region: Tojalabal jungle (border area)
Junta de Buen Gobierno: Toward the Hope
Meeting at: La Realidad
Autonomías: General Emiliano Zapata, Libertad de los Pueblos Mayas, Tierra y Libertad, San Pedro de Michoacán

5
Name: Resistance and Rebellion for Humanity
Region: Highlands
Junta de Buen Gobierno: Center of the Zapatista Heart Before the World
Meeting at: Oventik
Autonomías: Magdalena La Paz, San Andrés Sakamch'én de los Pobres, San Juan de la Libertad, San Pedro Polhó, 16 de Febrero, San Juan Apóstol Cancuc, Santa Catarina

Thanks to Sigfrido of the Barcelona Colectivo de Solidaridad con los Zapatistas for the information on this map.

Preamble:
In Their Own Words

We are the Zapatistas of the EZLN, although they also call us "neo-Zapatistas." OK, well, we the Zapatistas of the EZLN rose up in arms in January 1994 because we were tired of all the evil the powerful did to us, that they only humiliated us, robbed us, killed us, and no one ever said or did anything. For all that we said "¡Basta!" that is we weren't going to permit that they treat us worse than animals anymore.

And we also said that we wanted democracy, liberty, and justice for all the Mexicans, although mostly then we were talking about the Indian peoples. Because you see, we of the EZLN are mostly Indian people from the state of Chiapas, although we don't want to struggle alone for our own good or only for the Indian people of Chiapas and all of Mexico, but also we want to fight alongside the humble and simple people who are like us and that have the same great necessities and that suffer the exploitation and the thievery of the rich and their bad governments here in Mexico and in the rest of the world.

And so our brief history is that we got tired of being exploited by the powerful and we organized to defend ourselves and fight for justice. At first we were only a few, running from one side to the other, talking and listening to other people who were like us. We did this for many years and we did it in secret without making any noise. That is we gathered our forces in silence. It took us about ten years but we began to grow and soon there were many thousands of us. So we prepared ourselves well politically and learned how to use arms and all of a sudden, when the rich were having their big New Year's Eve fiestas, well, we fell upon them in their cities and let them know that we are here, that from now on they had to take us into account.

And so we really frightened the rich ones and they sent their big armies to finish us off like they always do when those who have been exploited rebel. But they didn't come close to killing us, because we had prepared well for the war and we had strength up in our mountains. And there the army walked looking for us and giving it to us with their bullets and their bombs and making their plans to kill all the indigenous people, but they couldn't figure out who was a Zapatista and who was not. And we were running and fighting, fighting and running, just like our ancestors had done, without ever surrendering or giving up or being defeated.

And then the people in the cities went into the street and cried out that we should stop running and fighting and so we stopped the war and began to listen to these brothers and sisters of the cities. And they told us that we should try and reach an arrangement or an accord with the bad government so the problem could be resolved without any more killing. And so we listened to these people because they are like we say here the Mexicans, that is, the people of Mexico. And so we put aside the Fire and pulled out the Word.

And the result was that those who governed said, yes, they were going to behave themselves and they were going to dialogue with us and make agreements they were going to keep. And we said fine, but we also thought it would be a good idea to get to know the people who had jumped into the street to stop the war. And so while we were talking with the bad government, we were also talking with these people, common and regular people like us, humble and simple.

But of course in the end the bad government didn't want any arrangement. It was all a trick so that we would go and talk with them and make accords but at the same time, they were preparing more attacks to finish with us forever. And so then they attacked us many times but they couldn't overcome us because we resisted well and the people all over the world mobilized to stop the attacks.

And so the bad government thought the problem was that many people were watching what was going on with the EZLN, and they started a plan to make it look like nothing was happening here. And all the while, they were surrounding us, putting a fence around us so that we would withdraw into our mountains and, well, the people would forget all about us because it is really far, the Zapatista lands.

And every little while, the bad government would test us and try to trick us or attack us, like in February 1995 when they dropped soldiers from the sky upon us but still they couldn't defeat us. They couldn't defeat us because as they say, we were not alone and lots of people supported us and we resisted well.

And the bad government had to make an agreement with the EZLN and these accords were called "The Accords of San Andrés" because San Andrés is the name of the town where they were signed. And this dialogue wasn't just us talking to the bad government alone, because we invited many people and organizations that are or were in the struggle for the Indian peoples of Mexico, and all of them said their word and we agreed upon what we were going to say to the bad government. And so that was the way it was, not just the bad government on one side and the Zapatistas on the other, but with the Zapatistas were all the Indian peoples of Mexico and those who supported them.

And in these accords, the bad government said it was going to respect the rights of the Indian peoples of Mexico and their cultures and that they would put it into a law in the constitution. But of course after we signed these accords, the bad government forgot all about them. Instead the government attacked the Indians to set back their struggle on December 22, 1997. That was the date the Zedillo ordered 45 men, women, old people, and children murdered in the town in Chiapas called Acteal. This great crime cannot be easily forgotten, and it shows how the bad government will always attack and kill those who rebel against injustice. And while all this was going on, the Zapatistas were saying and saying to the bad government that they had to fulfill the accords of San Andrés. And we were resisting in the mountains of southeastern Mexico.

And then we began talking to the other Indian people of Mexico and the organizations that they have and we reached an agreement that we would march together for the same things, that is, the recognition of indigenous rights and culture. And, well, a lot of people from around the world expressed their support and so did a lot of people whose word is very respected because they are important intellectuals and artists and scientists.

And also we conducted an international survey, that is, we met to talk with people of America and Asia and Africa and Europe and Oceania and came to know their struggles and their ways. And we called these encounters "Intergalácticos" just to make a joke and because we invited those from other planets, but it seems like they didn't show up, or if they did, they didn't make it clear where they came from.

But as we said before the bad government never completed its word and we made plans to talk with as many Mexicans as we could so they would support us. And so first in 1997, we marched up to Mexico City—here they call that march the March of the 1,111 because one man and one woman from each Zapatista village went along. But the bad government didn't listen to us.

In 1999, we held a consultation with the whole country to see if the majority of Mexicans agreed with the demands of the Indian peoples but the bad government didn't listen to us again. And finally in 2001, we made what is called the March for Indigenous Dignity, which won the support of millions of Mexicans and peoples of other countries. And we arrived where the deputies and the senators are, that is the Congress of the Union to urge the recognition of indigenous Mexicans. . . .

From the Sixth Declaration of the Lacandón Jungle. The words of the Clandestine Indigenous Revolutionary Committee (CCRI)–General Command of the Zapatista Army of National Liberation. June 2005

Prologue:
What Came Before

1

Corn. *Maíz.* That is where it begins. Out there in the *milpa*, the green shoots taking root if there has been enough rain this year. The new *elotes*—the sweet kernels the farmers will roast by the side of their fields, the first fruits of the season. The hard corn of December that will be ground into *masa* for the tortillas that keep Mexico fed. *¡No hay país sin maíz!* There is no country without corn.

And in this country that cannot survive without its corn, the Mayan people are designated by their sacred texts, the Popul Vuh and the Chilam Balam, as the People of the Corn—that is to say, they were made from corn.

In Chiapas, the corn was grown on the great fincas where the Indians were bound to the owner by a feudal system of peonage that resembled chattel slavery. Land on which to grow their own corn was so limited that Indian farmers measured their holdings in rows rather than hectares. What holdings the Indians had—thanks to so-called agrarian reform— were often on mountainsides so steep they had to tie themselves to the trees to plow. The cattle ranchers ran their herds on the rich bottomland of the valleys.

Fifty years ago or so, the Mexican government had the brilliant idea of opening up the Lacandón jungle, one of Mexico's last rain forests, to landless Indian farmers and those displaced from their communities in the highlands. The *indígenas* came by the tens of thousands to this New Agrarian Frontier. Invited in by their government, they were pioneers come to form their *ejidos*, or villages organized as communal production units, clear the trees and plant their corn and coffee.

The inhospitable jungle was at first their enemy, and they cut down the precious hardwoods and sold them off for a pittance to the wood merchants and planted on the cleared land. But without the trees to nourish the soil, the land burned up, and pretty soon the *campesinos* were petitioning the government for extensions of their ejidos. Few were forthcoming and the ejidos began to form themselves into unions of ejidos to back up their demands. Radicals from the north of Mexico saw Chiapas as fertile ground in which to recruit and added their mulch to the fermentation.

By the 1970s, the destruction of the Lacandón was a glaring wound and the Mexican government was forced to yield to international pressures and put an end to the New Agrarian Frontier. Luis Echeverría, a president once responsible for the massacre of hundreds of striking students, deeded the entire forest—a million hectares—to 66 Lacandón Indian families and issued eviction orders to all other indigenous peoples living within the forest, which had traditionally been a sanctuary for beleaguered Mayan communities. The Lacandones promptly leased the jungle to the timber corporations and became Seventh Day Adventists or else just got drunk.

Then in 1978, Echeverría's successor, José López Portillo, lobbied UNESCO to declare the rain forest a protected World Biosphere site, and the military moved in to force the non-Lacandón Indians to leave. It was just then that a handful of outside agitators from the north interjected themselves into this volatile dynamic.

2

The well-kept white house at the end of the gravel driveway out in Apo-
daca looked like it might be the getaway home of an upscale Monterrey
professional, which indeed it was. Dr. Margil Yañez was a respected
physician on the outside and a dedicated revolutionist on the interior.
Along with Rosario Ibarra and her husband, Jesús, they raised funds and
provided sanctuary for urban guerrilleros in that northern industrial city
during the troubled '70s.

My colleague Raúl Rubio was then a member of a 23 de Septiembre
Communist League cell at the university—the "Liga" was notorious for
"expropriations" (bank heists) and the foiled kidnapping of a Monterrey
oligarch that resulted in his death. Under Echeverría and López Portillo, the
government waged a "dirty war" against the Liga and 15 other guerrilla *focos*
operating around Mexico in the wake of the 1968 student massacre. Many
members disappeared. Rosario and Jesús Ibarra's son, Jesús, was only one.

The Yañezes were not Liga people. They had a more ambitious plan to
build guerrilla military strength into regional armies in the north and
south of the country, a concept that drew upon the 1910–1919 Mexican
revolution in which Francisco Villa and Emiliano Zapata had joined
their rebel forces. The Forces of National Liberation (FLN) was a
Marxist-Leninist formation but not as deeply attached to the model of
the Cuban revolution as the Liga was.

Raúl threw back the iron gate just as a young caretaker came to escort
us up to the big house, now a sort of private museum. Dr. Yañez is long
dead, but his son, the EZLN's legendary Comandante Germán, is still
quite active. Another Yañez brother, "Comandante Pedro" was captured
and killed by the Mexican army near Ocosingo in the mid-1970s.

The large dining room and kitchen area was neatly preserved. A staid
portrait of Dr. Margil hung on the wall. "Give me a hand with this!" Raúl
laughed—he was pushing on an old cast-iron stove. Suddenly, the stove
rolled back into the kitchen to reveal a set of stairs descending into the
basement. "This was where they hid the comrades," Raúl explained,
striking a match to locate the light switch.

The basement was about the size of the room above, with several smaller rooms running off it that had served as the FLN's arms bunkers. Raúl pointed out a chimney that was equipped with ladder-like rungs reaching to the top, a quick escape route for FLN members when the police and military came knocking. On the walls, black-and-white photographs of FLN members were hung in cheap frames. Many of those depicted were long dead—a 1976 raid in Nepantla, Mexico state, had wiped out seven leaders.

Raúl directed my attention to one photo in particular—a group of eight young men and women kneeling in a jungle clearing, dated 1984. One smooth-faced, unmasked young man in the front row, Raúl told me, was the guerrillero they now call Marcos.

3

The interlopers from the north set up camp around Lake Miramar, one of the deep jungle's scenic wonders, and began to make contact with the local Indians—the FLN had been sending brigades to the jungle for several years, and the surrounding communities knew who they were but were not always very clear about what they wanted. The *brigadistas* spoke an odd Marxian jargon back then, and communication was not easy, concede both Subcomandante Marcos and Gloria Benavides, AKA "Comandante Elisa." "We were Marxist-Leninists armed with what we thought was the truth, but few understood what we were preaching," Elisa remembers. Indeed, the Zapatistas were every bit as much missionaries for their cause as was the bishop of San Cristóbal de las Casas, the liberation theologist Samuel Ruiz García, with whom the Monterrey group would compete for the souls of the Indians.

For several years, the Zapatista nucleus had a difficult time penetrating the communities, and then, as Marcos tells it, they met Old Antonio. In Zapatista literature, El Viejo Antonio is the teller of myths—Marcos's numerous Old Antonio stories have been anthologized and several, such as *The Story of Colors*, have been published in the United States. But the old Mayan farmer was a real person, the first to invite the Zapatistas to his community—on the condition that they would just listen, not try to convert the villagers.

The plan was that the EZLN would take the town at night. The Subcomandante tells of sneaking down the mountain and advancing silently on the center of the hamlet, where the whole village was assembled on the basketball court to welcome them.

And so the Zapatistas learned to listen. By the late 1980s, the Zapatista Army of National Liberation was more than a dream and less than a reality. Having paused long enough to hear out their hosts, the EZLN had been converted to the Indians' communitarian principles. In each of the villages in the jungles and canyons and mountains of southeastern Chiapas, it was the community assembly that was the basic decision-making body. Nothing could be decided until consensus had been reached.

One by one, like petals from a blown rose, the comrades from the north drifted off until only two of the original brigadistas were left. But the connection with the communities had been made. The EZLN began life as a sort of self-defense squad, preventing evictions from the Montes Azules biosphere in the deep jungle. In the canyons leading down to the Lacandón, the *compas* defended the communities from the depredations of the *Guardias Blancas*, the White Guards, the private armies of the ranchers who ran their cattle on the Indian land. Gradually, the EZLN acquired arms, sometimes buying them from the very same White Guards who so tormented them, whenever the ranchers distributed new weapons to their gunsels. A village would sell a cow and invest the receipts in an AK-15, which would be held collectively.

Meanwhile, the *comandantes* frequently visited the villages in the Cañadas and invited the young men and, more pertinently, the young women, up to their training camps in the sierra, where they would learn how to use weapons and also learn Spanish—not to replace their Tzeltal or Tzotzil or Tojolabal or Chol, all Mayan languages spoken in Zapatista communities, but to open up access to the larger world beyond the jungle mountains.

For the women, the camps proved to be a revolution. For the young women, often sold into forced marriages before reaching puberty, kept monolingual, and chained to the cycle of producing one baby after another, the camps represented liberation. By 1994, a third of the EZLN's fighters were women, and women held important positions in the maximum leadership body, the Clandestine Indigenous Revolutionary Committee (CCRI). Major Ana María led the celebrated takeover of San Cristóbal on January 1, 1994.

4

In 1988, the long-ruling Institutional Revolutionary Party, or PRI, lost the presidential election to Cuauhtémoc Cárdenas, son of the beloved Depression-era president, Lázaro Cárdenas. But the PRI was determined not to give up Los Pinos, the Mexican White House, so it stole the ballot boxes and burnt the paper ballots and altered the precinct tallies and even crashed the vote-counting computers for ten days following the July 6 vote. When they came back on line, former budget secretary and Harvard-trained neoliberal economist Carlos Salinas de Gortari was named president. In the few polling places in and around the zone where the EZLN was consolidating its base, every vote, as if by magic, was recorded for Salinas. It taught the Zapatistas what they had known all along: Elections could not be trusted to bring change.

The new president was determined to put his black mark on history by annexing Mexico to the United States in the shape of a free trade pact with Washington, the North American Free Trade Agreement (NAFTA), as it was about to be known. But to get there Salinas had first to put his house in order to accommodate the first George Bush.

Article 27 of the Mexican Constitution set the guidelines for land ownership, and its inclusion in the post-revolution magna carta passed in 1917 was really the accomplishment of the agrarian martyr Emiliano Zapata, the incorruptible Nahua Indian leader of the armed campesinos he had organized into the Liberating Army of the South in Morelos state.

Indeed his assassination on April 10, 1919, by the Carranza government is considered by many to be the death day of Mexico's historic revolution, the first rising up of landless peasants in the Americas.

In the Zapatista zone, their namesake is considered a demigod and his image decorates schoolhouse walls and home altars: Votan Zapata, the Guardian of the Heart of the Mayan People.

Salinas proposed an overhaul of Article 27 to pave the way for U.S. agribusiness to buy up the Mexican countryside. The ejido, along with *la comunidad* in Indian territories, were the two forms by which poor campesinos could hold land. Such land could be passed on from father to son (or daughter) but could never be sold. Now Salinas introduced reforms that would permit the ejidos to sell their land outright, or rent it or enter into "association" with national and transnational agricultural interests. And that wasn't all. The 1991–92 amendment of Article 27 put an end to the distribution of land to the landless, the abiding principle of Zapata's revolution. By canceling land distribution, Salinas drove the final nail into the revolution's coffin.

5

Corn. *Maíz*. It is always at the roots of this rebellion. In 1992–93, as corn quotas were being set by NAFTA negotiators in Washington and Ottawa and Mexico City, the Zapatistas were preparing the war. "We had no other option," Marcos explained. It was chillingly evident that NAFTA would inundate Mexico with cheap, petroleum-driven corn harvested by one man and his tractor on huge spreads that were subsidized by Washington to the tune of as much as $21,000 an acre. This flood of imports would soon drive Mexican corn, often produced on tiny five-acre plots by farmers who have to pull the plow themselves, from the internal market.

Corn to the People of the Corn represented not just a livelihood but nutrition and culture and religion and language as well. "NAFTA is a death sentence for the Indians," Marcos wrote in an early communiqué.

As we shall learn, the EZLN was tragically on the mark.

6

The EZLN moved early to foil NAFTA. At a New Year's 1993 meeting in La Sultana in the Cañadas, where so much of Zapatista history has been written, the Clandestine Revolutionary Indigenous Committee voted to declare war on the Mexican government, a seemingly suicidal gesture, but the bases could not be held back. The declaration divided the Zapatista leadership. Some, like Lázaro Hernández, a key figure in the indigenous church Bishop Ruiz was building in the San Cristóbal diocese, and Salvador Morales Garibay, "Comandante Daniel," the last brigadista to have accompanied Marcos from the north, left the organization—Daniel later became the government's star *soplón* (stool pigeon).

But for a year the declaration of war was a secret outside of the jungle and highlands of southeastern Chiapas. Even after a chance firefight with Mexican army patrols in the Sierra of Corralchén, above what is now the autonomous municipality named Francisco Gómez (La Garrucha) in May 1993, the secret was never divulged.

"These are the people who brought us pinole and tostadas in the mountains," Comandante Tacho would intone to thousands of visitors at the Zapatistas' National Democratic Convention, when Mexican civil society was invited into their rain forest for the two weekends before the August 1994 presidential elections, the first face-to-face meeting between the two. As the Zapatista bases marched silently past the great podium, Tacho told the crowd: "These are the people who kept the secret."

7

In a previous volume, *The War Against Oblivion* (Common Courage Press, 2001)—the title is a free translation of what the EZLN calls its "*guerra contra el olvido*"—I told the story of the Zapatista rebellion season by season, because seasons are the most coherent time blocks through which to chronicle a rebellion of Mayan farmers, and then grouped those seasons into distinct times. The Time of the Secret (November 1984–January 21, 1994) was the first.

The Time of the Talking Guns (January 1, 1993–April 10, 1995) was a compact and dizzying chapter in Zapatista history, in which events followed upon events so quickly that we reporters could barely report them and the EZLN's fate often hung in the balance. The drama unfolded after the rebels, as they say in the Sixth Declaration, "fell upon the rich at their big New Year's fiestas." The taking of seven municipal or county seats in southeastern Chiapas was not without cost. Fifty fighters were lost in Ocosingo after being trapped in the public market by the army. As many as 450 more, almost all of them civilians, may have been killed in the first 12 days of the fighting before 100,000 marched into Mexico City's great Zócalo plaza to demand that Salinas call off the army's advance into the jungle.

Negotiations in Bishop Ruiz's cathedral followed, but the assassination of PRI presidential candidate Luis Donaldo Colosio in Tijuana in late March so unnerved the EZLN that it called off consultations with its bases over a series of pledges that the "*mal gobierno*" (bad government) promised would make life better for the Indians. Rather than entrust their fate to Salinas and the mal gobierno, the Zapatistas convoked the National Democratic Convention deep in the jungle.

Although the Zapatistas did not support Cuauhtémoc Cárdenas, the leader of Mexico's electoral left, they did back crusading newspaper editor Amado Avendaño for Chiapas governor in a vote held the same day as the presidential election. And when fraud prevailed at the polls, the rebels warned new president Ernesto Zedillo, a PRIistas like the rest of them, that if Avendaño were not sworn in as governor in December, the war would begin again. Which it did.

On December 18, 2004, the EZLN broke through the army's encirclement of their jungle bases and established 39 autonomous municipalities that swore allegiance to the rebels, mostly in the highlands.

The next day, the Mexican economy collapsed, the peso lost half its value against the dollar, and the nation plummeted into its steepest economic decline since 1932. Zedillo, who had only been in office a little over two weeks, immediately blamed the crash on Zapatista destabilization, an explanation laughed at in international finance circles. Nonetheless, the collapse threatened Washington's grand plans for Mexico, and Bill Clinton and the World Bank cobbled together a $30 billion USD rescue package, the first installment of which was due on February 8, 1995. The loan would be paid back in Indian blood, Marcos predicted.

On February 9, the president appeared on national television to unmask Marcos as a onetime university professor and order the military back into the Lacandón to capture the EZLN leadership. Once again, the civil society chanting *"Todos somos Marcos"* ("We are all Marcos") filled the capital's Zócalo plaza, and support for the Mayan rebels ran so high that the Mexican congress was forced to pass legislation ordering Zedillo to open a dialogue with the Zapatistas.

8

The Time of the Armed Word lasted from April 10, 1995, through January 11, 1997. For 22 months, both sides would glare at each other across a table in a building on a corner of the plaza in a highland town named San Andrés Larraínzar on government maps and Sakamch'én de los Pobres on the Zapatistas'. In the white caves near the rugged mountaintops above Sakamch'én, the Tzotzil people—the people of the *tzotz* or "bat"—had first drawn their breath.

To everyone's amazement, after months of snarling and snapping, on February 16, 1996, the comandantes and the representatives of Zedillo reached an agreement on Indian rights and culture that would have granted all 57 Mexican Indian nations limited autonomy over every aspect of their lives—agrarian policy, the exploitation of natural resources, the environment, their own justice system, education and health, and the way in which they elected their own authorities, but the agreement would never be translated into law. Instead, Zedillo vetoed the accords his own representatives had signed, on the pretext that it would allow the Indians to secede from Mexico. We are Mexicans, the Mayans insisted, but we want to be Mexicans on our own terms.

Zedillo's veto killed the dialogue—there was nothing left to discuss. On January 11, 1997, the comandantes rode off into the mountains above the jungle outpost with the haunting name of La Realidad (The Reality), and Mexico did not hear from them for the next year and a half.

9

The Time of Silence and Blood (January 11, 1997–July 15, 1998) was a terrible skein. Bolstered by the rebels' quiescence, the army encouraged paramilitary formations to terrorize Zapatista communities under a Chiapas Strategy Plan for developing counterinsurgency forces in all municipalities where the EZLN had influence—the plan was implemented by a general trained at the Center for Special Warfare in Fort Bragg, North Carolina, in low-intensity warfare.

The Chiapas Strategy Plan took its most chilling pound of flesh on December 22, 1997, when paramilitaries opened fire on Zapatista sympathizers who had taken refuge at Acteal in the highlands—49 women, children, unborn children, and old men, all members of a grouping of devout Catholic farmers called Las Abejas, or "The Bees," were massacred that terrible day. The unborn babies were cut out of their mother's wombs.

Soon the military was once again marching into Zapatista villages and the women would meet them with sticks and stones and force them off the land. Pedro Valtierra's prizewinning photograph of the resistance in X'oyep says more about this rebellion than any book I could ever write. Later, the mal gobierno would send troops and police to tear down the autonomous municipalities, and ten more were butchered at San Juan de la Libertad/El Bosque on June 10, 1998. During this difficult period, 400 non-Mexican solidarity workers were deported from the country as the Zedillo government tried to close down the zone to prying foreign eyes.

The Time of Reconciliation and Resistance (July 15, 1998–January 2000) was a brief breath of affirmation in the rebel continuum. The EZLN sought to form alliances with workers and students and other Indians in struggle all around the country, and in March 1999 held a national referendum on the moribund Indian Rights Law, in which

2,000,000 Mexicans voted to make it the law of the land, but still the mal gobierno would not budge. As 2000 dawned, the upcoming presidential elections dominated all political discourse and the EZLN once again lapsed into silence. "Elections," they wrote, "are not our time."

10

Zapatistas: Making Another World Possible, Chronicles of Resistance 2000–2006 carries this history into an uncertain future. During these past six years, bookended as they are by Mexican presidential elections, the world has been visited by the bloody crusades of the second Bush and aggressive retaliation by Islamic militants. In Latin America, the neoliberal machine ran out of steam and the pendulum has swung back to the left. Although the Zapatistas live far away from these events and were in fact marginalized by them, they heard the story of worldwide horror and resistance—the Fourth World War—unfold on their transistor radios and in the daily newspapers that occasionally reached their villages, and they responded. In this globalized world, many have grown tired of being victimized by the evil wrought by the powerful few and have banded together across traditional boundary lines to fight back. As the poet says, my veins do not end in me.

Among other goals, the current volume seeks to translate the Zapatistas' vision of these tumultuous and ultimately hopeful years as they looked out on a world that would never be the same as it was when their lonely rebellion began.

This book is once again divided into seasons and times—the Time of the Fox, the Time of Autonomy, the Time to Move On. The title, of course, derives from the cry that has served the antiglobalization movement since the battle of Seattle. In a very real sense, the struggle of the Zapatista Army of National Liberation over the past six years has been a dramatic and inspiring effort to make this possibility a reality.

Book One

The Time of the Fox

1. Summer/Fall 2000

What Is to Be Done?

The stunning defeat of the PRI in the July 2, 2000, presidential elec-tion ended seven decades of a "perfect dictatorship" that controlled the lives of the Mexican people from the cradle to the grave, looted the economy and the nation's resources, kept the masses in unspeakable poverty, demanded their votes at election time, and savagely repressed those who dared to stand up to the party's arrogance. But rather than unbridled joy, the defeat of the longest-ruling political dynasty in the known universe must have stirred up mixed emotions in the jungle mountain camps above the village of La Realidad, where the Coman-dancia of the Zapatista Army of National Liberation was then ensconced.

Indeed, the PRI had been the only government they and their fathers and their fathers' fathers before them had ever known. They had declared their war against the *PRI gobierno*, fought it tooth and nail for six years. Now the PRI gobierno was about to be replaced by an even more flaming neoliberal named Vicente Fox, the candidate of the right-wing, tradi-tionally Catholic and anticommunist National Action Party (PAN) founded by conservative bankers in 1939 to confront the "Bolshevik" intentions of President Lázaro Cárdenas.

Fox, once the director of Coca-Cola operations in Mexico and Central America and now Mexico's first-ever opposition president, had proved himself a master huckster, mounting a U.S.–style campaign replete with negative hits and wall-to-wall TV spots assembled under the mindful eye of Dick Morris, the PR whiz and self-confessed toe fetishist who had steered Bill Clinton into a second term in the White House. But Dick Morris was not the reason the Mexican people voted up Vicente Fox. After seven decades of magnum abuse and bullshit, they had had enough, and Fox was just a convenient excuse to dump the PRI.

The impact of Fox's victory cannot be overblown. Political gurus likened the PRI's defeat to the fall of the Berlin Wall. Washington spun Fox's victory as if democracy had magically taken root south of the border, purposefully forgetting that for 71 years it had overlooked the outrages of the PRI, an aggregation of thugs it never failed to commend for bringing democracy to Mexico in exchange for a free hand in pillaging the nation's natural resources and keeping dread communism at bay. Similar salutations of glee at the long-awaited democratization of Mexico radiated from the European Union and the former dictatorships farther south.

But in the mountains above La Realidad, Fox's victory carried ominous baggage. The Zapatista Army of National Liberation is, as its name suggests, an armed organization, that is, it supports the armed option. Although in recent years the EZLN's best weapon has been its words, the tension between *El Fuego* (The Fire) and *La Palabra* (The Word) had been their rebellion's best defense.

Moreover, the Zapatistas loathed the political parties for corrupting and dividing Indian communities, and they rejected elections as being a meaningful measure of real democracy. Fox's victory strengthened the electoral option, deceiving people into believing that true change can come from the ballot box.

In a nation that suffers grievously from an imperial presidency, voting for a new *tlatoani* (Aztec kingmaker) like Fox was grossly self-defeating,

Subcomandante Marcos suggested in a mid-June communiqué. "Infamy, insult, and banal gossip" had characterized the campaigns, and the Sup warned that mass media, not the Mexican electorate, was selecting the new president.

The Zapatistas had been silent for much of the electoral season—"elections are not our times," they wrote and signed out for six months save for the June 19 comunicado that also predicted no matter who won, the PAN or the PRI, the *mal gobierno* would use the election as a pretext to wipe out the EZLN.

Even though the comandantes had given their supporters the green light to vote if they thought it made a difference, disdain for the candidates was palpable. The compas on the Ejido Morelia had returned 19,000 pesos in Procampo farm subsidies designed to cadge their votes, and there was patent indignation in La Realidad, reported Hermann Bellinghausen, the diligent *La Jornada* correspondent, because the PRI was dangling 500 pesos each before hungry farmers (July is the hungriest month) in return for their votes.

Despite the momentous events sweeping Mexico, the EZLN's only comment on the outcome of the elections, or for that matter on any subject whatsoever, was no comment. The days ticked by, July melted into August, and there was still no word from the *compañeros* in the celebrated mountains of the Mexican southeast.

PRI—RIP

As might be anticipated, the trauma of losing a presidential election for the first time in modern Mexican history plunged the PRI into dark depression. Founded in 1928 by strongman Elías Calles to bring troublesome regional parties into the big tent of the post-revolution, the Official Party (it had various sets of initials before it became the Institutional Revolutionary Party) was consolidated under Lázaro Cárdenas in the 1930s when a corporate structure that included farmers, workers, business, and the military was installed to run the show. But after World War II, the business sector devoured the PRI, and the revolution institutionalized itself as the scions of the generals franchised out the wealth of the nation.

So long as the people were fed and could find a job, the PRI had a free ride. But by the 1960s, growth was shrinking, the income divide widening, and the masses restless for change. When a PRI president— Gustavo Díaz Ordaz—unleashed the military to murder hundreds of striking students in downtown Mexico City on October 2, 1968, the shit hit the fan and guerilla armies blossomed throughout the Mexican landscape. During the 1970s, the mal gobierno waged a "dirty war" against armed insurrection, most perniciously in Guerrero state, where Lucio Cabañas and his Party of the Poor roamed the sierra.

The roof fell in 1982 when oil prices collapsed and Mexico went into default on 100 billion dollars of loans from the international banking community. Bailed out by the IMF, the next three PRI presidents— Miguel de la Madrid, Carlos Salinas, and Ernesto Zedillo—were Ivy League–trained free market economists who annexed Mexico to Washington's interests and left the people dispirited and disconnected.

Ernesto Zedillo, an inflexible globophile (he now heads Yale University's Globalization Studies program) was the worst of the bunch. During his presidency, he had presided over economic collapse, widespread corruption, the exponential expansion of the narco trade, three bloody massacres, and the ruthless persecution of the Zapatistas. On July 2, he became the first PRI president to preside over his party's defeat. The dinosaur, if not demised, was at least critically wounded.

The last PRI president had infuriated the party rank and file by conceding victory to Fox on election night even before Francisco Labastida, the institution's inept standard-bearer, could make his concession speech. Now the faithful were howling for Zedillo's expulsion from the PRI. "Nos llevó a la chingada" (more or less, "he brought us to the big fucking"), a hastily called council of notables cursed. Mass desertions to the PAN on the right and the Party of the Democratic Revolution (PRD) on the left were anticipated. There were cracks in the PRI-run House of Labor: Víctor Flores, the thuggish leader of the rail workers union, literally prostrated himself at Fox's feet on election night. Now PRI Security was combing the party's monolithic skyscrapers on north Insurgentes in the heart of the capital, shredding incriminating documents and wiping out hard drives.

In addition to its damaged image, the PRI was broke. The campaign budget, inflated by $110 million USD purloined from PEMEX, the national oil conglomerate, and laundered through the oil workers' union into Labastida's coffers, had run dry, and massive lay-offs added to the general gloom and doom pervading party headquarters. Row after row of office cubicles were evacuated and the upper floors went dark. At the stout iron gates in the courtyard below, fractious power groups battled each other for control of the premises, and out in the provinces the factions were going nose to nose over the bones of the party. The most egregious violence took place in Chimalhuacan, a misery belt slum on the edge of the capital, where 14 were stabbed or shot to death and 67 wounded as two PRI bands, one led by "La Loba" (The She-Wolf), Guadalupe Buendía, and the other by a gang of goons hiding behind the insignia of Antorcha Campesina (Farmers' Torch), squared off over control of the local garbage dump.

Yet when the dust of defeat had lifted, the PRI proved not so dead after all. The Institutionals maintained skinny majorities in both houses of congress, and by browbeating and bullying the smaller parties into submission could still get its way. For the next six years, the PRIistas would bottle up every single piece of legislation Vicente Fox sent them.

The big loser really had been the leftish Party of the Democratic Revolution (PRD), which saw its congressional delegation reduced to 60 in a 500-member Chamber of Deputies. Its presidential candidate Cuauhtémoc Cárdenas, now a three-time loser, had garnered just 17% of the popular vote, and it looked like 2000 would be his Last Hurrah as the moral leader of the Mexican left. His successor: the feisty Tabasco state militant Andrés Manuel López Obrador, who had just been elected Mexico City mayor, albeit by a narrow margin, over Santiago Creel, whom Fox would soon appoint as the nation's new interior secretary.

The PRD had been decimated by what the Foxistas tagged *el voto útil*, the useful vote, i.e., Cárdenas-doesn't-have-a-chance-so-you-might-as-well-vote-for-someone-who-can-turn-the-PRI-out-of-office. Civil society, which usually gravitated leftward, saw the light and rectified. The result was that Fox beat the PRI by 2,000,000 votes and put a deep hurt on the PRD.

Fifteen Minutes

The victor was a lanky pseudo-rancher from the fertile *bajío* (lowlands) of Guanajuato, whose family had made a fortune freezing winter vegetables for the gringos. A maverick who had dropped out of graduate school to drive a Coca-Cola route, he had risen rapidly to become president of the soft drink titan's Mexican operation before cashing in his chips to plunge into politics, twice winning the governorship of Guanajuato (the PRI stole it away once) before the PAN fingered him as their presidential candidate.

Fox's Coca-Cola roots had made him an indefatigable marketer. He sold himself just like he sold his product, barnstorming the country in his trademark cowboy boots (the family owned the factory), big silver belt buckle, and bushy *bigotes* (mustache), stomping out the PRI varmints. Vicente Fox positioned himself as the candidate of *la gente decente* (the decent people), and his zealous Catholicism (he actually wrapped himself in the banner of the Virgin of Guadalupe) greatly offended the anti-Church Jacobins in the PRI and the PRD.

Fox's flamboyance and deeply personal style also offended his fellow PANistas, a staid bunch who never quite trusted him but tolerated his candidacy because he was their only ticket to Los Pinos.

As a salesman, Vicente Fox was a Mexican Og Mandino, reportedly his favorite author. For months in the run-up to July 2, the PAN candidate boasted that he would "fix Chiapas in 15 minutes," a very Warholian time frame. But what Fox meant by "fixing Chiapas" was open to interpretation. The grand plan offered by this ranchero with a ranchero's mind-set (underage Indian workers toiled on his plantation) seemed to rest on elevating the indígenas of Mexico into the middle class via micro-credits that would allow them to open a *changarro* (street stand to sell Chiclets to other poor Indians) and buy a *vochito* (Volkswagen Bug) and a *tele* (television set.)

In the long run-up to actually taking office, the president-elect repeatedly affirmed that he would meet with Subcomandante Marcos and fix things right up. Contacts had already been established with the Zapatista Comandancia, Fox spokesperson Rodolfo Elizondo bragged, but the contacts, a certain "Comandante Arcadio" and "Clandestine Director Felipe," turned out to be bogus. Notwithstanding, the incoming president appointed 85-year-old PAN patrician Luis H. Alvarez as his personal representative in Chiapas to follow up contacts. Alvarez, who became peace commissioner for Chiapas when Fox was sworn in December 1, spent the entire *sexenio* (six-year term) motoring through Chiapas without ever meeting a single EZLN commander.

So the rains poured down upon the jungles and mountains of Mexico's southeast, filling the ravines with white water, swelling the muddy rivers, and growing the *maíz* tall and green out in the milpas (cornfields). The compas listened and waited, although the promises of the Fox must have been met with smiles of derision. The 15 minutes came and went. Nothing changed.

¡Pablo!

Chiapas is the first state following the *presidenciales* to elect a governor. The governorship of Chiapas is hardly a steady job—the state has had a whopping 197 governors in its 183-year history—five alone in the six years since the Zapatistas went public. Some governors have been revolutionary heroes like General Belisario Domínguez. Some have been bloody tyrants like General Absalón Domínguez Castellanos, whom the Zapatistas once arrested and tried for his pillage of Indian lands and lives and then pardoned so that he might live the rest of his days with the shame of knowing he had been pardoned by the very people he had so humiliated. Most had just been bad governors.

Perhaps the worst of them was Roberto Albores Guillén, a substitute governor for a substitute governor appointed by Zedillo in the dark days after the Acteal massacre (his predecessor Julio Ruiz Ferro, who must have had prior knowledge of that tragedy, was bounced upstairs to the Mexican embassy in Washington, D.C., as an "agricultural attaché").

Known universally to the Zapatistas and their sympathizers as "Croquetas" (an allusion to his croquet-shaped physique), Albores was a vengeful persecutor of the EZLN, destroying three autonomous municipalities—Tierra y Libertad, Ricardo Flores Magón (where a Zapatista muralist was arrested and imprisoned for a year), and San Juan de la Libertad, where ten were killed in a furious exchange of gunfire between Albores's state police and EZLN sharpshooters.

When chastised for his caveman tactics by the left daily *La Jornada*, Albores Guillén would send his agents into the streets of the state capital, Tuxtla Gutiérrez, to confiscate the offending edition. He once pressured the San Cristóbal de las Casas municipal council to declare premiere actress Ofelia Medina, a longtime EZLN backer, persona non grata, and issued arrest orders for any striking student at the national university (UNAM) who inadvertently crossed the state line into Chiapas. Up to his ears in kickbacks, three members of Albores's cabinet have subsequently been charged with such crimes as illegal enrichment.

Given this sleazy dossier, Croquetas was a natural ally for Roberto Madrazo, the outgoing governor of Tabasco next door, a politician legendary for electoral intrigue, who already had his eye on the PRI's 2006 nomination. Having lost out to Labastida in 2000, Madrazo now proposed to use the turmoil churned up by his rival's defeat to take over the party.

Albores Guillén was a small pawn in Madrazo's chess game. Like a good PRIista, he had delivered Chiapas for Labastida in the presidenciales, one of the few states the PRI won. Although he had other ideas about who his successor should be, Croquetas kowtowed to Madrazo and endorsed the

Tabasco governor's *gallo* (rooster), a colorless political hack of Lebanese descent, Sami David David, most recently a PRI senator, whose most endearing quality was that he just followed orders.

David David's opponent was also a senator and a PRIistas, albeit a former one, Pablo Salazar Mendiguchía (Basque blood pulsed in his veins.) Known to Chiapanecos simply as Pablo, Salazar was an evangelical Presbyterian (in Chiapas there are such things), but this hadn't prevented him from striking up a warm relationship with the now-emeritus bishop of San Cristóbal, Samuel Ruiz, the *"Tatic"* (father.)

As the first president of the COCOPA, the congressional commission that had overseen 22 months of ultimately foiled negotiations between the EZLN and the mal gobierno, Pablo had borne a key responsibility for framing the San Andrés Accords in legislative language the Zapatistas could agree with. Salazar quit the PRI in 1999 after Zedillo vetoed the accords. Although not at all a booster of the "EZeta," he had learned in his years on the periphery of the conflict, much as Vicente Fox would soon understand, that challenging the Indian rebels was like poking a sharp stick into a very active hornet's nest.

Pablo would run under the nonpartisan banner of "The Alliance for Chiapas," a knockoff of Fox's "Alliance for Change," and a coalition of PANistas, PRDistas, and disaffected PRIistas, who didn't look at all comfortable together.

As is the rule in Chiapas, the race was ugly. David David campaigned with the bloody ex-governor General Absalón up there on the podium. Pablo was exposed as lying about his license to practice law. Sami may or may not have been gay but he was viciously attacked for being so. Up in Soyaló, angry Pablo supporters conked the PRI candidate with a flurry of stones, putting him out of commission for days.

Pablo, meanwhile, sought to be all things to all people, promising favors that he could never hope to deliver in exchange for endorsements, even reportedly cutting a deal with the vicious PRI paramilitary with the unlikely name of "Development, Peace, and Justice," pledging to cut loose their imprisoned leader, Samuel Sánchez, in exchange for their votes. Just days before the election, Sánchez's boys had evicted 31 pro-Zapatista families at gunpoint in El Paraíso outside Yajalón.

Violence was augured in the August 20 forecast. Prominent observers poured into Chiapas to oversee the vote, among them Rigoberta Menchú and Don Samuel himself, returned home to San Cristóbal for the first time since he had been so unceremoniously retired by the Vatican.

Pablo's people assured the press that the Zapatistas would turn out in big numbers for their candidate on August 20, but it sure didn't look that way on election morning. Hermann and I jammed down the Cañadas in the battered old jeep *La Jornada* gives him to tool around the jungle. We were looking for voters. At La Garrucha, the public center of the autonomous municipality called Francisco Gómez, a religious procession was in progress and the young women were primping for the afternoon dance. The *chavos* were, as always, clustered around the town basketball court. Chickens scratched the mud at our feet. There wasn't a voter in sight.

Similarly, back down the Cañada at San Miguel, a single volunteer observer from Santa Cruz, California, had not counted a voter all day. Cruising through Ocosingo, we spoke with voters lined up in the plaza, serious Tzeltales who did not want to say the name of the person they were going to vote for—such reticence usually translates to an anti-PRI vote, i.e., Pablo. Salazar had gone into election day with a 20-point edge in some polls.

A pair of judicial police agents tailed us in a commandeered taxi as we headed north out of town. In such situations, surveillance should not be taken lightly—Mississippi Burning is not all that far from Ocosingo. But as we sped toward Chilón, the agents braked and U-turned back to Ocosingo. I suppose they already figured the PRI's goose was cooked and hassling two itinerant journalists wasn't going to turn back the tide.

Up by Chilón, there were the usual complaints of "pregnant" (stuffed) ballot boxes in PRI-dominated precincts. At least one ballot box in a pro-Pablo polling place had been torched, but Salazar was kicking ass. This time around, Chiapanecos were not going to be bamboozled into voting the PRI up—the Fox factor was at work. By the time we drove back up to San Cristóbal, the bottle rockets were popping off and the marimbas pinging. Hundreds were partying in the town square waving *chelas* (cold beers) and honking horns: "¡*Pablo!* ¡*Pablo!*"

As had transpired just 50 days previous, when the PRI lost a country it had never lost before, now the once-ruling party had lost Chiapas, and that too had never happened before.

While Salazar's victory narrowed as the night wore on—he took 52% of the vote, 57,000 votes ahead of David David, who petulantly refused to concede. On the other hand, the PRI retained 11 out of 12 federal districts, a majority in the state congress, and most of the 117 municipal presidencies in the state.

Nonetheless, the political landscape had been irrevocably altered. The PRI no longer occupied Los Pinos. It no longer held the governor's mansion down in Tuxtla Gutiérrez. "An epidemic of democracy has arrived in Chiapas," grudgingly acknowledged Carlos Herrerra, who has grown old covering the Zapatista rebellion for *Cuarto Poder,* a PRI scandal sheet published in the state capital.

The Zapatistas' silence drove the pundits nuts. Marcos was obligated to respond to the wave of democracy that was sweeping the republic. *El Cambio* (The Change) had come and the EZLN had better get on board, a fresh start with a new president! After all, the rebels had declared war upon a PRI-run government and Fox was a whole new ballgame. Talks could begin immediately—Pablo would be a perfect broker!

"The Zapatistas will now turn in their guns and disappear," astutely predicted Carlos Tello Díaz, great-grandson of the dictator Porfirio Díaz, whose book *Rebellion in the Cañadas,* based on Mexican intelligence files, "exposed" the EZLN as Marxist-Leninist dupes. Six years later, the Zapatista Army of National Liberation has adamantly refused to disappear.

In response to all these overtures being tendered by those who never were their friends anyway, the silence from the jungle was deafening. Some, however, heard what the Zapatistas were saying quite clearly. "They are speaking," counseled Miguel Alvarez Gándara, once Don

Samuel's personal secretary, who managed the Church-run mediation body, the CONAI during 22 months of negotiations. "What they are saying by their silence is that they have no confidence in the political process. They will wait and see."

Uncle Sam's Mexican Election

The election season was hardly done with. The next showdown would unfold under swaying palm trees in a swampy southern state where alligators, mostly of the political persuasion, are a mainstay of the tropical ecosystem. This outing would feature a governor who considered the candidate to be his brother, a call-up of the state police to keep darker-skinned voters away from the polls, spoiled ballots and foiled ballot counts, cybernetic chicanery, a court-ordered recount that went on and on for a month after election day, the disputed "victory" of the governor's "brother" by the narrowest of margins, and even the eventual intervention of the nation's supreme court. Sound familiar?

The Tabasco gubernatorial election took place October 15, three weeks before the *fracaso* in Florida. Outgoing governor Roberto Madrazo threw the weight of the state behind his handpicked successor, Manuel Andrade, a roly-poly specimen he often referred to as his "brother." Andrade's opponent was Raúl Ojeda, like so many candidates posted by the purportedly left-wing PRD, an ex-PRIistas miffed at his party because he didn't get kingmaker Madrazo's nod. When Andrade was declared the winner by a few hundred contested votes, some saw it as being the last flail of the dinosaur's tail. Unlike in the U.S., Mexico's supreme electoral tribunal, the TRIFE, ultimately voided the vote and ordered new elections.

The U.S. *presidenciales* held on November 8 have earned a well-deserved asterisk in the history books as the most redolent election in the history of Gringolandia. Mexicans who noticed (only 31% professed they did and many of them could not tell the two 40-something-year-old gringo candidates apart) had a hard time grasping the concept of an electoral college, let alone dimpled chads and butterfly ballots, or how come the candidate that won the most votes didn't win the election, or, most of all, why no one was in the streets hollering fraud. Nonetheless, in the end, the monthlong meltdown of the U.S.'s vaunted "free elections" left a lot of those Mexicans who stayed tuned gasping for breath at the sheer brazenness of the Bushites.

Whereas Vicente Fox had won Mexico with a U.S.–style media blitzkrieg, the United States celebrated a very Mexican election on November 8, 2000. The flimflam in Florida must have made many PRI-istas nostalgic for 1988, the year of maximum ruling-party robbery, when Carlos Salinas was awarded a tarnished victory over Cuauhtémoc Cárdenas. PRI "alchemists" adept at turning the dross of defeat into golden victories must surely be counseling Bush, the neighbors at La Blanca Café in downtown Mexico City hooted at me over the Formica counter. The fact that Roberto Madrazo maintains a getaway home in Boca Raton was lost on no one.

The electoral burlesque in Florida chagrined Ted Lewis, who was then running the Mexico Program at the San Francisco NGO Global Exchange. Each year Global led delegations of well-meaning gringos to observe vote takings south of the border and pontificate on the deficiencies of Mexican democracy. Now, in light of a Florida election that made the U.S. the butt of crude jokes from Cancún to Casablanca and Calcutta, Lewis canceled his overseas program. In fact, in 2004, Global Exchange invited a dozen Mexican electoral observers to the United States to ogle George W. Bush's reelection debacle.

The absence of a confirmed president of the United States of North America did not stay Fox from extending his congratulations to Bushwa. Every 12 years, the U.S. and Mexico elect presidents together, and the fates of the winners are often intertwined. The chemistry between Fox and Bush was already heady. Both were fake ranchers (Fox farmed broccoli on his Guanajuato *rancho*, and Bush bought his Crawford spread because it is mandatory for Texas governors to own one.) By contrast, Fox had spent an icy half hour in Washington with Al Gore and came away with the impression that the Veep, whose real estate interests are elsewhere (Africa), was not sure which U.S. border Mexico occupied.

Later that August, Fox and Bush had huddled in Dallas and exchanged gifts—Dubya presented Vicente with a splendid Stetson, and the Mexican president-elect passed the still–Texas governor a pair of hand-tooled cowboy boots from the family factory. The two even had family ties— Jeb's wife, Columba, the mother of "the little brown ones" (*los morenitos*) the first Bush had made much of during his losing 1992 election campaign, hailed from León, Guanajuato—Fox's hometown.

Both Fox and Bush had no foreign policy credentials—the former had sold Coca-Cola in Central America, and the latter's expertise was limited to cutting ribbons on new international bridges along the border— and both needed each other to enhance the illusion that they knew what they were doing. Bush, in fact, needed Fox to bolster his stock with Latino voters—he would take 34% in November.

So when the U.S. Supreme Court finally selected George Walker Bush as the next president of the United States, an audible gush of relief emanated from inside Los Pinos, into which Fox was just moving. The honeymoon would not last a year.

Is a Change Going to Come?

It had been more than 100 days since Mexico had heard from the rebels and over a year since any of the comandantes had appeared in public. Momentous changes had come and gone and still the Comandancia maintained its stony mumness. Mail left for the Sup with Max, the usual drop in La Realidad, gathered moss.

That jungle ejido seemed strangely quiet and abandoned in the autumn of 2000. The usual dark rumors gave urgency to the speculation. The Clandestine Revolutionary Indigenous Committee was hopelessly split as to what to do now. Marcos had quarreled with Tacho and was being held in a secret prison deeper in the Lacandón wilderness. At the checkpoints, the soldiers closely questioned the Indians: "*¡Pinche revoltosos!* Tell us where Marcos is hiding!" they snarled.

When Hermann jumped aboard a jungle truck, "The Candidate," in late October, a grizzled soldier was yelling at the passengers, accusing them all of being Zapatistas. When one compa denied EZLN affiliation, the army man grew even more belligerent: "Well, if you're not a Zapatista yet, you better hurry and join up—we're not going to be here forever, you know, and they are going to win."

Sardos and Frankensteins

But the silence of the comandantes did not echo down below. As the "*sardos*" (soldiers) and their Frankensteinian creation, the paramilitaries, torqued up the pre-Fox pressure, the autonomous villages reached out to the civil society. These were the last days of the PRI, and the party faithful would be determined to settle scores before they vacated power.

After a secret October 31 head-to-head in Comitán, President Zedillo and his defense minister, Enrique Cervantes Aguirre (about to receive the Legion of Merit from the Pentagon for "containing the guerrilla offensive in Chiapas with minimal violations of the human rights [*sic*]"), helicoptered into bases at Guadalupe Tepeyac and the sprawling Vietnam War–size complex at San Quintín. Although their orders were not publicly acknowledged, aerial overflights soon resumed and movement through the checkpoints was closely scrutinized. For the first time since the 1998 crackdown on internationalists, migration authorities issued deportation orders when an Italian crew stopped at an Ocosingo immigration station was discovered to be holding plans for a potable water system in an unnamed autonomous municipality.

Out on the periphery of the Montes Azules biosphere, the standoff at Amador Hernández marked its first year. Now the military, which so far had been frustrated from punching a road through the ejido, was digging in for the long haul, building barracks and cementing in the farmland, which the soldiers had appropriated without the Indians' permission, into a permanent installation.

The unique face-off, which had both sides cranking up their sound systems to drown the other out (the military played Richard Clayderman, the EZLN speeches by Sub Marcos) sent up a din that terrified the local wildlife. Sometimes the EZetas would write leaflets urging the soldiers to desert and "return to the houses of your mothers," fold them into paper airplanes, and fly them at the army troops, "the Zapatista Air Force."

At Río Euseba, on the western flank of La Realidad, the military was adding second stories to their encampment, and each day an army convoy of at least 20 light tanks and Humvees rolled through La Realidad, the soldiers fixing their machine guns and video cameras on the villagers and the international peace campers who accompanied them.

In mid-November, troops showed up at the gates of the Zapatista community named for Moses and Gandhi, near Altamirano, and demanded that the rebels open up their ejido land to allow soldiers to train there. In the *autonomía* named after two prophets (a big mural on the schoolyard wall depicts them arm-in-arm), the authorities told the soldiers to just go away: "We don't want your militaries running around here. It scares our people, and we feel offended because you do not respect our communal territory."

During the autumn of 2000, 18,000 troops were thought to be camped out in the conflict zone, although some estimates ran as high as 60,000. Most were kept under wraps behind chain-link fences at San Quintín, Monte Líbano, Guadalupe Tepeyac, and Maravilla Tenejapa, strategic centers from which the military could lock down the Lacandón if need be.

Meanwhile, Fox was honing his Chiapas strategy. He talked of a general amnesty for 100 incarcerated rebels, of sending the San Andrés Accords on to Congress at long last, and of "repositioning" the soldiers, all conditions the EZLN had set years before to return to the negotiating table. "We only need a signal from the other side and we are ready to return to the dialogue," Coca-Cola Man eagerly bubbled. But there was no signal. Inside, the Zapatistas were preparing for a full-scale military onslaught. Whether or not the generals would obey any orders to the contrary was of the utmost concern.

And as the military prepared for the PRI's end-time, the paramilitaries they had suckled were again on the move throughout the Zapatista zone.

Although former local PRI deputy Samuel Sánchez and his military chieftain Marcos Albino plus 11 other goons were now locked up in crumbling Cerro Hueco prison for the armed attack on Zapatista families in El Brillante near Yajalón on the eve of Pablo's election, their paramilitary formation, "Peace and Justice," was as active as ever in the north state municipalities of Salto de Agua, Tila, and Sabanilla, where 500 Chol Indian supporters of the EZLN reportedly had been pushed off their land.

Fifty miles south in Bachajón, another armed band—the Chinchulines—dusted off their long guns after one of their leaders, another ex-PRI deputy, was jailed, and farther south still, the autonomous hamlet of San Manuel, just outside of Ocosingo but pertaining to the Zapatista municipality of Francisco Gómez, was threatened with attack from the anti-Zapatista Indian Revolutionary Movement (MIRA), headed up by yet another ex-PRI deputy.

Tensions in Los Altos ran just as high. Two Zapatista supporters were ambushed by PRIistas in Pantelhó on October 20. Across the county line in Chenalhó, where 49 were massacred at Acteal at Christmas 1997, the venerable French anthropologist Andrés Aubrey interviewed a paramilitary in Los Chorros, the PRI village where the massacre was prepared. "Only the PRI saves," the gunman warned, brandishing his automatic weapon to make his point, "and only this weapon is the salvation of the PRI."

Alarmed by the prospect of another Acteal in the making, 250 Abejas (Bees), the Tzotzil religious community that had lost so many at Acteal in 1997, and the Xi Nich (Ants)—Chol and Tzeltal farmers from Palenque in the north of Chiapas—began to walk toward Mexico City, 1,300 kilometers uphill, to ask protection from the Virgin of Guadalupe.

Whether the PRI—at least in Chiapas—would really relinquish power on December 1, when Vicente Fox was to be sworn in, looked more and more dubious.

On November 12, exactly 18 days before The Change was supposed to come, the Zedillo government acted to head off a second Acteal, a tragedy that would have given Mexico a permanent black eye and soured the outgoing president's reputation for all time. Before dawn, 1,000 federal police agents stormed into Los Chorros looking for weapons, but the PRIistas had been forewarned and a brief firefight cost one agent his eye. Smashing down doors and ransacking homes, the police confiscated only a single revolver before a furious mob drove them from the community. A military detachment stationed at Mahomet just down the road was never sent to back up the police, and the raid seemed more a simulation than a serious strike on the paramilitaries. Down in San Cristóbal de las Casas, Felipe Arizmendi, Don Samuel's replacement as bishop, scratched his head. Why had the Zedillo waited until the very end of his six years in Los Pinos to take on these killers?

Promises, Promises

The not-quite-president-yet, preoccupied with headhunting a new cabinet (Jesus of Nazareth himself took out an ad in the PANista daily *Reforma* pleading for a job in the new administration), didn't see any danger. Chiapas was "tranquil," he pronounced. He would take care of the whole mess in 15 minutes. In Paris, accompanied by his just-appointed foreign minister, Jorge Castañeda, who, along with new national security advisor Adolfo Aguilar Zinser, had defected from the PRD, Fox assured the French that he would "pacify" Chiapas, and in Bonn, he promised Gerhard Schroeder that peace was at hand. After a visit to a Volkswagen plant, Fox promised to lobby the German conglomerate to set up an assembly plant in the rebel zone so that the Zapatistas could find happiness cranking out vochitos.

November 17 was the sixteenth anniversary of the founding of the Zapatista Army of National Liberation, usually time for a display of gala militancy in rebel territory, but this year there was no one to sing "*Las Mañanitas*" to—the comandantes were just not home. Indeed, Chiapas suddenly seemed emptied of all the star players in this six-year-old armed psychodrama—gone were Don Samuel and his fiery coadjutor Raúl Vera. Governor Croquetas and Zedillo himself would soon be part of bad history. Marcos had vanished into the ether. In the end, as in the beginning, only the Indians remained.

On the eve of the Big Change, really nothing had changed for the Zapatistas. But all that was about to change too.

The Same Old Nightmare?

The first communiqué from the Comandancia of the Zapatista Army of National Liberation since mid-June was dated November 29 and published by *La Jornada* on November 30, the eve of Vicente Fox's inauguration. "*¡Yepa! ¡Yepa! ¡Yepa!*" it began—Sub Marcos sometimes uses this peculiar expression of alarm, pioneered by the popular cartoon mouse Speedy Gonzalez, to draw the attention of the press and the public.

What followed was "a play in two acts" that featured a pointed dialogue between "Mrs. Civil Society" and "The Political Class." The play proved to be merely a curtain raiser. The meat of the text was directed at outgoing president Ernesto Zedillo (and indirectly at his successor), bidding him a not very fond farewell.

"Six years ago I wrote you in the name of the Zapatista Army of National Liberation to welcome you to this nightmare, and your six years in office have been one long nightmare for millions of Mexicans," Marcos recalled.

> In your capacity as supreme commander, you could have chosen peace and negotiation, but you did not. You did everything in your power to destroy us but we continue to live in our lands.
>
> Our nightmare with you ends tomorrow. Another one could follow, or maybe it will be a new dawn. We don't know, but we will do everything in our power to make tomorrow flourish.
>
> From tomorrow on, you will know how it is to be persecuted day and night. For you, Señor Zedillo, your nightmare will go on.

When the ex-president entered the halls of Congress the next day to hand over the scepter of power, many members of his own party turned their backs on him. Zedillo knew from his own bitter experience with his predecessor, Carlos Salinas, that there was no glory in being an ex-president of Mexico, and his bags were already packed.

Or a New Dawn?

The next noon, Vicente Fox, looking very presidential in the tricolored sash slashing across his powerful chest, batted his cow-eyes into the camera and addressed Mexico's 10 to 20 million indigenous peoples: "A new dawn," he chose to declare, careful to utilize the Zapatista code word. "Never again a Mexico without you!"—a refrain he had lifted from the militant National Indigenous Congress (CNI), a Zapatista-inspired pan-Indian confederation.

As the first order of his new administration, Vicente Fox would send the San Andrés Accords, now codified by the COCOPA into the Indian Rights law (Ley Cocopa), on to congress for its approbation. Although in my heart of hearts I knew the new president was selling snake oil, or at least Coca-Cola, a tear welled in my usually dry and cynical eye. It had been five years since San Andrés was signed, and now finally it would be presented to the congress of the country. Although prospects for its passage were tenuous at best, Fox seemed genuinely committed to risking his considerable political capital on passage of the Indian Rights law. Of course, it proved to be a trick.

Inauguration Under Seige

The inauguration of Mexico's first-ever opposition president was a picaresque affair witnessed by the usual crazy quilt of foreign dignitaries, among them Fidel Castro, U.S. "Drug Czar" General Barry McCaffrey, and Bill Gates, as well as a Mexican viewing audience who had never seen anything quite like it.

Vicente Fox began the day by breakfasting with street kids in Tepito, the roughneck thieves' kitchen in the crumbling center of the old city. The next stop was the basilica in the far north of the capital, where he prayed before the *tilma* (cactus-fiber shirt) upon which the Virgin of Guadalupe had purportedly revealed herself to the Indian Juan Diego, an exhibition of faith that raised the hackles of Jacobin PRI and PRD legislators awaiting the new president in Congress.

When Fox addressed "the republic of my family"—his three adopted children (the new president was divorced when he took office)—before addressing the Republic of Mexico, the boos and catcalls rained down. The new president couldn't string two sentences together without being interrupted by cries of "*¡Mentiroso! ¡Mentiroso!*" (Liar! Liar!) and "*¡Juárez! ¡Juárez!*," a reference to Benito Juárez, Mexico's most secular president. After one protracted interjection by the PRI's "Bronx" backbenchers, Fox stood at the podium smiling down patronizingly until the Bronx ran out of breath. "Good, very good, my *muchachos*," he beamed, his humor unsullied by all the abuse.

Fox would in fact have to endure this PRI-led barrage for the next six years as it insulted him at every opportunity (and there were many), gridlocking virtually every piece of legislation passed on by Los Pinos. This was the legislature to which President Fox was about to throw the raw meat of the San Andrés Accords.

Outside the Legislative Palace that day, police fired rubber bullets at the first anti-neoliberal demonstration of the new regime. Led by the Ultra rump of a student strike council whose strike had ended more than a year before, the young street fighters, dissuaded by the police from invading Congress, dismantled a McDonald's instead.

¡Hola Vicente!

The EZLN was ready to deal. At a hastily called press conference down in the jungle at La Realidad the next day (December 2), the comandantes put their own spin on the new government 1,000 miles away up in the capitol. A pack of reporters—local, national, international—swerved down the canyons to that jungle ejido to the delight of young Clinton—the oddly named eight-year-old darling of the media—and his pals. It had been a long time between press conferences for the kids of "The Reality."

Marcos, Tacho, and Moisés formed a troika on the stage inside the amphitheater. "We want to remind the Fox that he has inherited a war here in Mexico's southeast," Marcos upbraided, "and he will not win it—not with *changarros*, not with *vochitos*, and not with *teles*." Chiclet stands, Volkswagens, and TV sets weren't going to do it this time. "Mister Fox, you start at zero in confidence and credibility with us."

In an effort to persuade the Mexican congress that it had an obligation to the nation's indígenas to pass the Indian Rights law, a Zapatista delegation would travel up to Mexico City to defend the law before the legislature: 23 comandantes, members of the Clandestine Indigenous Revolutionary Committee–General Command (CCRI-CG) plus Subcomandante Marcos, the bridge between the Mayan leaders and the urban world. Their appearance was already opposed by the PRI and Fox's own party, the PAN.

Moreover, if Fox was really interested in getting peace talks back on track, he would have to sign on to the EZLN's long-standing prerequisites for restarting the dialogue: passage of the San Andrés Accords into law, the release of all Zapatista prisoners, and a military retreat—in this case, the rebels were not asking Fox to withdraw the military but to dismantle bases closest to the EZLN's public centers, or *Aguascalientes*. The bases in question were Guadalupe Tepeyac and Río Euseba on either side of La Realidad; La Garrucha in the autonomous municipality of Francisco Gómez; Cuxulja, adjacent to the autonomía of Che Guevara; Roberto Barrios in the north near the ruins of Palenque; Amador Hernández, on the edge of the Montes Azules biosphere; and Jolnachoj, down the road from Oventik in the highlands.

In an ancillary document, "Windows Open, Doors Not Yet," presented at the December 2 press conference, the EZLN adjudged the July 2 vote as being a great "*¡No!*," a coup de grace at the base of the brain for the ruling party. But what had happened since confirmed that Fox's victory was not the long-awaited "transition to democracy" but just another branch of the oligarchy whose license to govern needed to be seriously questioned. There was a power vacuum in the country, and how it would be filled would determine Mexico's future. "The hour is still in dispute."

Making Adjustments

In respect to the Zapatistas' "signals for peace," Fox probably had enough juice with the new governor, Pablo Salazar, to spring the prisoners, but coaxing the military into abandoning key bases would be much more ticklish. Convincing Congress to make San Andrés the law of the land was totally out of his hands.

Hearings on the Indian Rights law would be held during a special session of Congress in March—the EZLN announced it would be arriving in the capital on March 11 after a lengthy caravan ride around the country to raise support for the measure. Fox would be awaiting the rebels with open arms at Los Pinos—*"Mi casa es tu casa."* But the EZLN had no intention of doing a photo op with the Fox.

The Prisoners

Deciding who exactly was a Zapatista prisoner would be a Solomonic determination. "The Voice of Cerro Hueco," the Zapatista prisoners' collective at that damp old penitentiary above Tuxtla, counted 97 prisoners—42 inside Cerro Hueco (Hollow Hill) and the rest spread around the state in six prisons. Five others listed as Zapatista prisoners—three in Tabasco and two in Querétaro in the north—were beyond state jurisdiction. As might have been expected, the PRI opposed the release, labeling them common criminals and demanding that imprisoned paramilitaries be released instead.

The prisoners' attorney, Miguel Angel de los Santos, sometimes dubbed "the Zapatistas' lawyer," told me that most of the 97 were from the north of Chiapas and had been jailed on trumped-up charges lodged by the PRI-aligned Peace & Justice paramilitary formation, whose own leaders were then imprisoned in Cerro Hueco.

On December 30, in a pre–New Year's PR caper, the Foxites announced the release of the first 16 Zapatista prisoners. Dozens of foreign correspondents were flown at government expense to Chiapas to await the release outside the walls of the old prison. As the prisoners emerged one by one in a blaze of floodlights, Governor Pablo, very much a part of the Fox show by now, announced his intention of shutting Cerro Hueco down for good.

Later, I spoke with the released prisoners up in San Cristóbal. Francisco Pérez Pérez had been framed on a kidnapping charge by the paramilitaries and had spent the last three years in various state prisons before finally being cut loose. Now he was going home to Sabanilla in the north to find his family. He hadn't heard from them for a long time and was anxious. "As political prisoners we know that we can lose everything in the struggle—even our families."

Blood Solstice

Winter solstice marked the third anniversary of the savage massacre that had taken the lives of 49 Tzotzil supporters of the EZLN at Acteal in the highlands on December 22, 1997. The "Bees"—whose ties with the San Cristóbal diocese were always more significant than their Zapatista connections—had invited emeritus Bishop Samuel; his thwarted successor, Raúl Vera, now bishop of Saltillo in the northern desert; and the new bishop of San Cristóbal, Felipe Arizmendi, to their settlement for Mass.

In the three years since the killings, Acteal had become a full-fledged Christian shrine, particularly for Liberation Catholics, and the solemnities garnered enough front-page ink to make the Foxites salivate.

Acteal was a perfect vehicle for the Catholic, huckster president to boost his credibility with the EZLN. On the morning of December 22, after conveying condolences to the families of the dead, Fox ordered, as commander in chief of the armed forces, the dismantling of the first military base on the Zapatista list, Amador Hernández in the far-off savannas fringing the Montes Azules biosphere.

Trading with a military that had always sworn its allegiance to PRI presidents could be treacherous. Fox, in fact, had already miffed the brass by selecting his own secretary of defense—selection is traditionally the domain of the generals and the admirals. In fingering General Ricardo Clemente Vega for the job he had jumped his man ahead of senior officers such as Miguel Godínez, once chief of military operations in Chiapas.

To patch up the rift, the president had appointed chief military prosecutor Rafael Macedo de la Concha, an army general, as the nation's attorney general. Giving the job to a military man tempered the armed forces' irritation but angered human rights advocates. In his years as military prosecutor, General Macedo had repeatedly blocked civilian prosecution of troops accused of abuses.

Would Macedo de la Concha's appointment relax reluctance in the upper echelons of the military? Amador Hernández was the first test.

Jungle Boogie

Amador Hernández was the easiest of the seven bases on the EZLN list to take down. So distanced from other Zapatista autonomías that observers had to fly in to check out what was happening, the ejido was named for a PRI *cacique* (rural boss) but had been an early EZLN outpost.

Then, in August 1999, Governor Croquetas, who was promoting an ambitious road-building scam designed to encircle the Zapatistas' autonomous municipalities, sent his crews in to open a road through the settlement into the deep forest. The road crews had been accompanied by troops, and the villagers refused to allow them to move in, beginning a standoff that had now endured for 515 days. Both sides faced off at the chain-link fence behind which a sprawling military base had grown up during the long confrontation—a base built on confiscated land without the community's consent.

Now the fence had come down. The villagers came and inspected the recovered land, now bald and scarred where the heliport had been gouged from the forest floor, but the jungle would soon move in to cover the naked ground and the memory of the desecrators would be reduced to a bad joke.

The dismantling of Amador Hernández left only 258 more military outposts in the conflict zone, according to data kept by the Fray Bartolome de las Casas Human Rights Center in San Cristóbal.

On the eve of the feast of the Virgin of Guadalupe on December 12, 250 members of the Abejas and the Xi Nich arrived at the Basilica of the Brown Madonna in Mexico City. They had been on the road since early October, had marched 1,300 kilometers, and they were foot-weary. Now they asked the protection of the Virgin from the paramilitary gangs that infested Los Altos. During the Mass, they asked also for special protection for the San Andrés Accords, which, given the mounting PRI-PAN opposition, was going to need a lot of it.

WE DO NOT EXIST, WE JUST ARE

We are wind, Us,
not the breath which blows on us.
We are word, Us,
Not the lips which speak to us,
We are step, Us,
Not the foot upon which we walk,
We are heartbeat, Us,
not the heart that pulses,
We are bridge, Us,
Not the soils which the bridge joins,
We are roads, Us,
not the point of leaving or arriving,
We are place, Us
not who occupies that place,
We do not exist, Us
We just are,
Seven times we are,
Us, seven times,
Us, the repeating mirror,

The reflection, Us
The hand which just opened the window,
Us, the world calling out
to the door of Tomorrow.

—*The words of Comandante David and Subcomandante Insurgente Marcos. Read at Oventik,*
Chiapas, on the Seventh Anniversary of the Zapatista rebellion, January 1, 2001.

New Year's at Jolnachoj

New Year's eve at Oventik was chilled by the glacial wind blowing down off the steep mountain that fronts the ejido. Marimbas ponged and rockets flared. The Indians clustered around flickering fires in a futile stab at staying warm. Better to dance the herky-jerky cumbias. At midnight, the Zapatistas and their visitors joined voices to mark one more year of struggle, and soon after, many toddled off to their bedrolls.

It had been a long day. The Zapatistas of Oventik had begun early with a surprise, unarmed assault on Jolnachoj, the military outpost four kilometers down the road from the Aguascalientes; the base, like Amador, was on the EZLN hit list. In the early morning mist, the rebels had marched shoulder to shoulder up the hill of Oventik, their breath coagulating in the cold mountain air like vapors from a past perhaps only the Indians can remember now. At each crossroads up on the highway, they were joined by more masked people of the Tzotz. Even the PRI villagers joined in—the soldiers were occupying a school that used to serve their kids. Perhaps there were 800 up there on the road, 1,000. In the morning mist, it was hard to distinguish between the real people and the ghosts.

They stopped outside the base, bunched up at the gate chanting softly *"¡Chiapas Chiapas, no es cuartel! ¡Fuera el ejército de él!"* ("Chiapas Chiapas is not a military base. The army must leave here!"). Suddenly, with one determined lunge the Indians pushed over the first fence, gathered their strength, and put their shoulders to the second.

Now the Zapatistas and the soldiers were only a hand's length apart. One young man bravely reached out and put his fingers around the muzzle of an AK-15. "Kill me!" he screamed, "you can kill me if you like."

But the soldiers only continued to back up, and pretty soon they were surrounded by the Indians and isolated from one another. A group of women cornered one of the troops, an Indian like them, and pelted him with words. "Go home to your mother," they shouted, "she is crying for you every night." "You are killing your own brothers!" "I don't want to be here!" the soldier sobbed and threw down his gun.

By late afternoon, the soldiers had torn down the base at Jolnachoj. Army transports stood ready to truck them to the bigger bases where the troops were being concentrated. At Fox's ranch up in Guanajuato, press secretary Marta Sahagún, soon to be Mrs. Fox, advised the press that the president had ordered the soldiers to vacate Jolnachoj as part of his crusade to achieve peace in Chiapas, but of course it was a lie—the People of the Bat had forced the army to flee.

Free at Last!

Driving up to Oventik for the big party, one didn't know quite what to expect. The San Andrés immigration and military checkpoint had always been a tough one to get around. The previous New Year's, the migra had corralled 42 dread *internationalistas* here, including the serial do-gooder Kerry Appel, father of the EZLN's organic coffee trade, who faced his third deportation.

Soon after his inauguration, the new president had ordered the removal of 53 military checkpoints in Los Altos, the canyons, the jungle, and the north of the state, in addition to 30 provisional encampments. Had the San Andrés checkpoint been evacuated?

At the fork in the highway bearing northeast out of San Andrés, no one appeared in the road to block our advance. We glided through what had once been the most feared checkpoint in Zapatista territory in silence, holding our breath tightly, and when safely down the road, all the compañeros in the car let loose with a great yell of victory. Since that day, no one—migra or military—has barred access to the Zapatistas again, perhaps the most enduring of the sudden changes that occurred in the first days of the Fox regime.

The new administration also made it clear from its earlier hours that the xenophobia that Zedillo had spread in the months following Acteal, when so many were deported "for life" from Chiapas, would not be a hallmark of the Fox presidency. The deportation of Italians who had come to install a potable water system in La Realidad was cancelled only hours after Fox was sworn in. Now 160 Zedillo-era deportees were invited to return to Mexico—the notorious Señor Appel included. So was the even more notorious Pedro Café, AKA Peter Brown, an avuncular bilingual teacher from San Diego whose NGO "Schools for Chiapas" had helped to build the rebel middle school in Oventik. Pedro Café spent New Year's Eve holding court up in the Oventik general store.

One of the more amazing examples of government turnarounds was the failure of either the military or the migra to take action against a group of internationals who had donned ski masks and marched with the Zapatistas to the gate at Jolnachoj. In the bad old days, such subversion would have bought you a permanent ticket home.

Selling Peace Like Coca-Cola

Vicente Fox got to trot out his pitchman's act at the annual conclave of Mexico's diplomatic corps up in the capital during the first week of the year. The ambassadors were given new videos produced by PR whiz Carlos Alazraki lauding Fox's fixing of Chiapas. "We're already negotiating," the president lied, "everything will be all fixed up when we sit down to dialogue." Peace was just weeks away, he enthused, urging the diplomats to put a fresh face on Chiapas in the countries to which they were posted.

The next sell-peace-like-Coca-Cola stunt came on January 10 at Cuxulja, a military outpost between Ocosingo and Altamirano that sat cheek by jowl with the autonomous municipality of Che Guevara. This time, the Fox image-makers flew in 14 ambassadors to inspect the dismantled barracks. Newly appointed peace commissioner Luis H. Alvarez and Governor Pablo were on hand to take questions. Reporters buzzed around them like jungle flies.

Then, abruptly, hundreds of ski-masked Zapatistas appeared on the road, marching right up to the ambassadors and demanding to be heard: "*¡Chiapas, Chiapas, no es cuartel! ¡Fuera el ejército de él!*" The military tried to shush the Indians up, but it didn't take. Getting rid of Cuxulja was a good start, the Zapatistas conceded, but what about the bases Roberto Barrios and La Garrucha and Río Euseba, and most of all, Guadalupe Tepeyac? What about the San Andrés Accords and the poor political prisoners? *Chiapas, Chiapas, no es cuartel . . .*

"I don't know what more I can do," an exasperated president told listeners on his Saturday morning radio show, "Fox Alive! Fox With You!" In six weeks, he had made more progress toward peace than Zedillo had made in six years. But pushing the military to remove the last of the bases was like navigating a minefield. One had to pick one's way with utmost caution, and Cuxulja could be the last base the army would be willing to withdraw from for a long while, he warned. The Zapatistas needed to start making some concessions of their own.

At the end of January, the 18th Motorized Calvary moved in to fortify Roberto Barrios near the great ruins at Palenque. The president seemed to suggest that the EZLN must lay down its arms before it would be allowed to march up to Mexico City—the rebels had already made it clear that the march would be unarmed. Fox needed some demonstration of reciprocity to convince the generals that "repositioning" the troops would lead to resolution of the conflict. But the more Fox gave, the more the EZLN demanded.

Guadalupe Tepeyac

The base at Guadalupe Tepeyac was the biggest bone of contention. The generals insisted that the installation, which was located on the site of the first Aguascalientes, where the EZLN's National Democratic Convention had been held in August 1994, was vital to controlling the region around La Realidad, 15 kilometers deeper into the jungle.

On February 9, 1995, Zedillo had ordered army paratroopers to fall upon Guadalupe Tepeyac in a frustrated attempt to arrest Subcomandante

Marcos and the rest of the Zapatista leadership. Just hours before the invasion, the 80 families of Guadalupe Tepeyac (the village is named for the hillside in northern Mexico City where the Virgin of Guadalupe and the Indian Juan Diego purportedly first hooked up) had packed their meager belongings and headed into the mountains, where they trekked in a biblical wilderness for weeks until they decided on a new location for their community. They had been in the "new place" for three years now, but they still returned to Tepeyac to visit with their dead and poke through the ruins of their homes.

Up in the mountains, life was brutal. The children suffered horribly from black fly disease—*leishmaniasis*, or mountain leprosy as it is some-times called. But despite the hardships, they were determined not to return for good until the soldiers were finally gone from Guadalupe Tepeyac.

In early December, three members of the U.S.–based Christian Peace Team sat down in front of the entrance to the military base and began a hunger strike, praying and fasting for the safe return of the villagers. Each night they lit 80 candles and distributed them among the collapsed houses. The army was sensationally disinterested in what the Christians were up to. Now soldiers posted large signs on the front gate that were inscribed with unintentional poetry. DANGER! The signage shouted, HIGH TENSION!

The Rating Game

Both the Fox and the Sup were media-made inventions (at least Marcos could remove his mask and become someone else in his off hours), and rather than engage in the full-blown hostilities that had colored interchanges between Zedillo and the rebels, the media massaged the message. As the rebels tooled up for their next great adventure, the dis-course between their ski-masked spokesperson and the first opposition president turned into a relentless rating war.

The Fox had the bully pulpit of Los Pinos from which to solicit national sympathies, but Marcos had proven adept in the past at deviating public focus from the center of the country to the periphery. In this "banquet of vanities," as publicist Carlos Alazraki dubbed it, the Sup didn't have a budget for TV spots like the Fox, but an endless river of communiqués, flowing out of the jungle and into the national consciousness via the pages of *La Jornada*, kept him in the ball game.

Now big-city reporters lounged around La Realidad fiddling with their sat phones as they waited for an interview with Subcomandante Marcos. Just as back in the mid-'90s when the Zaps were still a hot media property, the *Wall Street Journal* and the *New York Times* were rolling down the canyons—Ginger Thompson reported in the *NYT* that the Zapatista spokesperson had just married a woman who had insisted upon teaching him to dance. Later, the Center for Investigation and National Security, Mexico's CIA, disclosed that the Sup had recently become a father, and the pundits speculated that this would diminish his more militaristic instincts.

Mexico's most rigorous critic and essayist, Carlos Monsiváis, made his third trip to the Lacandón (the very urban Monsi hates jungles) to rap with Sub Marcos on a more existential plane—and Hermann sat in. Even Andrés Bustamante, a TV comedian sometimes known as "El Guiri Guiri" for one of his personas, pitched a tent. Bustamante had come to La Realidad in the guise of another one of his absurd characters, "Ponchito," a sort of Mexican idiot savant, to request an interview. "But who will interview me—you or Ponchito?" Marcos asked, genuinely confused. "Ponchito!" Bustamante was adamant, "I'm not my best character." "I feel that way sometimes too," the Sup mused.

The Fox Goes on the Road

Vicente Fox was all over the map in late January. The new president made his international debut at the World Economic Forum in Davos, Switzerland, and assured the crème de la crème of the corporate elite that peace was at hand in Chiapas. Mexico was a good place to invest—rather than be leery of the EZLN's upcoming march to Mexico City, the world's leaders should see the act as a measure of the strength of Mexican democracy.

While the Fox preached from the ice mountain, globalphobes chanting Zapatista slogans battled Swiss police in the deep snow outdoors.

The new president made his first trip to Chiapas on January 17 with Xochitl Gálvez, his new director of Indian programs, in tow. Gálvez, what North American Indians label an "apple" (red on the outside, paleface inside), is an Otomí girl who has mostly obliterated her cultural past and had become a successful businesswoman when Fox tapped her to run his microcredit scam designed to pacify Indian ardor with changarros, vochitos, and teles.

When "Chente" and Xochitl helicoptered up to San Cristóbal to announce a further troop withdrawal from Roberto Barrios, he was not received with much enthusiasm. *"¡Vicente! ¡Vicente! ¡Tus Tropas Chingan Gente!"* Indian women greeted in the plaza: "Vincent, Vincent, Your Troops Are Fucking Over the People!"

Pinche Plan Puebla Panama

Fox retuned to Chiapas on February 9, the third anniversary of Zedillo's invasion of Guadalupe Tepeyac, but did not venture farther than the state capitol at Tuxtla Gutiérrez, where he would officially unveil his grandiose development scheme for the impoverished, resource-rich, and highly indigenous Mexican south, the Plan Puebla Panama. This time there would be no announcement of further troop withdrawals.

The PPP would integrate Mexico south of Puebla state with Central America all the way to Panama, where the U.S.'s Plan Colombia would presumably take over. Superhighways, bullet trains, a new Panama Canal, and cross-border electricity generation would knit the region together and open up its interior to "investment" from the usual transnational energy exploiters. Indeed, the Zapatistas' trip north would run the PPP route in reverse.

Marcos already had his own vision of Plan Puebla Panama. The *pinche* PPP would lower the nation's northern border all the way to Mexico City, and the capitol would become a customs house for all the wealth the transnationals suck out of the south. The plan would destroy forests, rivers, the corn, and indigenous culture. Only by winning their autonomy as envisioned in the San Andrés Accords could southern Mexico's indigenous peoples send the PPP back to where it came from.

The Zapatista Itinerary

The itinerary for the journey was published in *La Jornada* in early February. "We are going to where the Señor who has much tongue and no ears to listen lives." But the comandantes were not going to Mexico City to have their picture taken with the Fox. If the president wanted a photo that much, the comandantes would give him a poster and he could have his picture taken with that.

The Zapatistas had some hard traveling to do before they even set foot in the capital. Pushing off from San Cristóbal on February 24, the 23 members of the Clandestine Indigenous Revolutionary Committee plus Subcomandante Marcos (19 men, only five women) would embark on a 3,000-kilometer odyssey that took them from Chiapas to Oaxaca, then up to Puebla, east to Veracruz and Tlaxcala, and north again through Mexico state, Hidalgo, and Querétaro, veering west into Guanajuato, Michoacán, Guerrero, and Morelos before following the route of the first Zapata down into Mexico City for a March 11 mass rally in the Zócalo, the great Tiananmen-like square in the center of the capital.

The journey would take them into the heart of Indian poverty. The comandantes would, in fact, spend two days as guests of honor at the National Indigenous Congress's special session in Nurio, Michoacán.

Between San Cristóbal and Mexico City alone, 53 presentations were already programmed, nearly four a day. The comandantes would be traveling in a Gran Turismo luxury liner followed by an international contingent led by the White Overalls ("Los Monos Blancos"), the Italian antiglobalization collective, and Peter Brown's Little Yellow School Bus plus any other vehicle that might attach itself to the caravan.

The caravan would be escorted and surveilled by the Federal Preventive Police, ultimately under the direction of attorney general General Macedo de la Concha. Interior minister Santiago Creel justified the presence of the PFP because the caravan would be traveling through zones where "subversives" like the Popular Revolutionary Army (EPR) and several spin-off guerrilla bands had influence. A last-minute hitch threatened to derail the rolling march when foreign minister Jorge Castañeda nixed the participation of the International Red Cross, but the White Overalls were promoted to take the IRC's place as the Zapatistas' security escort.

"We Will Go and See for Ourselves"

The caravan would be the EZLN's fourth foray outside of Chiapas. In 1996, tiny Comandanta Ramona, "*la más pequeña*" (the smallest of the small), journeyed to Mexico City to attend the inaugural session of the National Indigenous Congress and ask the CNI for its support of the San Andrés Accords. In 1997, 1,111 representatives of all the Zapatista communities' caravaned up to the capital to seek the backing of a then-resurgent electoral left, and in 1999, 5,000 Zapatistas spread into every corner of the republic to conduct a referendum on Indian rights.

This time, there were formidable roadblocks to be circumvented. Just getting out of Chiapas could be a problem. Jorge Constantino Kanter, the top gun in the ranchers' associations, was agitating his members to barricade the highways. The gunsels of the heavily armed paramilitary band "Development, Peace, and Justice" were out hunting trophy Zapatistas. Who really knew how the police, military, and migra might behave—particularly when confronted by hundreds of internationals who had been granted special visas to accompany their heroes up to Mexico City? "In a globalized world, people will come here and want to observe," Immigration Subsecretary Jesús Preciado explained, a far cry from the dark days of Zedillian xenophobia.

Beyond Chiapas, the welcome wagon was not out everywhere. A deranged deputy from Morelos, the ex-guerrillero Salomón Salgado had threatened to whack Marcos for allegedly being a *maricón* (faggot.) Ignacio Loyola, the PANista governor of Querétaro, called the Zapatistas "traitors" and demanded the death penalty for the rebels. Three members of Fox's cabinet insisted that Marcos be arrested the moment he set foot outside of Chiapas—this was the Subcomandante's first known trip outside of the state's borders, and it was unclear legally whether suspension of Zedillo-issued arrest orders was in effect outside of Chiapas.

The PAN leadership was backed up by the elite business confederations COPARMEX and the CANACINTRA—the latter labeled the Indian march "a grotesque symbol of Third Worldism." If the EZLN was really serious about addressing the congress, they had best leave their ski masks and *paliacates* (kerchiefs) back home, warned PAN senate leader Diego Fernández de Cevallos and the speaker of the lower house, Ricardo Cervantes García—"El Jefe Diego" (Diego the Chief) was famous for his refusal to negotiate with anyone "wearing a sock on their head."

In response to the PAN's woofing, what remained of the Student General Strike Committee marched up to the gates of the interior ministry wearing nothing more than their ski masks. "Like the Zapatistas, we have nothing to hide," they told the police.

The leaders of the PAN and PRI had openly scorned the Indian Rights law. "We want to make it perfectly clear that the PRI will not permit San Andrés to clear congress in its present form," the old guard senator Manuel Bartlett bluntly assured.

Other Zapatista efforts had been universally unsuccessful in convincing Congress of the righteousness of their cause. Why should this caravan succeed? And then, of course, there was the minor matter of gas money. There was none, Marcos emphasized. Up in Monterrey, women from El Barzón, the national debtors' organization, hocked their wedding rings to buy petrol.

Many of the comandantes had never traveled farther than their municipal seats before, but despite the obstacles they were eager to know a Mexico that had never let them in the door. "The women who went before came back to tell us how it is in the cities and all the people that are in our favor there," Comandante Susana, her eyes brimming with determination, had told Guiomar Rovira, author of *Mujeres de Maíz*, up in Oventik on the eve of the departure. "Now we will get to go and see for ourselves."

Mi Rancho Grande

Just days before the EZLN set sail on its epic voyage, Vicente Fox had a prestigious visitor from the north to his Guanajuato rancho. George Bush had selected Mexico as his first foreign stop as U.S. president because "no other relationship is more important to us." The two new heads of state would spend the day—February 15—riding the range. Bush would palaver with his new amigo "Chente," chewing over the bilateral agenda. Way up on the top of the list held by foreign minister Jorge Castañeda was immigration reform that would legalize as many as 3,000,000 undocumented Mexicans living north of the border. In those heady, pre-9/11 days, anything seemed possible.

At 9:30 that morning, just as Bush was touching down in Guanajuato, the Pentagon in Washington disclosed that the U.S. and Great Britain had carried out a joint bombing assault on Saddam Hussein's Iraq. The attack was described as "preventive," and although it was the second Bush's very first bombing of Iraq, the president characterized it as "routine." Purportedly aimed at "illegal" missile emplacements in the southern no-fly exclusion zone, the bombing had killed one and injured eight in distant Baghdad.

The attack came less than a month after Bush's inauguration, upon which occasion the president instructed White House terrorism chief Richard Clarke to develop regime change strategies for Iraq.

The bombing, of course, dominated the press conferences. Fox could hardly get a word in about immigration reform. In effect, George Bush had converted his Mexican visit into a platform from which to bomb Saddam, not a diplomatically friendly gesture. Yet, hours later, Castañeda's foreign ministry issued its qualified support of the bombing—an indication as to just how far Castañeda would bend over to win his cherished immigration reform. Six days later, Bush and Blair would resume their bloody bombing spree, killing three and injuring 11 this time out.

If the truth be told—which it so rarely is—George Bush's war against the people of Iraq was launched from a Guanajuato broccoli farm posing as Vicente Fox's *rancho grande*.

¡Zarpazo!

Under a thin silver crescent of a mountain moon, the March for Indian Dignity disembarked from San Cristóbal for the capital on February 24. Inside the big bus, behind polarized windows, the comandantes sat quietly, occasionally waving to a comrade as the *despidida* (farewell) swirled outside but mostly now fixed on what lay before them.

Yesterday, each had said their good-byes to their families and neighbors at the Aguascalientes closest to their villages. In La Realidad, Marcos made a great show of stripping off his AK-15, the bandoliers of ammo, and his Colt .38 sidearm and turning them over to Major Moy before stepping on a low-slung local dog, who squealed indignantly. The *banda de guerra* blared, the rockets flared, and the compas began the climb up to San Cristóbal, where they would hook up with their comrades from the Cañadas and the highlands and the north of the state.

In San Cristóbal, Marcos was in messianic mode. He spoke in the packed cathedral square about the march, which he called the "March of the People Who Are the Color of the Earth" and, more formally, the March for Indigenous Dignity. "We are the heart of this land. We are the first memory. We are the Zapatistas, the smallest of the small. . . .

"For 200 years, much more, we have walked this land crying out for justice, and the *mal gobierno* offers us only alms. Now we go to where he of the long tongue but little hearing lives, not to beg but to demand justice for the people who are the color of the earth." The Sup's voice barely rose above a sinuous monotone, but his words were those of a Mayan Martin Luther King.

On the Road: Day One

To the acute discomfort of their respective guts, the comandantes, already trailed by ten busloads of national and international supporters, various strata of the press, and shadowed fore and aft by elements of the Federal Preventive Police (PFP), wound down the 365 twists and turns from San Cris to the state capital of Tuxtla early on the morning of February 26.

The EZLN had never visited Tuxtla before, at least under its own name, although in 1992, the comandantes marched here against Salinas's revision of Article 27, disguised as the National Association of Farmers and Indians–Emiliano Zapata, or ANCIEZ. Now 10,000 mostly Indian Tuxtlans gathered on the broiling esplanade in front of the state capitol building to hear Marcos and the comandantes demand the release of Zapatista political prisoners from Cerro Hueco and the jailing of Croquetas Albores in their place.

Then the compañeros hopped back up on the Gran Turismo, now renamed *The MarcoPolo,* and headed west toward Cintalapa, where the mountains of the Chimilapas descend to the Tehuantepec isthmus. The Chiapas PFP patrols handed the caravan over to their Oaxaca counterparts, and the march of those the color of the earth ambled up the coast highway toward Juchitán.

The first sign of trouble showed up at La Ventosa, an extraordinarily windy stretch of the coastline where tractor-trailers are sometimes blown over on their backs. What appeared to be a ramshackle barricade strung across the road forced the *MarcoPolo* to brake. The Sup and Comandante David descended cautiously from the Gran Turismo and saw that what they had taken to be a roadblock was merely a collection of broken-down farm trucks piloted by nearby Huave Indians who just wanted to join the caravan in solidarity. *¡Vámonos, muchachos!*

Running hours late, as would be its natural rhythm, the march put into Juchitán after dark. A fabled Zapotec city of flowers and iguanas where matriarchal succession determines power relations, Juchitán is also the home base for the Workers, Students, and Farmers Alliance of the Isthmus (COCEI), which has dueled with the PRI for control of the region for decades, and the plaza was covered with enormous banners displaying the heads of Che Guevara and Lucio Cabañas, a neighboring Guerrero state guerrilla martyr.

Oaxaca is Mexico's most Indian state—1.9 million indígenas compared to Chiapas's 1.3—whose ethnic patchwork quilt includes 16 distinct indigenous cultures, and Zapotecs, Huaves, Chinantecos, Mazatecos, and Chontales shared the podium with the Mayans.

Comandante Esther spoke of the triple burden of Indian women ("We are Indian, we are women, and we are poor"), and Marcos told a previously unpublished Old Antonio tale, "The Story of Language," about how the young gods liked to tease the people of the corn and blow up the women's skirts with bursts of wind. So the men and women of the corn had a meeting to decide what to do and discovered they had no words to express their thoughts. The more they thought, the more they needed the words to say things, and so as not to lose the new words they were forming, they inscribed their language on a rock in the mountain. Now, whenever the young gods—not the first gods who made the world but those who are made from excrement—tried to trick them into forgetting their words, they would return to the rock and remember them all over again.

When the Sup was done, a treeful of birds behind me on the crowded Juchitán plaza abruptly erupted into song. Magic realism infused this odyssey at every stop.

Blood on the Sand

Meanwhile, the mask of benevolence that Vicente Fox had so carefully constructed to mute his more authoritarian urges was being torn asunder in the luxury Caribbean resort of Cancún, where he was presiding over a mini Davos-at-the beach. This road show version of the World Economic Forum required $12,000 USD in registration fees before you could get in the door of the deluxe Gold Coast hotel where it was being mounted. Demonstrators were kept penned up five miles away.

In early 2001, the Nation of Seattle was still a tenderfoot on the barricades. It had cut its teeth at the World Trade Organization fiasco in Seattle, December '99, moved on to Washington for the World Bank–IMF spring meeting, and then headed to Prague for the fall session. The year 2001 had begun up in the Swiss Alps at the original Davos. Up ahead on the antiglobal agenda was the Summit of the Americas in Quebec City in April, where Bush would push for the ALCA, the Free Trade Area of the Americas that would extend the dubious benefits of NAFTA all the way to the tip of Tierra del Fuego. Cancún was a tune-up for the summit.

Fox saluted the masters of the universe assembled in the Grand Ballroom of the Cancún Westin with embarrassing self-congratulations for having achieved peace with his Indians in Chiapas and, in passing, tossed out a plug for the Plan Puebla Panama to visiting investors: "While the Zapatistas march north, we are bringing sustainable development to the south."

Barricaded out of the hotel zone, a handful of globalphobes had infiltrated an adjacent beachfront, where they were quickly encircled by three layers of police—on the outer circle, the PFP kept the press at bay while local cops smashed the demonstrators with stunning headshots. Blood stippled the sand. Defenseless, the poor protesters could only think to strip off their trunks in protest, and 60 were arrested for indecent exposure.

Others were rounded up and loaded onto buses that took them out of state. Some eventually joined the Zapatista caravan.

Indian Heartland

After a morning stop at Tehuantepec on the isthmus, where the comandantes were blessed by involuntarily retired bishop Arturo Lona, Don Samuel's crime partner, the March for Indian Dignity climbed from the coast into the Oaxaca sierra and then down into the hot central valleys. Much as in 1997 when I ran this route, the roadsides were lined with *los de abajo*, those from down below, who waited all day under the scathing sun for a glimpse of the comandantes whenever they passed by.

In Oaxaca city, 10,000 pressed into the old colonial plaza to hear Marcos respond to Fox's vision of the Plan Puebla Panama. Warning that the PPP would divide the country and its national unity and destroy ancestral cultures, the Sup led the multihued crowd in a fist-thrusting chant of *"¡Oaxaca No Se Vende!"* (Oaxaca Is Not for Sale!)

From Oaxaca, the march reached into the altiplano of Mexico. An early morning meeting was held at Tehuacan in Puebla, where corn was first domesticated ten millennia ago and which now had become a vast blue jeans *maquiladora* where subcontractors for The Gap and Calvin Klein keep 20,000 Indians—Popoluca, Totonaco, Mixteco, Nahua—in thrall. Thousands of brown faces pressed in around the buses.

The motorized March for Indigenous Dignity was on a roll. First it went over the top of the Sierra Negra before dipping down into the mountains of Veracruz, where 20,000 greeted the comandantes in Orizaba, the largest political gathering in that city's history. The caravan set out for Puebla, Mexico's fifth-largest city, with a full head of steam, arriving after dark in a plaza so packed that spectators were dangling from the trees. Everywhere the Zapatistas traveled, the cry was always the same: *"¡No están sólos!"*—"They are not alone!"

White Ghost

The Comandancia was indeed not alone. Each time they filed out on stage, the Indians were accompanied by a ghost from their past: Comandante "Germán," AKA the architect Fernando Yañez, the father of the once-upon-a-time Forces of National Liberation, from whose loins the EZLN had sprung. One of the leaders cited for arrest by Zedillo in his February 1995 invasion of the Lacandón, Germán had been arrested later that year in Mexico City on cocaine and gun possession charges, taken to the infamous Military Camp #1 for questioning, and quickly released because his detention was screwing up delicate government-EZLN negotiation on Indian rights in Chiapas. He had not been seen in public since.

On the evening the comandantes set sail, Marcos had introduced Germán to the partygoers in San Cristóbal as an old and trusted comrade. Although he had no known legislative experience, Yañez was designated as liaison with the Mexican congress to establish the ground rules for the EZLN's defense of the Indian Rights law before that not-so-august body. In guerrilla-speak, the designation of a clandestine military chief to discuss terms of peace usually indicates a turn away from war.

Now each time the comandantes took their place on the podium, Germán would follow them out, careful to stand behind them, often hovering like a tall white ghost in back of Marcos. It was eerie, almost as if the old guerrillero was winding up a key in the comandantes' backs to make them move. And then there was this headset that Marcos had taken to wearing. He seemed to receive frequent messages on it, but then again, maybe it was only a device for keeping his cracked old Mao hat firmly atop his head.

The First Circle

From Puebla, the March for Indian Dignity extended north, describing a first circle that would soon form a *caracol*, a spiral, around the capital. The route of the caravan, which had now grown to 40 buses (700 internationals were said to be aboard), took the comandantes into the Nahua lands of Tlaxcala beneath the eternal snows of soaring volcanoes, and then into Hidalgo, waving to lively crowds in tiny Indian towns like Tepeapulco and Actopan.

Under threatening skies, the march of those the color of the earth put into the Mexquital valley, one of the nation's poorest rural regions, where the arid rocky soil was fruited by endless rows of spiny maguey cactus whose heart rendered the cool nectar of the Aztec beverage, *pulque*. A biblical rainstorm, replete with hail the size of frozen honeybees, pelted the comandantes when they spoke in Ixmiquilpan, but the mostly Indian audience wouldn't let them stop. "*¡No están sólos! ¡No están sólos!*" The miracle of the Zapatistas had brought rain to a place where it never rains, Hermann marveled.

Dangerous Curve Ahead

Querétaro, the conservative Catholic state where you couldn't even buy a condom in the local pharmacies, came next. Ignacio Loyola, the governor whose family ran the largest funeral home in the state, had threatened to have the rebels shot atop Campana Hill, where Benito Juárez had once thrust the ersatz French emperor Maximilian before a firing squad. "The Zapatista army?" Loyola scoffed, "Mexico only has one army, so we must be at war." Querétaro would not be a good spot for disaster to strike.

Riding the rain-slicked road up to the state capital, the brakes on the IndyMedia bus apparently failed and the vehicle caromed into the CIZ (Zapatista Information Center) van, which in turn plowed into the *MarcoPolo*, where the comandantes were innocently catching some zzzs. In all, nine buses and other vehicles were enmeshed in the *carambola*. Six compañeros in the CIZ van were taken to hospital. A federal police motorcycle officer was pancaked between buses—Carlos Martínez was DOA at the Querétaro hospital.

The contingent of White Overalls, fearing an assassination attempt on the Comandancia, formed a tight cordon around the dented *MarcoPolo* to fend off the federal police. The Frente Zapatista de Liberación Nacional, the EZLN's weak-sister political action front, was already telling reporters that the incident had been set up to give the Fox a pretext for calling off the March for Indian Dignity before it got to Mexico City.

After a six-hour standoff, the buses were allowed to continue north to Querétaro city, where Nanhu Indians and anarcho-punks had been waiting all the day in the plaza for their idols to show up. Marcos was on fire that night, blistering the mal gobierno and attacking the governor as a "lap dog" and less artful epithets. "Before we came here, an insurance salesman tried to sell us a policy against ordinary firing squads. We should have bought it.

"If they do put us before a firing squad, I don't want them to blindfold us. Ever since January 1, 1994, it has been a crime in Mexico to hide one's eyes." "*¡No están sólos! ¡No están sólos!*" the mob howled back.

Stretching the Circle

The torrent of turmoil had subsided by the following morning, March 2, and Querétaro authorities urged the comandantes to get back on the road. Skirting the Sierra Gorda, the caravan dropped off into the *bajío*, the fertile lowlands of Guanajuato, Fox country. In Acámbaro, a mestizo farming town that breeds massive migration to the U.S., the Zapatistas preached that the work of the first Zapata was not complete. "Mexico needs the *lucha* of the Zapatistas," Comandante Gonzalo warbled, concluding the final stanza of the EZLN anthem, *"Horizontes,"* and then the compas were back on the bus.

The march of those the color of the earth crossed Lake Cuitzeo, one of three great west-central Mexican lakes, which are drying up at an alarming rate, into what some call the Independent Republic of Michoacán, the Purépecha nation. In Zinapécuaro, thousands blocked the highway to Morelia, and Senator Lázaro Cárdenas Batels (now governor), the son of Cuauhtémoc and the grandson of the first Lázaro, came and shook the comandantes' hands.

In damp, cold Pátzcuaro by the side of the sacred lake, Purépecha fishermen from Janitzio Island protested the jailing of two comrades accused of taking the lake's delicate, disappearing white fish. "The mal gobierno thinks it knows how to care for our land better than we do," Marcos commiserated. *"¡No están sólos! ¡No están sólos!"*

At nightfall, the convoy headed into the Meseta Purépecha, the steep mountain range rising on the far side of the lake. Tomorrow, they would be guests at a special session of the National Indigenous Congress in the Purépecha village of Nurio.

Under Purépecha Flags

In the white morning mist hanging low over the wide valley, where the ochre-colored earth was being prepared for the spring planting, Tata Gregorio Alvarez, 103, fixed tea from the nuriti bush for an old friend with all the dexterity of a Japanese tea master. The old Purépecha farmer was curious. The legendary Subcomandante Marcos had just arrived in these distant mountains and Tata Goyo wanted to know what he wanted.

"An Indian Rights law," I explained, "one that will give the indigenous peoples autonomy over their lands so that they will never stop being farmers." "But Juanito, we are still farmers here and we grow our own corn and set our own price for it. No one tells us what to do. Why do we need a law for that?" the old Purépecha cackled toothlessly.

I had to admit that Tata Goyo had a point. Did the EZLN really need the government's permission to declare itself autonomous?

Two mountains south in the Meseta at Nurio, the National Indigenous Congress was unfurling under the enormous purple flag of the Purépecha Nation. The CNI had been created in 1996 by pro-Zapatista Indians to build support among Mexico's 57 indigenous nations for the San Andrés Accords—Comandanta Ramona, the smallest of the small, had accompanied pan-Indian activists at the CNI's first congress. But the CNI could never really figure out if it was a national organization or a broad-based network that connected up local struggles, and its fortunes had ebbed and flowed depending on the Zapatistas' focus on San Andrés.

The March of the People Who Are the Color of the Earth had lit a fire under the CNI, and now there were 12,000 people gathered on the deep green hillside above a local school. Humpbacked mountains newly shorn of their forests spired into the stark blue heavens above a sea of many tongues and multiple skin tones—41 out of the 57 distinct indigenous peoples of Mexico were represented at Nurio. The delegates of the First Peoples were now no longer fiery young activists but older, more serious men and women of consequence in their communities, who carried heavy briefcases stuffed with land grants, boundary maps, and decisions of the Agrarian Reform ministry.

Marcos was at his most Popul Vuhish in Nurio, salting his cant with references to Votan-Zapata and *los más antiguos* (the oldest people.) *"Camina, camina, y habla"*—"Walk, walk, and talk, learn the heart of he who walks with you," he sang to the rainbow gathering: "It is the hour of the word—guard your machete but keep it well-sharpened." And then in slow, painful cadence he began to read the names of those "who walk with us."

"Brother and Sister Aguacateco, Amuzgo, Cakchiquel, Chatino, Chichimeca, Chinanteco, Choho, Chol, Chontal, Chuj, Cochimi, Cora, Cucapá, Cuicateco, Guarijío, Huasteco, Huave, Huichol, Ixcateco, Ixil, Jalcateco, Pápago, Pima, Popoluca, Purépecha, Quiché, Serí, Solteco, Tacuate,

Tarahumara, Tepehua, Tepehuan, Tlapaneco, Tojolabal, Kanjobal, Kekchí, Kikipú, Kiliwa, Kumiai, Lacandón, Mam, Matlatzinca, Maya, Mazahua, Mayo, Mixe, Mixteco, Motocintleco, Náhuatl, Ocuilteco, Opata, Otomí, Paipai, Pame, Papabuco, Totonaca, Triqui, Tzeltal, Tzotzil, Yaqui, Zapoteco, Zoque . . . If our pain can unite us, if our hope can unite us, than it makes sense that we march together for tomorrow."

By acclamation, the CNI proclaimed itself in permanent assembly and voted to accompany the comandantes up to Mexico City. But what will happen if Congress refuses to consider the Indian Rights law, I asked Abelardo Torres, a leader of the Nación Purépecha. "Then the Indians are just going to have to declare themselves autonomous without the government's permission," he replied cheerfully.

Closing the Circle

As the pageant that had been the National Indigenous Congress packed itself up behind us, the Zapatistas headed east to finally close the first circle around Mexico City. A noontime meeting turned out the usual 10,000 in Morelia, closing down the Michoacán state capital to traffic. Among those on hand were 46 uniformed fifth graders with notebooks in their hands, who studiously jotted down what the comandantes had to say. "History has come knocking on our door and I could not resist the opportunity to let the children learn about it firsthand," the *profe*, an Indian himself, explained.

By midafternoon, the caravan had driven into Mexico state, which surrounds the capital on all sides. The first meeting was set in the high pine hills at Temoaya. The Otomí Ceremonial Center is actually an archly modernist temple erected by President López Portillo during the oil boom and is occasionally rented out to film James Bond epics. Perhaps the kitsch provoked the Sup into railing against the despoiling of Indian culture: "For the whites, we are an object of decoration, a painting, a photo, a weaving, but never a human being. . . ."

Then the increasingly mystical Marcos emitted the first of seven what he called "keys," Kaballistic messages for the Mexican capitol: "Do not only count the yeses and the nos. But also count the silences in between."

Back down in the Valley of Mexico in the sprawling metropolis of Toluca, before a boisterous mob of *chavos bandas* (gang kids) and street vendors, Marcos thundered, "They are afraid of the color of the earth! They believe the poor will rise up to pay them back their aggravations. So let them renationalize the banks if they don't want that to happen, let the factories become the property of the workers, and tell the army to surrender!

"*Hijos de María Félix*, don't get so hysterical. This is a new Mexico in which the Indians only want to take their place. . . ."

The comandantes doubled back that afternoon heading southwest through the industrial landscape into Morelos, where gilded Zapatas still stood or rode in every plaza in the state. On the highway to Cuernavaca an old man, all in white, crouched by the side of the road, lighting copal and blessing the Zapatistas with its sweet smoke when they passed by.

The day had been an enormous one and Subcomandante Marcos was exhausted by midnight when the convoy arrived in Tepoztlán, the Nahua power spot where they would bed down for the night. In the mid-1990s, the town had taken the Zapatista message to heart and risen up against the installation of a multimillion-dollar golf course, which the developers wanted to site on community land. "John, we don't play golf here," Mayor Lázaro Rodríguez, who had led the rebellion, explained to me.

"Marcos does not exist. He is a shadow behind the comandantes. They are my bosses. Listen to them," rasped the Subcomandante, but could not restrain himself from issuing the next key: "The silence of those of us the color of the earth is broken. Over the pieces, we rise. It is no longer possible for us to return and be like we were once and are not now. We are now those who will write the laws and make the history."

The Armed Option
In order to complete the circle, the EZLN had to make one obligatory detour south to the rebel-ridden state of Guerrero, an entity whose history is etched in the blood of martyrs. The massacres at Aguas Blancas (17 killed in 1995) and El Charco (11 in 1998) still dripped fresh red on the Mexican map. Lucio Cabañas, the grandson of one of Zapata's generals,

and his Party of the Poor had risen here in 1968 and ruled the sierra for six years until he was gunned down by the army during the dirty war in 1974. In 1996, the Popular Revolutionary Army (EPR), composed of Lucio's sons and nephews and steely Maoist ideologues, had once again picked up the gun. There had been hostile interchanges between the EPR and the EZLN, even a feint at encroaching on Zapatista territory in Chiapas, but since then the Popular Revolutionary Army has apparently split into factions—the FARP and the ERPI were two of them.

The plaza in Iguala was strung with banners of Lucio and Genaro Vázquez, who had risen in the same era but in a distinct Guerrero sierra. One huge *manta* called for the release of the *campesinos ecologistas* (ecological farmers) Rodolfo Montiel and Teodoro Cabrera, falsely charged with drug cropping by the army after they forced the U.S. timber titan Boise Cascade to pull out of the Sierra of Petatlán. Rodolfo and Teodoro were then in their second year of incarceration at the Iguala state penitentiary.

You could feel the tension on the back of your neck. "Guerrero Bronco" (Wild Guerrero) is just a hair-trigger from wholesale slaughter, and it felt like gunfire could break out without much provocation.

The EPR, the ERPI, and the FARP were there and not there in the plaza that hot breath of a noon. But they were listening attentively. Marcos thanked them for allowing the Zapatistas to pass through their lands and then invited those who opted for armed revolution to join with the EZLN in getting an Indian Rights law passed by Congress. It was kind of a "give peace a chance" argument, and the Zapatistas got out of town fast.

The Route of the Zapata

In order to descend into the city, the neo-Zapatistas had to follow the route of the first Zapata.

"I welcome them to the land of Zapata, but they must come with their weapons only in their minds or else this trip could be very difficult for them," greeted 101-year-old Emeterio Pantaleón, a onetime officer of the Caudillo's Liberating Army of the South. But not everyone shared Pantaleón's cautious warmth. Emiliano Zapata is mercantile property along the route, and outsiders in ski masks calling themselves Zapatistas were viewed as interlopers.

Out at the chokingly dusty fairgrounds to which the rebels had been consigned by a Cuautla city government not eager to host them, Omar, Esther, Yolanda, Fidelia, Zebedeo, Tacho, and David but not Marcos spoke of the devastation of Mexican agriculture and Comandante Gonzalo led the big, enthusiastic crowd in the EZLN anthem.

The event was marred by an ugly clash between the White Overalls and the press, and suddenly the bad gas of xenophobia was soaking the front pages just like back in the bad old Zedillo '90s. "Foreigners protecting a march of indígenas?" the daily *Reforma* sneered. "What's that all about?" And TV Azteca asked bluntly, "Do Italians ever bathe?"

On their way to the liberator's birthplace in Anenecuilco the next morning, the *MarcoPolo* was stoned by young thugs who kept shouting that they were the real Zapatistas. As the caravan traveled from Anenecuilco to Ayala, where Zapata had once promulgated his agrarian reform program, then to the general's military headquarters at Tlaltizapán, and on to the Chinameca hacienda where the Great Zapata fell victim to his government's treachery, the new Zapatistas drank deep at history's well. But supporters lining the backcountry roads of rural Morelos were sparse. A final homage in Cuautla's Plaza of the Southern Revolution, where the Caudillo's bones are buried under a colossal statue of whom else, had to be cancelled because a man with a gun had been seen stalking the neighborhood.

On the Edge of the City

The comandantes would take the old road down into Mexico City for the March 11 rally in the Zócalo, following the route through the town of Milpa Alta that Emiliano Zapata had taken in December 1914 to hook up with Francisco Villa at the apogee of the Mexican revolution. History is always the EZLN's copilot.

The compas were tired and sick when they reached Milpa Alta on the night of March 8. *"Tanta anda pa'arriba y pa'abajo"* (so much walking up and down), Esther muttered. But beat as she was, it was International Women's Day, and the comandante felt called upon to speak to the townspeople about the Triangle Shirtwaist Fire and "the 148 compañeras of New York" who had lost their lives in the conflagration. Then she offered the next and most arcane "key" to the city: "We do not have two faces, but two feet, yes, and one and then the other are necessary to walk. When the moon with three colors reigns, our force will be greater than the force of the color of the earth." Say what?

In Milpa Alta, there was sweet atole and warm tamales, the same as the neighbors had once fed the first Zapata on his way down to the big city. From Milpa Alta one can look down on the lights of the capital, and now the moon that had been but a sliver when they left their homes was swelled almost full, and the rebels basked in its wide arc as they gazed down. What would it be like inside this urban monster? they pondered.

The Zapatista Army of National Liberation was about to enter the most indigenous city in the Americas—as many as 5,000,000 Indians from every culture in the country make Mexico City their home. They wouldn't be alone.

At 3 a.m. that Friday morning, the Sup, who sleeps little, was summoned to a nearby colonial chapel for a tete-à-tete with *Proceso* magazine founder Julio Scherer, one of the most astute *politólogos* in Latin America. Televisa would be filming the encounter.

Scherer had just heard that Fox was inviting Marcos to Los Pinos to chat about "the state of the country and the Indian question." Would the Sup be going? "Just me alone—not the Indians?" The rebel spokesperson's voice oozed weary irony. "No, we didn't come all the way here just to visit the Fox. We have plenty on our agenda."

Concert for Nothing

Although Televisa and TV Azteca, which together own 90% of the television dial, conducted a near-religious rating war, the two megacorps struck a deal to stage a supernova "Concert for Peace" at the 150,000-seat Azteca Stadium on the first Friday in March. Some suspicioned that the concert was actually organized out of the interior secretary's office to counter the rebels' soaring popularity. The Concert for Peace was just for that, not for "Peace and Justice" and certainly not for the Zapatista Army of National Liberation.

Despite what the Foxites and the two-headed TV monopoly proposed, the March of the People Who Are the Color of the Earth was not a march for peace—although it was accomplished in peace—but one for an Indian Rights law that now stood before the Mexican congress. Peace would come later. To reduce the Indian Dignity March to a mobilization for an amorphous peace was a veiled jab at the "intransigent" Zapatistas for not abandoning their conditions for dialogue.

Was Marcos eager to attend the concert, Scherer probed? "Who do you think I am," the Sup shot back, "the Ricky Martin of the Zapatistas?"

The Concert for Peace featured Maná and Los Jaguares, the best pop rock money could buy, and more than 150,000 *fresas* (literally, "strawberries," slangly "petit bourgeois") jammed the Azteca to wiggle their petite boodies. Carlos Santana, a wildly popular homeboy, bowed out at the final moment. Both of the remaining groups did their damnedest not to mention the Zapatista Army of National Liberation on prime-time TV although they both played *rolas* that spoke to the war in Chiapas.

A ska-athon that same weekend that, *sí*, was dedicated to the compañer@s (admission was a kilo of beans for the autonomous municipalities) drew 25,000 ska-atics to hear 20 bands, one of which was actually called "The Accords of San Andrés."

The Televisa–TV Azteca cabal lost interest quickly in packaging up the Zap shtick as a viable commodity after that, and neither even bothered to carry the rebels' phantasmagoric arrival in the capital on Sunday the 11th, the first time since before 1521 that an Indian army had entered Tenochtitlán in triumph, inscribed Carlos Monsiváis.

Floating Gardens
On the eve of their descent into the maw of the city, the comandantes

played public meetings in the small plazas of Xochimilco, named for the Aztecs' fabulous floating gardens, or *chinampas*, in that southernmost *delegación* (borough) of the capital—technically Xochimilco was inside the Mexico City limits. Villa and Zapata had met here nearly a century previous when Xochimilco was still out in the country. It is still, in fact, quite rural.

Before retiring behind locked doors to plot logistics for the morrow, Esther advanced one further indecipherable key to the city they were about to be ingested by: "Our march has aged the silence. The brown voice will be one of many. Its eyes and ears sing of the color of the land as we pass in. We are the repeating mirror and our rebellion will not retreat into history." Then it was time to sleep. The sweet promise of tomorrow drew the rebels through the dawn.

The Zócalo

The 16 kilometers between Xochimilco and the city's "Historic Center" were lined with "*¡Vivas!*" and "*¡No están sólos!*" and "*¡E-Z-L-Nes!*" every millimeter of the way. Spectators hung from lampposts and rooftops as a giant Kenworth tractor pulled the long flatbed filled with comandantes and inexplicably outfitted with bales of hay as if in preparation for a square dance, through the entire length of the teeming city, arriving in the great central plaza at approximately 2:30 p.m. on the afternoon of March 11, 2001, my 63rd birthday. "*¡No están sólos! ¡No están sólos!*" 250,000 people the color of the earth packed between the walls of the bubbling plaza at the political heart of this ancient nation cried out with one throat.

The stage had purposefully been erected in front of the National Palace, the supreme seat of the mal gobierno's power, although the EZetas had not come here, as Marcos emphasized, to take power. Serious as the occasion was, the Sup could not resist cracking jokes like a stand-up comedian. "The government has often stood in back of us before—with their helicopters and their tanks."

"We want to say to those who govern here that you must listen and listen up good so that now you will put an end to the obliteration of our race, and the racism against all the Indians of Mexico," Comandante Tacho barked just to make it clear that the March of the People Who Are the Color of the Earth had been about color all along.

"The seventh key is you!" Marcos exhaled, and the enormous throng slowly modulated its "¡No están sólos!" and lapsed into profound silence. For once, everyone was listening—the people, Fox, the government, the political parties, even the cardinal inside the Metropolitan Cathedral adjacent to the speakers' platform. But what the Sup had to say seemed hesitant and even anticlimactic:

"We do not belong up here but we are up here along with all the men and women of our peoples, the first peoples, the Indian peoples. We are not your spokespersons but just one voice among many. We do not come to tell you what to do but to ask humbly to be heard. We are a mirror of you, not the reality. Look upon us and look upon yourselves.

"The march of those the color of the earth is done with. It is the hour of the Fox and those who govern him to speak."

"¡No están sólos! ¡No están sólos!" the crowd kept calling as Gonzalo stepped forward to strike the first chords of the Zapatista anthem.

Just as the Sup was abandoning the stage, an itinerant reporter remembered to ask him just how long he would be staying. "Until Congress passes an Indian Rights law," the Sup waved at me.

As always, the New York Times managed to trivialize this historic moment. "The crowd included many Indians in colorful clothing," Ginger Thompson and Tim Weiner wrote. Some people, they scribed, thought "the EZLN's support was no deeper than a T-shirt." The photograph of the monster gathering in the Zócalo unmasked this lie.

The Chess Game

Since the San Andrés Accords and their legislative offspring, La Ley Cocopa (the Cocopa Law, or more popularly, the Indian Rights law), were first signed in February 1996, they had always lived outside, orphaned by Congress and the commission that had godfathered them, kept alive in Zapatista imaginations, in communiqués and corridos, forums and street marches. Now at last the accords were going indoors, and the next chapters would be played out by men in suits who lurked in the dark corridors of the congress of their country, where Indian Rights was a tradable commodity that could be bartered for fiscal reform, the privatization of petroleum production, and even the governorships of certain southern states. Such scenarios did not much augur *un final feliz* (a happy ending) for this solemn saga.

While waiting around for the mavens of the Mexican congress to make up their minds about inviting the ski-masked rebels to address that tarnished chamber, Subcomandante Marcos swapped stories with a coterie of eminent foreign visitors—Nobel laureate José Saramago, the Catalán detective fiction genius Manuel Vázquez Montalban, the famous French globalphobe José Bové, Hebe de Bonafini of Argentina's Mothers of the Plaza de Mayo, and *No Logo* guru Naomi Klein, to name-drop just a few.

One of the stories with which Marcos regaled his audience that afternoon he titled "The Other Player," but Zapalogues like myself more often code-name the tale as "The Story of the Boot and the Chessboard."

It seems an Indian just arrived in the capital from the countryside was vagabonding down the street one morning when he saw a group of men sitting over a chessboard. For nearly an hour, the visitor looked on, trying to sort out the nuances of the game. Each time he asked a question or sought an explanation about why a move was made, he was rudely shushed by the learned chess masters. All of a sudden, the Indian, who had learned certain rudiments of the game by watching, unloosed his muddy boot and dropped it heavily down on the chessboards, scattering pawns and knights, bishops and rooks and queens everywhere. "Checkmate?" the Indian asked cheerfully, reclaiming his boot as he sauntered off down the avenue.

The opening gambit in the EZLN-Fox chess match was played on March 12, the day after the great Zocalo celebration. The COCOPA, the legislative commission that had overseen the San Andrés talks and then shaped the accords into legislation, knocked on the thick iron gate of the National History and Anthropology School next door to the jewel box ruins of Cuicuilco in the south of the city, where the rebel delegation was holed up. The EZLN and the COCOPA had not met for four years, and few of the original members who had drafted the Indian Rights law remained on the commission. The legislators left the Zapatista high command a sealed invitation to speak before the presidents of 20 legislative commissions in the chamber and the senate who would redraft the Indian Rights law.

The invitation, which was written on letterheadless paper and unsigned, offended the comandantes on two counts. First, they had always insisted that the Ley Cocopa be passed by congress without "altering a single comma," and second, as Marcos growled, "We did not come all the way up here to speak to a subcommission. Indian rights are a national clamor. The COCOPA wants to humiliate us."

Comandante Germán, who had shown remarkable diplomatic dexterity as the EZLN "courier," was sent back up to Congress with the rebels' flat-out repudiation of the COCOPA's offer. The Zapatistas intended to speak to all 628 of Mexico's federal deputies and senators from the highest tribune in the land, and nothing less was due them. President Fox, watching his Grand Plan to fix Chiapas in a lot more than 15 minutes unraveling at the edges, counseled patience, but the runaround had touched a Zapatista nerve.

They were farmers, after all, who long before they took up the gun and the mask, had occasionally journeyed up to Mexico City to petition for extensions of their ejidos. They had always been ignored, told the Licenciado was out, or to take a seat and wait until the official would see them. He never did. Congress's hesitation to invite the Indians in was not unsimilar.

Led by members of Fox's own party, PANistas and PRIistas irritably rejected the contamination of the Legislative Palace by grubby, masked Indian rebels. There were no provisions in the protocol for Marcos to address Congress, argued the PANista president of the lower house,

Ricardo García Cervantes. His Senate consort, El Jefe Diego, decreed similarly, suggesting that it was about time for the Indians to head back home anyway. "But we never asked that Marcos should address Congress," the comandantes countered: "We only asked that the EZLN and the CNI be allowed to speak."

What was the problem, the Indians' advocates asked? Lots of citizens had addressed Congress before, even foreign citizens (Jimmy Carter, Jacques Chirac, François Mitterrand, Jiang Zemin, Erich Honecker, and two different presidents of Venezuela), but also Mexican sports heroes and medal winners and even the rehabilitated sex murderer Goyo Cárdenas. Why not the Sup?

A Masterful Stroke

As Congress tried to find coherent legal ground to keep the Indians out, the comandantes lobbied down below, sending delegations into the Indian neighborhoods and barrios in this most Indian of cities to keep their constituencies abreast of the political class's devious efforts to exclude them from speaking before Congress.

Meanwhile, phalanxes of reporters were lining up outside the Escuela Nacional de Antropología y Historia (ENAH) begging for just ten little minutes with the Sup. One of the luckier communicators was *Paris Match*'s Mexico correspondent, who got an excloo with the Subcomandante in which he professed great admiration for Brigitte Bardot.

As the days ticked by and Congress proposed no new formula for the EZLN's defense of the Indian Rights law, Sami Nair, representing the European Parliament as an observer, suggested that if the Mexican congress could not provide a forum for the Indians, the European Parliament would be honored to hear them out.

On Monday, March 19, with the legislators still stalling, the boot hit the chessboard with a mighty thud. The comandantes were tired of waiting around and were going home. Congress had slammed shut its doors on Mexico's Indians with a resounding bang. Why should they waste any more time up here in the capital? It was planting season in the jungles and the highlands of Chiapas. They had plenty to do back home.

The move hit President Fox like a ton of boots. He had to head the comandantes off at the city limits. This would look terrible in the *New York Times*! WUXTRA WUXTRA! INDIANS REBUFFED BY MEXICAN GOVERNMENT! How much Coca-Cola could he sell that way?

Fox really didn't have to fret about the *New York Times*. The Zapatistas were leaving because Marcos had been denied the congressional podium, the paper's all-star Mexico team reported, as if the Indians couldn't speak for themselves.

On March 22, in a last-ditch concession to keep the EZLN in dialogue range, the Fox ordered the dismantlement of the three military bases still outstanding—La Garrucha, Río Euseba, and, after six years of occupation, Guadalupe Tepeyac. The offer failed to persuade the Zapatistas to call off their scheduled departure. We're going home, the rebels insisted. A farewell rally was called outside Congress on Friday afternoon, the 23rd. By now, Fox was wondering when the other boot was going to fall.

Five-Card Stud

Was the bye-bye just a big bluff or the real deal? Had the rebels cashed in their chessboard for a game of five-card stud? On their side of the big table, the Indians sat implacable behind their ski masks. There was no way the Fox could call them out. He pleaded with Marcos for "an eye-to-eye, face-to-face" meeting. No matter where he went the Indians haunted him. On an overnight junket to California, 20 demonstrators showed up at the Sacramento airport to demand that he fulfill his obligation to make the San Andrés Accords law.

Meanwhile, the EZLN mobilized its Mexico City support bases for the big good-bye party outside Congress, touring the federal district's three most important university systems. On the Red Plaza at the National Polytechnic Institute (IPN), with many Indian students and their parents in attendance, Marcos rapped long poetic lines that asked "*¿hasta cuándo?*"—"until when?" How long would this humiliation continue?

"The answer is ours," the Sup posited. The people had the power to end it now.

The next day, the comandantes spoke at all three campuses of the Autonomous Metropolitan University (UAM)—the Subcomandante had been a professor of communication philosophy at the university's Xochimilco branch, and now he talked to the students in the voice of his Quixote-like pet beetle Don Durito of the Lacandón.

On the 22nd, the Zapatistas were invited to the National Autonomous University (UNAM), the oldest institution of superior education in the Americas and Marcos's probable alma mater, where they spoke from what looked like the prow of a ship to a sea of 60,000 young people, most of whom had been preteeners when the rebellion erupted on January 1, 1994.

The UNAM was a tricky stage to work. The university was still bruised from a prolonged and ultimately fruitless student strike during which Marcos had seemingly sided with the ultra leftists. To counter charges of sectarianism, the comandantes had refused to come to campus until the whole university community agreed to issue the invitation, and the Subcomandante's words that afternoon sounded more like a motivational speech than a fiery appeal for action. "Finish your studies but stay in the struggle," he counseled, "and remember to always keep looking at what is happening down below."

Fox Dodges a Bullet

Good political theater requires a modicum of tension. On Friday afternoon, 20,000 rebel supporters gathered outside the Legislative Palace at San Lázaro in the east of the capital, to bid the EZLN adios. The president had summoned El Jefe Diego to Los Pinos near midnight the evening before to impress upon him the need to force a favorable vote on the Zapatistas' petition for an audience before Congress, but Fernández de Cevallos wasn't buying it. At 3:30 p.m. that Friday afternoon, the bristly-bearded senator engineered a frosty no vote in the upper house by a skimpy 52-47, to ratchet up the rebel supporters' frustrations. Now with thousands of enraged Zapaphiles pounding on the doors of the chamber and threatening a *"portazo"* (to take the doors down), the deputies began a crucial roll call vote on inviting the comandantes in. *"¡Portazo! ¡Portazo!"* the mob howled. *"¡No están sólos!"*

When the sound system that was broadcasting the proceedings to the thousands massing outside repeated the results of the vote, the gasp was audible: 220 in favor of hearing the Indians out, 210 opposed. At a late-night ENAH press conference, the comandantes announced their decision to delay departure until after the compas had addressed Congress. Fox had dodged a bullet. But the closeness of the vote did not bode at all well for the Ley Cocopa's chances of passing Congress.

What History Looks Like

The March 28 appearance of the EZLN before a joint session of the Mexican congress has been described as "historic" so often that the use of that descriptive probably set an all-time record for the repetition of a single adjective to describe a historic occasion. Certainly, there was plenty of the stuff afoot. The specter of ski-masked rebels taking their position behind the most political podium in the nation, for example, seemed a historic moment in the history of surrealism.

Historic sessions necessitate protocol. The March 28 conclave was to be a plenary session. All deputies and senators were invited but not required to attend—the PAN promptly declared a boycott—but the presence of the presidents of the 20 congressional commissions that would redraft the law was mandatory. The governors of Mexico's 31 states and Andrés Manuel López Obrador, the mayor of Mexico City, were invited to attend the session, but only four chose to. There would be seven speakers in all, four comandantes and three representatives of the National Indigenous Congress, and legislators would be permitted two rounds of questions. Unlike the Zapatistas' arrival in the capital, both Televisa and TV Azteca would carry the presentations live. The upper galleries would be open and the EZLN and the CNI permitted a total of 210 guests—six of the seats in the Zapatistas' section were left vacant, five for the prisoners still on ice in

Tabasco and Querétaro, and one for Francisco Gómez, Comandante Hugo or "Señor Ik" (Mr. Wind), who had fallen in the taking of Ocosingo on the first night of the war.

For weeks, the big showdown was ballyhooed as a mano-a-mano between Subcomandante Marcos and The Demon Political Class, and the attention lavished on the one mestizo in the Zapatista hierarchy was rancid with racism. Now the masked comandantes filed into the high-domed chambers one by one—David, Tacho, Zebedeo, Esther, Moisés, Omar, Mister, Gonzalo, Javier, Isaías, Bulmaro, Susana, Fidelia, Yolanda, Abel, Eduardo, Filemón, Alejandro, Maxo, Sergio, Abraham, and Bruce Lee . . .

Where was Marcos?

Tightly shoehorned into the press box, dozens of international correspondents corresponded their incredulity. That son-of-a-bitch didn't show up! What about my story? Count 'em again! Fuck. Now they were going to have to listen to the Indians for the next five hours. A sizable number of my colleagues defected posthaste to the nearest cantina, where presumably they would audit these historic proceedings on the telly with a cold Corona in hand.

The Whole World Is Watching

The first masked rebel ever to address the nation's congress stepped up to the mic, and she was a woman. "I just want to make one thing clear," Esther began. "Some of you are wondering where Marcos is today, but he is not here. Marcos is a subcomandante—that is, he works for us. We are the comandantes of the Zapatista Army of National Liberation and we speak for ourselves.

> My name is Esther, but this doesn't matter, I'm a Zapatista and a woman. This is what's important. Through my voice speaks the voice of the Zapatista Army of National Liberation.
>
> No one remembers us, the Indian women. We live on the edge of the mountain and no one sees how hard it is for us. . . .

By now, the legislature had grown so still you could have heard a fat cigar drop on the cushioned carpet.

> It is the women who give birth and see their children die in their arms, and there is nothing that we can do about it but cry. . . .
>
> We are always carrying, carrying wood, carrying water over the mountain for two or three hours, always carrying our children, carrying the corn for the tortillas. Always carrying. . . .
>
> The man goes off to work on the fincas and never comes back, and the woman is left only with her pain. . . .
>
> The ladinos and the rich make fun of us because of how we dress, because of our language, our prayers, our ways of healing, of our color, which is the color of the earth. . . .
>
> This is the life and the death of the Indian woman. I'm not telling you all this to hurt you or make you run off to help us. We ourselves struggle to change these things. . . .

There wasn't a dry eye in the house when Esther was done. All except for the PANistas. Diego had ordered party members not to attend, but 22 had come anyway and now huddled together frozen-faced, like an island in an ocean of empty seats. Those who had defied the Jefe's orders were acutely embarrassed. Marcos had sandbagged them by not showing up, and now their benchmates' boycott looked disrespectful to the Indians.

Despite all the guests, the Chamber of Deputies seemed a cavernous and lonely venue. Only 211 out of a possible 628 legislators had bothered to turn out, a third of a congress that had to pass on 12 constitutional amendments by a two-thirds majority if Indian Rights was to become law, an ominous portent for the legislation's future.

Others spoke that afternoon, perhaps not as plaintively as Esther, but all pleaded with their government to recognize their identity as both Mexicans and Indians. The EZLN still seemed to believe back then that the mal gobierno somehow could do something about their condition— or even wanted to if it could.

David and Tacho and Zebedeo spoke about war and peace and how there could be a dialogue if the San Andrés Accords became law. Representing the CNI, Mixe lawyer Adelfo Regino focused on autonomy and how disingenuous it was to think the indígenas would secede from Mexico if the Indian Rights law were passed. There were ample legal precedents for the free determination of indigenous communities. "Autonomy is not made out of air. It is a living space. It is where we live."

Juan Chávez from the Purépecha Nation spoke softly about the land and how Indians hold it between them collectively because "the earth is our mother." María Patricio, a Nahua healer, defended uses and customs, i.e., doing things in the old way. "We have many good uses and customs. One of our best is to look upon government as a way of serving our communities and not to acquire power over others." She looked hard at her audience when she said this.

The questions the deputies and the senators asked that afternoon were an x-ray of what was in store for the Indian Rights law. Didn't voting openly by consensus as contemplated in the Ley Cocopa violate the sanctity of the secret ballot? Didn't collective ownership infringe on private property rights? What about the rights of non-Indians in Indian territories? And, by the way, just who is an Indian anyway? Didn't legalizing uses and customs mean that human sacrifice was legitimate? Didn't uses and customs mean the persecution of women?

"Listen," María Patricio interjected, barely concealing her rage, "women are not only abused in Indian communities. I'm sure a lot of this goes on in your own homes. . . ." As the interchanges mounted in heat, the legislators discreetly broke for their sumptuous luncheons.

The session was winding down, and Marcos motored up from the south of the city to embrace his comrades as they exited the Legislative Palace to the applause of thousands. "We have done what we have come to do," the Sup told the adoring multitudes. "The buses are ready. This time, we are really going." "¡No-o-o-o!" moaned the mob, "¡No están sólos!"

Then the musicians climbed up on the stage, and Marcos asked Oscar

3. Spring/Summer 2001

Hello, I Must Be Going

The rebels broke camp on the morning of March 30. Many came to wave so long, toodle-ooo, until next time, *¡hasta la victoria siempre!* Even as "the city began to lose its name" (Hermann) out in the misery belt, the pueblo was still waving its good-byes. *"¡No están sólos! ¡No están sólos!"*

The return was a straight shot south and the comandantes dozed. The *MarcoPolo*, accompanied by 20 busloads of CNIs, the civil society, and wandering internationalists, pulled into Oaxaca city that afternoon, stayed the night, and moved on to Juchitán the next morning, where Marcos told another Old Antonio story, this time about trying to find oneself on all the roads of the world. Then the returning caravan pushed onto San Cristóbal, where it had all begun 37 days ago. There was a new moon and several thousand compas crooning in the plaza just as they were when the comandantes left: *"¡No están sólos!"*

In his public pronouncements, Sub Marcos almost exuded optimism. Fernando Yañez had flown on ahead with old Luis H. Alvarez, now the peace commissioner, to inspect the purportedly vacated Guadalupe Tepeyac military base.

The comandantes traded in the *MarcoPolo* for Suburbans the next day to make the rounds of the Aguascalientes and *rendir cuentas*—inform the community bases—of what had transpired on the road. Nine thousand greeted their arrival up in Oventik. "The door to dialogue is opening," Marcos opined and the marimbas pinged. The Subcomandante had not been in Oventik in seven years, not since that first night so long ago now when they had descended the mountains to take San Cristóbal.

Marcos and David embraced. Oventik was his bailiwick and he would stay here. At each of the stops, the comandantes would embrace and take leave—Esther on the Ejido Morelia, others in La Garrucha. There were only seven left by the time they came home to La Realidad, having traversed the Cañadas under a steady drizzle of confetti.

At each of the meetings in the canyons, Marcos had spoken in tongue—Tzeltal and Tzotzil and Tojolabal—something he had never done in public before. The words he left behind in villages that had enjoyed precious little good news from the world out there seemed full of hope.

Back in La Realidad, Major Moy handed Marcos his weapons, and he strapped them on and resumed the command of the EZLN's military forces. Now the Sup and Tacho embraced and the old Tojolabal farmer climbed up on his horse and disappeared into the darkness. Tacho still had a two-hour ride before he reached his house.

Seeding the Earth

Behind their masks, the comandantes were all campesinos, and now it was practically Holy Week already and they still had no seed in the earth. The good news was that the rains had held off and there were still a few days to prepare the ground, to plow and to plant. *"No hay país sin maíz"* for the People of the Corn. There might not even be anything to eat if those who are the color of the earth didn't get busy fast.

Even on the feast day of their demigod Votan Zapata, April 10, the day when poor farmers all over the country march to commemorate his assassination at the hands of the Carranza government back in 1919, the compas were too busy in the *roza y quema* (burning the old fields to enrich the new) to party. During Semana Santa, when middle-class Mexico goes to the beach, the Indians labored on their collective plots, and when they were done, they wiped their collective brow with a red handkerchief, smiled at what they had accomplished, and prayed to the Virgin for rain.

What's It All About?

The San Andrés Accords were signed on February 16, 1996, after several months of arduous negotiations with the representatives of Ernesto Zedillo's government, during which the comandantes were coached and counseled by dozens of experts on Indian issues, most of them non-Indians.

The resulting hodgepodge was a landmark document that could have given Mexico's 57 distinct indigenous peoples autonomous control over their own destinies in every aspect of community life—agrarian policy, use of natural resources, the environment, their health and education institutions, their own judicial system, even time on the nation's Morelos communication satellite to conduct their own native-language programming.

The accords and, later, the Ley Cocopa were founded on the bedrock of the International Labor Organization's Resolution 169, the universally accepted benchmark for defining an indigenous people. OIT (for its initials in Spanish) 169 stipulates that indigenous people have both territory or habitat and "territoriality"—that is, they get to say what goes on inside that territory, i.e., they are autonomous. Although the Mexican congress ratified OIT 169 in 1991, few legislators had ever read it.

Six months after San Andrés was signed and the COCOPA had codified it into a proposed law, then-president Zedillo deep-sixed it, even though his own personal representatives had put their Juan Hancocks on the document, because, he maintained, the autonomy provisions would have permitted Mexico's indigenous peoples to secede from the union, taking with them important resource assets that belonged to the whole nation. The EZLN had protested that nothing could be further from their true intentions—they were in fact Mexicans but wanted to be Mexicans on their own terms. That is what autonomy meant.

Zedillo's veto had shipwrecked San Andrés and killed the dialogue. For the past five years, as the status of the accords hung in limbo, San Andrés had become a kind of sacred creed for the Zapatistas and their supporters. Making the government live up to the commitment it had once so blithely signed had become an obsession for the comandantes that pushed all other political initiatives to the periphery.

The Gutting of Indian Rights

Now the fate of the Indian Rights law was in the hands of a legislature in which Indian blood coursed the veins of only seven out of its 628 members. Five of those seven were members of the PRI.

Moreover, the fight for Indian Rights constituted the first showdown between the new congress and the new president. Inside the congress, the PAN and the PRI split a majority, with the PRD limited to a spoiler rule. Indian Rights was a thorny playing field on which to test-drive the new legislature.

Both the PRI and the PAN (despite the president's ostensible support for the law) expressed grave misgivings about the Ley Cocopa. The lily-white Acción Nacional's program for indigenous rights had a lot more to do with "changarros, vochitos, and teles" than autonomy and free determination. The PRI was not against Indian rights, just these particular Indian rights. The EZLN did not represent all Indians, certainly not the PRI's Indians. The PRI would *"perfeccionar"* ("make more perfect," in the PRI lexicon) and "enrich" the Ley Cocopa. Their legislative surgeons whipped out the scalpels.

The PRD, on the other hand, wanted pretty much to leave the law as it had been drafted by the COCOPA. The Zapatistas, who had no standing in this debate, kept insisting that "not one single comma" be altered.

On April 27, the senate commission charged with preparing the *dictamen,* or proposed law, emerged from behind locked doors to unveil their handiwork, and it was not a pretty sight. The Ley Cocopa had literally been drawn and quartered. Gone were the autonomy provisions—"autonomy" would now be defined and implemented not by the indigenous peoples themselves but by 31 state congresses, the most corrupt legislative level on the republic's political map. Indian nations that transcended state lines—the Nahuas, for example, who live in 15 separate contiguous states—would not be able to associate into autonomous regions.

Indian communities were not autonomous but submissive to the state according to the PAN-PRI rewrite of the Indian Rights law—the essence of the change of a single word from "entities of public right" to "entities of public interest."

The principle of collective ownership of land and natural resources was erased in favor of preserving private ownership. This change opened Indian lands for transnational exploitation, paved the way for mowing down forests and installing junk tree plantations, the pillaging of mineral rights, the piracy of native plants, the privatization of water sources, and the poisoning of indigenous habitat.

There was more. Uses and customs were made subservient to state and federal laws. Indian justice was reduced to the prosecution of chicken thieves, the selection of authorities by consensus made a meaningless ritual. All the rest—education, health, satellite time, etc., would have to wait for the introduction of 72 secondary laws sometime in the dim and distant future. "If the Zapatistas reject this Indian Rights law it won't be the legislature's fault anymore—Vicente Fox will be to blame," PRIista Salvador Rocha, one of the architects of this travesty, boasted.

On April 28, the entire senate voted up the "Indian Rights" law by consensus—the PRD under the baton of Senator Jesús Ortega and Cárdenas's son Lázaro ("It's about as good as we can get . . .") joined in, to the party's eternal shame. The next night, the senate bill went over to the Chamber of Deputies for approval and there was more opposition, mostly from the PRI's Oaxaca section and the PRD, which this time walked out. But the final count was a laugher—388 to 60, not even close.

Once 15 out of 31 states ratified the legislation and President Fox signed on, "Indian Wrongs" would become the law of the land.

There were, of course, a few caveats. PRD chamber leader Hector Sánchez, a full-blooded Zapotec, declared that passage "means war not peace." Félix Castellanos of the Party of Labor (PT), the COCOPA president for the month, complained the law was "stillborn and will change nothing." "This law looks nothing like the one we asked for," insisted Adelfo Regino, the Mixe lawyer, throwing up his hands. He.was still in shock. "They will never listen to us." President Fox, who must have felt a little like he was on the poop deck of the Titanic as an iceberg hove into sight, babbled on about the glass being half full and that there was much work to do.

The EZLN waited 24 hours and then released a nine-point statement rejecting the new law:

1. *The Reform passed by the Congress does not respond to the demands of the Indian peoples.*

2. *This Reform betrays the Accords of San Andrés in substantial points—autonomy, free determination, public rights, land and territory, uses of natural resources, the election of authorities, and the association of municipalities among others.*

3. *The Reform actually restricts our rights and is a grave offense to the Indian people.*

4. *Señor Fox knows perfectly well this is not an Indian Rights law but a simulation.*

5. *With this law, the legislature and the President have slammed shut the door on the dialogue and avoided resolving the principal causes of the rebellion.*

6. The EZLN formally refuses to recognize this reform.

7. As a consequence, we have asked architect Fernando Yañez to suspend his function as our courier. There will be no more contact between the EZLN and the government of Fox. The EZLN will not return to the dialogue until the San Andrés Accords are constitutionally recognized.

8. We call upon international civil society to protest against this joke and demand the passage of the recognition of the constitutional rights of the Indian peoples.

The ninth point was directed at the National Indigenous Congress asking the CNI to organize demonstrations around the country. The Clandestine Indigenous Revolutionary Committee–General Command had nothing more to say. Silence is an Indian weapon.

Indian Wrongs

Although the EZLN had washed its hands of "Indian Wrongs," like the Frankenstein monster it was, the law had taken on a life of its own and eventually wormed its way through enough state congresses to achieve the 16 votes needed for ratification.

In what would turn out to be the comandantes' final communiqué for nearly two years, the rebels' general command turned over the task of organizing resistance to the National Indigenous Congress. With a thriving network down below in the states of the union, the CNI was well suited for the job and called out its troops to lay siege to the state congresses through which the law would lurch.

On May 9, the CNI launched the resistance to Indian Wrongs with the presentation of 60,000 signatures protesting its passage to the Mexican senate and taking back its slogan that the Fox had expropriated in his inaugural address: "Never Again a Mexico Without Us!" The next day, those words were inscribed on a banner that flew from the Eiffel Tower in Paris, France.

The Indians invaded the Michoacán and Guerrero state congresses and urged rejection, 100 Chichimecas were forced out of the Guanajuato state house, and in Puebla, Nahuas threw heavy coinage at local Congress members from the galleries upstairs. Yaquis in Sonora danced around a crackling bonfire on the state capitol lawn in Hermosillo. "Listen to our word!" demanded the three nations of the Tarahumara—the Rarámuris, the Tepehuanes, and the Pimas. Juan Chávez took the voice of the Purépecha Nation to the Quebec City Summit of the Americas in April. Mayans tossed eggs at Chiapas deputies, and Otomís chased a PRI congressperson out a bathroom window in Querétaro.

From the Río Bravo to the Suchiate, Mexico's Indians were dancing and drumming, guarding their sacred fire, shaking their eagle feathers, and generally bringing down a lot of bad mojo on the state legislators. Although the crusade was inevitably doomed, the mobilization of activist Indians all over Mexico was a hopeful sign that the Comandancia of the EZLN, silent but not inattentive to the national dynamic, duly noted in charting its next steps.

In early June, Veracruz, a PRI stronghold, became the first state to ratify the Indian Wrongs law, and the bill's backers quickly ran up a 6-0 lead by maneuvering it through PRI-dominated state congresses. But Chiapas and Oaxaca, the states with the largest Indian populations, soundly rejected Indian Wrongs on the grounds that the new law would not do what it was supposed to do—bring peace between the Mexican government and its indigenous peoples. On June 28, four states voted against ratification, narrowing the count to 11 in favor and eight against. Nonetheless, a late flurry of PRI states held off the on-charging nos, and on July 12, Michoacán became the 16th state to ratify Indian Wrongs. Police battled hundreds of embittered Indians in front of the state congress in Morelia.

The tally sheets from the state legislatures were rounded up and sent on to the senate, which rubber-stamped them in a secret session during the second week in July and forwarded the paperwork on to the Fox to sign and promulgate in the *Diario Oficial*, the federal government's legal daily. Because the measure was a constitutional amendment, Fox, who had sent Indian Rights to Congress in the first place, had no veto power over Indian Wrongs, but by not publishing the law, he could exercise a sort of pocket veto that gave opponents unwarranted hopes.

Eyeball to Eyeball

On July 15, hundreds of CNI militants and Zapatista supporters stormed into the Mexican senate behind a banner that mocked the "Congress of the Apes." They pushed three great boulders into the ornate doorway behind them to make certain no senator could escape. The boulders were clearly labeled "Cevallos," "Bartlett," and "Ortega."

Once inside the chambers, the protesters demanded to speak with the leaders of the PAN, PRI, and PRD, but only El Jefe Diego was available. Faustino Santiago, a Mixtec teacher and translator, was chosen to speak for the National Indigenous Congress.

The two men glared at each other over the long oak table whose high patina reflected the glittering chandeliers of the old palace. There was little love lost between the two men. The Indian had come to ask the senator, a multimillionaire hacienda owner, to fix the wrongs he had committed in gutting the San Andrés Accords. "We ask you to look into your heart and give us back our autonomy and our territoriality."

"Autonomy!" snorted the bristle-bearded senator, jabbing a foul-smelling cigar at Faustino, "Listen, with your damn autonomy you are dividing the nation!" *("¡Oyes! Con tu pinche autonomía estás dividiendo la nación.")* Cevallos had slipped into the *"tú"* voice, the personal pronoun used when addressing children and personal friends. Outside of his servants, Faustino Santiago was probably the first Indian the senator had spoken to in a long while.

"Why do you think we have to do what a bunch of farmers or a clandestine committee with socks on their heads tells us to do? We are the guardians of the whole nation. Our laws are not made in the jungle!" The PANista chieftain was hitting his stride now, playing for the cameras. Faustino had become just a prop. The Mixteco twisted his soft, wide-brimmed sombrero nervously and couldn't contain himself any longer. "How can you say these things?" he blurted. "We are the first people the gods put here in Mexico, and you treat us like a bunch of mental retards!" But Cevallos only waved him off. "The Indian law is decided. It is out of our hands. Do not let your people obstruct this any longer. They will only starve." Faustino rose from his seat and turned to go. "Come," he signaled his comrades, "we do not speak this man's language."

Out of Fox's Pocket

Having received the Indian Wrongs law from the senate, the Fox promised to sign and promulgate it forthwith, but he did not.

The days passed into weeks and the law was not published. Maybe the Indians' magic had pervaded Los Pinos and frozen the president's hand, maybe it was just the distraction of a new bride, Marta Sahagún, his perky, Barbie-like former press secretary. But ultimately, on August 15, Fox gave Indian Wrongs the green light and six years of the Zapatistas' bitter struggle for San Andrés ended in a dry legal notice in *El Diario Oficial*.

There was no general uprising, although the FARP (the Revolutionary Armed Forces of the People), a Guerrero-based breakaway from the EPR, did attack a police barracks in Iguala to retaliate for the betrayal. Neither was there a mass declaration of Indian autonomy as the Purépecha Nation's Abelardo Torres had predicted in Nurio. The guilt-ridden PRD promised to sponsor a "reform of the reform" and reintroduce the Ley Cocopa in Congress, but that proved to be idle chatter. The Fox himself quickly distanced himself from the issue and turned his back on the Zapatistas, rarely ever mentioning their name in public, even when he visited Chiapas. Indian Rights was as dead as a doornail.

Indian Wrongs Goes to Court

But by now, the struggle to achieve San Andrés had become reflexive for activist Indians, and the CNI went to work organizing appeals and *amparos* (injunctions) to test Indian Wrongs' legitimacy in court. One lawsuit led to another. Pablo Salazar and José Murat, the governors of Chiapas and Oaxaca, enlisted all the majority Indian municipalities in their respective states as plaintiffs. Forty of the nation's 57 indigenous peoples filed to protect themselves from the very law that was supposed to protect them. The Indians claimed that Indian Wrongs violated international treaties like OIT 169 and that the states had not ratified the law by a two-thirds majority as is required by the constitution.

By summer's end, 387 legal complaints had been filed with the Mexican Supreme Court to test Indian Wrongs. Since, under Mexican law, the Supreme Court had to judge each case separately on its own merits, the paperwork proved a Herculean task. A hundred clerks had to be hired just to copy the filings and whole warehouses rented out to accommodate the paper trail.

In the end, Indian Rights or Wrongs became the realm of lawyers, and as it did, the fine points for and against became even more indecipherable.

Selling the PPP Like Coca-Cola

In June, the president and Marta Sahagún de Fox went on a working honeymoon in Central America to sell the Plan Puebla Panama to his neoliberal brethren. Fox took all of Mexico's southern governors with him, including Pablo, to pitch the PPP. The presidentes and foreign ministers of Guatemala, Honduras, Costa Rica, Nicaragua, Panama, and Belize were summoned to San Salvador on June 15 to sign off on the primary documents. The Fox was jubilant. When questioned about Chiapas, he insisted the region was in *santa paz* and the EZLN "deactivating." The Plan Puebla Panama was worth "a thouand times more than the Zapatistas or any Indian community."

To seed Vicente Fox's transnational pipe dream, the InterAmerican Development Bank (known as the BID in Latin America) would back the PPP with a $2.5 billion USD grant for its first five years. The presidents toasted their new prosperity.

But although they were all smiles during the photo ops, the rulers of Central America looked at the PPP with a dose of healthy skepticism.

Despite the extravagant promises of electrification, highways, communications, development, and even a dry Panama Canal across the Oaxacan isthmus, they had been burned before. Mexico's power relations with Central America are a mirror image of the U.S.'s domination of Mexico. Like the U.S. migra, the Mexican migra mistreats Central American migrants and returns 100,000 of them to Guatemala each year. The Central American leaders' caution was understandable.

At the beginning of their administrations, every Mexican president unveils his development strategy with great bombast, but the projects just never seem to get done. A road is built to nowhere, a forest is torn down, white elephants litter the countryside, someone steals the money, or the money just runs out, and by the time public demands an accounting, the president is gone from office. The Fox's scam fit nicely into this frustrating mold.

¡PUKUJ!

On the same weekend that Fox was fixing the PPP up with the Central American oligarchs, people's organizations from the lands to be blessed by the Plan Puebla Panama met in San Cristóbal de las Casas to dissect the megaproject, develop a defense, and propose alternatives. Representatives of more than 200 farmers' and indigenous organizations, environmentalists, women's groups, and NGOs from 15 countries decried the PPP's impacts on forests, corn, mineral exploitation, water resource, biomass, and Indian culture. One speaker after another reminded their colleagues that only indigenous autonomy as guaranteed in the San Andrés Accords could give Indian peoples the tools to fight off such impositions.

One theme under intense scrutiny at the gathering was the charge of transnational biopiracy in the Altos and Selva of Chiapas. Rumors had floated for years that the Monterrey-based biotech titan Pulsar had enlisted the notorious Monsanto Corporation in a plot to map the genome of the Lacandón jungle for profit—an experimental station had already been established near Laguna El Suspiro in the deep jungle of the Montes Azules biosphere reserve.

Ten years earlier, biotech had visited the Mayans when *pozol*, a corn gruel that Indian doctors say has curative and digestive value, was "discovered" by a team of University of Minnesota scientists. Professor Larry McKay had successfully isolated an enzyme from the native beverage, taken out a patent, and leased it to a Dutch food processor for millions as a preservative. Now if the Mayans wanted to export pozol to the U.S., they had to pay the professor sizable royalties.

The theft of native medicines was happening all over again up in the highlands. The 1992 Río treaty had led to the creation of the International Biodiversity Group, which sponsored a project in the highlands—IBDG-Maya—ostensibly designed to identify and collect native plants in Los Altos of Chiapas. Under the direction of ethnobiologist Brent Berlin of the University of Georgia, an anthropologist with 40 years of experience in Chiapas who claimed *compadrazgos* (extended family relations) with village leaders, communities were contracted to supply plant collections to the San Cristóbal–based College of the Southern Border, a local research institute, which would receive and cull the samples and ship off promising materials to Berlin—the University of Georgia reputedly has the largest collection of Chiapas native plants on the educational map.

But the leaves didn't stop there. Utilizing the University of Georgia as a front, Berlin had helped to establish a Welsh laboratory, Nature Molecular Limited, which would probe the materials for byproducts with commercial value. Some call this process "bio-prospecting" and others, such as those in attendance at the San Cristóbal conclave, "bio-piracy." In a large photograph displayed at the entrance to the conference, Brent Berlin and his trim scientist wife appeared to have vision problems. Both had been adorned with pirate eye-patches.

The Indians were not happy with Brent Berlin. The owners of Nature Molecular Limited stood to make millions should they develop a salable commodity from the biomass Berlin sent them. The lab would keep the sales price to a manufacturer and reimburse itself for research costs. The Indians would be part of a four-way split of 1% of the royalties from any commercial products developed from their forests.

Antonio Pérez, a Tzotzil healer and member of the COMPICH—the Council of Organizations of Indian Doctors and Midwives—was furious and called Berlin a *pukuj*—a devil—right there on the conference floor. "This man is a pukuj—he is stealing our ways of healing!" Sebastián Luna, a second Tzotzil doctor, agreed with the designation: "I have nothing against Doctor Berlin personally, but he is making a profit on the sacred medicines Madre Tierra"—Mother Earth—"has gifted us with for the benefit of the people, and this makes him a pukuj." Matías Santiz, an elder from Oxchuc, even had a song about it. "He steals our corn and beans / He steals our plants and flowers / Pukuj! Pukuj! Be warned / The Pukuj is coming."

When Berlin's representative at the conference tried to speak in defense of the ethnobiologist, he was shouted down with cries of *"¡Pukuj! Fuera!"* (Devil! Get out of here.)

Berlin's scam soon fell upon hard times. The communities canceled their contracts—they had been signed with the now-ousted PRI caciques and would not be honored. The think tank, fearful of damaging its already tarnished reputation, pulled out. Berlin, who told me he was "a Zapatista in spirit," had failed to learn a basic lesson of the new Chiapas. Anthropologists had to find a new way of practicing their profession in the Zapatista zone now. First they had to ask the communities for permission to pursue their investigations, and then they needed to demonstrate how their research would benefit that community. This was the Zapatista way.

Jumping Genes

Not far away from the highlands of Chiapas, as the wind blew, an even greater threat to Indian culture and the indigenous way of life was taking root that summer up in Oaxaca's Sierra of Juárez in the tiny Zapotec-Chinanteco town of Calpulalpan.

When Mexican-born but Berkeley-based microbiologist Ignacio Chapela took a look at corn samples under a microscope in a rustic laboratory he had set up for the local farmers, something seemed very wrong. He had never seen maize DNA that looked so odd—"The genes were jumping around," Ignacio would tell me later, "this couldn't be."

Then he realized that he was looking at the first genetically modified corn to have spread into the Mexican milpa.

Intifada

Whether actively challenging the rulers of Mexico or brandishing silence as an Indian weapon, the Zapatista Army of National Liberation was one wing of the Global Intifada that rose like the phoenix in the first years of the millennium.

It began, as usual, in the Holy Land. During the high Jewish holidays in September 2000, in a coldly calculated stunt to enhance his prime ministerial aspirations, Ariel Sharon, the butcher of Lebanon, responsible for the murder of nearly 2,000 Palestinian refugees in the Sabra and Chatila camps on September 14–15, 1982, led a walking tour of one of the catacombs beneath the Temple Mount in the old city of Jerusalem. The ploy was, of course, designed to enrage the Muslim Palestinians who hold the Al Aqsaa Mosque that sits atop the Temple Mount, to be one of the most sacred shrines in Islam.

As Sharon anticipated, rioting promptly broke out in the cities of the West Bank and Gaza. Young men marched out of the kasbahs of Nablus and Jenin, hurling rocks and firebombs at the so-called Israeli Defense Force. In late September, the second Intifada was proclaimed—the first had ended with the now-disregarded Oslo Accords. A wave of suicide bombers terrorized Israeli cities—some of the bombs were delivered by women, the first women *shuhada*.

Sharon was elected prime minister in February 2001, and Israeli troops celebrated by hammering what remained of Yasser Arafat's Palestine—the Muqata, Arafat's walled compound in Ramallah, was severely damaged in the shelling, and Sharon ordered the "selective assassinations" of leaders of the resistance. By the end of the first year, 609 Palestinians had been killed in combat, four times the number of the Israeli dead, and the Arab world was on fire.

The Palestinian Intifada was one of several such social thrusts from down below that defied the global elite during summer 2001.

On June 15, ski-masked demonstrators armed with stones and Molotov cocktails confronted usually placid Swedish police during a European summit in Guttemberg, and for a second that staid old city bore more than a passing resemblance to Ramallah. The globalphobes had been on the warpath since Quebec City in April, a face-off with the Royal Canadian Mounties that looked a lot like one extended fire-bombing as the Nation of Seattle repeatedly tried to burn down the walled old citadel inside of which the Masters of the Universe were plotting the Free Trade Area of the Americas, or ALCA in Spanish.

The Main Event

The main event was slated for Genoa on July 20–21, when the cryptofascist Silvio Berlusconi would be hosting his first G-8. A hundred thousand police were mobilized to control the antiglobalization mobs, but three times that number of protesters showed up and took the old port city. Urban warfare was the order of the day—helicopters flopped overhead and the acrid taste of tear gas filled Genoa's narrow, twisty alleyways. Banks were torched on the Via Tripoli and fancy cars reduced to charred hulks. Ominous billows of black smoke from tire fires and pyres of garbage set by the dread Black Bloc cast a pall over the summit. The Free World's leaders had to be quarantined to ships in the harbor because it was too risky to set foot on dry land. "You can't let these demonstrators keep us from meeting," Baby Bush complained to his host.

Hundreds were arrested and 248 injured severely enough to be taken to hospital, most after the police encouraged the Black Bloc to mingle with peaceful demonstrators and then used vandalism as a pretext to clobber everyone. There was one death.

Carlo Giuliani, 26, a Black Blocker from Padua, was shot in the head at point-blank range after he pointed his fire extinguisher at a carabiniere. Italian police had not shot and killed a demonstrator since 1977, and Giuliani's death upped the ante in this instant Intifada. Protesters wept with rage and impotence as the police helicopters roared in over their heads and the truncheons flew.

Up until the killing of Carlo Giuliani, the antiglobalization move-ment had been kind of a game, a shadow play between security forces and demonstrators. Now the first blood had been drawn. Movements must have martyrs to flourish. Throughout Europe, stone-throwing youth gangs rampaged through the cities to avenge the young Italian's murder.

So what does this have to do with the Zapatista Army of National Lib-eration? Just this—the Carlo Giuliani Brigade of Italian activists now makes an annual pilgrimage to Chiapas in solidarity with the EZLN. They have even gifted Oventik with an ambulance.

Bombing the Banks with Doves

Mexico got a fresh taste of the Global Intifada on August 7 when three Mexico City branches of Banamex were "bombed"—well, not really bombed. Incendiary devices, large firecrackers known here as *palomas*, or "doves," were set off outside the branches, shattering windows and doors and setting off alarms but not doing mortal damage. The explo-sions occurred after hours and no injuries to passersby were recorded. Banamex, the nation's oldest bank, dating back to the 1870s, had just been sold to Citigroup.

The Banamex bombings were the first in Mexico City in the seven years since the Zapatista rebellion had exploded and radicals had shown their support by detonating a car bomb in a university parking garage. The bombings were also the first acts of terrorism under the Fox's regime, and cranked-up security forces went into action.

The FARP—the Armed Forces of the Revolutionary People—took on-site credit for the deed, leaving their initials spray-painted upon a blasted wall. The sale of Banamex to the gringos had been an affront to "the decorum and dignity of all Mexicans"—the FARP action may have been the first time in Latin America that a guerrilla army had come to the defense of a bank.

The FARP was also ticked off at the gutting of the Indian Rights law and Carlo Giuliani's martyrdom in Genoa. Finally, the guerrillas demanded that

Bolivia's ambassador to Mexico, Colonel Gary Prado, famed for capturing Che Guevara and cutting off his hands, be declared persona non grata.

The FARP first came to public notice on April 10, 2000, Zapata's death day, when it staged an armed press conference in the delegation of Xochimilco—the Banamex attacks took place on the eve of Emiliano Zapata's birthday. Sometimes tagged a Generation X guerrilla because it used the Internet as a tool of communication and had its roots in the 1999 student strike at the UNAM, the FARP had been one of the groups whose support for Indian Rights Marcos had asked in Iguala during the March of the People the Color of the Earth. On May 31, the FARP had been one of three guerrilla bands that attacked a military outpost in Iguala to protest passage of the Indian Wrongs bill.

Ten days after the dove bombings, three young brothers—Hector Cerezo, 26, Antonio, 23, and Alejandro, 19, all of them UNAM students, were rounded up at their Xochimilco home and charged with terrorism. They would become the first accused terrorists to be sentenced in the wake of the 9/11 New York and Washington attacks. Two of the three brothers are still in maximum-security prisons at this writing.

Although the FARP attacked Banamex with firecrackers, the message was crystal clear—the Fire Next Time.

Hours after the smoke cleared in Mexico City, across the planet in Jerusalem the Palestinian Intifada struck with stunning ferocity when a suicide bomber blew himself up inside a jam-packed Sbarro pizza parlor at lunchtime. Eighteen were killed outright and 90 others shredded by the nail bomb. Severed limbs were scattered for blocks around. Sharon retaliated in kind and turned the West Bank into a killing floor. All of this horrendous violence took place almost exactly a month before 9/11. Was anyone noticing?

4. Fall 2001

The Whole Enchilada

On September 3, President Fox, his increasingly Svengali-like foreign minister Castañeda, and, indeed, his whole cabinet touched down in Washington for the first state visit of the Bush regime. Much as Mexico had been the destination of Dubya's first foreign foray, Fox would be the first foreign potentate the Bushes would entertain at the White House.

The two presidents had not met since February when Baby Bush had ordered a routine "preventive" attack on Saddam's Iraq, converting Fox's Guanajuato rancho into a launching pad for the Fourth World War. As they had planned back then, immigration reform was on the front burner for the White House talks.

In the scenario that Jorge Castañeda had cooked up, immigration reform was the cornerstone of U.S.–Mexico bilateral relations, and the legalization of the status of 3.5 million undocumented Mexican workers living in the shadows of the United States was the cornerstone of that cornerstone. The Bush administration had proposed instead an expanded guest worker program, a virtual rerun of the flawed Bracero program of the 1940s and '50s, really a species of indentured servitude.

But Jorge, who was broadly mistrusted in Washington (particularly by Senate Foreign Relations Committee honcho Jesse Helms) as a deceitful leftist opportunist who had cast his falling fortunes with the Fox (not an off-the-mark judgment at all), would not settle for anything less than the "Whole Enchilada" as he dubbed it—both "legalization" ("amnesty" had become a dirty word in the Bush lexicon) AND a guest worker program that could produce as many as 600,000 jobs a year for Mexican workers.

Castañeda met with secretary of state Colin Powell on the morning of the 4th, and the two emerged from behind closed doors with amiable smiles on their mugs. There were still differences, but maybe something could be worked out after all. Later that day, the Fox lobbied a special joint session of Congress, urging the solons to find a new approach to this age-old dilemma; received an award from the National Endowment for Democracy (NED), the moneybags for the conservative opposition in Latin America; and schmoozed with national security adviser Condi Rice, who dubbed the towering president "the living personification of democratic change." Alan Greenspan even lined up to shake hands. Things were going very well, *espléndido*, Fox waved to reporters.

The presidentes posed for the official photo and got down to brass tacks on the 5th. "It is a great honor for us to be amigos and partners for prosperity," the Bush oozed in welcome. "Our two nations are constructing a singular relationship in the world," the Fox boomed back, and both disappeared to palaver, first privately deep in the bowels of the White House and then with their respective cabinet ministers. Once again, the *banda* filed out with big grins on their mushes. U.S. attorney general John Ashcroft assured reporters that Bush was "firmly committed to making immigration reform a reality"; Castañeda boasted that an agreement could be signed within the year, at the latest early 2002.

In addition to positive movement on immigration, Castañeda had wrung several key concessions in other areas that Mexico had long sought from the White House. Washington would no longer "certify" Mexico's willingness to wage the War on Drugs as it had every March for a decade, a source of much ill will and nasty name-calling, and the Bush administration would review the long-standing ban on the importation of Mexican tuna fish enacted because the Mexicans killed too many dolphins in the process. Things were going splendidly, *espléndido*.

The White House visit pulsed with pomp and circumstance: a 21-gun salute to honor the Mexican president and a patriotic pageant featuring an honor guard dressed in Revolutionary War costumes tootling "Yanqui Doodle Dandy," followed by military marching bands and contingents carrying flags that marked great American military victories. David Brooks, the sharp-eyed *Jornada* U.S. correspondent, watched as banners celebrating "Kosovo," "Vietnam," "Pine Ridge" (*sic*), and, incredibly "Mexican Incursion 1846–47" (which resulted in the theft of half of Mexico's territory) and "Mexican Incursion 1916–1917" (Black Jack Pershing's futile chase of Pancho Villa) marched solemnly by.

Then it was State Dinnertime. The presidents, both dressed in tuxedos and cowboy boots, and their respective spouses—Marta in four-inch heels and chiffon and the more zaftig Laura in a Scaasi gown—greeted guests in the East Room for cocktails. Among the luminaries in attendance: Chief Justice Rehnquist; Secretary of State Powell; Jeb and Columba, his Guanajuato-born wife; prominent Republicans (John McCain, the odious Helms) and Democrats (Joe Biden and Tom Daschle); Archbishop Roger Mahoney of Los Angeles; all-star Latinos like Plácido Domingo, NFL Hall-of-Famer Antonio Muñoz, the then–Dallas Mavericks Mexican Eduardo Nájera, and President Bush's attorney, Alberto Gonzales; a pack of billionaire businessmen and women from both sides of the border; and representing Hollywood, movie tough guy Clint Eastwood.

"Our relationship is incredibly important!" the Bush toasted, hoisting a flagon of 7-Up (the president, a dry drunk, didn't drink alcohol then). Dinner was White House kitsch and gluttony at its most flagrant: Maryland crab, buffalo steak crusted with pumpkin seeds, fava and chantelle ragout, chorizo pozole, and a miracle mango whip dessert sprinkled with red chile peppers and a tequila *sabayón*. You could have fed a whole village in Chiapas with what the guests stuffed down their craws that night.

Significantly, there were no enchiladas.

After supper, the Bushes and the Foxes mounted the balcony for a 20-minute display of fireworks that lit up the White House switchboard with complaints from the neighbors. The photo op of the two presidents and their elegantly coiffed wives waving frenetically from the balcony to a passel of flunkies down below was worth the price of admission.

Across the street in Lafayette Park, Zapatista supporters had gathered to give Fox the finger. "*¡Zapata Vive! ¡La Lucha Sigue!*" they yodeled and waved signs that demanded the Fox make San Andrés the law of the land.

Five days later, there were, of course, additional fireworks. Mohammed Atta and his merry band flew commercial airliners into the World Trade Towers and the Pentagon, and thousands died, some of them Mexicans. Overnight, Mexico went from being "incredibly important" to a "trampoline for terrorists." Castañeda's whole enchilada was dead and stinking. "Everyone coming in here now is a potential terrorist," an unidentified customs agent in Laredo told the *New York Times*.

TERROR WAR

Era un once de septiembre,
Cuando los hechos pasaron,
Un martes en la mañana,
Dos torres detumbaron
El orgullo de Manhattan.

(—"The Tragedy of Manhattan," Los Rancheros de Terán)

The psychosis spread south at the speed of CNN. "Attack on America!" flashed on every screen in the republic—Mexico is a part of America. The towers collapsing over and over again on the tube struck a nerve—the desolation reminded many of the terrible 8.1 earthquake that had buried 30,000 and changed the political landscape south of the border exactly 18 years and eight days earlier.

At least 16 Mexicans were lost on Black Tuesday up there in the towers, walloping pots and bussing tables in Windows on the World on the 108th floor. The real number of Mexicans lost remains a mystery. The Tepeyac Center in New York tried to keep count, but many of the missing never were found in the rubble—the Center estimated that there were 500 Mexicans working in and around the WTC that fateful morning.

The workers in Windows on the World were mostly Mixtec and Nahua Indians from Puebla, Oaxaca, and Tlaxcala, states that have been sending their young men to New York for a decade. Once, at a wild Indian fiesta in Tlaxcala, I was approached by a young man wearing an "I Survived the World Trade Center Bombing" T-shirt. He told me that he had been working in a delicatessen at street level when the Blind Sheikh detonated his fertilizer bomb, and had been cut badly by flying glass.

There are now an estimated half million Mexican workers in the greater New York area, most from the farming towns of the bone-dry altiplano of central Mexico, and taco stands line the streets of Manhattan these days—when I was growing up in Gotham, there were perhaps four Mexican restaurants on the whole island. The newcomers work long hours for below-minimum wages at 24-hour Korean greengrocers, as night cleaners in the skyscrapers, taking care of rich people's kids, washing cars, selling flowers in the street, and stitching in the sweatshops, the kind of labor that every immigrant population that has ever come to this city of immigrants has always done, and like those who came before them, they send as much money as they can back to their families and dream of going home rich.

> *El Pentagon, señores,*
> *No puede hacer la excepción,*
> *Lo cuidan como un diamante,*
> *Y lo es de la nación,*
> *No pudieron salvarlo,*
> *Y nunca de la tercer avión.*
>
> (—*"The Tragedy of Manhattan"*)

The attacks of 9/11 put a big hurt on Mexican workers in the Gran Manzana. The collapse of the economy dried up their jobs, and they couldn't send home the *remisas* that kept their families and their villages going. Moreover, tightened border security in the wake of 9/11 kept them from ever going back to Mexico, because they knew they would never be able to return to Manhattan when the shit storm blew over. In a word, they too had been buried under the rubble of the Towers.

Incredibly, Vicente Fox was at the World Trade Center himself that very morning—but the Mexico City WTC, a modest 28-story structure, addressing the usual gaggle of impresarios. His reaction to news of the catastrophe was reflexive: "This is a crime against humanity that cannot go unpunished!" Fox immediately cabled off his solidarity to George Bush, who, by now, was cowering in a Colorado bunker. Mexicans had died in this terrorist attack, and now Mexicans would do their part in Bush's War on Terror.

Privately, the Foxistas had to concede that the future wasn't coming up roses. Immigration reform was the first casualty—a nation that has just suffered grievous terrorist attack does not easily open up its borders. The economic downturn ushered in by 9/11 would slow the flow of the remisas, the country's second-largest source of income, and the economy would be in the toilet for a year at least. The border crackdown would stall trade, and mountains of Mexican produce would spoil waiting in the endless lines to get across to the Other Side. The border-based maquiladoras would go belly up without orders for U.S. consumer goods.

> *Por cielo, por mar, por tierra*
> *Osama Bin Laden te anda buscando,*
> *Bin Laden, el terrorista*
> *Que la CIA ha preparado,*
> *Este fue el error más grande*
> *Del gobierno americano*
>
> (—Rigoberto Cárdenas)

Although the Fox tendered copious condolences, the Bush wanted more. "You are either with me or with the terrorists," he had howled to the rest of the world at a joint session of the U.S. Congress in his September 19 declaration of the War on Terror. What Bush wanted from Mexico was impossible for Fox to deliver: a symbolic commitment of troops for his crazed crusade in the desert. But the Mexican president's hands were tied by his country's constitution—Mexico does not intervene in foreign wars.

Nonetheless, Castañeda thought he could change all that. Bush had "the right to revenge" and Mexico should back him up. I suppose he thought he might be able to salvage his cherished enchilada, but Jorge's idea was not an idea whose time had come. For many Mexicans, 9/11 was a case of the chickens coming home to roost.

Marching off into battle with a nation that had invaded their country eight times has rarely been on the agenda of most Mexicans. Like all Latin Americans, they remembered another 9/11 back in 1971 when Henry Kissinger toppled the socialist government of Salvador Allende, assassinated the president, and installed a brutal tinplate dictator named Pinochet in La Moneda Palace. About 3,000 lives had been snuffed out in both 9/11s.

"This is not our war," wrote political guru Miguel Angel Granados Chapa in the daily *Reforma*. "The U.S. has many enemies that are not Mexico's enemies," former national security chief Jorge Carrillo Olea observed in *La Jornada*. One unheralded citizen took it upon himself to pass out leaflets in front of the U.S. embassy reminding passersby of Hiroshima and the genocide of North American Indians. The conspiracy-minded recalled the U.S.S. *Maine*, the Reichstag, and the Gulf of Tonkin subterfuge, and figured that Bush, a president without a mandate who had stolen high office in a bogus election, had bombed himself to win sympathy.

"*¡Bush! ¡Colón! ¡Al Paredón!*" ("Bush, Columbus, to the firing squad!"), demonstrators chanted as they marched past the much abused statue of Christopher Columbus on Reforma Boulevard on October 12, now the Day of Indigenous Resistance. "*¡No a la Guerra! ¡Bush Es una Perra!*" (No to the war, Bush is a female dog), Zapatista supporters whooped as they stormed into the plaza in San Cristóbal that day.

Hours after the attack, I ran into my ultra-left comrade Alejandro in a local *panadería* (bakery) here in the Centro Histórico of Mexico City where I live. "Did you see that? What pilots! What balls they had!" he gloated, expressing an opinion that many who live in the south of the world must have entertained that startling day. I ran into Alejandro about a year after Black Tuesday. He was more subdued. Now he was certain that Bush had staged the whole thing to consolidate Yanqui control over the rest of the planet.

Fox's problem with contributing even a token force to Bush's Terror War on Afghanistan provoked Washington's umbrage. Mexico had not held one single display of public mourning to express solidarity with its nearest neighbor to the north. Mexico was on a par with Axis of Evil countries on the condolence meter, equal to Cuba and one step above Saddam, who did finally express his sympathies one month late, on October 20. A campaign to boycott Cancún was hatched. Fox had to go on Larry King to explain Mexico's lack of enthusiasm for the War on Terror, but the damage had been done and Bush and Fox would eye each other with mutual distrust for the next five years.

Terror Time in Tacoland

The U.S. southern border was the gateway for Al Qaeda. Any halfway-witted terrorist could penetrate this 3,000-kilometer swatch of No-Man's-Land. The mujahideen were already on the way north—Hezbollah secret cells operating on the Triple Frontier out of Ciudad de Este, Paraguay. Bin Laden was recruiting suicide bombers among the Mara Salvatrucha, the tough, tattooed Central American youth gangs now congregating on the Mexican border at Tapachula, Chiapas. Members of the Revolutionary Armed Forces of Colombia, the FARC, which heads the White House list of narco-terrorist organizations, had been busted in Tijuana on the U.S. border. The Zapatistas were lurking in Chiapas. Batten down the hatches!

It was sort of like the bad old Red Dawn days with the Soviet Army and the Cubans pouring into Colorado to take "what we have" and the Red

Chinese massing in Baja California, and Harlingen, Texas, only a 48-hour ride from Sandinista, Nicaragua. When a truck hauling cyanide was stolen at gunpoint in Puebla a few thousand miles from the U.S., the FBI received permission to parachute in to thwart the hijacking.

As in El Norte, the racist backlash was palpable. A Mexican citizen was beaten to death in Los Angeles after reportedly being mistaken for a "raghead." In Mexico City, the windows of the Islamic Cultural Center were punched out. A Palestinian visitor was detained and interrogated by federal police while seeing the sights on Reforma. The terror waves swooshed when 41 Iraqis, Chaldean Christians trying to reach Detroit, were rounded up by the Mexican migra near Tijuana precisely on 9/11, and on the 22nd, 14 paperless migrants from Yemen, Bin Laden's mother's place of birth, were collared in Tapachula. All arrests of Arab travelers were to be immediately reported to Washington, undersecretary of the interior Ramón Martin Huerta instructed.

Air travel in and out of the capital triggered nervous breakdowns. The FBI had taken over Benito Juárez International Airport, to the great disdain of Mexican nationalists, profiling the passengers, ransacking their luggage, compiling no-fly lists, and groping the potential terrorists. Several Aeromexico flights to Los Angeles, the airline's most popular route, were turned back in California air space, one with a fighter jet escort.

On October 9, two Israeli agents, Saur Ben Zvi and a Mexican citizen living in Tel Aviv, were stopped inside the congressional complex with a suitcase containing timers, wires, and fuses—but no explosives. Ben Zvi was deported before reporters could get to him, and his partner disappeared back into the gnarliest megalopolis in the western world. The incident remains notoriously unexplained.

Bin Laden Comes to Chiapas

Chiapas, with hundreds of miles of dense border jungle, was a known terrorist den. At least 18,000 troops and probably a lot more, who had been confined to barracks since the Fox had ordered them to stand down, were turned loose to patrol the frontier with Guatemala for incoming terrorists—the border zigs and zags just 20 miles south of La Realidad, and the Zapatistas fretted that an invasion was on the army's menu.

I traveled to San Cristóbal at the end of September. There was still a crowd of Chamula men gawking at the planes plowing into the towers time and time again on the bank of screens at the Elektra store on Insurgentes. The manager confided that the Indians thought they were watching a movie but I doubt it. There had been Mexican air force bombings here in the first days of the rebellion.

Gustavo Castro, a savvy researcher who heads up the San Cristóbal think tank CIEPAC, told me that when he visited the villages now, the compas would ask him for the "New York" video. Gustavo figured that they had seen that the American Cyclops was vulnerable and that maybe the Lilliputians of this world could, in fact, put out its one good eye if they ever got together.

The Mayan people are very attuned to apocalyptic scenarios. Their sacred books predict an end to the present cycle in 2010–2012. The Apocalypse was something that the evangelicals, many of whom were Mayan, could get with too—but the Jehovah's Witnesses were not convinced. Two conditions were lacking for Gog and Magog to square off, Esther Díaz told me one morning in San Cris as she passed out tracts in the plaza. Not all the lands of the earth had received the word of the Savior yet—18 nations were still unblessed , including Afghanistan, but she hoped the U.S. would soon take care of that. The second condition was the reconstruction of Jehovah's Temple, which would involve the eviction of Muslims from the Al Aqsaa Mosque, a move Ariel Sharon was already plotting.

A few yards away inside the Cathedral of Peace, the Diocese, once a lair of liberation theology, was singing a different psalm than the Jehovah's Witnesses. "The United States has sown violence all over the world and now it has reaped what it planted," Don Samuel's successor, Felipe Arizmendi, preached in his homily at Sunday night Mass. Bush must reflect on why the whole world hates his country. "September 11 cannot be fixed by committing injustices against the poor nations and exploiting them." Bush should not regard the poor as his enemy but rather lower their national debts instead. "We pray against war and terrorism," the bishop intoned from the altar, sounding for all the world like his sainted predecessor.

But the Spirit House where the 9/11 dagger stuck its deepest was out on the periphery of town at the Sheikh Hamdan bin Rashid al Maktoum *madrassa,* or Islamic training center, located at the foot of the Hormiga colony, a swarming kasbah of Tzotzil evangelicals expelled from Chamula for not honoring the saints with Tzotzil white lightning, or *posh.* The Hormiga, an enclave landscaped by the bones of stolen cars, is where the PRI paramilitaries bought the heavy artillery that murdered 49 at Acteal.

The Sheikh Hamdan madrassa sat catty-corner to the Strong Fort Pentecostal House of Prayer, forming a kind of fundamentalist ghetto on the edge of San Cristóbal. The Islamic training center is pretty much the handiwork of two stern-looking Spanish converts from Granada (once a Muslim city), Esteban López and Aureliano Pérez, who have baked San Cristóbal's best whole-grain breads for years. Both are married to Tzotzil women and make many babies. Whenever Zapatista tensions max out, they are visited by immigration authorities.

One day, Esteban and Aureliano passed a copy of the Holy Koran to a pistol-packing Hormiga preacher, Domingo López Angel, a PRD deputy who had been expelled from the state congress for fomenting one too many ruckuses. López Angel and his fellow firebrand preacher Manuel Collazo were both affiliated with the left-center party, and Governor Croquetas tossed them into Cerro Hueco on trumped-up charges just before the presidential election and urged them to convert to the PRI. Collazo did and was released in time to vote. Domingo refused to recant, stayed in his cell, and studied the Koran, Malcolm X–like. Eventually, he took Allah as his personal savior, and when he was released he moved his flock to Mohammed at the madrassa.

Now the Muslims of San Cristóbal were on the hot seat. Since 9/11, military surveillance had been intensified. Televisa had run a tabloid clip,

"*Escuela de Terroristas*" (Terrorist School) that showed the community at prayer. Collazo, who had split with López Angel, accused the Muslims of being in league with Bin Laden. There had been death threats in several languages. "We are afraid they will come take us and our families as they are doing with Muslim men in your country," Esteban sullenly smoldered at a U.S. reporter.

They Must Be Terrorists

The Comandancia watched the towers tumbling down, the business suits plunging into the abyss, and the subsequent devastation and hysteria, probably on a tiny black-and-white screen hooked up to a car battery in their camps above La Realidad. What they thought of it all is not recorded in any communiqué.

The EZLN had frequently been tarred as terrorists—they wore the obligatory ski masks, didn't they? In the first days of the rebellion, the media made them out to be green-eyed Guatemalan terrorists. A score of Zapatistas, including Javier Elorriaga and Elisa Benavides, were locked up in February 1995 by Zedillo on terrorism charges. More recently, a U.S. Drug Enforcement Administration circular had coupled them with the EPR and the FARC as "narco-terrorists," an absurd charge for a group that carries out its own stringent war on drugs. Terrorism is still delicate terrain for the compas to navigate. They don't like to talk about it much. And besides, the comandantes had taken a vow of silence.

But the EZetas had their defenders in high places. Governor Pablo vouched that they were *luchadores sociales* (social strugglers), not Bin Laden's henchmen and -women. In his heart of hearts, Fox probably did think they were terrorists, but peaceful ones who only terrorized his peace of mind, not like the EPR and the FARP, the bad guerrillas.

"This is one of the worst stages for the Zapatistas. They have been overwhelmed by events and marginalized in the press. No one thinks about them anymore because of the international situation," Miguel Alvarez, Don Samuel's secretary, told *La Jornada*, "but still silence is not paralysis. It is a way of speaking out. . . ."

But if the Comandancia remained mum, the bases had their own analysis. On October 5, the Italians and their turbines finally kicked in and the lights came on in La Realidad. News of 9/11 and Bin Laden, the Taliban, and the War on Afghanistan boomed from every radio and TV. "We never thought airplanes could be turned into bombs," Rubén, a Zapatista campesino, commented to Hermann one jungle autumn afternoon, eyeing the heavens for low-flying aircraft. "In this country now, Afghanistan, many people will suffer, no?" the farmer asked, but he knew the answer already. The Afghanis were Lilliputians like themselves, *otros* (others) like all the Indians and non-Indians who have come to call themselves Zapatistas, and now they would all catch a little piece of hell.

The Fourth World War

In the absence of any text from the Subcomandante and his cohorts during this painful period, *La Jornada* (Oct. 22) published an excerpt from a 1999 document that Marcos had presented to the visiting International Observation Commission (mostly Italians and Spaniards), which he had slugged "The Fourth World War." I excerpt from the excerpt here—remember Marcos is the EZLN's military commander.

> *Every war up until now results in territorial realignment. The First World War, the Second, the Cold War. But in a uni-polar, globalized world, the territory that is conquered is the globe. In the Fourth World War, the enemy is humanity. . . .*

> *The idea now is to conquer and reorganize the people rapidly. In the first Gulf War, the U.S. had assembled a massive force and inflicted rapid mass destruction but abandoned the conquered territory before the body bags started coming home. In the end, there was no conquered territory. The first Bush seemed to hope that Saddam had learned his lesson. Clinton had a similar strategy, saturation bombing the civilian population of Kosovo to save them from genocide.*

> *The world is not the world anymore—now it is a village. Everything is close. The United States makes itself out to be the big police. They claim to have the right to intervene anywhere to protect their own internal security and they define what is a threat, from Sri Lanka* [read Afghanistan] *to Chiapas.*

And then, in an eerie future-think coalescence with Baby Bush's concept of the War on Terror, the Sup adds:

> *The Fourth World War will be fought everywhere, without fronts. . . .*

Was Marcos in Afghanistan?

In the Belly of the Beast

Months before 9/11 had induced mass psychosis in North America, I had pieced together a tour of the U.S. to tout my then-latest Zapatista chronicle, *The War Against Oblivion*. Now I hesitated. The trek would take me through a U.S. heartland where patriotic paranoia topped 10 on the Richter. Nonetheless, I was determined that the story of indigenous struggle for social justice and against the perfidy of their government not be muzzled by Bushwa's terror war and Ashcroft's malevolent U.S. Patriot Act.

Getting my Zapatista dolls through Customs was the first challenge. The ski-masked dolls, each carrying a wooden stick gun, are stitched together by Chamula women and have been big sellers for a decade on the streets of San Cristóbal.

I rehearsed my spiel to Homeland Security. "They are not what you think, my friend. These are Mayan Indians who defend their cornfields." To my chagrin, Tom Ridge and his newly deputized Praetorian Guard didn't give a rat's ass for my little Zapatistas. I was just some toothless old gaffer, tottering along on senior citizen discounts. Little did they suspect that they had just released the Zapatista plague into the breadbasket of the nation.

I have crisscrossed my native land many times, the Willie Loman of the Zapatista Army of National Liberation trundling my volumes from one North American tank town to the next, preaching revolution from down below and howling "*¡Basta Ya!*" at the masses. This time, though, it was different. The pain on the land was palpable. Fraying flags flapped from whitewashed homes, a talisman against the next attack. Everyone had the jitters and people did not look you in the eye on public transportation.

It was truly a terrible moment to be traveling. The FBI was unwinding turbans at the airports and the white powder was in the mail. "They want what we have!" Bush vomited—his ratings were in the 90s—and 1,000 Muslims were swallowed up by Ashcroft's dungeons. "The United States should bomb all Muslim centers, kill their leaders, and convert them to Christianity," Fox News Barbie doll Ann Coulter advised.

My travels in the Midwest coincided with the Bush bombing campaign "to soften up" Afghanistan. Bin Laden was wanted dead or alive and Mullah Omar was on the run. Forty-six thousand U.S. Special Forces were raking that ragged, dirt-poor land under the rubric of "Operation Enduring Freedom." Meanwhile the Northern Alliance was mowing down anyone who got in the way of their murder machine. It was a hard act to follow.

My first gig was at a small Catholic college 80 miles north of St. Paul, Minnesota. I would deliver a riff on "Fixing the Zapatistas in History." I've done this act many times. The auditorium was sparsely filled and the professor who had invited me to lecture apologized for the turnout. He mentioned that something was wrong with the VCR—it seemed to be stuck on CNN. Not far into the rap, I sensed that the small audience was listening intensely, watching my every word. Then I realized that they were not focused on me at all but rather staring past me where Bin Laden was mouthing silent imprecations against America on the big screen behind my back.

Chiapas was clearly not a priority for the U.S. Left during those dark days. In Madison, I spoke about the March of the People Who Are the Color of the Earth to three young people in a student union auditorium that could have sat 600. Outside, hundreds of demonstrators were protesting bloody Sharon's clampdown on the West Bank, launched under the umbrella of Bush's Terror War. It was not the Zapatistas' moment.

Not unsurprisingly, one of the few rads who were still listening to the comandantes' silence was the Great Chomsky. I was ushered into his book-lined office just outside the linguistics department at MIT for my 50-minute hour. His *9-11* had just hit the bookstores and was selling its way to the top of the *New York Times* paperback list. I had pertinent questions and flicked on my tape recorder: Would Iraq be the next domino after Afghanistan? Noam raised a palm to stem the barrage. He had some questions of his own to ask me. Would I explain the Indian Rights law? Autonomy? The silence of the Comandancia? What about the PRI? Fox? Land tenure? What was happening to the corn? I never got a question in edgewise before my "hour" was up. No wonder Noam Chomsky knows so much.

But outside of the Great Chomsky, the Zapatistas didn't have much scratch. In Chicago, I read the heart-wrenching section from *Oblivion* about the Acteal massacre at the Heartland Café, Mike James's long-standing social experiment in the far north of the city. Spoken word performers usually do their act during dinnertime at the Heartland, and my mournful tale of the ruthless massacre of 49 Tzotzil men, women, and children at Christmas in 1997 was drowned out by the clatter of platters and gales of dinnertime laughter. Chiapas seemed very, very far away.

The high/low point in the 53 *charlas* (talks) I offered during this pestilent season came at Lane Technical High School on the north side of the Windy City, a multiracial (read black and brown) educational detention center with 8,000 inmates. First you passed through a metal detector and a pat-down and showed your picture ID. Burly security personnel escorted me to the classroom. The *Star-Spangled Banner* blared from the loudspeakers on every floor.

Chloe, the 16-year-old daughter of radical parents, had convinced her teachers to have me in for a sort of first-period show and tell. Three classes had been gathered together for the presentation and there was a lot of scuffling in the room. Ms. Renteria, the lead teacher, was nervous.

"This isn't going to be about overthrowing the Mexican government, is it?" she wanted to know.

I pulled out my Zapatista dolls to draw in attention. "What do you think these are?" I asked the kids, sort of like a left-wing Mister Rogers. "Terrorists!" the kids yodeled back. Oh yah, why? "Because they have those masks on. The terrorists wear those masks," one young Latina up front ventured. Did she know why the Zapatistas wore the ski masks? Because before they put on the masks, no one saw them, I explained. They were Indians, they were worth nothing, people looked right through them as if they weren't there. They had no name or face, but the moment they put on the *pasamontaña* everyone knew right away who they were and have never forgotten since. The Zapatistas put on the ski masks to unmask Mexican racism.

I had them in the cup of my hand now and punched in the video of the March of the People Who Are the Color of the Earth. Suddenly, Ms. Renteria flipped on the lights. The class was over. The kids started scuffling again. I had lost them. Even if the Latina who had thought the Zapatistas were terrorists came up and asked me to speak at the school's Latin American Club, I felt defeated.

The next afternoon, Chloe came home from school with 29 letters from her classmates dissing Ms. Renteria for cutting me off, and thanking me for having shown up at Lane Tech. "Before you came, I had a bad impression of the Zapatistas. Now I support their struggle for human rights," one young compañera had written. Such moments greatly lightened the load for the Willie Loman of the Zapatista Army of National Liberation.

Digna Ochoa—The Movie

On October 19, while I was wending my way through the post–9/11 rubble, the indomitable human rights lawyer Digna Ochoa was found murdered in her small Colonia Roma office in downtown Mexico City. I read about this black deed online in *La Jornada* and started making phone calls right away.

Digna had been one of the lawyers who had successfully defended Javier Elorriaga and Elisa Benavides and a score of compas taken in raids in Yanga, Veracruz, and Mexico state on the night Zedillo ordered the invasion of the jungle. Many of the defendants had been charged with terrorism. She had just taken on the defense of the Cerezo brothers, the first Mexicans to stand trial in the wake of 9/11.

But her most celebrated clients at the time of her assassination were the *campesinos ecologistas* (ecological farmers) Rodolfo Montiel and Teodoro Cabrera, framed and tortured by the Mexican military after they had organized a campaign to drive the U.S. timber giant Boise Cascade out of the Petatlán Sierra on Guerrero's volatile Costa Grande. Rodolfo and Teodoro had just been awarded the Goldman Prize, sometimes described as an environmental Nobel, and the $125,000 USD that came with it had made them the wealthiest inmates caged up in the Iguala state penitentiary.

Digna Ochoa's body had been discovered by a young attorney with whom she shared the office. Mail left for her the day before was still stuck in the door. Lamberto González found Digna pitched forth on the floor, her head nestled in the seat of a chair. She had been shot twice, once through the right temple and the other in the left thigh. The presumed murder weapon, a Czech-made revolver, was found near her body. There were no prints on it. Oddly, Digna was wearing red latex gloves lightly dusted with cornstarch. An anonymous note thrown down on the blood-stained rug threatened those who lawyered at the Miguel Pro Human Rights Center, a Jesuit institution where Digna had once toiled, with multiple deaths.

Digna Ochoa and the Pro Center were the recipients of countless death threats from 1998 through 2001. Digna herself was often followed, and in the summer of 2000, two unidentified security agents (later she would tell me they were military intelligence) broke into her apartment and interrogated her all night about suspected members of the EPR she was defending—she had charged the military with abuse. Before the agents left they tied Digna to an open propane gas tank, from which she was able to escape in the nick of time. Rescuers found her distraught. She was wearing red latex gloves lightly dusted with cornstarch that her captors had forced her to don.

Digna and I spoke often during 2000 when I was doing a piece on the campesinos ecologistas for *Sierra Magazine*, most often in a darkened cell-like room at the Pro Center, where death threats were then being found almost daily in planter boxes and desk drawers, and a police car stood perpetual watch outside. She seemed tired and depressed and was about to take a leave of absence. Her good friend Kerry Kennedy Cuomo had arranged for her to come to Washington. Her caseload was turned over to her associates.

Digna's murder was the first political crime of Vicente Fox's administration (he was selling Mexico to Shanghai at the time of her death). For the president of "Change" the killing was an international black eye—it looked suspiciously like countless acts of intimidation committed by the PRI in its seven decades in power.

Digna had unexpectedly returned to Mexico in March 2001 and the death threats had resumed. Her friends and sister lawyers Pilar Noriega and Barbara Zamora demanded to know why the police had not provided protection. (They had offered but Digna refused because she distrusted the cops.)

Digna's death was "without a doubt, a political crime . . . *terrorismo* of the extreme right," Mexico City chief prosecutor Bernardo Bátiz denounced—Bátiz had taken charge of the case after attorney general (and general) Macedo de la Concha recused himself from the investigation because, as former chief military prosecutor, his many confrontations with the dead lawyer over cases of military abuse of the civilian population would have made his presence look mighty fishy.

Bátiz, a congenial people's attorney and ex-PANista before he became Mexico City chief prosecutor, now found himself in the eye of the storm. Amnesty International and Human Rights Watch issued jeremiads and called for an end to the military's impunity. Kerry Kennedy, who runs the Robert F. Kennedy Human Rights Foundation, expressed anguished outrage, and the U.S. State Department decried Ochoa's "brutal" murder. Now other human rights groups were receiving similar sinister threats. Marina Patricia Jiménez at Fray Bart in San Cristóbal thought she was being followed and her phone bugged.

Digna Ochoa was buried in her hometown of Misantla, Veracruz, an excruciatingly poor sugarcane-growing region where she had been raised, the daughter of campesinos active in the liberation Catholic Church. Digna herself had once been a nun and sometimes still wore her habit to court.

In the years since, no one has ever been charged with Digna's murder. A cacique up in the Petatlán Sierra was questioned by Bátiz's boys but didn't seem to know who Digna Ochoa was. Soldiers whom she had accused of torturing the campesinos ecologistas all had perfect alibis. Maribel Gutiérrez, a crack investigative reporter at *El Sur* in Acapulco, ran a scoop identifying several *pistoleros* who had bragged that they had done the hit, but by the time she got to them, they were all dead.

At the end of October, the Comandancia of the Zapatista Army of National Liberation broke its silence for the first time in six months and the last time in the next 13. This is what Sub Marcos wrote to Digna's survivors:

I speak to you in the name of the elders, the children, and the men and women of the EZLN. We have just been informed of the death of Digna, so long expected and so irresponsibly ignored. This crime stirs the indignation of all honest people. When those who struggle for justice are eliminated, those in power celebrate fiestas and let a few coins drop to promote indifference.

Down below, there is pain and fury but not impotence. Certainly, the crimes committed against Digna Ochoa and all human rights defenders darken our road, but everywhere, we can construct the light that will chase these shadows and vanquish yesterdays of impunity and cynicism. We cannot find the words to express the pain that veils our gaze but not our path. Find in our silence a timid embrace because, you know, even without words, we accompany you. Health and long life to those who carry on the vocation and the destiny.

Digna Ochoa—The Sequel

If "Digna Ochoa—The Movie" (Felipe Cazals has made an excellent film about her life, *Digna Ochoa: Hasta el Ultimo Aliento*) was spooky, "Digna Ochoa—The Sequel" was even more twisted.

Within days of Digna's death, there were suggestions that all was not as it seemed. *Chisme* (gossip) hinted at serious friction within the Pro Human Rights Center, and it was said that director Edgar Cortez, a Jesuit priest, had encouraged Digna to take the leave of absence and seek psychiatric counseling. Cortez was thought to be suspicious of the lawyer's complaints that she was being harassed by security agents, and questioned the authorship of the death threats that had been scattered throughout the offices. They were usually composed of words carefully scissored from newspapers and sometimes quite obscene and violent.

While Digna Ochoa was on leave in Washington, D.C., the Miguel Pro Human Rights Center asked for her resignation, and she returned to Mexico immediately, upset at the center's action but determined, friends said, to make a fresh start as an independent human rights attorney. For the first time in years, Digna had a boyfriend, an evangelical preacher she had met on the Internet.

Renato Sales was Bátiz's third investigator to work the case. The son of a prosecutor who had bungled the murder case of the 1980s—the assassination of star investigative reporter Manuel Buendía—Sales finally said what others could not: Digna Ochoa had committed suicide in a demented attempt to retaliate against the Pro Center for having fired her. There was plenty of circumstantial evidence to back up Sales's hypothesis. The murder weapon, it turned out, belonged to Digna—her brother Jesús had given it to her after the agents had invaded her apartment. There were no prints anywhere in the apartment other than Digna's—none on the gun or the mail that had been stuck in the door. The mysterious red latex gloves lightly dusted with cornstarch apparently saw to that. Sales even produced a volume of poems about death that his investigators had discovered open to a poem by St. Teresa of Avila, a meditation on Christian martyrdom.

Often over the top and pandering to the press (he gave the *New York Times* an exclusive interview disclosing the suicide investigation), the ambitious Sales ran head-on into a wounded human rights movement not at all ready to concede his suicide hypothesis. Confirmation of the sainted Digna's self-inflicted demise would be a traumatic blow to the credibility of Mexican and international human rights organizations such as Global Exchange, which had just presented her with a prestigious, posthumous award. Digna's suicide, and her theoretically spiteful motives for making it appear to be a murder, was a devastating scenario to swallow.

In his eagerness to impress, Renato Sales made many mistakes. He deconstructed Digna's office and set it up in his own, reportedly destroying valuable evidence in the process, and Bátiz had to cut him loose. A new prosecutor was selected on the recommendation of a blue-ribbon commission headed by the moral leader of Mexico's human rights movement, Rosario Ibarra de Piedra, the diminutive Big Mama of the Disappeared. After evaluating the evidence for months, the chosen prosecutor, Margarita Guerra, concluded that Digna Ochoa had committed suicide and closed the books on the case. Her family—and Subcomandante Marcos—continue to demand that it be reopened.

5. Winter/Spring 2001–2002

A Silent Anniversary

Chiapas was on the other end of the flyway when I returned to Mexico to mark the eighth anniversary of the uprising. Up at Oventik, with the Comandancia submerged in silence, this year would be austere compared to the hurly-burly of the takeover at Jolnachoj the previous New Year's.

The autumn had been a fretful season and the Zapatistas had harvested with caution, one eye over their shoulder. After Governor Pablo's release of Samuel Sánchez and his gangster band with the proviso that the paramilitaries lay down their arms, "Peace and Justice" had split into three equally dangerous factions that intimidated Zapatista bases all over the north of the state. Down in the Cañadas, Tzeltal coffee farmers from Ocosingo organized into the ORCAO (Organization of Coffee Cultivators of Ocosingo), affiliated with the PRD, and overran the Zapatista community store at Cuxulja, which serves seven autonomías, including Che Guevara, and destroyed a mural, *The Dawn of the Rainbow*, that festooned the premises. Tensions were running on high octane. Meanwhile, Vicente Fox had just returned from visits with the pope, Spain's José

María Aznar, and Italy's Silvio Berlusconi, and gleefully reported that the Zapatistas had dropped off the European agenda.

In Los Altos, three perpetrators of the Acteal massacre were released from Cerro Hueco, putting the fear of God in Las Abejas. At the fourth anniversary of the tragedy, December 22, the Misa and the ritual reenactment of the massacre had been closely watched by Pablo's police to prevent a rerun of that slaughter.

The comandantes' autism, punctuated by the condolences to Digna Ochoa's family in October, was reinforced in November and December. The seventeenth anniversary of the founding of the EZLN out there in the jungle between Plan de Guadalupe and El Calvario passed without fuss.

Municipal elections on October 7 had been dominated by the PRI, which took 72 out of 118 municipalities and 11 out of 12 districts in the local congress. The Zapatistas abstained as they always do, but in San Andrés, one of the first autonomías, the compas had just installed new authorities in defiance of the PRI's claim that the municipality officially belonged to them.

Finally, the Indian Wrongs law remained in stasis, with the Supreme Court promising to start delving through the more than 300 appeals in February. Sporadic efforts to revive the Ley Cocopa in Congress sputtered on inconclusively. There was little that the politicos could or would do to remedy the slap in the face with which they had rewarded the nation's first peoples. The fate of Indian Wrongs was now in the hands of the court.

There were no comandantes in sight up at Oventik and the annual festivities were low key. A huge bruised moon hung heavily over the snaggle-toothed mountains, bathing the Aguascalientes in an eerie light. The EZLN's year had been a bruised one too—the guts had been wrenched from the San Andrés Accords and Indian Rights mutilated by Mexico's political class. The painful retreat of the Comandancia into silence had been complemented by a world gone kaplooey, pushing the Zapatistas even further into the shadows.

There was not a whole lot to celebrate but the compas made a go of it anyway, bouncing to tropical cumbias to keep the cold at bay. The autonomous municipal council—the men in beribboned hats, the women wrapped in warm shawls—welcomed a handful of international visitors to Oventik. "Tonight we mark the eighth anniversary of our war against oblivion," their New Year's greeting began. For the Zapatistas, there was only one war and it was right here at home.

After midnight, I stepped up Oventik's main drag. The bruised moon-beams put a shine on the roofs of the new middle school, the library, the church, the auditorium, the clinic, the boot workshop, and the general store. Critics say the EZLN is losing support because the rebellion has not translated into material gain for the Indians, and they have good reason. These new structures were not much to show for eight years of rebellion and repression.

But these buildings were theirs—they had raised them up with mortar and brick and their own callused hands and aching backs without the per-mission of the mal gobierno, and they were beholden to no one for them. Indeed, I had never seen the Zapatistas as determined to transform their dreams into concrete reality. They said what happened here on this land now. Although the mal gobierno—and maybe the Zapatistas themselves—did not know it yet, they were already autonomous.

Argentinazo!

It had been a long hot summer down at the other end of the continent in Argentina. Just as the comandantes were settling in for their long winter nap, the "Argentinazo" flamed into Latin American political legend. All year that southern cone nation had been on the brink of collapse. The money had run out and the IMF would tender no more moolah to pay off the $150 billion debt the generals had accrued. It had apparently been quite expensive to dispose of 30,000 suspected leftists by dropping their drugged bodies into the Río de la Plata and the Atlantic Ocean from air-planes. To add insult to injury, the Argentinean people, those who sur-vived, had been bled dry by IMF debt service that totaled $220 billion.

The Videlas and Violas and Galtieris had been heinous jackals, but the IMF was the harshest dictator, experimenting like a Dr. Mengele upon the broken economy with "shock therapy," "structural adjustment," and the wholesale privatization of the nation's natural riches and resources.

With default and disaster right around the corner, President Fernando de la Rúa had brought back Domingo Cavallo, who had run the Menem kleptocracy, to save Argentina from going belly up. Cavallo's first act as economy minister was to proclaim an extended bank holiday, sealing the vaults and freezing the life savings of the middle class. The scheme was to issue worthless bonds in lieu of cash. The scenes of elderly pensioners throwing themselves at padlocked bank doors was heart-rending. Out-of-work workers swung sledgehammers to smash ATMs to smithereens. The Argentine peso, once pegged one-to-one to the dollar, lost 90% of its value between 2001 and 2002, and it seemed like half the population was booking steerage back to the old continent for extended visits with their Italian and Spanish forebears.

For the industrial proletariat, times had been tough for a long time. But now 35% of the workforce was not working, and those who still were had not been paid since October. Argentina, the breadbasket of the world, could not feed its own. Grown men and women grappled for scraps in the better garbage dumps of Buenos Aires, and a wave of supermarket lootings in the misery belt surrounding the city had De la Rúa and Cavallo particularly jittery.

The *piqueteros*, laid-off workers who no longer had a workplace to picket, lit tire fires and blocked access in and out of the capital to demand unemployment benefits, further paralyzing the economy.

On December 18, the president proclaimed a state of siege. The military poured into the streets and it smelled a lot like the bad old days of the dirty war. But this time around, the people could not be cowed. Millions stood on their balconies and out on the central avenues of the cities banging on their cooking pots, a grand *cacerolazo* that could be heard all the way to Chiapas. Hundreds of thousands—*los de abajo,*

Evita's eternal *decamisados*, arm-in-arm with a devastated middle class—crammed into the Plaza de Mayo facing the pinkish Presidential Palace or Casa Rosada where the mothers had mourned their children for 30 years, and this time the crowds would not go home. Even after the security forces opened fire and eight were killed, they just kept banging on their pots and jumping up and down and calling their president a gorilla. At 1 p.m., Cavallo, who had grown so afraid to appear in public that he hired a stunt double, resigned, and by 8 p.m. that evening, De la Rúa was gone. Argentina would have four presidents in the next three weeks. "*¡Qué se vayan todos!*" (That the political class must go!) resonated throughout Argentina.

The Argentinazo rearranged the land of Che. From creative disorder arose a new revolutionary-minded order based on spontaneity, solidarity, and above all, autonomy. Workers took over factories—Zanon Ceramics and the Brukman textile factories were the most celebrated, but also dozens of bakeries and ravioli makers, machine shops, and even a five-star hotel whose owners had gone bankrupt, formed collectives and went back to work. Neighborhood assemblies coalesced to take charge within their own turf—like the Zapatistas, they formed education and health commissions to deal with needs the busted government could or would not fix. The Movement of the Unemployed ran day-care centers, grew community gardens, fed folks in "economic kitchens," created barter marts free of the money economy.

The *escraches* (to scratch off, expose) smoked out the dirty war criminals and invited in the masses to drive them from the neighborhoods. Popular culture exploded in a carnival of anticapitalism. Drag queens ran tango schools in the expropriated factories. It was all improvised, antihierarchical, very down below, and eminently reminiscent of Zapatista constructs. The piqueteros even sometimes donned ski masks.

The more cutting-edge connoisseurs of real political change took notice of the parallels between the uproars in Chiapas and the Argentine. Irish anarcho theorist John Holloway (now teaching at the University of Puebla) was quick to publish. Brigadistas setting out for Chiapas to help build Zapatista infrastructure often carried Holloway's *How to Change the World Without Taking Power* tucked away in their backpacks. The Irishman's reasoning had a lot of resonance: " *'¡Qué se vayan todos!'* What a beautiful dream! Imagine a world without politicians! A world without their cronies, the capitalists! A world without capital! Imagine a world without power!" Holloway wrote in April 2002.

Like the Zapatistas, the piqueteros did not want state power. The state was corrupt, had no credibility, was hopelessly in debt. No one believed in it as an institution anymore. Why kill or be killed to take the state when the power was really down below in the barrios and the fields, the Zócalo, the Plaza de Mayo? Like the Zapatistas, the piqueteros and their allies were profoundly opposed to the political parties and the elections they staged. *"¡Nuestros sueños no están en las urnas!"* (Our dreams are not in the ballot box.)

In early 2002, Buenos Aires became the hot stop on antiglobalization itineraries. There was even talk of chartered flights from San Cristóbal to the Argentine and then on to Porto Alegre for the second World Social Forum, where both the EZLN and the piqueteros received standing ovations.

The Argentinazo was the first social upheaval in Latin America with a decidedly Zapatista imprint, but the parallels are actually a bit tenuous. The Zapatista experience is a rural one, very rooted in place and race and really non-exportable to an urban setting. The makers and shakers of the Argentinazo had little contact with the Mapuches, Argentina's historic Indian population, who are deeply marginalized in the south of the country. The piqueteros demand that McDonald's fork over 10,000 Big Macs to feed the hungry. The Zapatistas defend corn.

But what is the same is that both dare to dream that another world is possible and are, in fact, building that dream into concrete reality.

Such lofty ideals, most of all the impertinent concept that fighting for state power was unnecessary because the people already had the power, would eventually prove subversive to the old Latin Left, and undermined the bedrock upon which Lula and Chávez and Kirchner and their burgeoning band of social democrats have based their claim to power.

The Exodus Comes Home

Even when the Mexican army was the only game in town, Guadalupe Tepeyac was always the secret chamber at the heart of Zapatista geography. In the months following the uprising, the village served as headquarters for the Zapatista General Command, and the Clandestine Indigenous Revolutionary Committee (CCRI) met daily in the safe house atop the grassy hill just south of town. It was also the site of the Zapatistas' first Aguascalientes, where in August 1994, thousands attended the National Democratic Convention, the first face-to-face between the rebels and civil society.

It was in Guadalupe Tepeyac that the rebels entertained Bishop Ruiz and the peace negotiator Camacho Solís, and Zedillo's interior secretary, Esteban Moctezuma, along with Cuauhtémoc Cárdenas, Andrés Manuel López Obrador, and a full house of national and international luminaries. And it was here that on February 9, 1995, hundreds of paratroopers had dropped from the sky "like turkey buzzards," driving the Zapatistas of Guadalupe Tepeyac into the surrounding jungle mountains.

Guadalupe Tepeyac takes its name from the angular mountain that rises high above the town—it has always looked more to me like a great eagle about to unfurl its wings and take flight, but the Tojolabales saw it more as a metaphor for the hill in northern Mexico City where, so the story goes, the Aztec Juan Diego first encountered the Virgin of Guadalupe, a meeting that became the cornerstone of the evangelization of indigenous America and one that many think was a trick played on the Indians.

The Tojolabales trekked into Tepeyac from Comitán in the Fifties when the Lacandón jungle was opened up to landless farmers as Mexico's "New Agrarian Frontier" and by the 1960s had achieved ejido status for the hectares the settlers had hacked from the jungle. But like all farmers in far-off forests, they were immediately forgotten by their government. For decades, they masqueraded as members of the PRI's National Confederation of Farmers (CNC)—in 1989, Comandante Tacho (then Humberto

Trejo) was even invited to Los Pinos along with other Indian campesino leaders in a press stunt to legitimize the illegitimate presidency of Carlos Salinas. But Salinas's determination to alter Article 27 of the Mexican constitution and the havoc it foreshadowed for the nation's small farmers drove the campesinos of Guadalupe Tepeyac to rise up in arms.

The first public service ever bestowed upon this distant jungle hamlet was an enormous hospital built under Salinas's Solidarity Program. Construction was pure PRI boondoggle. Outlying villages would have had to walk their sick for days through the jungle to receive medical attention, if they made it there alive. Anyway, the hospital didn't have much in the way of functioning medical equipment. In fact, when Salinas and his soon-to-be handpicked (and eventually assassinated) successor, Luis Donaldo Colosio, who ran Solidarity like it was his personal fiefdom, came to inaugurate the facility in August 1993, truckloads of gleaming dialysis and x-ray machines, incubators, and operating tables were hauled down to Tepeyac to stock the hospital for the ribbon-cutting. After the photo op, Salinas and Colosio ate lunch (Tacho was supposed to have been a waiter) and climbed back into their helicopter. Soon after, all the gleaming new machines were trucked back up to Comitán, leaving the hospital a hollow shell.

The rebellion exploded three months later.

After January 1, the rebels rebaptized the hospital in the name of the immortal Che and used it as a kind of dormitory for visiting internationals. But Zedillo's paratroopers put an end to all that on February 9, 1995. For the past 12 years, the hospital had been shunned by the Zapatistas and today is patrolled by private security agents, the ultimate white elephant in this part of the jungle.

The displaced villagers wandered in the wilderness for many months, dragging their chickens and *comales*, cooking pots and marimbas after them from one provisional camp to the next until neighbors invited them to reestablish their village on a rough mountain hillside. They hacked a few acres of corn land from the jungle mountain. The chickens began to lay eggs, and the nomads of Tepeyac settled in—but it was never like home. Every once in a while, a representative would come down to the ghost town they had abandoned to retrieve a forgotten item or clean off the grave of a relative, but the villagers never considered going back while the military occupied Guadalupe.

The army had established a base that resembled a Fort Apache–like enclave. Strategically, Tepeyac served as a chokepoint on movement in La Realidad, a dozen kilometers farther inside. The *putas* from the whorehouses up in Margaritas and Comitán took over the schoolhouse on the hill. The soldiers butchered the town's prized peacocks, which in their haste to get out of Dodge, the villagers had left behind. The beer trucks stopped here now, and the *soldados* got drunk and went out and pissed on the empty, crumbling houses. The jungle grew back.

The army's first act had been to bulldoze the Aguascalientes, setting fire to the historic EZLN safe house on the hill and a public library that held thousands of donated volumes. The military lied that the destruction was due to a government tree-planting program.

Then the Fox became president and pulled the military back. Guadalupe had been the last of the seven bases the EZLN demanded be dismantled as one condition of the return to dialogue with the mal gobierno. The president had only ordered the garrison to stand down when the comandantes, then in Mexico City, threatened to return to Chiapas because Congress had refused to hear them out on the Indian Rights bill.

Overnight, the military installations became "Indian Development Centers" under the auspices of the SEDESO, the government subsecretariat that runs Mexico's antipoverty programs. But those who had been exiled from these lands strenuously objected. The military had expropriated their ejido, and the ejido had to be turned back to them whole and not transferred to some other agency of the bad government.

Once they were assured that the *sardos* had really pulled out, the villagers began returning. They had left with 80 families and now there were 102. Six villagers had died in the mountain. New homes needed to be built, collapsed walls raised up again. The cornfields were overgrown and unproductive. Coffee production would take years to revive. The town's water lines had been chopped up by the military. So the autonomous council of Guadalupe Tepeyac called out to the civil society to help them put their town back together.

The Italians arrived to fix the water lines. Brigades from the UNAM and the National Polytechnic Institute patched the walls and painted spectral murals. Schools for Chiapas cleaned out the condoms from the schoolhouse.

One day while Guadalupe Tepeyac was returning to life, I wandered out to where the Aguascalientes had been and sat down on a log to listen. In the distance, 50 hammers tack-tacked, crows and macaws chattered, butterflies floated by—and then I heard it, the great roar that had erupted from thousands of throats that rainy August night nearly ten years ago to applaud the comandantes and the bases, "those who kept the secret." It was as if that moment was still preserved here, planted in the earth, bursting from some subterranean sound trench. Or maybe it was only the wind.

So finally, on February 9, 2002, the sixth anniversary of their exodus, the Zapatistas in Guadalupe Tepeyac came home at last, marching through the dusty settlement from the hospital, past Fort Apache, out to the Aguascalientes behind the banner of the Dark Virgin and the flag of their country. "Today we do not want to celebrate the leaving of the military but, rather, the resistance of our town," a member of the autonomous council spoke the word. "Many thought we would never return. The mal gobierno did everything they could to finish us off while we were in the mountain. They destroyed our village and destroyed our houses. But now we have come back to build up Guadalupe Tepeyac and live with our dead."

Crazy February

"Crazy February" is the way Carter Wilson describes *carnaval* in San Juan Chamula in his excellent novel of the same name. And Chiapas is really crazy in February. For one thing, it is carnaval, that last burst of Indian energies before the stern Lenten season comes in. For another, the month is filled with military holidays like Armed Forces Day on the 19th—one reason why Zedillo chose February as the month the turkey buzzards would fall upon Tepeyac.

February holds significant memories for the EZLN too. February 16, for one, the date of the signing of the San Andrés Accords on that date in 1996. Now the accords, promulgated at Sakamch'én de los Pobres, were as hollow and punched out as the great chalet where the government and the rebels had tried to negotiate for 22 fruitless months on the corner of the plaza in that autonomous municipality.

Far away, in the capital of the country, the accords were barely clinging to life. A posse of 168 guilt-ridden members of the PRD, the PT, and a few PRIistas (no PANistas) announced their intention to reintroduce the Ley Cocopa in the congress, but everyone knew they didn't have the numbers. Meanwhile, El Jefe Diego and most of the PRI were busy writing the secondary laws that would lock Indian Wrongs in place.

The National Indigenous Congress had correctly concluded that Congress was a dead pigeon and placed their fate in the paws of 11 all-white justices (one blonde), although some former advisers, like Magdalena Gómez, were already looking toward international courts and forums like the International Labor Organization and the Inter-American Human Rights Commission (CIDH) as the ultimate arbiter.

By midwinter, the court had winnowed down the caseload from 351 to 331—each case had to be decided individually. The court's chief clerk kvetched to the press that his team was xeroxing about 4,000 pages every day to keep up with the caseload.

The first audiences were anticipated for early spring. The first to be heard would be the Totonaco-majority municipality of Molcaxac, Puebla, whose advocates argued that Indian Wrongs violated their rights under OIT 169, ratified by the Mexican congress in 1991, narrowing the issue down to whether international treaty or constitutional amendment prevailed as the law of the land.

February had one other anniversary that seemed almost to mock the EZLN—February 24th, the day the comandantes had set sail for Mexico

City a year earlier. With their hopes crushed once again by the mal gobierno, the comandantes had sunk into stubborn silence.

"Our words were not listened to by the powerful," the Comandancia had written under Sub Marcos's hand before dropping off the face of the earth. Who knew how many years it might be before they spoke again?

In the first days of spring, the International Civil Observation Commission on Human Rights came again to Chiapas to appraise the situation in Los Altos and the jungle. The CCRI had declined to speak with them, the commission reported, but they had heard in the villages that the comandantes would only speak again when Indian Wrongs was declared unconstitutional by the Mexican Supreme Court. Given the glacial pace of justice in Chiapas, that could mean no word might be forthcoming from the compas until the 25th century.

Poison Spring

Spring planting is always a problematic season filled with maximum tensions between farmers' organizations as the campesinos seek to recuperate wedges of ejido land and get their seeds in the soil before the first rains fall in May. The 2002 planting season was poisoned by such toxic conflict throughout the Zapatista territories, where the rebels went nose to nose with a fistful of organizations whose initials formed baffling acronyms but which inevitably were aligned with the PRI, and increasingly the PRD, which by now was hopelessly in Pablo's corner.

Since fall, the compas had been confronted by a cluster of PRD farmers' groups—the CIOAC in the Tojolabal region around Comitán; the ARIC-Independiente, long the rebels' running partners but now Pablo supporters and PRD bases, out in the Montes Azules and at San Marcos in the Cañada of Francisco Gómez (La Garrucha); the Ocosingo small coffee farmers in ORCAO, which had risen up with the Zapatistas on January 1, 1994, and now were part of the growing PRD structure in the Zapatista zone of influence.

ORCAO and the EZLN had scrimmaged over the community store at Cuxulja last autumn. Now they were hassling over a ranch in Sitalá near

Chilón—and, more bruisingly, at Nueva Patria, also in the canyon of Francisco Gómez, where the two sides exchanged machete blows and in classic Mayan war mode took hostages. The police rushed in to separate the combatants.

Farther in, on the fringes of the Montes Azules sanctuary, the autonomías of San Manuel, Francisco Villa, and Ricardo Flores Magón were under fire from a PRI front, the OPDIC, which took direction from an Ocosingo state congress rep, Pedro Chulín. The skirmishes were mostly fought with clubs and machetes and no fatalities were registered.

Much of this push and pull was over land that had been reclaimed from the elite cattle ranchers and smaller *finqueros* who had fled the rebel zone after the January 1, 1994, uprising. The EZLN had moved rapidly to take back those lands and distribute them among their bases even when an allied organization like ARIC staked a claim. Although they had been indemnified by the state, the ranchers continued to insist the properties in dispute still belonged to them and sometimes aligned with local campesino groups to press their claims.

As every spring, the Montes Azules was on fire. Dense smoke surrounded the tiny communities of Asia (60 settlers) and Africa (15) on the north flank of the sanctuary. Conservation International, which bought a wedge of the rain forest through a 1980s debt swap and now thought it was responsible for the whole Lacandón, and the Environmental Table, a state-federal task force designated to remove "illegal" Indians from the forest, blamed the fires on 49 settler communities, a dozen of which were Zapatista-affiliated. Others attributed the blazes to deliberate arson or just simply to the incendiary nature of Nature in her driest season.

Fox government strategy this spring had been to deputize the 66-family Lacandón Indians who had been deeded the reserve in a discredited 1972 decree by President Luis Echeverría, as "Guardians of the Forest," sort of like paramilitaries with powers to evict settler communities in defense of both the environment and the land they had so dubiously been awarded.

But toxic as social tensions were that spring, a new menace edged the planting season with anxiety. Ignacio Chapela's discovery of genetically modified corn in Oaxaca's Sierra del Norte in September had sounded an alarm among the nation's campesinos. Mexico was importing about six million tons of NAFTA corn each year from the U.S. Because of European Union and Japanese restrictions, Greenpeace calculated that 60% of the load big gringo corn producers were dumping on Mexico, subsidized by their government at up to $21,000 USD an acre, was contaminated.

What was more alarming was the speed at which contamination was spreading. Gracias to the North American Free Trade Agreement, GM corn began flooding into Mexico in 1998. Now, just four years later, its DNA was being found in the remotest sierras of Oaxaca and Puebla. A 2003 survey performed by the National Ecology Institute and never published found GM corn contamination of up to 60% in 11 out of 22 corn-growing regions in the two states.

How had this happened? Mexico had temporarily suspended cultivation of transgenic corn in the late 1990s. Yet the transgenics poured in with cheap corn allegedly destined for animal feed but that wound up being consumed by the poor—the Cargill Corporation, which now dominated the privatized grain distribution system, claimed it couldn't sort the transgenics out.

Some of the GM corn came across the border in the pockets of *indocumentados* who thought they were bringing home miracle seed. Chapela's Calpulalpan corn came from the nearby government-operated DICONSA supermarket distribution center, said to be originally from Michigan and sold cheap by the PRI to bribe farmers to vote its ticket in the 2000 presidential election. There were 22,000 DICONSA stores all over Mexico, and the GM corn fell off the battered trucks that hauled it into the sierras, and the wind blew the pollen into the cornfields by the side of the road. The wind was the vector.

Maíz was first domesticated in the Tehuacan valley near the Puebla-Oaxaca border. Harvard paleo-botanist Richard McNeish, an Indiana Jones type who also documented the first rice and the first potato, carbon-dated Tehuacan corn as first being planted seven millennia ago. Although McNeish's findings are disputed, Coxcatlán, where the Harvard man found the first corn, continues to tout itself as "the birthplace of corn." That corn is now threatened with genetic contamination and ultimately homogenization and obliteration. Ignacio Chapela's chance discovery implies the death of 300 distinct strains of Mexican maiz and the loss of millions of years of genetic history.

The threat to Mexican corn was the hot environmental horror story of 2002. First came Chapela's discovery of Monsanto BT corn in Calpulalpan. Next came Monsanto's Terminator seed, named for the future governor of California, which went sterile after one growing cycle—Monsanto pressured farmers to sign contracts that forced them to buy their seed from the St. Louis–based corporation. Farmers whose crops had been contaminated by wind-borne transgenics were prosecuted for stealing the seed—one Canadian farmer up in Saskatchewan, poor Percy Schmeiser, had lost his farm to the courts.

Even Chapela had his own horror story. The presumably ethical journal *Nature* had published his findings on the contaminated corn of Calpulalpan and then buckled under a biotech industry bulldozer blitz and retracted the article, an editorial decision that nearly cost Ignacio his tenure at U.C. Berkeley.

The horror stories terrified the Zapatistas. Like all farmers, they were seed savers, culling the previous year's harvest for choice kernels to replant. Now the globalization of GM corn would make this a crime. The future was in the wind blowing through the milpas in the mountains and down in the jungle.

Up at Oventik, the compas had a solution. They culled their best seed and packed them away in clay pots mixed with eucalyptus leaves and topped by a brilliant swatch of embroidered cloth tied down by twigs, the traditional way of preserving their seed stock. Later, the NGOs would chip in to buy a freezer and the Madre Tierra Seed Collective was created to safeguard the germ plasma of the People of the Corn. Madre Tierra now sells its uncorrupted Mayan corn on the Internet (www.schoolsforchiapas.com).

Not Listening

Rodolfo Hernández, a Mixe Indian farmer and town official in the village of Santa María Yavesia in the pine-forested mountains of eastern Oaxaca, arose before the roosters and dressed in his clean white *cotones*. He wanted to look his best for the task the community assembly had entrusted to him.

Rodolfo's wife was waiting for him in the kitchen with strong coffee and warm tortillas that she wrapped in a colorful *servilleta* for him to take along on his trip.

Rodolfo grasped the briefcase with the town's treasured documents and started down the dark dirt track for the hour's walk out to the highway. Dogs barked suspiciously as he tramped through the ghostly fields.

The stars were still twinkling when the early bus picked him up, and by midday Rodolfo was down in the state capital, where he met with the *licenciados* at the NGO Mixe Services. Others joined them—representatives of the Mixe and Zapotec villages of Santiago Zacatepec, Santa María Tlahutoltepec, and Santa Catarina Lachatao. Money was short and the men pooled their resources to come up with the 1,000 pesos Rodolfo, Agustín Cruz from Lachatao, and the Mixe lawyer Marcelino Nicolás needed to put them in court in Mexico City the next morning.

The three men caught the night bus up to the capital—they slept on the bus so as not to pay for a hotel room. The Indians washed up at the bus terminal and arrived at the Supreme Court of the nation at the stroke of nine.

The great granite building with marble floors and huge brass doors adjacent to the National Palace is an imposing edifice designed to intimidate humble petitioners into abandoning their cause without even crossing the threshold. You better have a good case to be heard here.

This was not the first time that Rodolfo and his compañeros had journeyed up from their remote mountains to plead for their villages. They had been here on May 5 when the case was first called. They had come with their village elders to substantiate how Indian Wrongs would deny them rights previously held under OIT 169 and to demonstrate how the community assemblies were the authentic voices of their villages and should be granted constitutional standing. But the justices would not hear them and decreed that they would only accept narrowly focused written arguments. The Indians' lawyers had filed an appeal, and the men had returned to their communities to await a hearing.

Meanwhile they sat the elders down and took their testimony to submit to the court in the form that had been ordered. Now they had returned "to speak our word with dignity. We ask just the right to be listened to," Rodolfo, a serious man in his forties who struggles with the pronunciation of legal jargon, told demonstrators outside the courthouse.

The Indians knew the rules by now. They would be given 30 minutes to litigate 500 years of oppression. Everything had to be typewritten and framed in a bloodless legalese. They complied. They hoped that although not one of the 11 justices had a drop of Indian hemoglobin pounding in their veins, they would finally accept the testimony of the elders that they had come to present.

But the Supreme Court of Mexico had no time for the Indians today. The justice of the court who was scheduled to hear the matter, Mariano Azuela, had other business to attend to and hadn't bothered to inform the clerk, a flagrant snub. Rodolfo and the others would argue their case in the street. "These compañeros have traveled a long ways from a great distance to be heard this morning, and the justices did not even have the courtesy to notify them that they wouldn't be here," Carmen Herrera, who was arguing the case for the Miguel Pro Center, said with weary disgust to the few demonstrators who walked a picket line pinched between multiple street vendors.

Supporters had turned the granite walls of the Supreme Court into an art gallery, hanging dozens of drawings by kids in the conflict zone, hoping to attract the attention of the justices. "I drew my dog because the paramilitaries took it away," a 12-year-old from Yaxjemel in the highlands wrote in block letters. "They also stole the chickens. . . ."

The Supremes had been hearing the cases since early May, 12 cases a day, 30 minutes a hearing. Molcajac, Puebla, was the first to be called, but most plaintiffs were from Oaxaca, which has 410 majority indigenous municipalities. Most argued the OIT 169 gambit, the failure of Congress to have consulted with the Indians as mandated by OIT 169, and the tainted majorities for ratification in the state congresses. The written arguments took up reams for the Supremes to sift through. Preventing the Indian elders from giving testimony had meant the justices were literally not listening.

So the campesinos came and tried to tell their stories and couldn't and went home again to mull it all over in the remote mountains where the stultifying pace of Mexican "justice" drives men to guns. On May 31, in the Sola de Vega district of Oaxaca, two communities that had bitterly contested the ownership of local forests for decades detonated in a feast of blood. Twenty-eight men and boys from the Zapotec community of Xochiltepec were slaughtered by rivals from Amoltepec at a rural bus stop. The courts had given one group the forest, and then the other.

Fifteen years previous, in early 1987, I had traveled to Sola de Vega after learning of a similar massacre in Santa María Zaniza on April 11, 1986. The names of 28 dead farmers and 70 widows and orphans had been given to me by a rural schoolteacher at a campesino forum in the north. The killings had involved the ownership of these same forests. The men of Amoltepec had been adjudged the aggressors back then too. Their leader, Antonio Roque, had been sent to state prison for ten years. Now he was the municipal president. The courts still had not decided who owned the forest.

Is Marcos a Goner?

Don Samuel Ruiz had returned to San Cristóbal during the first week of July, the protagonist of "The Extraordinary Encounter for Peace and Justice in Chiapas." The event was a kind of Last Hurrah to restart the peace talks through sheer moral suasion in a state where limbo between war and peace continued to reign.

Resplendent in a spotless white cassock and visibly overjoyed at having come home "to the city where I was born again," Tatic moved the usual actors on and off the stage at the city theater—González Casanova, Gilberto López y Rivas, the poets Juan Bañuelos and Oscar Oliva, who had been members of Samuel's mediating body, the CONAI, through nearly two years of fruitless negotiations at Sakamch'én. The subtext of the encounter was to open up to the public the CONAI's archives, which contained 10,000 documents related to the talks. The empty spaces in the programming were filled by the Acteal Choir and the best Indian brass band in Mexico, from Tlayacapan, Morelos.

No other bishops attended the encounter, not even Tatic's old coconspirator Arturo Lona, who, like Samuel, had been put out to pasture by the Vatican. Felipe Arizmendi, Samuel's successor, with whom relations had been strained, did not bother to put in even a courtesy appearance.

Although Tatic had insured the diocese's continuing option for the poor with a last-minute synod before he was forcibly retired, most of his henchmen had disappeared in the changeover. The Vicar of Peace, Gonzalo Ituarte, had transferred to the Dominicans in Ocosingo. The Vicar of Justice, Felipe Toussaint, had married and left the priesthood. Bishop Arizmendi had a more corporate style of running the diocese. His homilies were posted on the Internet every Sunday for publication on Monday morning.

Still, despite their estrangement, Samuel and Felipe Arizmendi presided over Sunday night Mass together.

The diocese continued to suffer for Comandante Sammy's sins. In building an autonomous Indian church, Tatic had ordained 342 deacons, many more than any other diocese in Latin America. For years, Cardinal Joseph Ratzinger, soon to ascend to the papal throne, had persecuted Samuel for preaching a "Marxist" version of the Gospel and assembling an army of Indian deacons and catechists in the jungles and highlands of the diocese. It was whispered that Bishop Ruiz had even ordained Indian women, and the Vatican had sent a team of investigators from the Council for the Defense of the Cult and the Disciplines of the Sacrament.

Although Tatic had been cleared, Ratzinger had prohibited Bishop Arizmendi from ordaining any more deacons—the deacons often substituted for priests in the backcountry.

Don Samuel's Encounter came just days before the Church and the Fox focused their klieg lights on Juan Diego, the Indian who purportedly first revealed the Virgin of Guadalupe to Mexico, who was about to be elevated to sainthood. Pope John Paul II would be winging in for the beatification, his fifth and final visit to the Aztec nation. The pope would also canonize two other Indian martyrs, Los Mártires de Cajonos—Indian stool pigeons who were beaten to death in Oaxaca for ratting out their cousins to the Spanish conquerors for practicing forbidden rites.

Scheduled as it was on the eve of a papal visit and the impending World Cup, Samuel's encounter did not have much scratch. Mostly, the effort was sabotaged by one glaring absence—that of the very people who were the subject of the encounter, the Zapatista Army of National Liberation. The EZLN sent no representatives of the autonomous municipalities, made no reference to the meeting in the heavy traffic of denuncias that arrived from the Zapatista communities (the Comandancia continued its frosty silence), and otherwise emitted no signal that they even knew the Encounter was happening.

Indeed, the only evidence of the Zapatistas at Samuel's conclave was the images in the daily papers of the compas in the autonomía called Olga y Isabel, out by Chilón, mostly ski-masked Tzeltal women carrying stout staves as they advanced on government road-building equipment near Kan'akil on July 6. "This road is only for the military and the rich," the Zapatistas protested, an echo of the epic struggle at Amador Hernández. "No one asked us if we wanted a road." Unlike Croquetas at Amador, Governor Pablo retired the equipment the next day.

The lack of action at the Encounter begged diversion. The scandal sheets hadn't heard from Marcos in so long that they suggested he was defunct, so on each cab ride to and from Samuel's peace klatsch, I would ask the driver if he thought the Sup was kaput. "Por supuesto"(of course),

Luis Enrique responded. Marcos was definitely dead—*"definativamente."* He sounded quite happy about it.

On the other hand, Luciano thought the Sup was "in hiding, preparing for his next attack." Juan Ortiz was convinced that Marcos had "retired to be with his family, *¿no?*" "*¿Quién sabe?*"—Manuel answered my question with a bored question of his own: "Who knows?"

Of course whether the man was dead or alive was not the question. When, at the conclusion of the Encounter, the masses—or what was left of them—rose to sing the EZLN hymn, "Horizontes," the part about how much "the nation needs the Zapatistas" had particular poignancy. Where were they?

Los Macheteros

In October 2001 in the usual mega-hyperbole style, El Presidente had ordered the expropriation of nearly 6,000 hectares of corn land out on the dried lake beds of Texcoco, just east of the city, for the construction of a new international airport, a sumptuous $3 billion USD investment that would guarantee Mexico's spot as the commercial gateway to the south. Secretary of Commerce and Transportation Pedro Cerisola unfurled flow charts and displayed expensive mock-ups. At least 24 world-class constructors had already submitted preliminary bids. Construction would mean the creation of at least 32,000 jobs. The new airport was a win-win venture.

With all the superattenuated puff, no one seemed to pay very much attention to those who actually owned and lived on the land to be expropriated until it was too late. A total of 5,391 hectares would be commandeered from 12 Texcoco ejidos, 3,700 of them from San Salvador Atenco, 80% of the town's growing lands. And 2,000 more hectares would be subtracted from a nearby environmental sanctuary.

The Nahua farmers of San Salvador Atenco did two things right away: They got a good if irascible attorney, Ignacio Burgoa, an ace on expropriation law, and filed an appeal to the same Supreme Court that was hearing the Indian Wrongs cases, and they began sharpening the blades of their broad machetes.

There were plenty of reasons not to build Latin America's most garish airport in Texcoco. The ejidos were laid on dried lakebed lands that were already seriously sinking each year as more and more water was pumped out to slake the thirst of the neighboring metropolis. Moreover, the airport was to be sited on a major migratory bird flyway, and the danger of large birds crashing through airliner windshields should have been enough to dissuade the Fox. The zone in which Bechtel and the transnationals would build was also an archeologically rich area, once the domain of Nezahualcóyotl, the poet king ("We are only here for a little while / although life be made of jade / it will break / although it be made of gold / it will tarnish / although it be the feather of a Quetzal bird / it will blow away"), and the remnants of his reign lay just below the surface of the fields. Moreover, the descendants of Nezahualcóyotl, the Nahua farmers who still lived on the land, were not giving it up—at least for the seven lousy pesos per square meter offered, the land was not for sale. Upping the sale price to 50 pesos a square meter changed nothing. *La tierra no se vende.*

The machetes were the symbol of the lucha from the first day of the struggle: machetes, pitchforks, sharpened hoes, the work tools of the farmers of Atenco, their weapons. Throughout the spring and summer, the *macheteros* of Atenco marched every day everywhere, sometimes on horseback, clashing their machetes with a great clanging noise or scraping them along the sidewalk, a truly irritating sound. First they marched on the Mexico state capital of Toluca and then, inevitably, into the Zócalo of Mexico City, to the Agrarian Reform and the secretary of agriculture, communications, and transportation, Los Pinos, driving Mrs. Fox nuts with their clanging machetes. They marched on the U.S. embassy on Reforma Boulevard and chopped up the Stars and Stripes with their sharp field knives. I saw them in Monterrey at the United Nations Development summit, where they had come to welcome Fidel Castro.

The macheteros of Atenco sometimes wore the paliacate and the pasamontaña, but they were not Zapatistas, or rather they followed the dictums of Zapata and not Marcos. La tierra belong to those who work it. The tierra was not for sale. *No se vende, se ama, se defiende.* (The land is not for sale—it is to love, to defend.) The macheteros had organized the *ejidatarios* of Atenco and several other ejidos into the Popular Front to Defend the Land. The front was not necessarily even leftist. The farmers of Atenco described themselves as Guadalupanas. They had voted up the PRI in the 2000 election.

The Frente was most often spoken for by the farmer Nacho del Valle and his cut-glass-voiced daughter, América, who, the rumors flew, had ties to the EPR.

Hanging out with the macheteros of Atenco could be dangerous to one's visit to Mexico. When Professor Dan Leahy and a dozen visiting students from Evergreen, an activist university in Washington state joined the militant campesinos in the great May 1 march on the Zócalo, they were rounded up by immigration authorities and deported under Article 33 of the constitution, which prohibits political participation by non-Mexicans, the first political deportees of the Fox administration.

The battle for Atenco escalated to new heights on July 2 when the macheteros forced their way into the old Benito Juárez International Airport at peak tourist season in the midst of the War on Terror. The clashing machetes truly terrorized the *turistas.*

During the first weeks of July, the farmers captured a number of surveyors and electricity workers who were laying markers on ejido land, tore out the markers, and held the workers hostage. When the police arrived to rescue the hostages, their patrol cars were torched. Cordons of "civil society"—mostly ultras from the University General Strike Council—encircled Atenco and constituted an early warning system against evictions. During one fiery rally against the airport, a Coca-Cola trailer was expropriated, the bottles emptied out, and a crew of *jóvenes* (young men) set up a Molotov cocktail assembly line.

Then on July 24, the farmer José Enrique Espinosa died after a lethal police tear gas attack, the macheteros' first death, and Atenco exploded. The firebombs flew and the state police were forced to withdraw from the ejido.

When on July 31 Fox snookered the investors by abandoning plans to expropriate San Salvador Atenco, the business class griped loudly that he had given in to a mob of machete-wielding hooligans—but actually, it was the macheteros' other strategy that was working. Ignacio Burgoa had found glaring errors in the expropriation order, and the Supreme Court was about to deal the president a rude rebuke for having proceeded with dubious documents. To save face, Fox pulled the plug on the airport. The fiesta in San Salvador Atenco lasted a whole week.

Who Is Killing the Zapatistas of Chiapas?

Between July 31 and August 28, at least four members of Zapatista base communities met violent deaths and dozens were wounded in the seething lowlands of Chiapas. Who was killing them?

On July 31, a group of PRIistas described as paramilitaries attacked Zapatista bases at La Culebra in the embattled autonomía of Ricardo Flores Magón. Seven were wounded. On August 8, José López Santiz was gunned down in the autonomous municipality of 17 de Noviembre (Ejido Morelia)—his compañeros claimed paramilitaries were responsible. On August 19, a Zapatista roadblock at the Quexil crossroads in Flores Magón was assaulted by the same "paramilitaries" who had invaded La Culebra. Although no one was killed, a dozen Zapatistas were laid out by machete blows and beaten with clubs. On August 24, the paramilitaries shot and killed one or two Zapatistas in the schoolhouse at Amaytik on the edge of the Montes Azules, again in Flores Magón. On August 27, Zapatista base Antonio Mejía was cut down in Kan'akil, Olga y Isabel autonomía, by a gang of "paramilitaries."

All of these homicidal "events" took place under the drenching jungle rains of summer in mud so deep it could swallow a horse whole. Taken collectively, these five acts of murderous violence pointed to an uptick in the low-intensity war against the EZLN. In whose interests was this war being conducted? Who was jerking the paramilitaries' strings?

By political definition, a paramilitary formation is organized, trained, armed, and financed by the military to do its dirtiest work—mass killings, torture, selective assassinations, kidnappings, drug running.

In the context of the Zapatista conflict, the Chiapas Strategy Plan, the counterinsurgency effort implemented by the Fort Bragg–trained General Mario Renán Castillo in the mid-1990s, fomented the development of paramilitary groups in areas of Zapatista influence.

"Development, Peace, and Justice" appears to fit the classic paramilitary mode in that it had continual support from the Mexican military. *"Máscara Roja"* (Red Mask), which slaughtered 49 at Acteal, was trained by an army officer but bought its weapons on the private market. The attacks on EZLN bases in the summer of 2002 were strikingly out of character for Chiapas paramilitaries. The assailants did not use automatic weapons, wore no uniforms, and did not seem to have any connection to the army. Nonetheless, the attacks were universally adjudged to be the handiwork of the *paras*.

By the ninth year of the Zapatista rebellion, the word "paramilitary" had acquired magical properties. It had come to mean anyone who was not the military and who actively opposed the EZLN. The term was applied obsessively in the offended villages and reported without critical inquest by the press. *La Jornada*, its headline writers, and even Hermann were particularly culpable of spreading this misapprehension of the forces of friction operative in the Zapatista zone in 2002.

A brief revisit to each of these incidents yields dramatically distinct conclusions.

Item—The July 31 attack at La Culebra is attributed to Pedro Chulín's PRIista bases under the guise of the OPDIC (the Organization for the Defense of Indians and Farmers). In repeated communiqués addressed to "the people of the world," the autonomous council of Flores Magón denounced the OPDIC as paras—but paras carry AK-15s and the invaders at La Culebra were armed with machetes, sticks, stones, and a single revolver.

Item—The August 8 slaying of José López Santiz on the Ejido Morelia appears to have grown out of a dispute over a cow. López was reportedly shot eight times in the head, purportedly by a loan shark from Altamirano, and his body found out in the cornfields. He was buried immediately and no autopsy ever conducted. Alcohol is mentioned as playing a role in the killing.

But the Zapatistas of Ejido Morelia attributed López's death to the paramilitaries and marched into Altamirano, a dangerous cowboy town, to find his killer and force him to support their comrade's widow and children, as is the Indian way of justice. With mayhem on the eyeline, Governor Pablo had hastened to Altamirano to quench the flames of indigenous indignation. The rebels and the governor met in the middle of a cowtown street. *La Jornada*'s Elio Henriquez recorded this interchange: "Don't you know me? I'm your governor!" "What is your name?" the Indians asked. "Pablo, Pablo Salazar . . ." "Do you have identification that shows you are the governor?" Pablo rifled his pockets. He did not.

Item—The August 6 confrontation at the Quexil crossroads, one of three checkpoints the Zapatistas had established leading in and out of the jungle to prevent traffic in stolen cars, the poaching of illegal timber, and to keep the beer trucks out of the Zapatista communities in this part of the jungle. The attackers were identified as Chulín's posse, the OPDIC. They were ostensibly on their way down to Ocosingo for an anti-PPP rally in a flotilla of 22 trucks. The PRI, to which they pertained, opposed Fox's PPP too.

There had been bad blood at the crossroads for weeks now with the Zapatistas challenging timber trucks hauling precious hardwoods to mills in Ocosingo. As the price of coffee collapsed in Chiapas, the ejidos had taken to wood poaching to survive. Later the OPDIC would claim that the rebels were extorting them for 150 pesos a load. Someone said something to someone and the resulting *zafarrancho* (kafuffle) resulted in a number of cracked heads on both sides but no fatalities. *La Jornada* reported the scuffle as yet one more paramilitary attack. In fact, Hermann's account spoke of 11 OPDIC airplanes landing on a strip near La Culebra. Were bombing sorties next?

Item—The most lethal incident took place on August 26 in the school-house in Amaytik. Two families, one Zapatista and the other not, had been feuding over the elopement of their children. By Tzeltal uses and customs, the groom's family had to pay a 5,000-peso bride price, but they had welched. Lorenzo Martínez, representing the autonomous council of Flores Magón, was to mediate. Once again someone said something and someone pulled a pistol out of his pants. Martinez and possibly another Zapatista were killed (the second death was unconfirmed).

"PARAMILITARIES EXECUTE TWO ZAPATISTAS," howled *La Jornada*, but the attribution seems sorely out of whack.

By now, Governor Pablo was insisting that there were no longer paramilitaries in the state and that the skirmishes in and around the jungle represented "intercommunal friction."

Item—The August 27 murder of Zapatista farmer Antonio Mejía in Olga y Isabel may be the only paramilitary killing in this bloody skein—his assassins were apparently members of Los Aguilares, a local crime family with reputed ties to the military. But whether the Aguilar family was more than just a *gavilla*, or armed criminal band, that prowled the region depended on the perimeters of the debate.

So who was killing the Zapatistas of Chiapas if it wasn't the paramilitaries? At the bottom line were a bunch of pissed-off Indian farmers, PRIistas and PRDistas both. Land recovered by the EZLN after 1994 was often the fulcrum of contention. The PRIistas were especially aggravated because their party was no longer in power and so they no longer received the perks that being electoral clientele once afforded them. Also, the PRIistas and the PRDistas saw that the Zapatista communities, seeded by NGO money and selling tons of organic coffee to the gringo buyers, were at least doing better than they were. In fact, the price of coffee may well have been the source of this latest river of blood.

The Price of Coffee

In March of 2002, the price of coffee on world commodity exchanges hit rock bottom, 41 cents a pound Americano, the lowest price in 116 years. The last time coffee had touched bottom like this was in 1886.

The explanation was simple. The international coffee cartels were suffering a world glut, thanks largely to the World Bank and its export agricultural models that foisted credit on the Global South to grow coffee for the Global North. In 2002, Vietnam had supplanted Brazil as the Número Uno coffee grower on the planet earth.

Chiapas grows a lot of coffee, mostly on tiny plots owned by Indian and mestizo farmers, with larger German-owned plantations (fincas) in the sierra and the Soconusco region on the Pacific coast. For the small farmers 41 cents a pound for backbreaking labor—clearing a hillside and hauling 175-pound sacks down from the mountain—was not going to feed their families. Governor Pablo estimated that 500 coffee farmers were abandoning their patches each month and heading north to find work.

Chiapas has been a hub of out-migration for a long time. Each year 250,000 Central Americans poured north through Tapachula on the coast, but the flow had thickened after Hurricane Mitch struck in 1998. Now plummeting coffee prices in their own coffee-producing countries were pushing even more farmers into the immigration stream. Serious starvation was afoot in Nicaragua.

6. Summer/Fall 2002
("The Price of Coffee" cont.)

Now for the first time, Mexicans from Chiapas were moving north. "Travel agencies" had sprung up in 20 Chiapas coffee-producing towns, like Viajes Hernández ("the safest way to travel") in Huixtla—many had once transported coffee. A rusted old bus left once a week. You could reserve a seat for 1,500 pesos ($120 USD) all the way to the northern border. Passengers were advised to bring proof of citizenship because the Mexican migra was shipping Chiapanecos back to Guatemala.

Daniel Pensamiento, a reporter for *Reforma* who went along for the ride, noted that passengers were regularly extorted at the nearly 30 military, police, and immigration checkpoints along the way.

The first stop was El Altar out in the Sonora-Arizona desert, where hundreds perish each year trekking "the corridor of death." Last stop was Tijuana, where work had been promised in the maquiladoras—but the "maqs" were deserting the Mexican border in search of even lower-wage options in China and the Dominican Republic and Mexico's south. In fact, a maquiladora had just opened in San Cristóbal de las Casas in Chiapas, where the migrants had just come from—the owner, later accused of serious sex crimes, had been reportedly subsidized to the tune of $1,000,000 to move a striking plant there from Acapulco under provisions of Fox's Plan Puebla Panama.

Now the first farmers were coming home—in cheap coffins. Three men from Teopisca near Comitán in the Tojolabal zone died in the Arizona desert in 2002. Fourteen coffee pickers from Coatepec, Veracruz, another coffee region, died out there in the spring.

The Zapatistas grow coffee too, but the EZLN does not migrate. Its members are rooted on the land and responsible to their communities. The Zapatistas don't believe in the American Dream—they dream another world is possible—and those young men who are tempted to buy a piece of it know the trouble it will cost their family and that later they will be ostracized from the community for having left.

The Zapatistas cultivate excellent coffee, shade-grown and organic, mostly in the highlands. Hundreds of Zapatista farmers are certified as organic growers. Kerry Appel, the Colorado desperado, has been pivotal to the process. After the rebellion, Kerry began hauling sacks back up to Denver in his scarred VW van. Soon he was selling the stuff out of his Human Bean Company, "Zapatista" brand with a label starring a masked Zapatista compañera (really a Denver girl). One cup led to another. MutVitz, a cooperative of 27 communities and six autonomías around El Bosque–San Juan de la Libertad, came together and the EZLN was in the biz. The proceeds—Kerry pays $1.60 a pound—help to build the infrastructure of Zapatista autonomy.

Coffee is not a good development tool, however. It does not contribute to the nutrition of the farmers. All coffee in Mexico is grown for export. (Nescafé is often served in coffee-growing regions.) Growing coffee takes food-growing land out of production and inhibits biodiversity. And most significantly, the price of coffee is set by an international cabal in which Starbucks, which now buys 1% of the world coffee crop, is a prominent player. Building autonomy on coffee prices, even fair trade ones, is a contradiction in the making. But the EZLN has few other options. For better or for worse, coffee has at least kept them on the land.

Every crisis is pregnant with irony. As farmers from all over southern Mexico and Central America were abandoning their plots and jumping into the immigration stream northward, Starbucks was heading south. The pilot "coffee store" adjacent the posh Sheraton Hotel on Reforma was just a few yards from the U.S. embassy. A double latte cost 35 pesos, a day's wages for coffee farmers in Chiapas. Global Exchange stood outside in the street and passed leaflets to the pedestrians asking them not to patronize the place.

Starbucks buys Chiapas coffee—its purportedly "shade grown" and dubiously "all organic" Quetzal brand. The coffee is grown by four ejidos in the cloud forest of El Triunfo near the Guatemalan border, a project cobbled together by Conservation International. But according to published reports, the ejidos use chemical fertilizer, spray pesticides, and are not certified "organic"—not even by Transfair, the San Francisco–based scam that charges Indians an arm and a leg to okay the purity of their product.

The trail of coffee in Mexico drips with the blood of rebels. From Atoyac, Guerrero, on the combative Costa Grande, where Lucio Cabañas rose; to the Loxichas in the southern sierra of Oaxaca, another coffee-growing region, where the Popular Revolutionary Army (EPR) flourished; to the Altos of Chiapas, where 49 Zapatista supporters were massacred in Acteal at the height of the harvest, rebellion and repression and coffee go hand in hand in hand. Now, with the coffee harvest about to begin all over again in the highlands, the EZLN was bracing itself for an uncertain season.

QDEP

On the eve of the Supreme Court decision re the Indians vs. the Indian Wrongs Act, a group of NGOs headed by San Cristóbal's Fray Ba issued this caution: "We advise you that you are responsible for the grave consequences of your decisions. Peace is in your hands." But if indeed that was the case, the Supremes fumbled the dove badly.

On Friday afternoon September 6, the 11-member panel handed down a decision not to be released until they were safely out of the building, had folded away their togas, and were gone for the weekend—some for extended vacations.

The decision leaked out incrementally over the next few days. The gist was that the justices had rid themselves of this bothersome affair by declaring themselves "incompetent" to decide the constitutionality of constitutional reforms enacted by the congress and therefore could not render a decision.

This judicial dodge was a stinging slap at the Indians who had entrusted their fate to Supreme jurisprudence. The matter had been decided not on its substance but rather on the pretext of protocol.

The decision had not been unanimous. Eight justices had washed their hands of the affair but three did not—although two of the three thought the court had jurisdiction and were prepared to vote Indian Wrongs up. Of the three, only Mariano Azuela, the judge who had stood the Mixe farmers up, disputed the constitutionality of Indian Wrongs. Azuela warned a *Jornada* reporter that the Supreme Court decision would "inflame" indigenous peoples everywhere.

Rodolfo Stavenhagen, now a United Nations rapporteur on indigenous people and once the head of the COSEVER, a body invented to oversee the implantation of the never-implemented San Andrés Accords, was equally gloomy: "The decision means that the Indians will construct their autonomías on the margins of the law."

But despite all the doomsayers, only scattered acts of violence occurred. A disgruntled crowd broke out the windows at San Cristóbal city hall. On the steps of the Supreme Court, a single egg flew out of the small knot of concerned citizens who had gathered to mourn, and splattered against the façade of the great granite building. Mourners stood vigil over a coffin slugged "QDEP Ley Cocopa" ("Rest in Peace, Cocopa Law"). The dozens who had come for the wake drifted off into the afternoon. One felt a great sense of exhaustion.

Now that the Supremes had spoken and the final appeal had been blunted (some litigants would step up to international venues), the debate had reached its *punto final*—for both Indian Rights and Indian

Wrongs. Although Indian Wrongs was now the law of the land, it was rejected by the very group it was supposed to protect and could not be imposed upon free people without big trouble. Indian Wrongs would never be implemented. Secondary laws were never enacted. QDEP Indian Wrongs.

So "justice" had had its final say, and it was time for the EZLN to break its silence, which it did in mid-November for only the second time in 19 months.

¡Gora Euskadi!

The first communiqué snuck onto a public stage without much initial fanfare: a letter to Fernando Yañez, who was Comandante Germán, Marcos's self-appointed *gran hermano* (great brother). Dated September but not released until November 17, the 19th anniversary of the founding of the EZLN, it was read during the presentation of the zero issue of *Rebeldía*, a new EZLN journal that has become an invaluable— if wordy—resource. The Sup's prose was jokey and absurdist. It was almost as if the rebels had never gone away.

In response to Germán's invitation to participate in the presentation, the Sup explained, "As you know, we are in silence and silence is not to be broken but to be cared for, so we will not be able to be there with you [at the Casa Lamm in Mexico City]." And: "There is a rumor that the Zapatistas are finished but the only thing that is finished around here is our patience." The Sup roasted the political parties and thumbed his nose at the Supreme Court. The communiqué was sort of a *gran carcajada* (big cackle) with multiple mentions of the fabled G-spot. "I know, I know, for people in silence, we talk a lot," he wrote in his sixth postscript.

Marcos was also heard in the autumn of 2002 on *Meet Me in the Streets*, the Spanish troubadour Joaquín Sabina's new album, for which the Sup wrote the lyrics to *"Cómo un Dolor de Muela"* (Like a Toothache), with its punch line *"Rebeldía* is a pain that's not worth curing." Sabina toured Chiapas for eight days in October, donating all his concert receipts to the compas.

On November 23, *La Jornada* published a text that had been sent to the Spanish *rockero* Angel Luis Lara, AKA "El Ruso," to be read at the inauguration of the Madrid Aguascalientes. Bigwig Zapsymps were on hand at the Complutense University for the gala: Saramago, Manuel Vázquez Montalbán, Manu Chao. *La Jornada*'s Luis Hernández Navarro (a former adviser during the San Andrés talks) and Hermann were invited to present papers. Hermann spoke about the Zapatista silence that was slowly shattering all around him: The Zapatistas had advanced because of the quantity of words they say, because of the discourse they have constructed and their constant dialogue with society, which so contrasted with their lengthy silences.

The gist of this new communiqué proclaimed, "No to logic! No to prudence! No to immobility and conformism!" His writing sometimes out of control and over the top, the Sup soared high: "There are acts of rebellion that are the color of butterflies, and the task of a butterfly is to bring the rainbow closer to the ground so that children can learn to fly."

But the Subcomandante also swooped in low, straight for the scrotum of the Spanish political class. "Felipillo" (Spanish socialist prime minister Felipe González) was a dog; José María Aznar, González's Franco-style successor, was "the imbecile Pepillo." Marcos dumped on the "constipated little king" Juan Carlos. But the Sup saved his rottenest tomatoes for the "fascist clown" Baltasar Garzón, the chief investigating judge in the National Audience, Spain's most powerful court.

Garzón, who affects a Susan Sontag–like gray swoosh in his leonine mane, is widely respected in human rights circles as the jurist who unsuccessfully sought to prosecute Chilean ex-dictator Augusto Pinochet for dirty war crimes but was foiled by Blair's poodle, Jack Straw, on the grounds that the butcher of the Chilean people was suffering from selective Alzheimer's. Garzón had then gone on to hound the Argentine generals and was about to receive from Mexico one Ricardo Cavallo, "Serpico," adjudged responsible for the deaths of at least 5,000 leftists at the Naval Mechanics' Institute, or ESMA, in Buenos Aires. Garzón's quest for justice for the victims of South America's dirty wars was expected to land him on the Nobel Peace Prize short list.

But Baltasar had a dark side, a loathing for the Basque terrorists ETA (Euskadi Ta Askatasuna, or "Basque Homeland and Liberty") that led him to commit egregious human rights abuses against those he saw as "apologists" for ETA terrorism. He had closed down the Basque daily *Egin*, thrown the editor of *Oveja Negra* (Black Sheep) magazine in jail, and threatened the same for *Gara*, the successor to *Egin*. Although he had not personally tortured ETA suspects and "apologists," he had consigned them to a system that Human Rights Watch and Amnesty International says does so. He had just proscribed Batasuna, a Basque *abertzal*, or independent left party, that had members in both the Spanish and the Basque parliaments. Batasuna had been shut down, its offices sealed, its electoral registration revoked, and its leaders dragged in for interrogation.

Why Marcos was so exercised over the injustices committed against Batasuna in a world toxic with such noxious abuse is uncertain, but he came at Garzón full frontal for crimes against humanity.

"We had many Basques among us here and they did not show us how to make bombs. In fact, each Zapatista is a bomb. . . ." The Sup trashed Baltasar's pursuit of Pinochet as a farce and invoked the Mexican curse for the Spanish Conquistadores: "¡*Gachupín!*" (literally, "spur-wearer").

The Sup's defense of Batasuna was transmogrified into support for ETA by the time the morning papers were in the street, and his critics came for him with sledgehammers. Carlos Fuentes, a lover of all things Gachupín, accused Marcos of abandoning the Indians and becoming Kurtz of the Congo. Fernando Savater and Carlos Monsiváis, leading intellectual lights of the old and new worlds, threw bricks at the spoiled brat in the ski mask. Even Saramago and Vázquez Montalbán buckled—the Sup had overstepped literary decorum with his outburst. On the other hand, the Aznar government remained aloof despite the slurs cast upon Pepillo and his king, unwilling to descend to the level of "this deranged persona," as interior minister Angel Aceves asserted.

But Baltasar Garzón, afflicted perhaps with some morbid pathology for self-laceration, picked up the bait and threw down the gauntlet. The Subcomandante was "miserable" and "cowardly," hiding behind his silly ski mask and "ridiculous pipe." Marcos had brutally insulted the memory of more than 800 victims of ETA terrorism. In a letter to *El Universal* dated December 3, the judge actually challenged Marcos to a duel—well, a debate—"without masks, face to face."

Garzón had supplied the suddenly super-epistolatory Sup with a golden gambit. In the name of "Zapatista children, old people, men and women" he challenged Garzón to a debate to be conducted over five days between April 5 and 10 in Lanzarote, the Canary Islands, presumably at the home of Nobelist José Saramago and his translator wife, Pilar del Río. All seven judges would have to be Gachupines. If Baltasar Garzón won the tussle, he would be allowed to unmask Marcos in public and then have him tortured, as were the Basque prisoners. If Marcos proved triumphant, Baltasar Garzón would take on the defense of the San Andrés Accords before international tribunals and prosecute Ernesto Zedillo for war crimes.

Parallel to the debate and presumably in some other part of the Saramago compound, all Basque political forces, civil and military, would be convened to discuss a just solution to the conflict. The Sup attached invitations to Spanish and Basque civil society, the abertzales (Batasuna), and ETA. The note to the terrorists was particularly nervy, critiquing ETA for taking out civilians—"There is never any justification for that"—and respectfully asking the fighters to declare a 177-day truce beginning Christmas Eve. "In case you do not accept the truce, I offer myself to you as your next victim. You can accuse me of being a collaborator. The Spanish government already says that I am an apologist for terrorism." *¡Gora Euskadi!* The Sup tossed his old Mao cap high into the jungle sky. Eventually ETA would snarl back, warning Sub Marcos to butt out of a struggle that wasn't his to butt into and accusing him of using the Basque conflict to sell T-shirts.

The Subcomandante's literary tour de force brought Saramago and Vázquez Montalbán back into the fold. "Lanzarote will prove that Utopia is still possible," the Portuguese Nobel laureate waxed. "This offer will go down in history—but in literary, not political, history," the burly Barcelonan waned. Getting to Lanzarote might be a problem, the Sup rued: "All we have are our canoes."

The Basque interlude confused not a few. For the first time in 19 months, the Zapatistas were talking, but they were speaking Euskara. On December 29, when Marcos issued a stiff warning to the Fox government not to evict any of the Zapatista communities in the Montes Azules, as was being threatened almost daily now, he made his point sandwiched between acid commentary on the Basque-Zapatista dynamic. "They are not angry with us for our supposed support of ETA but because we left the house of indigenous rights in which they had us confined." His intellectual critics were just toadying up so they would be in line for the Príncipe de Asturias literary prize, the most prestigious in the Spanish language. Once again, Marcos used the term "Gachupín," which always touches a Mexican nerve. But this time he advised Garzón that he was not interfering in Spanish politics, because "a quarter of the blood in my veins is Gachupín." It was an unusual admission for a mouthpiece of an indigenous movement who often makes no distinction between his own mestizo background and that of the Indians for whom he speaks.

We Don't Need Permission

During the week between Christmas and New Year's, I traveled to Chiapas with a brigade of young people from the National Polytechnic Institute ("Poly") who were working on a project in Guadalupe Tepeyac. We found a truck to haul us down to the jungle from San Cris and set up camp under the *palapa* (open-sided shed) the town used to dry its coffee.

The village seemed oddly muted in contrast to the busy days of rebuilding that had preceded the Guadalupanos' official return the previous February. The ejido was divided—the farmers had not been able to reestablish their pre-exodus production, and the plummeting price of corn and coffee had laid the local economy flat. I spoke with the profe, "Carlos"—he was exasperated with not being able to keep kids in school.

"They get to be 10 or 11 and they want to work with their fathers in the milpa." The profe feared that they would soon be joining their cousins from neighboring PRI villages in the long trek north. "I have a hundred kids here—they are the Zapatistas' future."

I changed the subject. What was all this Basque stuff in the Sup's recent communiqués? But the profe clammed up. Would Tepeyac be celebrating the ninth anniversary of the rebellion this January 1? "What is there to celebrate?"

Down the road in La Realidad the story was much the same. The autonomous council had no plans to celebrate on New Year's. What is there to celebrate? The Vascos? There had been a few in the peace camp but they were long gone now.

Although the council steadfastly denied that anything was planned for January 1, we noticed the women at the washing hole in the river were scrubbing their ski masks and paliacates as if maybe they were getting ready for a trip.

We spent New Year's Eve up at Oventik, but there was no party—or at least none that was open to the outsiders. Instead, we hung out up at the general store chewing over the price of coffee with the NGOs. There were lots of internationals in town for the anniversary—Iñaki García from the Barcelona *colectivo*, Federico Mariani from the Italian group Ya Basta! and Hebe de Bonafini of the Madres de la Plaza Mayo had just landed in San Cristóbal.

Around midnight, I snuck down to the pine bough–scented auditorium and peered through the slats. *Milicianos* and *milicianas* were bouncing to the cumbias, their weapons casually slung over their shoulders. But it was a private party.

The bases began gathering even before first light down at the Coca-Cola plant on the periphery of San Cristóbal, where they had gathered that first January 1 to take the city and declare war on the mal gobierno. They kept arriving all day from the communities in the highlands in packed little farm trucks, the women in their brilliant *huipiles*, the men wearing rubber boots and straw sombreros and carrying their machetes and a hunk of *jocote*, or pine pitch, from which to fashion a torch. In late afternoon, I walked the line, which now extended several kilometers from the Coca-Cola plant to the new maquiladora out on the Pan-American Highway, counting heads. I stopped counting at 15,000. Coupled with another 7,000 from the jungle and the Cañadas who would join the march at the entrance to the old city, the January 1, 2003, retaking of San Cristóbal was the largest coming together of Zapatista bases I had ever witnessed. Only weeks before, the word on the street was that Marcos was gone and the compas finished.

As I strolled through the line of march, I began to notice small hand-lettered signs professing international solidarity. *"¡Vivan los Argentinos!"* *"¡Qué Vivan los Italianos!"* *"¡Carlo Giuliano Vive!"* *"¡Qué Vivan los Globalfóbicos!"* *"¡Qué Vivan los Vascos!"* *"¡Gora Euskadi!"* The EZLN seemed to have turned its attention to its support base outside of Mexico.

The march into San Cristóbal began at dusk. Machetes clanged like the best days of Atenco and the torches flared in the cold dark night. Unlike 1994, the cobbled streets were packed with both tourists and *Coletos* (the white and mestizo burghers of San Cristóbal who during the colony wore their hair in a ponytail, or *cola*, hence *Coleto*, or those of the ponytail). Some had panicked and closed their shops early but their Indian servants and porters had not. Some were quite drunk. *"¡Darle duro, muchachos!"* ("Give it to them hard, boys!"), they shouted as the compas filed past.

The line of march filled the cathedral plaza and extended down the spanking-new tourist walkway the city fathers were so proud of, all the way down to the Santo Domingo church, turned the corner, and filled Avenida General Utrilla back to the Indian market. Although it was a historic gathering, the Zapatistas were no longer on the media's radar, and there were few reporters other than Hermann and myself on hand to record the haps for posterity.

In the packed square fronting Tatic's yellow cathedral, seven comandantes declaimed for the first time in 19 months. Indeed, those who spoke included several who had spoken to the nation on the March of the People Who Are the Color of the Earth and later addressed the

Mexican congress—Esther, Tacho, David, Zebedeo, Omar, Mister, and Bruce Lee. As before Congress, Subcomandante Marcos did not accompany them.

Comandante Tacho worked the crowd, blasting the political parties, particularly the PRD, whom he accused of selling out Indian rights so "Cárdenas's son could become governor of Michoacán." By now, torch fires were wildly out of control, and David seized the mic and urged the compas to extinguish them before everyone was barbecued. The solemn David set the tone: "We don't need the mal gobierno and its lies anymore!" "We didn't rise up nine years ago to beg for alms," Esther warned, "we are autonomous with or without the law." "We don't have to ask the government's permission to be autonomous," insisted Bruce Lee.

We don't need the government's permission anymore. This was what the EZLN had come to San Cristóbal to tell the little bit of the world that was still listening. We are autonomous. We don't need to waste any more of our time asking the government if we can be autonomous. Then the comandantes were done and the bases climbed up into hundreds of those little farm trucks and drove back into the mountains and the jungle of southeastern Chiapas. The disappearing act did not take an hour. They left behind the new tourist walkway in shambles, which gave the Coletos one more thing to complain about.

January 1, 2003, was a parting of the waters for these resilient Mayan rebels. For nine years, they had cajoled, wheedled, demanded, and finally taken up arms to gain the attention of the mal gobierno and win their autonomy from it—but the one thing that the mal gobierno could never grant them was precisely that, autonomy. When finally in the fallout from the Indian Wrongs law they came to understand this, the Zapatistas realized that they had been autonomous for a long time, and really all they had to do now was organize that autonomy. They had the power now. The Time of the Fox—and, in fact, the whole political class (*"qué se vayan todos"*)—was done with. Now it was time for autonomy.

Book Two
The Time of Autonomy

7. Winter/Spring 2003

Coalition of the Killing

For a long time, this place has existed where the men are Zapatistas, the women are Zapatistas, the kids are Zapatistas, the chickens are Zapatistas, the stones are Zapatistas, everything is Zapatista. And in order to wipe out the Zapatista Army of National Liberation, they will have to wipe this piece of territory off the face of earth— not just destroy it but erase it completely, because there is always the danger of the dead down below. . . .

—Subcomandante Marcos to *Proceso*, 1994

The reader will recall that Bush's war against the Iraqi people began in Mexico on February 15, 2001, when the newly selected president had the chutzpah to deploy Vicente Fox's Guanajuato rancho as the launching pad from which to bomb Baghdad. The unprovoked attack by the U.S. and the U.K. was just a "routine" run, Bush lied to the cameras, although the assault was the very first strike on Saddam since Bush had stolen the presidency and signaled the opening salvo of his homicidal campaign to unseat Saddam ("He tried to kill my daddy"), engineer "regime change," and appropriate Iraq's petroleum reserves, the second largest under Mother Earth.

As we know only too well now, "Operation Iraqi Freedom" was in the planning stage from the very first day that Bush occupied the Oval Office. Ex–White House terror czar Richard Clarke wrote a best-seller that described how he was asked to dream up scenarios to topple Saddam not 48 hours after Dubya had been inaugurated. After 9/11, Clarke was pressed by Dick Cheney and Donald Rumsfeld to provide nonexistent links between al Qaeda and the Iraqi strongman. Not only did they not exist, but also, just weeks before Mohammed Atta and his gang took down the World Trade Towers, Bin Laden had called for Saddam's overthrow and execution.

By early 2002, Fox News was reporting the Iraq war as fact. As he rode the 9/11 tsunami of fear and loathing to 80% approval ratings, no lie was too grand for Bush and his associates to cram down the craw of the American people. John and Jane Q. Public wolfed it all down greedily: the WMDS, anthrax, democracy, Niger uranium, the strategic alliance between Saddam and Al Qaeda, the sweet victory that would soon be ours. Congress turned into the usual mush and granted the president war powers. The White House turned its attention toward strong-arming the United Nations into signing on to the aggression.

Mexico does not usually have a seat on the Security Council. Foreign Minister Jorge Castañeda's pop, also named Jorge and also a foreign minister, had made it a principle of Mexican diplomacy not to sit on the council after a disastrous experiment in the 1970s. Mexico's vote was just too susceptible to U.S. pressures. The General Assembly should be the lead decision-making body anyway.

But Junior had other ideas. Selling Mexico's vote in exchange for "the whole enchilada" was hailed as a "pragmatic approach" by the big business confederations like COPAMEX and pop historian Enrique Krauze. After a spat with Brazil about who should occupy the Latin seat the Dominican Republic was abandoning, Castañeda Jr., who had extraordinary influence over his president, not exactly a diplomatic fluorescent light, dispatched his longtime associate Adolfo Aguilar Zinser, then functioning as Fox's national security adviser (Adolfo and Jorge had both left the PRD together), to New York.

Mexico subsequently voted up Resolution 1449, which found Iraq "in material breach" of Security Council sanctions and issued an ultimatum to comply. The inspectors returned to Baghdad to uncover the WMDs. As the year turned, the Bush/Blair axis of evil was putting the hammerlock on council members like Mexico that were reluctant to rush into war, and relations between Washington and Mexico City grew ragged.

Both Fox and Zinser were agreed that a Mexican vote to unleash the U.S./U.K. assault on Iraq constituted a violation of the Estrada Doctrine, the governing principle of Mexican international diplomacy, which rejects all foreign intervention in the affairs of a sovereign nation (Mexico has frequently been intervened in—mostly by its neighbor to the north), a position that led Castañeda to accuse Zinser of being "out of control" at the U.N. Jorge resigned on January 27 and has never been back.

Vicente Fox is a devout Catholic and the Mexican Church had spoken out against the impending war—nine out of 10 Mexicans shared that view. But Fox's rejection of U.S. intentions in Iraq was not mere altruism. The Bush/Blair war was designed to wrest control of Iraqi oil fields, a takeover that could bring world prices tumbling to $10 a barrel. The resulting glut would pull the plug on Mexico's immediate economic future.

The Bush/Blair pressure on Fox was classic. Spain's José María Aznar was flown in to try to sweet-talk the Fox into joining the poodle club. The *Wall Street Journal* editorialized that Mexico was "a friend of Saddam's." Mexico would be cut out of reconstruction contracts, hinted new ambassador Tony Garza, a Bush crony. According to unidentified embassy sources (most probably Garza), Mexico's refusal to stand with Washington at the Security Council would stimulate the same sort of backlash as the Fox News–driven anti-France (remember "freedom fries"?) putsch had. Some 11,000,000 Mexicans living in the U.S. were at risk of being rounded up and interned à la the Japanese if Zinser was allowed to vote the war down at the U.N.

Inside that glass fortress towering over Manhattan's East River, Bush's much traveled envoy John Negroponte went for the throat. Once the proconsul puppet master who pulled the Contras' strings out of Tegoo and an ambassador to Mexico at the beginning of Carlos Salinas's painful stay in office, Negroponte was instrumental in enabling NAFTA negotiations. (Among other advantages, NAFTA would make Mexico so beholden to the U.S. that it would never again vote against Washington at the U.N., according to State Department cables leaked to *Proceso* magazine at the time.) Negroponte took to bugging the offices of the undeclared members of the Security Council. At this point, the U.S., the U.K., and their Bulgarian and Spanish poodle dogs stood in favor of invasion; France, China, and Russia threatened veto if a war declaration came to the council; Syria and Germany were equally opposed; Mexico, Chile, Cameroon, Guinea, Angola, and Pakistan had not yet formulated an appropriate response—Bush mouthpiece Ari Fleischer lied that Mexico was the lone holdout against invasion.

The Group of Six began to meet to draft a plan that would extend the March 8 deadline on weapons inspections and postpone a unilateral declaration of war by Washington. "The next morning, when we went to Negroponte's office to present the proposal, he read it back to us word for word," the owl-eyed, fright-wig-haired Zinser told this reporter. Adolfo's story was later corroborated by the disclosures of a translator, Katherine Gunn, who worked for Britain's signal intelligence outfit GCHQ.

The news of the bugging elicited little outrage either on the part of Zinser's new boss, Luis Ernesto Derbez, or even from Secretary General Annan despite it being an egregious violation of United Nations protocols. Zinser subsequently became Security Council president for April and officiated over the unanimous legitimization of the illegal aggression. Later, he would bridle at Yanqui arrogance, complaining that Washington still considered Mexico to be its "back door," and Fox fired him forthwith. Adolfo was killed in a wreck on the Puebla highway in August 2005.

The rest is more hysteria than history. On February 5, clown prince Colin Powell, in a last-ditch pitch to mau-mau the Security Council into compliance, spewed scabrous lies on international television. Ordinarily Powell would have spoken before a reproduction of Picasso's *Guernica*, a painting emblematic of the first aerial bombing of a civilian population (the Basques in 1937) that decorates the Security Council's chambers, but poodle Annan acquiesced to Negroponte's insistence that the painting be covered with a blue cloth to avoid influencing yet-undecided members.

By March, Bush and Blair saw that they were sunk at the U.N. and cut their losses by withdrawing their ultimatum from Security Council consideration. How Mexico would have voted in the end is unclear—I would bet abstention.

The invasion started to roll on March 19, and by the first week of April "coalition forces" were pulling down statues of Saddam in Baghdad and bombing public marketplaces, killing hundreds. By the end of April, at the U.N. Human Rights Commission in Geneva, Mexico was voting against an investigation into U.S./U.K. human rights abuses in Iraq and the targeting of civilian populations. On International Working Men and Women's Day, May 1, Bush was declaring the war won from the deck of an aircraft carrier off San Diego. Mission Accomplished.

As I write today, just a week from the third anniversary of this cruel crusade, perhaps 150,000 Iraqis have perished in the carnage. The U.S. dead were at 2,299 this morning, a number that fills out only a few slabs in the charnel house that Bush has built in Iraq.

When I was forced to leave Baghdad in the week before the bombing began, Mr. Chkashab, the director of the Daura oil refinery, invited us in for tea and told us verbatim: "This time we will not fight the Americans on the desert. There is no protection out there. Now we will invite them into our cities and resist them block to block with whatever we have—sticks, stones daggers—just as our grandfathers did to the British."

Iraq Comes to the Mountains of Mexico's Southeast

The Comandancia, which must have watched this pageant of horrors from the camps above La Realidad, would soon be postmarking their communiqués "from Iraq in the mountains of the Mexican southeast."

To butter up Bush, Fox had ordered the increased surveillance of Mexican borders and oil fields on the absurd premise that Iraq would counterattack the U.S. from the south. "Operation Sentinel" mobilized 18,000 Mexican troops, 3,000 assigned to the southern border, which skirts

EZLN camps in the jungle. Overflights darkened the sky, and Hermann reported U.S. Navy patrols were conducting maneuvers off Puerto Madero on Chiapas's Pacific coast. Although Vicente Fox had not signed on to the Coalition of the Willing, the number of troops involved in safe-guarding Washington's southern flank represented the third-largest contingent in that unholy alliance.

Iraqi Daze

As the buildup to the war crescendoed, fuming about it was not enough, and I put my life in order and headed out to Iraq in one last desperate effort to stave off the genocide. We would be human shields, interposing our bodies between Bush's bombs and the people of Iraq.

Small rallies against the coming war were frequent in Mexico City, and at the last act I attended before shipping out in late January, Andrés Contreras, "the Happy Troubadour," was caterwauling from the top step of the Angel of Independence on Reforma Boulevard about how Osama Bin Laden was *El Bueno* (a good guy) because "he has killed many a gringo."

We traveled up to Baghdad with the classic Casasola portrait of Votan Zapata staring sternly from a bus bulkhead and arrived in Ali Baba City on February 15, the maximum day of protest against Bush's mad war, when 15,000,000 souls around the world pounded the pavements in the loudest NO! to war ever heard in the known universe, a stentorian outcry from the bottom that Bushwa arrogantly dismissed as "a focus group" and relentlessly marched his troops off to war.

As the Apocalypse approached Baghdad, the days fused into nights and I lost track of the Zapatista Army of National Liberation. Internet access was closely monitored by the Saddamites, and I could not dial up *La Jornada* for news of the compas back in the mountains of Mexico's southeast. To salve my homesickness, I gabbed with a young woman who worked at the corner copy shop and was studying Spanish at the university. I wonder what has happened to her amid the carnage.

Then one icy night at a rally in Tahrir Square a week before the invasion, I heard a clarion cry: "*¡El Pueblo Unido, Jamás Será Vencido!*" and, yes, "*¡Zapata Vive! ¡La Lucha Sigue!*" A tiny delegation of Mexicans had just arrived, headed by the PRD's international secretary, Mario Saucedo. My longtime colleague Blanche Petrich, who had been the first to interview Subcomandante Marcos way back when, had tagged along to cover for *La Jornada*.

The Human Shields had borrowed a page from the Zapatista playbook and insisted upon autonomy from the Saddam government. We would choose the sites at which we wanted to be bombed and form our own committees to run the encampments. But Saddam and the Baathists, much like the mal gobierno back home, did not much appreciate the nuances of autonomous decision making, and although we were not treated with poison gases like the Kurds, five logistical leaders, this writer included, were deported on the eve of the war. (Many more stayed on for the bombing.)

Escorted to the Jordan border by burly men in leather coats and Saddam mustaches—dead ringers for the Mexican Judicial Police—like so many deportees collared by the migra, we crossed paths out in the desert night with a second group of Mexican shields on their way to stand under the bombs in Baghdad, among them Sister Luz from the Hospital San Carlos in Altamirano, where the nuns had treated wounded Zapatistas in the first days of the rebellion and were almost lynched for doing so by the local ranchers. On my map, all roads seem to lead back to Chiapas.

I returned to the Centro Histórico in early April. A number of pieces I had written from Baghdad had been published in *La Jornada* and the waiters at the Café LaBlanca had been following my travels. "So they haven't killed you yet," Carlos Díaz, the owner, clapped me on the back. The café con leche was on the house and it tasted like I was home at last.

Outside, it was Holy Week and Bush's head was being blown up on the streets. On Holy Saturday (*Sábado de la Gloria*), Mexicans delight in exploding papier-mâché figures of much despised politicos. Out behind the Sonora witchcraft market the Linares family, master crafters of Holy Week Judases, stuffed a 15-foot U.S. soldier with fireworks and hung an

"I liberated Iraq" sign around his neck, and along with a smaller figure of a one-legged Iraqi citizen ("He liberated me") blew them both sky-high. "What else can I do?" Miguel Linares told me, "I hate this damn war so much. . . ."

¡No En Nuestra Nombre!

"The architecture of this war is no different . . . the stones are our bones and the mortar our blood . . . there is little difference between Bush's smart bombs and the Roman catapults, only the technology brings it to us faster," Subcomandante Marcos wrote, studying the visuals of the Yanquis' obscene Shock and Awe show on the tube somewhere near La Realidad, in a document titled "The Other Geography," received in April.

> Geography has been simplified by the globalization of war. Now there is an up, which only accommodates a handful of people, and a down, which covers the rest of the planet. Now the simple and humble people of Iraq, the old people and the men and women and children, have much in common with prosperous North American arms merchants—they make the bombs and the Iraqis receive them. Bush and Blair are just amiable mailmen. . . .
>
> This war is not against Iraq or rather not just against Iraq but against all those who disobey, who rebel. But Bush and Blair have not learned their geography lessons well. Iraq is not just in the Middle East but also in Europe and Africa, Oceania, the U.S. and Latin America and the mountains of the Mexican southeast, wherever people continue to say no. . . .

The Mexican movement against the war was small but vibrant. Returning human shields died-in in front of the embassy once a week and shouted "¡Zapata Vive! ¡Inch' Allah!" at Garza and his gang; Palestinian kaffias ("Yasser Arafat turbans") were on sale in my neighborhood. Much of this defiance was put together by signers of the Not in Our Name initiative (No en Nuestra Nombre), who had gathered on

March 18 at the gringo embassy, where many U.S. flags were torched as Jacobo Zabludovsky, the grand old man of Mexican radio, reported on the first minutes of the invasion over the speakers. When hotheads tried to rush the 20-foot fence that protects the North Americans from the regular rage of Mexicans, they were repelled by the *granaderos* (riot squad). Later, ski-masked fedayeen would trash a swath through the Zona Rosa, the nearby tourist zone.

Mexicans flinched in horror at the brutality of the invasion. Unlike in Gringolandia, what was actually happening on the ground in Iraq was not blanked out. Televisa had an unembedded crew in the Palestine Hotel and recorded the deliberate U.S. tank assault on that building in graphic detail. Both networks featured Al Jazeera footage of the devastation of Baghdad's civilian population.

If that was not enough to piss the locals off, it became evident from the first days that Mexicans were dying in this imperialist outrage, "green card Marines," kids who had joined up to legalize their immigration status—many had been brought over as infants without papers by newly legalized parents under immigration amnesties in the late 1980s and early '90s.

Tracked into dead-end jobs, Mexican kids in Southern California were *carne de cañón* ("meat of the cannon") for the gung-ho Marine recruiters who invaded their high schools and their homes, spouting the kind of macho jive these young men liked to hear. Most of the Mexican recruits were concentrated at Camp Pendleton outside San Diego, and it was precisely the Pendleton units that led the invasion. In the first 90 days of the war, 14 Mexicans were killed—actually, the first to die, Rodrigo González, a farm boy from Salinas, Coahuila, died on February 23 in Kuwait when his helicopter went down.

One of the first to fall was Jesús Suárez near Nasiriyah on March 21. In those days, the only way a green card Marine could earn instant citizenship was to come home dead, and the Pentagon offered Jesús's father, Fernando, this posthumous honor. Enraged by the useless gesture, Fernando Suárez del Solar turned it down. "My son was a proud Mexican," he spat at the generals. Jesús had been a *conchero* dancer growing up in Tijuana, and Don Fernando has carried the spirit of his "Guerrero Azteca" (Aztec Warrior) to Iraq and back and into the high schools of Southern California to plead with the *vatos* not to sign up in Tío Sam's killer army.

April 12 was the next worldwide mobilization, and the political parties, noticing that 99.999% of all Mexicans despised the war, seized the opportunity from the civil society to convoke the march—only this time there were some caveats. "Violence-prone" groups, such as the General Strike Committee, the Macheteros of Atenco, and the Francisco Villa Popular Front, were barred from the line of march. So as not to offend the Yanqui masters, the route would be from the Monument of the Revolution to the Zócalo, studiously avoiding the U.S. embassy.

The EZLN and its proxies could not agree to such conditions. More pertinently, the rebels would never march with the very deputies and senators who had castrated Indian Rights. On April 5, Sergio Rodríguez Lascano, speaking in the name of the FZLN, a kind of Zapatista political wing, called a press conference to declare the antiwar movement was hopelessly divided between "those who just want to stop U.S. intervention in Iraq and those who want to change the world." How could there be a march that avoided the root of all this evil? With the blessing of the Comandancia, the EZeta, in conjunction with other independent struggle organizations, would lead a countermarch from the Zócalo to the U.S. embassy, "the Other March," on April 12. That Saturday, the two marches, moving in opposite directions, did indeed intersect, but there were no fisticuffs.

The senators and the deputies and the "good" peace movement droned on before 60,000 in the big square. I caught the metro down to the embassy, careful to avoid stepping on Don Durito of the Lacandón, who was purportedly carrying a sign that read, "A wall without graffiti is like a world without rebellion." Now 40,000 almost universally young people were already eviscerating the Stars and Stripes. Others were tossing tomatoes and rotten eggs at the fortresslike edifice. Sub Marcos's nasal twang began to blast from the speakers.

The EZLN condemned the war as a violation of international law—"This is a war against reason and humanity"—and signed on to a declaration being circulated by *Z Magazine* in the name of 77 comandantes and 2,222 communities (twice the number of Zapatista communities claimed in the 1997 March of the 1,111).

"Today the political class took advantage of the rising clamor against this war of the powerful against the poor," Marcos charged. "It isn't important if those who make this war are named Bush or Blair or Fox. It is not important if the flag they fly is that of the U.S. or the PRI-PAN-PRD. The principal aim of their war is the globalization of terror and submission—but what they have succeeded in doing is globalizing the rejection, the No. . . ."

When the rally broke up and headed out into the city, a bloc of young nay-sayers clashed with police on Reforma Boulevard. A patrol car was firebombed and 27 arrested, beaten, and jailed. Their parents searched frantically for them, running from one police lockup to another all through the night.

In a subsequent communiqué, "Seven Thoughts in May," directed at the Italian and Spanish solidarity movements, the Sup continued to hammer away at the U.S. aggression in Iraq.

> The U.S. makes itself the sheriff of the hyperpolis. They think if they destroy the culture they will win. The hatred of Hitler and Bush for culture is not the only similarity between these two. The other is their ardor for global domination.
>
> And if they win, then what? We can expect another war, interrupted by commercial announcements. Look, we are not trying to tear down the statues but rather we seek to construct a society in which statues exist only for the birds to shit upon.
>
> Our No to this war has become a generalized No. . . .

Ecotourism—Saving Nature for the Rich

At the end of the previous November, settlers in the Montes Azules were startled when a caravan of 30 or so jeeps flying weird little flags visited their far-flung villages in the heart of the jungle. Laden down with expensive camping gear, short-wave radios, walkie-talkies, lots of munchies, and cases of mosquito repellant, the visitors reportedly questioned the villagers about real estate values in broken Spanish, posed for snapshots with the colorful natives, and roared off back into the bush.

It took several months to verify that the denizens of the Blue Mountains were not hallucinating. The caravan proved to be one wing of the Isuzu Challenge Rally, which each year travels to environmentally sensitive regions (Namibia, Vietnam, Patagonia, and the Himalayas had been previous venues) under the banner "Man & Machine United for Nature."

Affluent businessmen (there were no businesswomen) from Japan, Israel, South Africa, Thailand, Mexico, and Guatemala (where the Isuzu franchise is owned by the military) had booked on for the ride. The weird little flags were those of Japan and Israel—the latter is a major supplier of the Guatemalan armed forces and reportedly pieced off Governor Pablo with 198 Galils for his state police as reward for having facilitated the Isuzu Challenge Rally. In fact, a retired Israeli general, Avihu Ben-Nun, captained the adventure.

After a few days of plying the Lacandón, the expedition moved on to Guatemala's Lake Tikal under escort from the dread Kaibiles, or Tigers, that neighbor republic's most feared security force, responsible for the genocide of tens of thousands of Mayan Indians in the 1970s and '80s. The fumes of internal combustion soon dissipated, but the Isuzu Challenge Rally was the harbinger of Big Ecotourism to come.

While bird-watching in the Montes Azules, the ralliers had lodged at a vest-pocket eco-ranch just outside of Ocosingo—the Rancho Esmeralda, whose North American owners, Glen Wersch and Ellen Jones, had picked up the spread for a song from a local ranching family that had been run off following the 1994 rebellion, and had converted it into a comfortable inn, one of the top 10 in Mexico according to the Lonely Planet tourist guide. Not the least of its attractions was that it was next door to the exquisite Mayan ruins at Tonina.

But Rancho Esmeralda had long been claimed by the autonomous council of "Primero de Enero." Compas from Nuevo Jerusalem had moved onto the land, which they had once worked as peons, immediately after the uprising, but retreated when the military began construction of a large base across the highway. The confluence of the gringo-owned eco-ranch, the Zapatista village with the Old Testament name of New Jerusalem, the millennial Mayan ruins, and the armed-to-the-teeth military base had all the elements of a good novel.

The arrival of the military-led Isuzu caravan at the Esmeralda exasperated the ranch's rebel neighbors. Jeeps raced through their community at all hours—the rancho was most easily accessed through New Jerusalem—and they blockaded the road. Now the guests had to park far away and lug their suitcases through the Tonina ruins on the Esmeralda's other flank, a violation of National Historical and Anthropological Institute rules and regulations.

By Christmastime, Wersch and Jones were in the middle of an angry *pleito* with the Zapatistas of Primero de Enero and claimed the rebels had ordered them to turn over the deed and vacate the premises. Wersch jumped on the Internet to advise past and future guests that the Esmeralda had been invaded by "terrorists." The *New York Times'* Tim Weiner substantiated the bogus charges without even leaving Mexico City. Soon Wersch and Jones were demanding military protection and Governor Pablo's intervention on their behalf, and when both turned a deaf ear, they appealed to the U.S. embassy. The State Department subsequently issued travel warnings to U.S. citizens visiting Chiapas.

With their business down the drain, the gringos hired lawyers and tried to wheedle 10,000,000 pesos out of the state (they had paid 21,000 for it), and when that ploy failed, they abandoned the eco-ranch and by the first of March, the Zapatistas were moving in.

THE BALLAD OF THE MONTES AZULES
*The people that live today
in the biosphere*

of the Montes Azules,
all are threatened
by the illegal invasion
by which the bad government
wants to kick out the communities.

We are the color of the earth
and no one can deny it
because we are the first ones
and the original settlers.

We are the color of the earth
and our memory is engraved
in the stone and the sea.

—The Two Winds of Voice and Fire, from "Ballad of the Eviction from Montes Azules"

The evictions began in mid-December—27 Chol Indians expelled from Sabanilla in the north of the state who, like many before, had sought sanctuary in the rain forest. The refugees, really just two families, lived under a tarp along the Lacanja River in a settlement they had named for the old guerrillero Lucio Cabañas. They had been removed by the authorities with little struggle and flown up to Comitán in the highlands, where they were promised new land that never materialized. Five months later they were threatening to return to the Montes Azules.

According to Environmental Secretariat (SEMARNAP) rosters, 42 communities in the biosphere were slated for removal—12 to 16 of them expressed affiliation with the EZLN, 14 with ARIC-Independiente, and the rest either to the PRI or to no political alliance. Eight settlements in a cluster around Chajul, where the Guatemalan border elbows north, were immediately under the gun.

Big Ecotourism was moving into the southern Montes Azules—the Tzendales River ecological station had been converted into a luxury hotel, a deal thought to have been brokered by the U.S. eco-titan Conservation International with big money from the Ford Motor Car Company, in participation with the private enterprise Espacios Naturales y Desarrollo Sustentable (Natural Spaces and Sustainable Development), on whose board Julia Carabias, Zedillo's environmental secretary and an architect of the eviction proceedings, was a prominent player. A night's lodging was payable in hundreds of Yanqui dollars. "Natural Spaces" was also the mover and shaker in a second "eco-hotel" under construction in Chajul.

Other ecotourist pipe dreams already on the drawing board: The Veracruz-based Turrent Corporation was planning a five-star hotel at Lacanjá Chansayub in association with the Lacandón community, and the Alquimia Group, which had converted the sacred Mayan *cenote* (well) at X'caret on the "Mayan Riviera" south of Cancún into a tourist playground, was reportedly looking thirstily at the Bascán cascades close by Roberto Barrios just outside the biosphere. Could Club Med be far behind?

Up in San Cristóbal, Bishop Arizmendi caught wind of the ecotourist development and mused, "Most of the people in the Montes Azules did not go there for ecotourism. . . ."

Policy for the reserve was set by the Mesa Ambiental (Environmental Table), a body that reflected the views of various government and nongovernmental bureaucracies—the SEMARNAP, Agrarian Reform, the biosphere management, Governor Pablo's people, and a representative of the Lacandón nation, which claimed to be the sole owner of the jungle. Although SEMARNAP chaired the table, it was the Connecticut-based NGO Conservation International that pulled the strings.

Founded in 1987 and now operating in 26 countries, CI advises transnationals like EXXON and Ford that have dismal environmental track records on environmental "investments." Conservation International had itself debt-swapped for a small swatch of the Montes Azules a decade ago and arrogantly foisted its designs to exclude all but the Lacandones from the reserve. Its strategy was positively Machiavellian: deputize the Lacandones as "forest guardians" and turn machete-wielding posses loose on the settler communities around Chajul, "inviting" them to leave the forest.

The Lacandones are indeed the titular owners of 600,000 hectares of the rain forest, including the entire Montes Azules. As previously noted, in a discredited decree promulgated by President Luis Echeverría, the whole Lacandón was deeded to 66 families belonging to that *etnia* (ethnic group) in 1972. The Lacandones immediately sold their logging rights for precious mahogany and cedar hardwoods to the timber companies. Hermann often contends that the Lacandones are not Mayans at all but rather Caribs who came from Campeche in the 18th century. "Why do they have more rights then we do?" a Mayan villager upstream from Chajul complained to him.

Mythologized by the anthropologists Franz and Trudi Blom, the Lacandones insist they are the legitimate heirs to the jungle and all other Indians have to get out. They even issue certificates to substantiate their bloodlines and have always been "government" Indians dissing the Zapatistas and opposing the San Andrés Accords.

Tensions rose precipitously in March and April when Mexican navy patrol boats began escorting armed Lacandón "forest guardians" up the river to the eight communities threatened by CI's grand plan. Offering to burn the settlements to the ground, they issued an ultimatum: Everyone must be gone by May 7. "The only way they will get me out of here is dead," a Tzotzil-speaking Zapatista told Hermann on the banks of the Lacanjá.

International solidarity was soon in the pipeline. Global Exchange sent a fact-finding mission to the Montes Azules, and the Barcelona camaradas raised a "No Evictions!" banner in the Plaza de Catalunya. By May, the solidarity networks were hyping the Montes Azules as the next Acteal.

As the deadline approached, the forest guardians showed up in court in Ocosingo accompanied by a white "scientist" and swore out arrest warrants for the trespassers. Finally, at the midnight hour on May 7, Pablo stepped in and offered the Lacandones an even bigger wedge of the ecotourism pie. The evictions were postponed indefinitely but the forest guardians remained on the warpath.

By late May, the jungle was a literal tinderbox. Forest fires seared the mountain wilderness and the settlers prayed hard for rain, danced, blew flutes, beat on drums and marimbas, recited rosaries for the first drop to fall. "We are born from the water like the corn," a young Zapatista poetized. Dry lightning crackled in the distance, thunder rumbled.

The first rains brought reasonable protection from eviction. The roads were soon impassable and the rivers swollen and dangerous. The settlers would be shielded by the white rain for months to come, thwarting all plans to move them out.

A bureaucratic permutation at the top also afforded the villagers a cushion. The SEMARNAP's term chairing the Environmental Table had elapsed and the Agrarian Reform Ministry took over. Attention would now turn toward the communities' possession of the land, which they had settled. The frozen pace of "regulating" land ownership in rural Mexico would buy time.

A Virtual Tour

During my own private winter of discontent, while I had been out in the world trying to forestall an unstoppable invasion, Subcomandante Marcos had been on a trudge of his own—a virtual tour of the Mexican republic, or at least the part of it that he had visited on the March of the People the Color of the Earth.

Traveling "like a rolling stone," Sub Marcos visited 12 *estelas*, or ancient markers, that defined each state. The journey demonstrated how keenly the EZLN had been studying the terrain. Replete with copious notes and combining black-and-white stats gathered from the National Geographical and Statistical Institute (INEGI) with the anecdotal evidence of those who had testified along the way, the "12 Estelas" were a census of resistance and a blueprint for what three years later would crystallize in "the Other Campaign."

Oaxaca, the first Estela, is the most indigenous state in the Mexican union, with 17 distinct etnias. Marcos visited each of their struggles, particularly those of the Mixtecos, or "cloud people," in the eroded moonscape of their sierra. In Puebla, the Sup displayed an uncommon knowledge of the number of Indian communities displaced by road building. The Sup rolled on to Veracruz, revisiting the dirt-poor Zongolica Sierra and lambasting the desecration of the sacred Totonaco ruins at Tajín by Governor Miguel Alemán for an annual high-ticket culture carnival. Alemán later invited the Subcomandante to visit in person, which the rebel chieftain promised to do only if he could bunk in the Perote and Papantla state penitentiaries, which hold a disproportionate number of indigenous prisoners.

In Tlaxcala, a state no bigger than the EZLN's home county of Ocosingo, Marcos wove testimony from ex-*braceros,* who had been cheated by the U.S. and Mexican government out of millions owed them for their labor in the 1940s and '50s, with the myths of Tlaxcalteca warriors. Tossing out incriminating gobs of INEGI statistics on the social conditions of Indian communities in Hidalgo, the Sup zeroed in on the Huasteca Mountains, where rural bosses have virtually enslaved the indigenous population. Visiting Querétaro, where the PANista governor had once offered to have him shot atop Campana Hill, the rebel leader reminded "lapdog" Ignacio Loyola that he still owed the EZLN two political prisoners and went ballistic against homeboy El Jefe Diego, the capo who had killed Indian Rights.

In Guanajuato, Vicente Fox's native turf, Marcos revisited the Chichimecas and dissected the terminal neoliberalism of the president. The Purépecha Nation took center stage in Michoacán and in Guerrero, the dead and disappeared of the Dirty War—the Sup somehow overlooked the Popular Revolutionary Army and its offshoots in his census of the forces of rebellion in that wild and woolly state. What was left of the legacy of Votan Zapata dominated the Sup's visit to Morelos. In his post-Atenco analysis of Mexico state, the peripatetic Subcomandante zoomed in on hard-edged punks in Atizapán.

Mexico City was the final Estela, and Marcos's vision was prescient, correctly anticipating even before the upcoming midterm elections in July that Andrés Manuel López Obrador would be the PRD's 2006 presidential candidate. AMLO (known by his initials) was making deals with big money—Carlos Slim, the richest man in Latin America—and co-opting the popular movement in a city that held a fifth of the nation's voters and remains solidly PRD, a party the Sup reamed on paper for its multiple betrayals.

Although the Zapatistas' turn toward autonomy had been critiqued in some quarters of the Mexican Left as a turning away from national concerns, the 12 Estelas signified that the EZLN still retained a healthy interest in changing the national reality from the bottom up.

The Real Tenth Anniversary

Although the Zapatista world was already gearing up for the January 1st tenth anniversary of the rebellion, the real tenth marking of the EZLN's first decade as a public entity had already passed on May 22. On that date in 1993, elements of the 83rd Infantry Battalion under General Miguel Godínez confronted an unnamed armed band off the road to the capped oil-drilling platform at Nazareth in the Cañadas, not far from what is now the autonomous municipality of Francisco Gómez (Garrucha). One civilian and at least one soldier were killed in the shootout.

Pursuing the rebels into the Corralchén Sierra, the soldiers stumbled into the Zapatista encampment at Las Calabazas and confiscated uniforms, propaganda, and a few weapons, leaving little doubt that something was brewing in the mountains of southeastern Mexico.

For a day, the 83rd Battalion scoured the mountain for signs of the rebels. Marcos was positive that the jig was up. But on the 24th, the troops did an about-face and retreated back to Ocosingo. The orders, the Sup concluded, could only have come from upstairs. From Salinas.

The incident at Las Calabazas became the inspiration for my first article on the Zapatista Army of National Liberation. No editor would believe that such an organization existed, but finally on October 12, Indigenous Resistance Day, the *Anderson Valley Advertiser*, an eccentric Northern California weekly, took a chance and scooped the world by seven weeks.

Throughout the summer of 1993, rumors of the impending rebellion were rife in the mountains and jungles of eastern Chiapas. Ranchers intercepted citizen-band communications between rebel detachments, and *soplones* (stool pigeons) spilled the beans to local newspapers.

The military, as it should have, reported this threat to national security to President Salinas, who did not want to hear about it. The North American Free Trade Agreement was about to hit the floor of the U.S. House of Representatives and any suggestion of instability down south could queer the deal. Salinas was maniacally obsessed with his historical legacy, which he saw as being intimately bound up with NAFTA.

Up in El Norte, Bill Clinton didn't really want to know anything about Indian rebels in southern Mexico either. Having attached useless side agreements on the environment, labor, and commercial dumping to the main agreement, he was ready to rumble. Despite intelligence being gathered by an alphabet soup of agencies—the CIA, DEA, NSA, DEA, and satellite reconnaissance—that red-lined subversive activity on the Chiapas-Guatemala border, Bubba sent RAND terrorism expert Brian Jenkins up to the Hill to testify behind closed doors that Mexico would have a revolution if NAFTA was NOT passed. January 1 unmasked that lie.

On November 17, 1993, the tenth anniversary of the founding of the Zapatista Army of National Liberation in a miserable jungle camp in the Lacandón, NAFTA cleared the U.S. Congress by a mere 34 votes. Clinton dispensed billions in pork to win the vote. After January 1, Ross Rogers, then chief political officer for the U.S. embassy, told me on deep background that if Congress had known about an incipient Indian rebellion, those 34 votes might not have been there.

8. Summer/Fall 2003
The Most Comical Elections

The July 6 midterm elections unfolded amid stupendous political scandal. The PRI stood accused of embezzling $110 million USD from PEMEX to finance Francisco Labastida's 2000 debacle. The boodle had been authorized by the national oil monopoly's director, Rogelio Montemayor, and was laundered through the petroleum workers union into Labastida's campaign coffers—some of the money was sunk into a series of rigged automobile raffles in which the winner had to return the prize to the PRI.

PEMEXgate constituted an outright theft of what belonged to the nation by a party that had always considered that it owned that nation. Multiple charges were filed by Fox's corruption czar—Montemayor fled to Houston and it took years to extradite him. Oil-worker union boss Carlos Romero Deschamps and his aide-de-camp, Ricardo Aldana, who had organized the swindle, were senators of the republic and enjoyed immunity from prosecution. In the end, the PRI was fined a billion pesos for the flimflam and no one ever spent more than an hour in jail.

One reason why PEMEXgate was soft-pedaled by the Big Huckster in Los

Pinos: Fox was up to his ears in his own unseemly imbroglio, code-named Amigogate, in which his campaign finance committee—"Los Amigos de Fox"—had triangulated multiple millions in illegal money from non-Mexican corporate contributors through foreign banks (a flagrant violation of what passes for campaign financing laws in Mexico). The scandal even featured a shades-wearing femme fatale, Carlota Robinson, the mistress of Fox's fundraiser and ex-Coca-Cola sidekick Lino Korodi. Both Amigo- and PEMEXgates were swept under the rug in the run-up to July 6.

Meanwhile, the PRD was imploding. Party prexy Rosario Robles had bankrupted the Democratic Revolucionarios and turned to her lover, a shady Argentinean tycoon who bankrolled her in exchange for lucrative Mexico City construction contracts. Videos of party officials stuffing wads of Yanqui dollars into their suit-coat pockets would soon flash incessantly in the nation's living rooms.

"The political parties seem to have an infinite capacity for self-ridicule," Marcos chortled. "These elections are the most comical in Mexican history."

Five hundred seats in the Chamber of Deputies, six governorships, and a variety of local offices were up for grabs on July 6. Eleven parties were franchised by the Federal Electoral Institute to contend, and together they fielded a record 11,000 candidates. The electorate had ballooned to 59,000,000 from the low 40s in 2000, but people did not really sign up to vote but rather to obtain the registration card, which served as useful I.D.

Ironically, July 6 was the 15th anniversary of the stealing of the 1988 presidential election from Cuauhtémoc Cárdenas and the civil insurrection that it had engendered—the protests almost brought the government of Carlos Salinas down before the Bald One was sworn in. But July 6, 2003, was another story.

And the winner was? Massive absenteeism with 60% of the vote. Whereas nearly 70% of registered voters had turned out to elect Fox in 2000, almost half that number saw no reason to cast ballots three years later.

The 2003 midterms were a referendum on Vicente Fox's first three years in Los Pinos, and Coca-Cola Man was cruelly punished—the PAN even lost San Francisco del Rincon, Guanajuato, where the Fox and his Mrs. retired each weekend to ride the range. The PANista delegation in the lower house was reduced by 60 seats, for a total of 155, while the PRI, seemingly on the rebound, clobbered the right-wingers by amassing 223 seats, close to an absolute majority, in addition to taking four out of six governorships on the ballot that day—prior to the election, the one-time ruling party had squeaked by with single-digit advantages in both the chamber and the senate. The 60 seats lost by the PAN went to the PRD, giving the purported Lefties 96 deputies, hardly enough to do much damage.

From July 6 until the end of his stay in Los Pinos in December 2006, Vicente Fox would now be a lame duck president.

Although the numbers appeared to put the PRI and its unctuous leader, Roberto Madrazo, in the driver's seat for Los Pinos in 2006, the real winner was Mexico City mayor Andrés Manuel López Obrador, who cleaned house in the capital, with the PRD taking 14 out of 16 delegation (borough) presidencies, 35 out of 40 federal districts, and an absolute majority in the local legislative assembly. Mexico City contains about 20% of the nation' voters, and AMLO's big sweep forced Washington to sit up and take notice.

Early presidential polling had the mayor running neck and neck with first lady Marta Sahagún, but after a long, slow tease Martita dropped out of the race when her big galoot of a hubby threw a hammerlock on her and dragged her from an impromptu press conference. "My wife is not a candidate. When our time is done here," the Fox concluded, "we will go home to the ranch and saddle up the horses."

In Chiapas, for the first election day since 1997, the EZLN laid siege to the polling precincts—2003 was, after all, the first federal election since the three parties had decimated Indian Rights. Up in San Andrés Sakam-ch'én, the PRI-controlled state election commission insisted on installing voting booths despite a banner in the plaza hoisted by the autonomous council forbidding their installation. The precinct was overrun before it could open and the ballots burnt in the usual ceremonial bonfire. There was scuffling outside the refugee community of Polhó at Majomut, where the voting station was similarly torched, and over the mountain in Cancuc, one Zapatista was shot and 10 injured in election-day brawling. "In synchronized operations, unknown masked persons" had impeded voting in 26 precincts, 23,000 votes in all, according to the state election commission. How many of those presumably disenfranchised would actually have cast ballots if the precincts were left standing is uncertain—absenteeism in Chiapas was 65%, five points above the national average. Even the Abejas, ardent supporters of Governor Pablo, sat this one out.

As usual, the PRI swept 11 out of 12 Chiapas federal districts, further humbling Pablo. Despite all the burning ballots, the EZLN did not really care much about the elections. The compas were busy fleshing out their autonomy. Elections came one day a year. Autonomy is forever.

Taproots of Autonomy

Historically, the Zapatista communities in the jungle, and to a lesser extent in Los Altos of Chiapas, had always been autonomous if only because of the vast distances between their settlements and the seats of government. In the huge county of Ocosingo, the nation's second largest, for instance, it was sometimes a two- or three-day trek (much more in the rainy season) to reach the *cabecera* (county seat), where the PRI was always in control, dispensing crumbs to the outlying *parajes,* or "stops," in exchange for their votes. If the communities needed services, drinkable water, or a schoolteacher, they had to suck up to the ruling party or fend for themselves. So they began to develop mechanisms to take care of their own needs.

Particularly in the jungle, where the Indians were originally *"colonos"* who had come from elsewhere to work the land, the communal assembly became instrumental in collectivizing decision making and pulling together energies to struggle for what they needed. This was a process the indígenas themselves had cultivated, not one brought to them from the outside by Marcos and his *"iluminados"* (illuminated ones). Indeed, the outsiders had to learn this lesson before they could begin to build an army.

The Zapatista rebellion has always been a rebellion of the periphery against the *cabecera* (literally "place of the head"), where all power was concentrated, and on January 1, 1994, it was not just happenstance that the EZLN overran four key PRI-controlled cabeceras that had tormented the outlying communities as long as anyone could remember.

The dynamic between the Zapatista communities and the county seats was an apt metaphor for the rebel construct: from the bottom up and the outside in. Chiapas was the nation's southernmost state, about as far away from the center as you could travel and still be in Mexico, and it has been the Zapatistas' peculiar genius to sometimes force national focus to swivel from the omni-powerful capital to the edge of the country, just a few kilometers from the Guatemalan border.

Reorganizing Autonomy

Autonomy had been in the rebels' bones since the beginning. The Comandancia's cry on January 1 that they did not need the mal gobierno's permission to be autonomous was only confirmation of their defiance. To hell with the congress up in Mexico City. They would apply the Ley Cocopa themselves right here in their own territory. The political parties that had stripped the figure of autonomy from the Indian Rights law had, in fact, spurred its construction in the mountains of Mexico's southeast.

How best to organize this autonomy that they always possessed had been the source of intense deliberation in the communities since January 1. The Zapatistas would no longer demand that the mal gobierno "enrich" their lives. Like La Realidad, where the Italian turbines now lit up the community, they were getting off the government grid for good now. But autonomy is a fiction if it does not provide an infrastructure. In truth, they had been building that infrastructure for a decade now as the schools and clinics blossomed in the zone, but the construction of these services, largely the work of health and education commissions in the autonomous municipalities, had been haphazard and overly dependent on the initiatives of the NGOs. The new income coming in from fair trade organic coffee offered alternative funding.

In an outpouring of nine closely written communiqués published in late July and early August, the CCRI, under Marcos's pen, proposed a radical reorganization of rebel structure. The first order of business was the death of the Aguascalientes—the name had been derived from a referential point in the Mexican Revolution when the representatives of the armies of Villa and Zapata met behind rebel lines in that tiny north central state under the rubric of the National Democratic Convention, and the EZLN had borrowed it for its own 1994 CND in Guadalupe Tepeyac.

Now the Zapatistas' five political cultural centers would be known as "Caracoles," or conch shells, which in Meso-America are used to summon the communities to meeting. The name change was as much conceptual as it was new nomenclature. A second definition of *caracol* is "spiral," and the Caracoles would be spirals through which the outside world could enter the Zapatista one, and the Zapatistas know the one outside. "What enters the heart from the outside and what leaves the heart to travel," Old Antonio whispered to the Sup while the two sat by the fire, smoking.

The voice of the old farmer had not been heard in several years, but now he was called upon to introduce the Caracoles. After the first gods, the oldest ones, had separated the night from the day by placing themselves between heaven and earth at the four corners of the world, Antonio explained, the *bacabes,* or those who stood as pillars, had a need to know what was happening out there in the firmament. So they wore the caracoles around their necks, and their hearts would listen and go forth. "For this reason, each man and woman was given a caracol in their heart with which to listen and communicate their word."

The names of the new Caracoles would be "The Mother of Caracoles–Sea of Dreams" (La Realidad), "The Whirlwind of Our Words" (Ejido Morelia–17 de Noviembre), "Resistance Until the New Dawn" (La Garrucha–Francisco Gómez), "The Caracol That Speaks for All"

(Roberto Barrios), and "Resistance and Rebellion for Humanity" (Oventik).

The second step in the reorganization of autonomy was the "MAREZ" (Zapatista Autonomous Rebel Municipal Zone), which would be administrated from the Caracoles by Juntas de Buen Gobierno (JBGs or "good government committees"—as opposed to the way the mal gobierno governed). Each of the five Juntas would include one or more representatives from the autonomous municipalities grouped together in the MAREZ. The MAREZes and the JBGs effectively established autonomous regions as contemplated under the right of association of majority indigenous municipalities in the San Andrés Accords. The EZLN was implementing Indian Rights where it counted most—where they lived.

The JBGs would operate on the Zapatista leadership ethic of *mandar obedeciendo,* or governing by obeying the will of the community, which, Subcomandante Marcos noted, was still "only a tendency" in Zapatista territory and not yet a universal practice. The Juntas would rotate each month with new delegates arriving from the autonomías—"so everyone will get to know how to govern everyone else" (dixit the Sup). A whole new generation of rebels had grown up since the EZLN's founding—in the last century now—and they needed to be put to work.

The names of the Juntas de Buen Gobierno and the autonomías they governed would be:

"Toward the Hope" (San Pedro de Michoacán–La Realidad, Tierra y Libertad, which ran along the Guatemalan border to the Pacific coast, and Libertad de los Mayas);

"The Heart of the Rainbow of Hope" (17 de Noviembre–Ejido Morelia, Che Guevara, Moisés Gandhi, Vicente Guerrero I, Lucio Cabañas, Miguel Hidalgo, Primero de Enero, and Olga y Isabel);

"Road of the Future" (Francisco Gómez–La Garrucha, San Manuel, Francisco Villa I, Ricardo Flores Magón, and hundreds of villages in the Tzeltal Cañada);

"New Seed That Will Fructify" (Roberto Barrios, El Trabajo,

Vicente Guerrero II, La Montaña, San José de Rebeldía, La Paz, Benito Juárez, Francisco Villa II);

"Center of the Zapatista Heart Before the World" (Oventik–San Andrés Sakamch'én, San Juan de La Libertad, Polhó, Santa Catarina, Magdalena de la Paz, Primero de Febrero, San Juan Cancuc, and extending to Chapa de Corzo, Tuxtla Gutiérrez and Cintalapa, where no autonomous municipalities yet existed).

The Juntas de Buen Gobierno would administrate five MAREZes grouping together 29 autonomous municipalities that included, according to the most recent EZLN accounting, 2,222 villages, a total population of perhaps 100,000 Zapatistas.

The Juntas were tasked with settling disputes between the autonomías within their respective jurisdictions. These could range from a wandering cow to a contentious elopement and relieved the CCRI from being the ultimate arbiter in these matters. The JBGs would not just serve rebel communities but were open to non-Zapatistas and even PRIistas living within the MAREZ.

A more pertinent function of the JBGs was to ensure an equal distribution of resources among the autonomous municipalities. Because the Aguascalientes had usually been located close to the road, they received the bulk of NGO largesse, while other autonomías in the deep outback, like Olga y Isabel, got little. Indeed, the Aguascalientes had been in danger of turning into cabeceras themselves. With the new income from fair trade coffee pouring in, changes could be made to offset a Zapatista landscape of haves and have-nots. Now the premiums paid by the fair traders would go to the MAREZ, and not just the coffee-growing coops, and be distributed by the JBGs among all the autonomous municipalities.

The reorganization of autonomy had a striking impact on the work of the NGOs. The Sup treated them roughly in his proposals to revamp the EZLN structure. After the rebellion, civil society and the NGO community had sent the rebels bales of old clothes "so extravagant that they were only fit for a stage play." The EZetas now had whole rooms of busted computers and medicines whose dates had long since expired. "We will not be treated like the mentally ill," Marcos parried. He himself had been carrying around in his rucksack for several years a single rose-colored pump, size six and a half, an example of what the Sup tagged the "Cinderella Syndrome."

The compas were tired of being told by the NGOs what they needed: "They give us an herb garden when the school is falling down." Moreover, the NGOs developed "special relations" with the autonomous councils and families in the communities that could lead to privilege and corruption.

Now things were going to be different. The nongovernment organizations must now submit their proposals to the JBGs, which would evaluate them to see how they fit into the EZLN's development agenda. Ten percent of the seed money for the project would have to be invested in infrastructure in an autonomous municipality that did not receive the resource. The JBGs would be open 24 hours a day to receive new proposals.

Were the rebels biting the hand that fed them? Kerry Appel, whose coffee sales were propelling this sea change, thought it was a good idea that more communities shared in the new wealth. Peter Brown, AKA Pedro Café, whose Schools for Chiapas had clashed with the Oventik education commission over curriculum, was more circumspect: "There will be a new relation with the NGO community."

Others were not so sure that the changes were for the best. Writing in *La Jornada*, Guillermo Almeyra feared a new level of bureaucracy in the rebel structure and cautioned against the growing dependence on coffee, which immersed the EZLN in the dread market economy.

Interior Secretary Santiago Creel did not like the way the Caracoles and the JBGs smelled. As had his PRI predecessors, he feared separation and secession, a parallel nation—PRI presidential hopeful Roberto Madrazo echoed the paranoia.

On the other hand, Governor Pablo philosophized that "anything that improves the lives of the indígenas must be legitimate" and did not undermine his ability to govern—Pablo was reportedly summoned to Los Pinos for rectification.

The whole deal was "bogus" interjected none other than his majesty Judge Baltasar Garzón, pointing out that the Mexican constitution only authorizes three levels of governance—federal, state, and municipal. Regional autonomy was patently criminal. Garzón also used the occasion to announce that he would be coming to Chiapas in coming weeks—on a "vacation," he sneered.

¡Caracoles Ya!

Sympathizers with the Zapatista cause the world over were advised to set aside the weekend of August 8–10 for a "hyper-mega-magna-super-dooper" *pachanga* up at the Caracol named "Resistance and Rebellion for Humanity," once known as Oventik. On the 8th, the EZLN would bury the Aguascalientes, a festive funeral featuring the rebels' increasingly electronic cumbia combos and a basketball tournament that pitted one Zapatista dream team against another.

On the 9th, the invitees would play midwives to the birthing of the Caracoles, and on the 10th, the Juntas de Buen Gobierno would be open for business. The dates were significant—August 8 was the birthday of Votan Zapata, and the 9th was United Nations Day of the Indígena, which gave the Fox and his authentic Indian maiden Xochitl Gálvez a pretext for forums and fiestas to paper over the inauguration of the Caracoles.

Zapatistas from the neighboring autonomías began arriving Friday morning for the big burial. Collectives of women weavers set up stands on Oventik's steep main street. Ski-masked men in beribboned sombreros—the ribbons correspond to Old Antonio's bacabes—smoked and joked among themselves. Internationals and brigadistas from the big city browsed the general store for singer-songwriter Comandante David's most recent tapes—many visitors wore little handmade caracoles.

The Comandancia was in place by mid-afternoon, 10 comandantes in all. Such a gathering of CCRI members had not been noted at Oventik since the March of the People the Color of the Earth. David, the highland commander whose base is Oventik, hosted the ceremony, and the one-time seminarian said what everyone already knew: The rebels did not need the mal gobierno's permission to be autonomous now. Esther sec-onded that emotion on behalf of the Zapatista women.

Zebedeo commented upon the evil afoot in the outside world: The Iraqi people were learning that you couldn't exchange a tyrant for for-eign invaders. He extended solidarity to the Cuban compañer@s, a rare mention of that embattled people. Globalization was the "new inquisi-tion." In September, the word of the EZLN would be heard in Cancún when the World Trade Organization came to that global resort.

Bruce Lee took on the Plan Puebla Panama—it would never be imposed on Zapatista territory. ("This is not a threat but a prophecy," the Sup had once pronounced.) Instead, the EZLN was proposing the Plan La Realidad–Tijuana, which called for a network of commerce and cul-tural workers. The PLR-T would promote self-government and autonomy throughout Mexico and encourage resistance and rebellion. The plan would struggle for the Zapatistas' original 13 demands—land, work, labor, bread, education, health, shelter, communication, culture, independence, democracy, liberty, and peace—and foster solidarity with the aggrieved.

Unfortunately Marcos was not able to attend the fandango in person, Tacho told a disappointed throng, because he had a *dolor de panza* (stomachache) from laughing too much. Nonetheless, the Sup had sent an audiotape, his debut on Radio Insurgente, which due to technical snafus was not yet up on the short-wave band. "We have heard that somewhere there is a better world," DJ Sup chimed in. "We didn't get that from Carlos Marx or even Groucho Marx. These are not the words of El Che or the Zapatista Army of National Liberation. The author of this subversive phrase is none other than B.B. King!" and then he punched in the cart, and the rumbly voice of the Indianola, Mississippi, bluesman and his faithful guitar, Louise, blasted sweetly from the speakers. For the next hour, Marcos spun his favorite platters: Cucu

Sánchez, Joaquín Sabina, Ely Guerra, Crosby-Stills-Nash-&-Young, El Piporro, Armando Manzanares, Tania Libertad, and Paul Simon ("Still Crazy After All These Years").

In late afternoon, the Comandancia moved the party uphill to the building that had been constructed to house the Junta de Buen Gobierno called Center of the Zapatista Heart Before the World. Bottle rockets flared against the sinking sun. The white ribbon across the doorway was snipped, and 14 members of the new JBG (warning—all were men) were presented with the *bastones de mando*, the ceremonial staffs that confirmed their authority. Indian violins, flutes, and guitars serenaded the ski-masked compas in the gathering twilight. A *torito*, a kind of bull figure stuffed with fireworks, was ignited and showered sparks everywhere to the oohs and ahhs of the children. I hunkered down in the patio of the house next door and tried not to get singed. The mural on the building's façade depicted a large, golden ear of corn. When I looked more closely, I realized that each kernel was the head of a tiny, ski-masked rebel.

The next morning, the Juntas de Buen Gobierno went to work at all five Caracoles. First on line to meet the members of the Center of the Zapatista Heart Before the World was a delegation of campesinos from Michoacán who were hauling a truckload of victuals and just wanted to know where to deliver it.

The JBGs were in business.

Basque Intrigue

There were plenty of "*¡Goras!*" at the big party. "*¡Euskal Herria! ¡Euskal Presoak!*" Comandante Zebedeo said, calling for Basque political prisoners to be returned to their homeland. "May this cry be heard in the torture chambers of Garzón!" And then, as an aside: "We have heard that Garzón had chosen to take a vacation in Chiapas from closing down newspapers and criminalizing political parties." The judge, Zebedeo insinuated, had not been invited to the fiesta.

Down on the b-ball court, a Basque five had trounced an all-star rebel quintet, and up on the road, handmade signs broadcast the EZLN's solidarity with the Vascos. The bond between the Mayan Indians and the Basque people is a mysterious one—both are "fourth world" nations, nations within nations, and perhaps that is the link.

Vascos in Mexico were right in the sights of Bush's terror war. The Fox, seeking to convince the White House that he was a staunch ally after all and hoping to make points with poodle Aznar, a role model, had ordered a crackdown on alleged ETA members. Since 1996, when Mexico and Spain signed an extradition treaty, 36 Basque citizens had been summarily deported into the torture chambers of the Civil Guard—one had died in Mexican custody. The Fox government was now holding Lorenzo Llona, a naturalized Mexican whom Garzón accused of a 1981 triple murder in Gipuzkoa—but Llona had a perfect alibi: He had been in Mexico City that day submitting his immigration papers (they were so dated).

Garzón was not to be satisfied. Having just arrived for a "vacation" and in bald violation of Mexican law, the judge forced his way into the Mexico City penitentiary where Llona was being held and tried to interrogate him. Garzón also sought to question six Basques, four of them naturalized Mexicans, who had been rounded up for purported ETA money laundering. At this writing, three years later, the six are still imprisoned pending deportation.

"Being Basque in Mexico these days is a lot like being an Arab under Bush," the FZLN's Javier Elorriaga, the scion of Basque hoteliers in Acapulco, worried. Basques had been in Mexico for a long time—the first Vascos arrived with the Conquistador Cortez.

"Marcos is a charlatan who is bamboozling the Indians," the judge gabbled to the Tuxtla tabloid *Cuarto Poder* upon touching down in Chiapas. What exactly Garzón was poking his proboscis into now was never clearly defined. During his stay, the judge was spotted at an amber exhibition in San Cristóbal—Chiapas amber is much valued in Spain. When an anonymous Zapatista supporter discovered that Garzón was appraising a tiny caracol fashioned from the precious pollen, he snatched the amulet from the judge's hand and shelled out a few hundred dollars' worth of pesos to prevent the Spaniard's purchase.

Garzón's visit presented intriguing possibilities. Had Marcos's "dolor de panza" that kept him away from Oventik been a smokescreen? Had the judge and the Sup met in some leafy jungle nook and finally consummated the Great Debate?

The WTC Kills Farmers

The Fifth Ministerial conclave of the World Trade Organization was scheduled to convene on September 10 in Cancún. Its negotiations would make or break the so-called Doha round.

Shaken by the fracaso in Seattle, the WTO had taken refuge in Doha, Qatar, in 2000, where demonstrators could not get at them. The prickliness of the Third World had to be addressed, so the Doha round was focused on development through trade but it had been snarled early on by angry interchanges over agriculture. The South demanded that the Industrial North lower protective tariffs on agricultural exports and abolish the system of obscene subsidies to corporate farmers that allowed them to dump their goods on Third World markets below cost, thus undercutting local farmers and, as in Mexico, driving them from the land. One example of such abuse: In Japan, farmers are awarded $7.50 USD daily for each cow grazing in their pastures, while one-half of humanity, 3,000,000,000 people, subsist on less than $2 a day.

The Group of 21 developing nations, led by Brazil, India, South Africa, even China, and with less enthusiasm, Mexico, insisted that meaningful cuts in subsidies had to be made before negotiations could advance. The North—the U.S., the European Union, Canada, and Japan—turned a deaf ear to their demands. Cancún was a do-or-die push to get the Doha round back on track.

In Yucatec Mayan, Cancún translates to "nest of snakes," and long before the WTO came to town, the Caribbean resort was a snake pit of globalization. Cancún was built on the bedrock of transnational package tourism. The big hotel chains dredged out the Caribbean floor and spread its sparkling white sands over the limestone shoreline of what once had been a minimal Mayan fishing village, recruited the locals to throw up the luxury hotel zone—the Sheraton was sculpted to look like an ersatz Mayan temple—and pretty soon, the spring breakers were flooding the resort every year for two-week package tours of drunken hooliganism.

Cancún was considered a "pole of development"—entire Indian villages migrated here to find work as maids and pot wallopers and hod carriers, disrupting the fabric of Mayan community life. The indígenas upon whose labor the tourist tycoons depended were assigned a loathsome swamp out by the airport with no electricity or drinkable water, one of the worst slums in all Latin America. The distinctions between rich and poor, white and Indian, made Cancún a congruent metaphor for the rewards of globalization.

Busloads of Zapatista supporters, including a contingent from the Italian Ya Basta! left San Cristóbal for Cancún during the first week in September. The concept was to transform this Caribbean tourist playground into a sort of tropical Seattle. Mindful of the blood that had splattered the white sands back in February 2001 when a fistful of globalphobes had tried to march on a road show of the Davos-based World Economic Forum, the key to successful disruption of the WTO was going to be assembling large numbers. For many participants, the Fifth Ministerial was a tune-up for the Summit of the Americas set for Miami in mid-November, where Bush would try and ram FTAA/ALCA up Latin America's ass, and police terror was on the menu.

Organizational initiative for the WTC protests was taken by Via Campesina (The Farmers' Way), the 70-nation alliance of millions of poor farmers, which along with big NGOs like Oxfam saw agricultural subsidies as sounding the death knell for campesinos everywhere. Delegations of farmers from Korea and India, the Sem Terras of Brazil, the dispossessed of South Africa, and even a few gringos from Iowa had been summoned to Cancún, and the marches were swollen by thousands of Mayans from the ejidos all over the Yucatán Peninsula.

Security was frightening. The Fifth Ministerial would coincide with the second anniversary of 9/11, and the presence of so many bigwigs in one spot afforded a golden opportunity for anyone who might want to do damage to the international ruling class. Eighteen thousand federal troops and police had been amassed to deal with the unruly, 15-foot barricades erected at the entrance to the hotel zone to keep the globalphobes at bay, and air and sea space was patrolled by a U.S. anti-terror task force. The usual blacklist was promulgated, identifying troublesome intruders like Noam Chomsky and José Bové (both were no-shows), but it didn't keep many globalphobes away.

Although the EZLN "shits on vanguardism" (dixit the Sup), the Zapatista Army of National Liberation has been in the vanguard of the antiglobalization movement since their 1996 "Intergaláctica," where the seeds of Seattle were sown. The rebels had never appeared in person at any of the mayhem that had ensued after Seattle, but their Word was always present. Now, true to their words, their Word was heard in Cancún.

The EZLN had much to say to say to the farmers gathered in Snakepit City. "We are farmers," Comandante David had once told the government negotiators way back at the beginning, "and all we want really is to keep being farmers." Now the comandantes' messages were flashed on the screen at the cultural center where the campesinos were encamped.

"With the weapon of resistance in one hand and the weapon of autonomy in the other, we call upon the farmers of the world to remember the words of our Zapata: The land belongs to those who work it," David intoned. "We are women who work in the milpa and we know the crimes of globalization," Esther told the gathering. Marcos seemed to be calling for frontal assault: "This is not the first time that those of money have hidden behind high walls . . . the high command of money has come to Cancún to dominate the world in the only way it knows how—destroy it! The hotel zone is a symbol of the world they would construct—the only way we ever get in there is as servants and maids. Behind those walls, they are plotting out how to change death into money. . . ."

Perhaps 12,000 marched out toward the barricades under scorching skies on the opening day of the Ministerial. Korean farmers had constructed a dragon from folded paper, which they carried inside a stout wooden box. It was the Korean Day of the Dead, Kun Hai Lee, a veteran of many such protests, explained to me as we approached the metal fence. The WTC kills farmers.

Now the Korean delegation used the wooden box as a battering ram to bring down the barricade, but there was little give. Then Mr. Lee jumped up on the box and used it to vault to the top of the fence. Behind him, a colorful billboard welcomed the tourists to Cancún. Mr. Lee dropped a hand-lettered sign around his neck. The WTC Kills Farmers!

With a warrior cry, Mr. Lee plunged a dagger into his heart, pitched forward, and fell to the ground dead.

Kun Hai Lee's suicide sent out shock waves and touched hearts on both sides of the barrier. Inside the Cancún Convention Center, where the negotiations droned on, the NGOs built an altar of white flowers and dripping candles, not just to Mr. Lee but for all the dead farmers under the sun—since April when crops had failed in Karnataka state, India, more than 200 farmers had committed suicide, often with rat poison and pesticides. Farmers' groups brought inside by the NGOs began to march around through the convention center, their dignity so powerful that it caused the delegates from the wealthy nations of the North to flinch, an uncommon posture for such Masters of the Universe. At a press conference, chief U.S. negotiator Robert Zoellick, later Condi Rice's top terror war lieutenant, termed Mr. Lee an "extremist" and said his death would not cause Washington to alter its trade policies. Just then, a group of Greenpeacers broke into the room and tossed handfuls of Indian corn at the U.S. trade rep.

On the closing day of the Fifth Ministerial, thousands walked up to the barricade where Mr. Lee had fallen and attached long, thick hawsers (Cancún is a shipping port) to the barricade, and the globalphobes collectively pulled the fence down—it took us about an hour to bring it to the ground. Now there was a no-man's-land between the protesters and phalanxes of armed-to-the-teeth robocops. The Black Bloc, looking for all the world like helmeted extras from a Mad Max extravaganza with their shopping carts of Molotov cocktails and sawed-off telephone poles, were poised to attack. Suddenly, a group of Indian women began to chant, "Sit down, sit down," and everyone did. "¡*Todos somos Mr. Lee!*" someone cried out, and the cry caught from throat to throat. "We are all Mister Lee!" The Black Bloc sheepishly retired from the scene.

Inside the convention center, the WTO was coming apart at the seams. The delegates from the poorer places on the planet now understood that their farmers were so desperate that they were dying on the barricades. The wealthy North had been unyielding, even trying to browbeat the Third World into opening their markets to their goods and services with nothing offered in return. When the U.S. and the E.U. double-crossed deeply impoverished West African nations on cotton subsidies, the delegate from Benin abandoned the negotiating table, and one by one his African brothers and sisters followed suit. By six that afternoon, the delegates were checking out of their hotels.

Foreign minister Luis Ernesto Derbez, the official host, slid behind the podium and in a profoundly somber voice, proclaimed the Fifth Ministerial meeting of the World Trade Organization adjourned without having reached agreement on any of the crucial issues that 148 nations had come together to resolve. Pounding his wooden gavel sharply, Derbez dismissed the remaining delegates, and the sound that echoed in the nearly empty auditorium was like that of nails being driven into the WTO's coffin. Score one for the Nation of Seattle.

Tierra Santa

"The planet has open wounds and bleeds all over its geography," Marcos wrote in September. "Naming these wounds will not cure them but it is a sign of humanity to do so. We say Palestine and we are wrapped in shame."

A traveler in Zapatista territory could be forgiven for imagining that she or he had suddenly been transported to the Holy Land. Everywhere one turns there is a New Jerusalem or a New Palestine. One crosses the

Jordan River to reach villages named Bethlehem and Canaan. The Lacandón was indeed once the Promised Land for those who flocked here a half century or less ago. Their exodus from their home communities and their arrival in Paradise was a trek right out of the Old Testament—the most popular text in the clapboard chapels of the lowlands is the Book of Exodus, translated into Tzotzil, Tzeltal, Chol, and Tojolabal many years ago by the Jesuits at Bachajón. With the surge of evangelical communities, most expelled from San Juan Chamula, the biblical names have multiplied like loaves and fishes.

The Zapatistas identify with the persecuted and dispossessed of the earth, and the occupation of Palestine by the Israeli Zionist state troubles them. Several years ago, a delegation from the Israeli peace movement—Gush Shalom and Women in Black—came to the Caracol Whirlwind of Our Word and met with the Junta de Buen Gobierno on the Ejido Morelia. Anthropologist Mariana Mora, who translated for Reuben and Daphne, was struck by how closely the compas followed events in the Middle East. The Junta members peppered the peaceniks with prickly questions: Why did the Israeli army shoot children? What was it like to live in the refugee camps?—the Zapatistas had their own refugee camp up at Polhó in the highlands. What was the land like? What grew in Tierra Santa? Was Sharon the father of Bush or Bush the father of Sharon?

That fall, I shipped out for Palestine to pick olives with an International Solidarity Movement (ISM) brigade. I had caught the Human Shield bug, I suppose. In March, the so-called Israeli "Defense" Force had crushed young Rachel Corrie to death under the wheels of a Caterpillar bulldozer while she tried to stop a home demolition in Rafah camp, Gaza. For months, her tattered face hung on the fence of the BART Station on 24th street every time I visited San Francisco. After Rachel, the Israeli military murdered young Tom Hurndall, who had been with us in Baghdad but so distrusted Saddam's ham-handed antics that he went on down to Gaza to work with ISM. He was crossing kids on the Rafah road, where Israeli tanks thundered up and down recklessly, when an IDF sharpshooter took him out—Tom was in a coma for nine months before death finally claimed him.

Other young activists suffered the Zionist bullets in this terrible period—Brian Avery shot in the face by soldiers on the West Bank, James Miller filming a home demolition when the Israelis blew his head off. An ISM recording of an Israeli officer screaming that he had orders to aim for the head confirms that the deaths and maimings of young international activists was state policy.

In late summer, the International Solidarity Movement put out an appeal for older Jewish volunteers to come to Palestine to pick in the autumn olive harvest. Operating under the illusion that both Jews and Arabs respected age, I saw us as standing in the front lines to protect the younger activists. I soon learned that age is a relative quantity in those ancient lands. Even the children seem old.

I crossed the muddy trickle of the Jordan River in mid-October into an Israeli military compound. The border police were weeding out subversives. Edward Said had just passed and I had promised to throw a stone on his behalf. "The Palestinian people have been orphaned," the translator Ramón Vera advised me when I left Mexico.

I had been to Israel once before, after the first Gulf War, and was appalled at what I saw. Jews were not supposed to behave like these monsters. "We do to the Palestinians what the Nazis did to us. We are in our Nazi phase," David Nir, a human rights activist frequently beaten by settlers, told me one day as we picked olives. "The Nazis too thought they were the Chosen People."

I grabbed a cab from the border up to East Jerusalem and bunked at the Faisal hostel just outside the Damascus Gate, a kind of ISM safe house. CNN and the BBC blasted from the TV monitors 24 hours a day. At the top of the news was Bolivia, of all datelines. Tens of thousands of Indians were marching on La Paz to overthrow the president, Gonzalo Sánchez de Lozada ("Goni"), who was trying to sell off the country's immense natural gas deposits to transnational energy titans. Up in El Alto, the Aymara city above the capitol, at least 50 had been gunned down by Goni's troops. We watched footage of masked young men hurling stones at the advancing tanks. "This looks like us in our Intifada," laughed Hassan, who guarded the door at the Faisal for the ISM.

We headed north into the Nablus Valley. Sharon was bombing Gaza and the Holy Land was on fire. We had to cross many checkpoints manned and womanned by snarling occupation troops—Chiapas too is an occupied land. We spread out into the villages—time was short. The Israeli army only gives the villagers a few days to harvest their olives, and there is never enough time. They are constantly harassed by rabid settlers.

Since Israel became a beachhead for Washington in a hostile Arab world in 1948, a half-million olive trees belonging to Palestinian farmers have been cut down, uprooted, burnt, their bark stripped (it kills the tree), or simply fenced off and confiscated. The evisceration of this ancient harvest cripples Palestinian agriculture. Olives are the backbone of their agrarian economy. They are everywhere in this afflicted land— on the flag and on the table and in the poetry of Mahmoud Darwish. As in Mexico, where there would be no country without *maíz*, there would be no Palestine without the *zitoon*.

The Israelis no longer value the land of the Holy Land—the Zionist "pioneers" had a brief romance with living on the land and built their kibbutzes on what they stole from those they had pushed off it. Ragged day-laborers from Thailand and China now work the farms. Some say Israel went crazy when it lost its connection to the land.

The Palestinians have never lost that connection. Even as the land of milk and honey became the land of bullets and suicide bombers, the farmers continued to tend their trees, eking out a hardscrabble living from the rocky fields and bare rolling hills that had always been theirs. As in Chiapas, the people of Palestine are the color of the earth and the earth is the color of the people.

It was harvest time in the Nablus Valley, just as it was back home in Chiapas and indeed everywhere that men and women still work the earth. In Awwarta, we picked from gnarled grandfather trees, some centuries old, careful not to damage their brittle branches. Suddenly, everyone stopped picking and turned toward the Itamar settlement that sits on the hill high above the town like a Martian castle. Was crazy Victor, who goes from village to village poisoning the wells, on the loose again? No, this time it was a lean gazelle streaking across the barren hillside as if it had just loped out of the Old Testament.

At day's end, the farmers hoisted up the bursting burlap sacks on the backs of the burros and hauled the zitoon to the town's gleaming Italian olive press. They dumped in their loads and stood under the starry sky, smoking and complaining like farmers the world over. The price of olive oil was down in the dumps; there was a world glut. Anyway, they could not export their product. For years, the Israelis had denied them an export permit, and now that the permits were available, their cost was far beyond their meager means. Sa'ad had barrels of olive oil down in his basement that he could not sell. Still he tended and cherished his trees.

In the last days of the harvest, the farmers prune the trees and drag in the firewood to feed their ovens. A special flatbread is baked and slathered with the new oil of the zitoon. Their stones will later be used as fuel in the snowy winter months.

Sa'ad hosted us to a full table. Roasted chickens, yoghurt from the goats, hummus from his garbanzo patch, nine distinct varieties of olives. He swept his hand over the groaning board. "This is why I will never leave this land," he rejoiced. The Zapatistas echo Sa'ad's blessing.

We picked our way down the valley. In Ein Abus we were set upon by crazed Zionist goons, the "Hilltop Youth," the police call them, racist Kahane kids from Brooklyn. They beat me with thick branches and threw rocks at point-blank range, and I survived only because of Rabbi for Human Rights Arik Ascherman's diversionary tactics. When I stumbled down the hillside to Ein Abus, Saleem from the town council commiserated: "Now you will know in your own bones what we have suffered for the past fifty years." Getting out of bed some mornings is a meditation on solidarity.

Later, in Yanoon, I watched the brigadistas pick their way up hill, accompanying the farmers and their families so they too would not be beaten. Down in the dusty valley, a lone donkey emitted a wistful bray and his song took me home to corn and Mexico. Corn, olives in Palestine, the sacred coca in Bolivia and Peru, now the date palms in Iraq. These are identity crops—the countries in which they grow cannot exist without them. Whether they are destroyed by genetic manipulation or the Israeli military, Bush's War on Drugs, or the giant U.S. Rome plows that have uprooted the dates that are the sweet soul of Iraq, the act is not just one of ecocide.

We charge genocide.

20/10

The 10th anniversary of the Zapatista rebellion began early. Actually, it wasn't just the EZLN's 10th birthday but its 20th as well—it had taken 10 years to build up the Zapatista Army of National Liberation before the compas marched into San Cristóbal that freezing New Year's Eve in 1994.

This is how it began.

One afternoon in late 1983, three Mestizos from the big city and three indígenas from Chiapas jumped down from a jungle truck near Laguna El Suspiro in the middle of the Montes Azules wilderness, grabbed their bulky backpacks, determined the trail, and trudged uphill through the muddy rain forest until it was too dark to move on.

The first camp was called La Pesadilla (The Nightmare), because it was, for those whose only jungle until now had been an urban one. The comrades strung up a tarp to stay reasonably dry, foraged for wood, and set a fire, using a plastic bag for tinder. The one they called Pedro fished a notebook from his pack and by the light of the glowing embers began to write: "November 17, 1983. Some meters above sea level. Raining hard. We have set up camp. *Sin novedad* [military parlance for 'there is no other news']."

Marcos arrived in La Pesadilla in early 1984 with two Indian comrades, he tells Gloria Muñoz in her *20/10*, a mosaic of Zapatista history that had been commissioned for the 20/10 anniversary, on whose pages the Sup repeats the now familiar tale of how a handful of iluminados came from the cities to liberate the exploited Indians. When they visited the villages to proselytize, the Indians thought they were speaking Chinese. This part of the story is about how they learned to listen to those they had come to save and were themselves saved.

The 20/10 season began on November 10 with the presentation of Muñoz's book at the swanky Casa Lamm (it has chandeliers) in the Colonia Condesa up in the capital. Muñoz, who had come to Chiapas with the rebellion and sometimes worked for the German DPA news agency, and Hermann had been the last two reporters to interview Sub-comandante Marcos before he fled into the jungle as Zedillo's para-troopers were falling on Guadalupe Tepeyac in February 1995. She and the Sup had been romantically linked (*"en el estado romántico"*) since the late '90s, and she is quite probably the mystical La Mar with whom Marcos sometimes shares his life. In 1997, Gloria settled in a Zapatista community and began to separate the strands of "20/10." "She is like a *bordadera* [embroiderer], sewing the fragments of our reality together," the Subcomandante eulogized long-distance at the Casa Lamm soirée.

The Zapatistas are great movie fans—"We are the People of the (Pop)corn," Marcos once cracked—and a pair of documentaries had been assembled to commemorate 20/10 (actually only the last ten). *La Jornada* produced a two-volume chronology featuring footage available to the public; Ramón Vera, Ana Bellinghausen (Hermann's daughter), Alberto Cortés, Chuchu Ramírez Cuevas, and a bunch more veterans of the War Against Oblivion put together a sort of home movie from bits and pieces shot by Arturo Lomelí and other diligent freelancers down the years, *La Palabra y el Fuego* (The Word and the Fire). Both the book and the documentaries made the rounds at cultural centers in the capital and then went on the road in the provinces.

The moment was an odd exhale of nostalgia for the EZLN, a period of looking back on where they had come from—just six damp compas on a muddy hillside in the middle of a an impenetrable jungle. There were photo exhibits, Comandante Germán converted the safe house in Monterrey into a museum, an art auction featured original works from the pen of the Sup, birthday cakes were baked, candles blown out, and a grand *bailongo* at the Salon Los Angeles, whose slogan is "Those who have not danced at the Los Angeles do not know Mexico," filled the house. An all-day rockathon featuring a mammoth mosh pit and every alternative band in town drew 12,000 young Zapsymps to a Mexico City soccer stadium. Admission was a kilo of rice or beans for the autonomous communities.

But on November 17, the day officially designated as the founding one, the EZLN went inside, closed down the Caracoles to prying eyes, and partied down in private.

Inevitably, the anniversary generated an avalanche of summing ups, some more lucid than others. Twenty and 10 years later, Chiapas and Mexico were not the same, would never be the same again—and yet everything was the same. The Zapatistas were still farmers, there was still corn (although threatened) and the seasons kept coming round again and again. The rebels were still as poor in pocket as they were when all this began, but now they shared a new dignity. They were free and autonomous of the mal gobierno, and in this walk they had shown the world a new way of wedding politics to life. In the process, they had renovated the left from the bottom up and sparked the struggle against the corporate globalizers. In many ways, the oldest had become the newest, and even if their dual weapons of the Word and the Fire had less *fuego* and more *palabras* in it these days, they were being heard all the way to Tierra del Fuego. In fact, 20/10 was a celebration of the Word over the Fire.

San Cristóbal on the eve of the 20/10 was a distinctly different burg from the stodgy, complacent city it had been that first January 1. The Indians no longer stepped into the gutter when the whites walked by, although the tourists never noticed. Most visitors now came to pleasure themselves and pig out in San Cris's cosmopolitan eateries, not for the revolutionary buzz. The *pintas* that splotched the whitewashed walls were more apt to mourn Kurt Cobain than extol Sub Marcos now. The

Casa Vieja Inn, where we reporters had holed up for months while the troops were in the streets—a glance at the hotel register tells the story of the first years of the rebellion—was overrun by Italian tourists definitely not of the Monos Blancos brand. Ground had been broken just outside of town for a megastore and a 10-plex. San Cristóbal had its own maquiladora now.

The real celebrations were out where it had all begun on the periphery, in the Caracoles and the autonomous municipalities in the jungle and Los Altos, in every hamlet and paraje, in every heart.

On New Year's Day, Hermann and Ana and Alberto Cortez drove down to the Caracol Whirlwind of Our Words on the Ejido Morelia to show *La Palabra y el Fuego* to the compañer@s. The community was crammed into the auditorium, and the video would be projected on a bedsheet. Some of the elders sat behind the screen and watched it roll in reverse. *The Word and the Fire* is a kind of home movie, and the rebels mostly saw themselves and their neighbors flash upon the makeshift screen. Some of the events depicted—the execution of the three elders on the Ejido Morelia by the military in the first week of the rebellion for instance—must have deeply touched the community, but the response was muted. They hated it, the filmmakers thought. One man rose to speak his word: "This movie did not make us feel good. We still suffer the pain of our compañeros in our hearts." Then a second hand went up, one of the elders who had sat behind the screen. "Would you show us the movie again please?" he asked.

"Twenty years? Ten years? They went by so fast," Major Moisés muses in *20/10*. "We've just finished beginning. . . ."

9. Winter/Spring 2004

Un Muy Otro New Year's

The EZLN was truly *muy otro* (very other). Whenever we expected the compas to speak out, they clammed up. When we believed they had taken a vow of silence, they would flood us with comunicados. Fiestas sometimes occurred on a few days' notice, but when we anticipated a big party, the Zapatistas were apt to go to bed early.

New Year's Eve 20/10 up at Oventik was like that, a cozy, sparsely attended soirée—perhaps the rebels were all partied out. We downed steamy mugs of Oventik organic (Very Other) up in the Che Guevara General Store and descended the steep street to the basketball *cancha*, where the stage had been strung with black balloons imprinted with Sub Marcos's ski-masked puss.

This was the first New Year's since the installation of the Juntas, and the members of the seven autonomous municipal councils that pertain to the Caracol Rebellion and Resistance for Humanity assembled for the occasion, the men in their beribboned chapeaus—there were few women. The message of the civil authorities did not expend much breath looking back to the 20/10 but rather gazed forward to resistance as usual.

The Zapatista Army of National Liberation had resisted the mal gobierno for 3,650 days and tomorrow would be no different. ¡*Vamos Vamos adelante en la lucha avante!* The wind whipped wickedly off the mountain, and the Zapatista bases drifted off to curl up with their partners for some well-deserved shut-eye, leaving the internationals snake-dancing down on the basketball court. One had the impression that the party had really been staged for them.

It wasn't even 11 o'clock yet and we piled into Bea's pickup for the descent to San Cristóbal. Navigating the icy two-lane with its suicide-curve contours required diligence. Suddenly, a horrible scraping noise filled the cab and Bea's brakes disappeared. We careened down the mountain with Beatriz fighting to keep the vehicle under control and God as her copilot. When we hit the San Andrés crossing, she swung uphill and the momentum was enough to carry us into the darkened plaza of Sakamch'én de los Pobres. The wild ride was enough to make us sink to our knees and give thanks to the Creator.

The soft, sweet voices of Indians at prayer seeped through the wooden doors of the pale yellow *templo* on the corner. The scent of flowers and fragrant incense filled the nostrils with celestial aromas. The saints looked down from their glass cases and smiled as midnight approached.

Abruptly, the church detonated in a shower of intense light and its bells clanged cacophonously. Various strains of bottle rockets whizzed off into the swirling heavens: *morteros*, *palomas*, *triqui-triquis* and other miscellaneous pyrotechnical devices contributed to the joyous clatter as the worshippers burst out of the church into the brisk night. On the lintel, the *imoles* (elders) quaffed posh and offered thanks to the bacabes who held up the four corners of the world. The Zapatista year had turned again.

No Happy Birthday for NAFTA

The EZLN did not have an exclusive franchise on January 1. New Year's 2004 was also the 10th birthday of the North American Free Trade "Agreement." But other than a fistful of transnational tycoons no one was hoisting jeroboams of champagne. NAFTA had wrought incalculable damage and inflicted palpable pain in the decade it had been imposed upon the Mexican people by their distant neighbors to the north without their permission.

NAFTA and the EZLN had risen together and their roots were intractably entwined. They had, indeed, been old adversaries long before January 1, 1994. Salinas's cabal to modify Article 27—the word of Votan Zapata—had been the fulcrum of rebellion. When Salinas touted NAFTA as marking the ascent of Mexico into the first world, the EZLN declared war in the name of the poor and reminded the world that Mexico was still very much a part of the third one. The masked Zapatistas' first victory had been to unmask NAFTA.

The "free trade" treaty's progenitors tried hard to put a smiley face on their flawed product. "Trade" between the U.S. and Mexico had quadrupled during NAFTA's first 10 years from $88 billion in 1993 to over $400 billion a decade later. Foreign investment in Mexico had boomed from $11 billion 10 years ago to $116 billion today—although much of this swag was speculation capital sunk in the Mexican stock market. In his self-serving 1,300-page defense of his much dissed presidency, *Mexico: The Difficult Road to Modernization*, Salinas boasted that NAFTA had saved the nation from bankruptcy after the Great Peso Plunge that sent Mexico into its deepest economic slide since the Depression. Actually, the crisis was caused in part by a current-accounts debacle induced by a sudden surge of imported goods from U.S. transnationals doing business in Mexico, although the immediate trigger was payback of short-term loans Salinas had contracted to keep his House of Cards stacked until after he exited Los Pinos. His successor Zedillo's maladroit bungling of a peso float had much to do with the 1995 economic collapse.

There was nothing free about "free trade," and "trade" was a grossly misleading way to describe this bunko game. Three hundred transnationals concentrated 70% of the commerce across the northern border—NAFTA had not bolstered trade between Mexico and the U.S. but rather between divisions of U.S. corporate empires; Ford Hermosillo did business with Ford Detroit.

Meanwhile, after NAFTA's first 10 years, much as during the 34-year reign of Porfirio Díaz in the past century, all of Mexico's banks were controlled by foreign financial octopi and all the railroads had been sold off to Union Pacific, on whose board of directors Ernesto Zedillo now sat. The mines and the airlines were now in private hands. Two million hectares of tropical forest had vanished in NAFTA's first 10 years, and junk tree plantations were sprouting up all over southern Mexico *gracias* to such global congloms as International Paper and Temple-Inland.

National industries—particularly textiles and plastics—had been deemed uncompetitive and forced to shut their doors, and even the "Mexican Maquiladora Miracle" (2,000,000 jobs) had gone pffft as the transnationals migrated to even lower-wage China. NAFTA had been lauded for creating 2.7 million jobs, but according to RMALC (Mexican Network Against Free Trade) it had cost the country about the same number, a wash. At the same time, real wages, RMALC noted, had declined 3.4% since 1994, and as wealth became even more concentrated, the divide between rich and poor now was more precipitous than on that winter night in 1994 when the Zapatista Army of National Liberation had reminded the world just how dirt poor Mexico really was.

Ahh, but the benefits—there must be some benefits, right? Wal-Mart's 600 megastores now accounted for over half the retail sales in the country, pushing Mexican chains into liquidation. The groundbreaking for a Wal-Mart Mega in the archeological zone of Teotihuacan, the City of the Gods and the New World's first corn culture, had just been celebrated. More than 2,000 McDonald's (not to mention thousands of Burger Kings, Wendy's, Carl Jr's, Domino's Pizza, Dunkin' Donuts, and Kentucky Fried Chickens) were now plastered across the Mexican landscape, and morbid obesity and childhood-onset diabetes were epidemic. Commercial strips in Mexican cities were indistinguishable from Dallas—all part of the plot to "homogenize" markets, that is, to sell the same product in the same stores at the same prices in the two countries. In San Cristóbal, the Coletos were flocking to the brand-new Cineapolis 10-plex, where Hollywood movies ran at the same time they opened in El Norte. But "homogeneity" was not an Indian word, and anyway, the indígenas, as we have noted, are very otro and did not make good consumers.

Big agriculture, corporate farmers like Fox who packed broccoli for the gringos or Maseca, the corn flour giant, were well served by NAFTA, but the campesinos were crushed under the treaty's iron heel. In 2003, tariffs had been abolished on dozens and dozens of agricultural products from apricots to zucchini and including basic grains like rice, wheat, and sorghum (but not corn and beans, which would receive minimal protection through 2008) and Mexican farmers had taken to blocking the international bridges—one disgruntled campesino even rode his horse on to the floor of Congress in protest.

UCLA professor Raul Hinojosa's worst-case scenario that 10,000,000 poor farmers would be forced off the land by NAFTA was fast becoming reality—a Carnegie Endowment–sponsored evaluation of the trade treaty's first 10 years counted 1.3 million campesinos as having already abandoned their plots and jumped into the migration stream. With farming families averaging five members each, the numbers weighed in around 6,000,000 and was climbing. The "travel agencies" that had sprung up like mushrooms in the small cities of Chiapas to ferry indigenous farmers to almost certain death in the Arizona desert were just one outcropping of this disaster.

Rather than decreasing out-migration, as the first Bush and Salinas had lied, it meant that 400,000 Mexicans were busting into the U.S.A. every year now, and since the treaty was signed in 1992, more than 4,000 Mexicans had perished trying to cross the border to take a job no North American would touch, considerably more than had fallen from the Twin Towers on 9/11, but because it was a slow, incremental catastrophe, no one seemed to notice.

Now the indocumentados were dying by the hundreds each year out in the wastelands west of Yuma, falling into ravines up in the snowy Rumorosa mountains, being shot down by the migra (now under Homeland Security and acronymed ICE for Immigration and Customs

Enforcement) or racist vigilantes on the Arizona line. They were flattened racing across freeways in San Diego or bitten by rattlesnakes scuttling across south Texas, suffocated in sealed boxcars on the rail sidings of the Great Southwest, and crushed in car crashes after high-speed chases by the law. They drowned in the All-American Canal outside Mexicali-Calexico, and their bloated corpses bobbed up and down on the currents of the river Mexico calls the Bravo and the U.S. the Grande. They came home to their families in cheap cardboard coffins if the authorities could determine where they came from in the first place. Hundreds of unidentified migrants are buried in a potter's field in Holtville, California. NAFTA had been pitched as raising all boats, but thousands had drowned in the flood.

The Zapatistas of Iowa

That January I taught "Fixing the Zapatistas in History" at a tiny college up in the wedge of tundra where Minnesota, Nebraska, and Iowa corner. Buenavista, named for a battle in the "Spanish-American War" and not the social club, had wheedled a grant from the Iowa State Humanities Council to spread cultural diversity in the frozen hinterlands.

On the first morning of class, I was confronted by 14 corn-fed, wheat-thatched farm kids who had never heard of the Zapatista Army of National Liberation and were mostly taking the course so they didn't have to go back to unhappy homes after the holidays. I put 20 words on the board—"rebellion," "Indian," "Mexico," "Zapata," "Corn," etc.—and asked them to write me a paragraph about one of them. Fourteen kids handed back their thoughts on corn. "Corn is everywhere in my life." "My family has grown corn for five generations." "Since I was a little kid, I've tasseled corn every summer." I knew I had them then. The People of Iowa are as much the People of the Corn as the Mayans.

"Fixing the Zapatistas in History" was kind of an immersion course— three hours a day, five days a week. I told them the story, showed them the films, made them read my books, and preached the Word of the Zapatistas, and some of the kids actually got it. One young woman who was married to a Mexican wrote a kind of futuristic screenplay in which the EZLN takes the Zócalo on January 1, 2010, and distributes power to the poor. Another found significant parallels between the Popul Vuh and the writings of Subcomandante Marcos. A third did preliminary research on the amount of transgenic corn Iowa was dumping in Mexico each year.

I had been hired to spread cultural diversity, but Storm Lake, Iowa, was already pretty diverse. Hmong farmers had been settled by church groups here in the 1970s. They too grew corn. Now there were many Mexicans.

If Iowans are the People of the Corn, they are also the People of the Swine. The fact is that while there are only 3,000,000 two-footed Iowans, there are 10,000,000 swine within the ample borders of the Buckeye State, and hacking them apart and packing them for market is a pillar of the economy.

Following the collapse of the peso in the mid-1990s, Mexicans began to arrive in Storm Lake in numbers and went to work in the packing plants, an industry that has thrived on low-wage immigrant labor long before Upton Sinclair wrote *The Jungle*. These days no chicken leg or pork chop would get packed in the U.S.A. if all the Mexicans were sent back to where they came from.

The Storm Lake economy was heavily dependent on the rendering of domestic animals. IBP, the misnamed International Beef Processors (it slaughtered porkers) running three shifts across the railroad tracks, is a wholly owned subsidiary of Tyson Foods. In the Clinton get-rich-now '90s, Tyson—a major Bubba contributor—and Cargill, the largest privately held corporation in the world masquerading as Springfield Farms, had bought out the small packers, busted the union, and replaced $15-an-hour chuckboners with $6 Mexicans. Tyson subcontractors prowled the country towns of Nayarit and Jalisco to recruit crews. Now a thousand Mexicans and a handful of Hondurans stood waist deep in the offal and entrails of dead oinkers on IBP's killing floor, and the indocumentados had become the newest tenants of the little house on the prairie.

Many were trapped here in this frozen wasteland. When plants in neighboring towns went belly up, the Mexicans working on phony social security numbers were not eligible for unemployment payouts. ICE had congealed the border and they couldn't go home again—not if they ever wanted to come back. Paying the heating bills was beyond their means. It was really cold in the little house on the prairie.

But across the tracks in Storm Lake there were warm spots. The Mexican stores in town were filled with jalapeños and piñatas, Guadalupana candles, *carnitas*, and warm tortillas. In the restaurants, lonely men wolfed down platters of *chile verde* and stared into the necks of their Coronas. Chente Fernández belched rancheras from the jukebox. One could live all day in downtown Storm Lake, Iowa, right here in the breadbasket of America, and never speak a word of English.

Storm Lake was the other side of the NAFTA tragedy. Stripped of their land and forced to flee to El Norte by Mexican imports of 6,000,000 tons of corn a year, much of it from Iowa, the *paisanos* were stuck here in the belly of the beast. Many had gotten here the hard way—one woman had been enslaved in a Houston whorehouse, and the bones of 11 indocumentados had been found inside a sealed boxcar near Dennison in 2001.

But whatever the cost, they were here now and had begun to re-create where they had come from so they would not forget Mexico. Even here in the beast's belly, the young Indian and mestizo men from the impoverished villages of western Mexico had found time to organize a troupe of Aztec *conchero* dancers—they were a big hit at the fiesta on the Day of Guadalupe—and the Indian heart of the south beat loud and strong here in the heartland of El Norte.

Tahuantinsuyo

Tahuantinsuyo: the mythic Inca confederation encompassing the majority-indigenous modern-day nations of Bolivia, Peru, Ecuador, and possibly Paraguay with a combined Indian population of 40,000,000 of the Americas' 65,000,000 First Peoples and hundreds of native cultures from the Andes to the Amazon.

What had Tahuantinsuyo learned of the Zapatista Army of National Liberation and its 20/10-year battle to be autonomous?

First stop on this inquiry was Cochabamba, Bolivia, where I touched down with a print of *La Palabra y el Fuego* and a copy of Gloria Muñoz's *20/10* in my backpack on the third anniversary of the now legendary War in Defense of the Water.

During the winter and spring of 2000, just months after the battle of Seattle, Aymara farmers from the dry high valleys, workers at the municipal waterworks, regional labor federations, and Evo Morales's *cocalero* (coca-growing) unions had faced down the Bolivian military and finally chased the Bechtel Corporation, which had taken over the local water company and raised rates 300%, back to San Francisco, California. The War in Defense of the Water had changed power relations in Cochabamba. On a wall near the plaza where the confrontations had occurred, a mural showed fanciful scenes of the peoples' victory. It was inscribed, "A city that is no longer afraid is capable of the impossible."

On my first night in Cochabamba, I was invited to a *challa,* or housewarming. The shaman, who it turned out worked at the municipal water company, burnt the fetus of a llama, added coca leaves and quinoa and other mystery seeds, and offered the smoke to the Pachamama. Elías explained that because he worked at the water company, he had learned of the Bechtel involvement (the corporation was doing business as "Aguas de Tunari") and spread the word. He had been predestined to become a combatant in that historic struggle. "We learned to dance in the plaza when the bullets were flying everywhere," the shaman laughed, "but our weapons were better than theirs because we had the pueblo."

The EZLN had name recognition in Cochabamba. Oscar Oliveira, one of the directors of the Committee to Defend the Water, did not need a video to learn about the Zapatistas—he knew the narrative in his heart.

"In 1994, we heard a new voice and it came from the Zapatistas who were Indians like ourselves. Bolivia had been sacked for 500 years. They took our gold, our silver, and now they wanted our water. It was time for us to shout *¡Basta Ya!* too.

"We did not want power, because we already had power and it came from the bottom. We found this out there in the plaza dodging their bullets. We didn't need to elect a president or overthrow the government to take power. Now the way it works here is that the people govern and the government obeys. We learned this from the EZLN. Here in Bolivia, we are changing the world from the bottom up."

The Zapatistas' rejection of taking state power, which has its roots in the great Zapata's rejection of the Mexican presidency in favor of the defense of his village lands during the 1910–1919 revolution, hardly met with universal approbation among Bolivia's radical class. Evo Morales, now Bolivia's first indigenous president, who was then constructing his campaign, was adamant. His cocaleros had survived 20 years of U.S. Drug Enforcement Administration eradication campaigns. More than 200 farmers had fallen in this heroic struggle and the jails were teeming with his comrades. "This is an absurd thing the Zapatistas are saying. To liberate the people, you must pass through state power. And that is precisely what we want—the power of the state. . . ."

"I do not agree with the Zapatistas," scowled Leonida Zurita, the handsome leader of the women's cocalera federations and Evo's onetime lover. "We will take state power next year when Evo is elected president, and then we will change the Law of the Coca. We have to have power to change the laws."

The image of armed EZLN rebels taking San Cristóbal on January 1, 1994, is stamped in Latin America's recent memory, and some were concerned that the Zapatistas had capitulated to civil society and abandoned armed struggle.

"I was in jail in 1994 when the news came to us that our brothers and sisters in Chiapas had risen up in arms and it gladdened our hearts," remembered Felipe Quispe, then a member of the Tupac Katari guerrilla and now the leader of the Aymara peasants union and the Pachakutik Party with seats in the Bolivian congress. Quispe's vision of Tahuantinsuyo is decidedly separatist—"We will tear up their constitution and write our own. Their flag will be changed for ours" (the rainbow-hued Wiphala), proclaims the Mallku ("condor"— an honorary title).

"We hear the Zapatistas want roads and schools. That's good. We want those things too. But you must warn the Zapatistas never to give up their arms. If you do not have an army to defend the revolution, there is no revolution." The Mallku is thought to be building an Indian army. We were seated across the table from each other in Quispe's ramshackle La Paz headquarters. I watched his long, strong fingers trace the veins in a coca leaf as if he were divining the future. "Here," he said suddenly and handed me a shopping bag of the sacred coca. "Take this to Subcomandante Marcos. Tell him that we are the coca just like the Zapatistas are the corn. When we are born, we give coca, and when we die. The eradication of our sacred coca is to us genocide and we will never permit that."

El Alto drapes itself over La Paz like a dark condor. This mountaintop Soweto of 700,000 Aymara and Quechua Indians controls the flow of protest down into La Paz nearly 1,000 meters below and was where the overthrow of President Gonzalo Sánchez de Lozada was hatched in 2003 after "Goni" had sought to sell off Bolivia's natural gas deposits (the second largest in Latin America) for a few shekels to transnationals like Repsol and the French Total. I had watched this Indian Intifada unfold from Palestine.

The War in Defense of the Gas—one war leads to another in Bolivia's volatile political climate—had lasted 41 days, and at least 80 comrades had been killed by the Bolivian military. Luis told me how the Indians of El Alto had pushed 10 freight cars out onto a railroad trestle and toppled them one by one from the bridge to the highway below to prevent the army from advancing. The incident was a measure of the collective power the people of El Alto have amassed from down below.

El Alto governs itself through a series of autonomous neighborhood councils (sound familiar?). I was invited to show *La Palabra y el Fuego* at a local community center that also housed a pirate radio station whose signal was heard all over La Paz down below. The young Indian audience was galvanized by the images of the rebellion, and there was applause and even a few *"¡Zapata Vives!"* when it was done. But one student's hand shot up right away and he would not be denied. "We have seen this video and heard the words of the Zapatistas"—Marcos offers an erratic narrative on the soundtrack—"but what we want to know is where is the fire? Words alone cannot take state power."

But there are two weapons, I explained on the defensive right away, and now the Word is the Zapatistas' best weapon. And besides, the EZLN doesn't really want to take state power. "How could that be? Didn't Che want to take state power?" the young man shot back—the figure of Che is heavily freighted with revolutionary reverence in Bolivia, and I thought it best not to pursue my defense of the compas. Later, the kid would fish a stick of dynamite out of his bookbag and put it in my hand—Bolivia is a country of miners and there is a lot of it lying around. "Bring this with you when you go back to Chiapas," he offered amiably. I filed the dynamite with Quispe's coca.

On the way to the hotel, Luis talked about the Aymara military structures in the Ayllus, the autonomous villages of the altiplano bound together in "markas," a rough translation of the Zapatistas' JBG/Caracol formations. "The Indians here have a different time, but they know when it is the right time to move." The Aymara villages were distrustful of modern communications—they didn't use the telephone or e-mail, because they were too vulnerable to government penetration. Instead, in the old way, they set fires on the bare hillsides to communicate among themselves.

After midnight, glancing out of the hotel's cracked window at the surrounding Andean peaks, I could have sworn I saw the fire on the mountain.

Tahuantinsuyo Too

Across the cordilleras down in Lima, the young Quechua organizers pressed me to explain the Zapatistas' rejection of the mal gobierno. How did this autonomy work? Did the EZLN take part in elections? What exactly did the San Andrés Accords say about OIT 169? CONACAMI, a coalition of 1,100 Indian villages that had been devastated by transnational mining, was demanding that abandoned mines be sanitized and turned back to the villages for much-needed farming land. The organization, like the EZLN, based its claim on OIT 169.

I traveled with Miguel Palacín, a CONACAMI director, up to his home turf near Cerro de Pasco, 15,000 feet up in the Andes and the highest city—really a huge strip mine—in all Latin America. All along the route, we had sampled the disasters that transnational mining has wrought upon the Andes—mountains sheared in two, mile-long cyanide stains, the venomous smelters, Indian communities living in misery under the slagheaps, a ragged woman, thin and taut as a stick of dynamite, clapping an emaciated baby to her breast by the roadside. Gold was about to hit $500 an ounce.

Out at Lake Chinchaycocha, so poisoned now by mercury that cows keeled over on the hoof when they grazed upon its grassy shores, Miguel mourned the desecration of Indian lands. As a child he remembered playing in the ruins of the Inca high road—the Capac Nan—that borders the lake, imagining that he could hear the Chaski runners bringing tribute and news up to the Inca in Cuzco from what is now Argentina and southern Colombia. "We are the Incas and this has been our land since time began. Now we are taking it back."

Sarayaku has earned the title of "the Chiapas of Ecuador." *"Todos Somos Sarayaku"* and *"No Están Sólos"* are neatly spray-painted on the walls around Quito University. Sarayaku, a Kichwa town along the Bobanaza River down in Amazonas, has been battling the oil barons for decades, first Shell and now new-style transnational resource mongers like Burlington Energy. Whenever they send seismologists onto their lands to drill test holes, Sarayaku gathers up its bows and curare-tipped arrows and fighting lances (*bodoqueras*) and journeys out to the limits of its territory to confront the outlanders.

The Kichwas of Sarayaku are members of the Amazon federation of Ecuador's Confederation of Indigenous Nations (CONAIE), the longest-lived Indian confederation in Latin America. In 2000, the CONAIE joined with young army officers to overthrow President Jamil Mahuad after he put Indian-killer Andrew Jackson on the money and dollarized the sucre.

The CONAIE has a credibility problem these days. Having thrown their weight behind one of the officers, Lucio Gutiérrez, the Indians rose to power under his aegis, and CONAIE founders Nina Pacari and Luis Macas occupied key posts in his cabinet. "We were in power but we had no power," Pacari told investigators Lucien Chauvin and Barbara Fraser. Meanwhile, Lucio began displaying alarming neoliberal tendencies—oil companies like Occidental and the much hated Texaco were given a free hand by Gutiérrez, who also granted the Yanquis permission to expand its anti-terrorist base at Manta. All of a sudden, Gutiérrez became a fan of the ALCA. The Indians left his cabinet after 204 days. "Now we have learned that power is in other places," admitted Leonidas Iza, outgoing CONAIE chairman. "The real question for us now is whether we exercise our power inside the state or outside it."

I caught up with Iza outside Puyo, a gateway city to the Amazon, at a congress of the nine-nation Amazon federation. One hot topic under debate: Were the Andoa people, tall serious-looking men with elaborate face tattoos, really a separate nation from the Shiwiar, among whom they lived? Only four fragile elders who spoke their language survived, and when they spoke before the assembly, the Schwar could not understand them, so the nine-nation federation grew to 10 by unanimous vote.

I caught the community puddle-jumper out to Sarayaku with two young teachers, Leopoldo and César—César was packing in two family-sized jugs of bright yellow Inka Cola—and they invited me to spend the night and speak to them of Marcos and the Zapatistas. I showed them maps and pictures—there was no electricity and I could not show the video, but they hung on to every word. *"Mandar obedeciendo,"* Leopoldo jotted down in his notebook. Howler monkeys were gooning out there in the trees. We talked about the Juntas de Buen Gobierno and the Caracoles and what being autonomous meant. The Kichwas of Sarayaku were physically farther removed from their government than even the settler communities in Montes Azules and had been effectively autonomous throughout their history.

The maestros talked about their community assembly. Each family sent its representative to hash out community problems. Decisions taken there must then be reviewed by the council of elders. This was their way of governing themselves. César excused himself to crush a tarantula with a shovel. In the morning I thanked the maestros with my last Marcos T-shirt, the one on which he gives the world the big finger. They promised to take turns wearing it to the school.

Don Sabino was a member of the Council of Elders. He was now somewhere in his 90s, a renowned *yacho*, or herbalist, and he graciously took time out from boiling ayahuasca root to take me on a run through the surrounding jungle. Each tree had a story. He grabbed off handfuls of leaves and stuffed them into my mouth. This one was for hunting, this one would cure diarrhea. "We have another story of life here in Sarayaku," he mused like Old Antonio's Amazonian doppelganger.

Power in Kichwa means "changing things together," I was told by Don Sabino's nephew Marlon, the president of Sarayaku, on the flight back to Puyo. I offered him my copy of *El Fuego y la Palabra* for when the lights came to Sarayaku. "They say that Sarayaku is the Chiapas of Ecuador," I reminded him. "Well, maybe that is true but it's too hot to wear those damn ski masks here," Marlon laughed.

Soon after Bolivia's popular movement booted Goni back to Miami, the miners of Huanuni went home. "If you ever need our help to overthrow another president, don't forget to give us a call," they advised the Aymaras of El Alto. Indeed since the new millennium moved in, the Indian peoples of Tahuantinsuyo have toppled three presidents (Mahuad in 2000 in Ecuador, Goni and his successor, Carlos Mesa, in Bolivia). There will be others before it's done.

A 2003 Central Intelligence Agency assessment anticipating what kind of bad juju for the U.S. was brewing in Latin America concluded that the growing militancy of the continent's indigenous peoples would be the most serious threat to Uncle Sam's hegemony over the next decade and a half. For once, the Company could be on the mark.

The Taco Factor

"We the People of the Corn are in continual struggle against the domination of your science. You have always depreciated our knowledge, repressed and ignored it," the young Zapotec challenged the distinguished scientists, many of them with significant ties to Big Biotech, who had gathered in Oaxaca to soft-pedal the dangers that GMO corn presented to the indigenous farmers of Mexico.

Members of an expert panel convened by the environmental commission of the North American Free Trade Agreement to investigate charges by 17 Mexican NGOs that massive importation and consumption of genetically modified corn was a clear and present danger to the country's 57 distinct Indian peoples, the men and women of science now found themselves confronted by a roomful of pissed-off indígenas and environmentalists.

"Do not believe what they say, comrades, these are not scientists. They have come to kill us!" a truckload of activists from Oaxaca's Flores Magón Indigenous Council barked into a bullhorn out in the parking lot as the management of the five-star hotel, the Victoria, celebrated for its panoramic vistas of Oaxaca city, fussed and fumed that the Indians were trespassing on private property. Alfa Squad rent-a-cops pounded at the ground with their batons. The only Indians who ever penetrated the perimeter of these exclusive grounds were maids and gardeners.

"The big liars of the market and the state appear among us as 'specialists' and 'investigators.' They say our seeds are no good and our ways of cultivation inadequate. They counsel us to buy their seeds and learn their ways of killing the corn and the earth," the young Zapotec Aldo González politely tongue-lashed the expert panel. Tall and straight with a long ponytail, Aldo was the National Indigenous Congress's delegate in Guelatao up in the Sierra of Juárez, where three years earlier Nacho Chapela had found the first signs of transgenic contamination in Calpulalpan.

Standing next to Aldo at the microphone as straight and tall as the Zapotec was a stalk of maíz pulled from a Guelatao milpa.

Whereas Chapela had isolated the BT strain of modified corn engineered to kill corn-boring caterpillars (it also wiped out Monarch butterfly chrysalises), Aldo's corn has tested positive for StarLink, a Novartis brand that had been barred from human consumption by the U.S. Department of Agriculture. Now here it was alive and kicking in the Oaxaca sierra.

By 2004, GMO corn was everywhere in Oaxaca, spreading silently like the plague from cornfield to cornfield. Scientists like Chapela who exposed the contamination were silenced and their investigations suppressed. When the 2002 Mexican Ecological Institute study found modified maize in 11 out of 22 corn-growing regions in Oaxaca and Puebla, 4,000-plus of the samples yielded an average contamination rate of 7.4%. But the institute's report had never been published. Instead, a survey taken two years later by the agricultural ministry found that all significant GMO contamination had somehow magically disappeared.

"Time and time again, you have sought to force us to abandon the cultivation of our corn in the way our grandfathers taught us. Instead of culling the seeds for the best strains, as our race has done since the beginning of history, you want us to buy yours." The Oaxaca conclave was indeed all about seed. Indian farmers were famous seed savers. Big Biotech wanted to sell them their souped-up killer seeds. It's the market, dummy!

High above Oaxaca city, in Aldo's sierra and in all the sierras of Indian Mexico, the ground was being prepared to drop in the new seed. Would it be the seed of their *abuelas* and their *raza* or the seeds the Monsanto Corporation of St. Louis, Missouri, marketed under the "Terminator" label? The Terminator is engineered to go sterile after one growing cycle, thereby obliging the campesinos to buy more.

"*¡Fuera semillas asesinas!*" the Indians for whom Aldo spoke chanted, and the chandeliers shook: "Get out of here with your killer seeds!" It seemed like a good moment to break for lunch. While the trinational panel of experts sauntered off to private banquet rooms, the protesters piled into the 16th-century courtyard of Santo Domingo church, where Mexico's most luminous painter, Francisco Toledo, fresh from having fought off a McDonald's in the jewel-box Oaxaca city plaza, served organic tortillas tastefully fashioned from blue and purple Indian corns.

"Corn is not just another crop for us. It contains our past, defines our present, and is the beginning of our future," Aldo read from the document "In Defense of Corn," prepared by the protesters the night before, deep in the bowels of Santo Domingo. "Corn is our brother and sister, the foundation of our culture, and the center of our daily lives."

The lunch break had not much cooled tempers. The Indians and their environmental allies were particularly piqued because key chapters of the panel's preliminary report had not been translated from English. What are you trying to hide, they yelled at the scientists. "You are using the Indians of Oaxaca as guinea pigs (*conejillos de Indias*) in your evil experiments!" "You killed your own Indians—now you want to kill us!" a Zapotec from the isthmus pointed accusingly. Peter Raven, a National Medal of Science winner who is reportedly married into the Monsanto clan, stared into his shoes.

The night before, the women of Za'aquila, a nearby Zapotec mountain town, put their maíz to soak into *nixtamal*. When they arose in the dawn, they emptied out the corn and ground it down to 100 kilos of *masa* on their stone *metates*. There are, I hear, 600 ways to prepare corn, but the tortilla is far and away the most ubiquitous. Tortillas are a staple of diet in rural Mexico. While urban dwellers tend to utilize the tortilla as a food scooper, for 13,000,000 Mexican children, the National Nutrition Institutes tell us, the tortilla is the only food.

"We have listened patiently to your scientists, but now we are tired. *¡Basta Ya* with your lies!" Aldo showed the NAFTA panel a Zapatista fist. "The dignity of Indian peoples is contagious. To defend our corn is to defend the sun, the earth, the water, the wind. In Oaxaca, we are building autonomy, which is the only legitimate sovereignty, that of the people to defend their corn in each municipality, each town, each neighborhood. . . ."

Just then, the salon doors swung open and the women of Za'aquila marched into the meeting, trundling enormous *tlaxcales* (baskets) of handmade, organic tortillas, which they energetically distributed among the distinguished scientists. The dubious men and women on the panel poked tentatively at the warm tortillas. The farmer Rubén approached the microphone and encouraged them to eat heartily. "Take a taco with us," Rubén cajoled, "it will help you feel more human."

Zipizapi at Zinacantán

Zinacantán, like its neighbor San Juan Chamula on the far side of the mountain above San Cristóbal, is a colorful, dangerous, sui generis Tzotzil municipality much favored by tourists for its Indian weavers. Because the Pan-American Highway bisects its geography, market transport is easy, and in modern greenhouses here transnationals grow roses that are shipped as far afield as Japan.

But this globalized touch is largely an illusion. Like Chamula, Zinacantán's homegrown "uses and customs" govern daily life. One such "use and custom" is the wholesale consumption of posh, the Tzotzil white lightning. Another is the dynastic rule of the PRI.

But the PRI had schismed in southeastern Chiapas, and a faction of ex-PRIistas who had defected to the PRD won municipal elections the previous October. Soon after the new municipal president, Martín Sánchez, was sworn in, a gunfight broke out between warring bands of Indians and two PRIistas were killed.

Like other municipalities in the Altos of Chiapas, power in Zinacantán is concentrated in the cabecera, but of the 40 outlying parajes, the EZLN had a presence in 13, and in four of the villages—Elambó Alto, Elambó Bajo, Jech'vo, and San Isidro (perhaps 150 families in all)—the Zapatistas were in the majority. Rumors were afoot that the four communities might break with Zinacantán and form their own autonomía, but, for now, they took their direction from the Junta de Buen Gobierno, the Center of the Zapatista Heart Before the World, at Oventik and were openly defiant of the official municipality, refusing to contribute tithes to the authorities for the fiestas of the saints because they knew their hard-earned pesos would just be spent on posh. The Zapatistas, it will be remembered, don't drink.

In retaliation for the four rebel enclaves' reluctance, Martín Sánchez suspended their water rights, ordered hoses to the houses cut, strung barbed wire up around the nearest water repository, and posted armed guards. If the Zapatistas needed water, he reasoned, let them go to Oventik. "They have their own buen gobierno, ¿no?" Now the Zapatista families had to walk four kilometers hauling 20-liter water cans on a tumpline around their foreheads, the *mecapal*. If they got the cans home, Sánchez's goons would come and kick over their tanks and fill them with stones.

As Martín Sánchez had anticipated, the Oventik JBG responded to the compas' troubles. "If someone wants to make trouble for the Zapatistas, they will bring down plenty of trouble upon themselves," the JBG warned pugnaciously. When the Zinacantán municipal president responded in kind, the rebels scoffed at his threats. "If the army couldn't scare us, a group of Indians like ourselves won't do any better."

Summoning all seven autonomías under its administration to bail out the brothers and sisters, the JBG rented water trucks (*pipas*) to slake their comrades' thirst, and when the PRD stoned the trucks, the *zipizapi* (running battle) endured for months.

April 10, the death day of Votan Zapata, often coincides with Holy Week, conflating Jesus Christ and the Liberator of the South into one crucifixion. That Holy Saturday, both the 85th anniversary of Zapata's assassination at the hands of the mal gobierno and a holiday marked all over Mexico by the dumping of buckets of water on unsuspecting passersby, the EZLN delivered several pipas to their thirsty comrades in arms and planned to march on the municipal offices at the county seat.

Five thousand set out behind banners that read *"Martín Sánchez—¡No Chinga Sus Hermanos Indígenas!"* ("Martín Sánchez—Don't Fuck Over Your Indian Brothers!") and "Zapata Is Not Dead So Long As We Are Alive!" When the rebels passed Paste, a PRD settlement, Sánchez's gangsters, many of them drinking, ambushed the rear guard of the march. Those contingents in the lead raced back to rescue their people but were cut off by two police patrol cars sent by Sánchez. Gunshots were heard. The fighting grew fierce and very one-sided. Twenty-nine Zapatistas were taken to hospital in San Cristóbal, eight or maybe 15 of them with gunshot wounds. One compa had been shot in the thorax.

The ambush was the most violent aggression against the EZLN since June 1998, when Croquetas attacked San Juan de la Libertad and 10 were killed, not all of them Zapatistas, and the incident would put the rebels and the PRD on a war footing for years to come. Although the PRD National Committee sought to distance itself from Sánchez, it ascribed the violence to "intercommunal rivalries," much as the Zedillo government had tried to explain away Acteal, and refused to apologize.

The 125 Zapatista families who had fled into the forest for safety did not return for weeks. When they did at the end of April, they were accompanied by the civil society, including Las Abejas. The children rode in the little yellow school bus that Schools for Chiapas now parked permanently at Oventik. Governor Pablo pressured Sánchez into negotiating with the Oventik JBG and the water was turned back on.

The zipizapi at Zinacantán was fraught with lessons for the Zapatistas' burgeoning autonomous infrastructure. Where the rebels constituted a majority population, such as at San Andrés–Oventik or La Realidad–San Pedro de Michoacán, they could guarantee services like electricity and water—some outposts like La Realidad were already off the government power grid. But where Zapatista bases were isolated and dependent on hostile authorities for such services, autonomy would always be just over the next mountain.

The War Against the Caracoles

Nine months after giving birth to the Juntas de Buen Gobierno, the Caracoles had come under fire. Road signs that read "You Are Now Entering Zapatista Territory, Where the People Rule and the Government Obeys!" were riddled by buckshot and blasted by shotgun shells. In some places, the signs were cut down, and when the rebels erected a replacement, that one was decapitated too. The fragging of the signage was a symptom of the hostility the EZLN had provoked in some quarters for daring to provide for its people.

The ambush at Zinacantán had not been the only flash point that spring. In the Tojolabal zone (the Tzotz Chuj MAREZ), the CIOAC, a farmers' struggle organization closely connected to the PRD, kidnapped and threatened to burn alive Zapatista *transportistas* who ferried comrades from distant ejidos up to the cities of the region—the CIOAC claimed the concession.

The counterinsurgency, as the EZLN was quick to tag it, was spearheaded by a well-oiled press campaign to paint the Zapatista autonomous zone as a hotbed of criminal anarchy. Although the report "Public Security and the Zapatistas' Juntas de Buen Gobierno" was leaked on state letterhead, Pablo denied authorship. The paper tallied more than 6,000 criminal acts committed in areas of Zapatista influence since the JBGs had been sworn in nearly a year ago. Zapatista *autonomías* provided a safe haven for drug smugglers, *polleros* (people smugglers), wood poachers, cattle rustlers, and car thieves. Opium poppies had been raided in Chanal in the Tzotz Chuj area—the first evidence of poppy cropping in southeastern Chiapas. The EZLN, of course, has its own War on Drugs, and growing or using drugs is severely punished.

A closer look at Pablo's stats told a distinct story. Of the 6,000-plus reported crimes, 95% had been committed in cities like Comitán, Ocosingo, Palenque, and San Cristóbal which, although located in areas where the rebels have support, are hardly controlled by the Zapatistas. In fact, the EZLN's autonomous justice system was keeping crime to a minimum in the villages they served.

The purported lawlessness in Zapatista territory paled when compared to the perpetual crime wave across the state in Tapachula, on the Guatemalan border, where the Salvadoran Mara Salvatrucha, a youth gang on steroids, perpetrated daily mayhem on hapless migrants, and three major Mexican drug cartels indulged in blood orgies for control of the border crossing. Eighty executions had been recorded in 2003.

The offensive against the Caracoles stepped up in June when a federal-state task force, the Chiapas Coordination Group (Mexico's top internal security spy agency, CISEN, the defense ministry, the navy, Federal Preventive Police, and Chiapas Public Security) spilled details to the PANista daily *Reforma* of an ongoing investigation into what was described as "the reactivation of the military wing of the Zapatista Army of National Liberation."

According to this ersatz intelligence, the EZLN was operating 20 training camps and preparing 2,100 militia members for "a resumption of the war." Sixteen of the camps were supposed to be in Ocosingo, with 1,758 militia members under arms. Major Moisés was supposed to be the commander in chief, although Subcomandante Marcos, who had not been heard from in some months, had his own camp, as did Comandante Zebedeo (*Reforma* listed his purported real name).

The only training camp visible to the public was supposed to be at Oventik, a few dozen meters east of the basketball court adjacent to the Primero de Enero rebel secondary school—the Chiapas Coordination Group repeatedly confused schools with "training camps." According to *Reforma* columnist Ana María Salazar, once a civilian flunky at the Pentagon during the Clinton years, the EZLN was preparing for a resumption of hostilities in late 2005. Early 2006 at the latest.

The "leak" appeared to have been floated to boost military intentions to augment the number of bases in the increasingly autonomous (and "lawless") zone. As usual, the mirror image of this twisted "intelligence" was closer to the truth.

According to the San Cristóbal NGO CAPISE, which studies the militarization of Chiapas, the army now maintained 22 units and eight battalions in the state, including five infantry units, four motorized units, one artillery regiment, one battalion of engineers, and one battalion of military police. Onésimo Hidalgo, another assiduous San Cristóbal researcher, listed 490 military and police positions in Chiapas—213 of them operated by the Mexican army and grouped in three military zones (31 at Rancho Nuevo, 36 at Tonina, and 39 just across the Usumacinta in Tenosique, Tabasco). In the Zapatista zone, the military had established 98 camps, 59 of them on ejido land without the ejido's permission. Military and police operated 29 permanent checkpoints and 57 mobile ones. Federal police agencies worked out of 62 sites in Chiapas, 15 under the auspices of the Federal Investigation Agency (AFI) and 23 more under the Federal Preventive Police (PFP). Immigration authorities operated 47 installations, the Mexican navy 18, and state public security listed 141 positions.

The actual number of troops in Chiapas and the conflict zone has been disputed for as long as the rebellion has been active. In the early years of the insurrection, 18,000 was an accepted figure among observers, but an ad hoc census taken by researcher Arturo Lomelí in 1996 doubled that number to 36,000, and the guestimates have just gone up since. Subcomandante Marcos insists there are 70,000 troops in the conflict zone, which would be about a third of the Mexican armed forces.

The military has sometimes claimed troop numbers to be no greater than 12,000 but in 2006 declared less than 3,000 remained inside the conflict zone. An additional 3,000 troops were sent to the southern border after the U.S. invasion of Iraq as part of Operation Sentinel. According to Secretary of Defense (SEDENA) sources quoted in *La Jornada*, the exact number will remain classified for the next 12 years. How many Mexican army troops are there in the jungle and mountains of Chiapas? Too many.

But the offense against Zapatista autonomy was not all military might. The Fox counterinsurgency plan was designed to co-opt or coerce the rebels back onto the government grid, and the smiley side was a plethora of federal and state social programs to put a check in the hands of EZLN base communities. Luis H. Alvarez was often the agent of co-optation, plying the fringes of the Zapatista zone with truckloads of corrugated cardboard roofing material and solar cells, trying to hoodwink the compas into being photographed with him. Maybe he was lonely.

In early July, the wily octogenarian snuck into La Realidad by the back road, accompanied by Televisa and TV Azteca crews to tempt six PRI families (50 folks in all) with his tainted wares. The cameras whirred and Fox's long frustrated "peace commissioner" was the top of the news that night. After so many years of abject failure, Luis H. Alvarez had finally penetrated a Zapatista autonomous community.

10. Summer/Fall 2004

An Accounting

As the Caracoles entered their second year, the Juntas de Buen Gobierno were called to account. Each JBG was to draw up a year-end report that included total income taken in, cash on hand, what had been paid out and for what, in addition to a summary of accomplishments, what had been learned, and what had not in the first 12 months of the Zapatista experiment in building autonomy. The reports were then summarized in a series of nine "videos you can read," a production of the "Zapatista Intergalactic Television System." The "videos" were only the second communiqués issued under Sub Marcos's pen more than halfway through 2004.

The cash balance was favorable: Together all five Caracoles had taken in 12.5 million pesos during their first year, with payouts of 10 million, leaving 2.5 million pesos in the kitty to begin a second year of operation. Oventik was the engine of the EZLN economy, taking in 6 million pesos, largely from sales of fair trade coffee—and now organic honey—and seed money from the NGOs. An Argentine soccer star named Javier "Pupi" Zanetti and the captain of Inter Milan donated 5,000 euros because "we believe in a better, unglobalized world enriched by the cultural differences and customs of all the people. This is why we want to support you in this struggle to maintain your roots and fight for your ideals." Zanetti also donated his soccer shirt and along with his teammates contributed an ambulance.

Meanwhile, 4 million pesos had been spent on the upkeep of the seven autonomous municipalities grouped together in the Caracol Resistance and Rebellion for Humanity. Other major expenditures included feeding the refugees at Polhó after the International Red Cross had abandoned the encampment—"There's no war here now," the ICRC told the Zapatistas, "we have to go take care of the people of Iraq"—and to hire the pipas that ferried the water to the compas in Zinacantán (Pupi paid for the pipas).

The other Caracoles displayed similar financial health—La Realidad had taken in 5 million with 4 million in expenditures; Roberto Barrios, 1.6 million with a million paid out; Morelia had 1.5 million incoming and 900,000 in expenses; and La Garrucha, 600,000 total income with half of that expended to pay the bills. Given the multimillion budgets allocated to official municipalities by the state and the feds, the Caracoles were a bargain.

The JBGs administrated the Zapatista zone on a shoestring. Junta members needed about eight pesos a day (80 cents USD) for the *combi* (collective taxi) that took them to Oventik, and sometimes they walked. They brought their own pozol and the community supplied the tostadas. They brewed their own tea from "weeds," the Sup noted. The JBG's parsimony contrasted starkly with the astronomical salaries the officials of the mal gobierno drew down.

Other Caracol/JBG expenses were offset by volunteer labor. The health and education commissions in the autonomous municipalities were made up of volunteer promoters whose home villages paid for their food, travel, and clothing and tended their corn while they were in the field. Zapatista underwriting of community projects was often ingenious. The JBG Heart of the Rainbow of Hope (Ejido Morelia) asked the parents of each student to donate a chicken when they enrolled their kids, and the poultry and egg sales from the Zapatista chicken farm helped to finance the autonomous educational system.

The EZLN health care system was similarly brilliant if bottom line, functioning on funds from European NGOs. Health promoters carried out vaccination campaigns, midwives were trained, and most autonomías had pharmacies where donated medicines were given away free.

The Zapatistas were even performing surgeries now at the hospital in San José del Río, just up the road from the notorious white elephant Salinas had installed in Guadalupe Tepeyac. The operations were minor—cysts, hernias, and such—but more ambitious cuttings were in the wings. Zapatista health services were as popular with PRI communities as they were with the rebels. PRIistas living alongside the autonomías were asked to ante up 10 pesos if they had it—if they didn't, *"ni modo"* (what else can we do?) Lucio, a health promoter in San Pedro de Michoacán, told Gloria Muñoz. Health care was free for all members of the EZLN's base communities. "The people here don't die as fast as they used to," Lucio wryly observed.

Despite skimpy resources, the EZLN's justice system was up and running. The JBGs now had volunteer "detectives" who investigated the allegations brought before the Juntas. Although the system was "one of dialogue and not penalization" (no jails), penalties could range from fines to ostracization for more serious infractions. Those judged guilty of minor transgressions could work off their crimes in the communities. If a homicide was committed, the killer had first to support the family of the victim, although should the perpetrator came from the outside, the Zapatistas would turn the culprit over to the authorities of the mal gobierno.

Like health care, the Zapatista justice system was attractive to the PRIistas living in the autonomías—Oventik had resolved 85 justice issues in 2003–04, with 15 of them involving non-Zapatistas. The stature of the Juntas was such that when a non-Zapatista teacher was raped on the road to Santa Rita near La Realidad by ski-masked scumbags who tried to pass themselves off as compas, she had no compunction about reporting the crime to the ski-masked local Junta.

The Caracoles were spirals through which the outside world came to know the Zapatista world—and the rebels, the world outside. During 2003–04, the non-Zapatistas who visited the Caracoles numbered 3,791, including 1,600 from all 32 Mexican states and the federal district, and 2,191 non-Mexicans from 43 counties. Tibetan lamas climbed the steep streets of Oventik; Alaskan Indians built a sweat lodge; Irish and Greek brigadistas toured through the region; a young man from Algeria came to the Ejido Morelia to show the compas how to cook couscous.

Not everything was hunky dory. Marcos noted two grievous kinks in the way the JBGs were functioning. There was an appalling lack of women selected as representatives by the autonomías to serve on the Juntas—1% of all JBG members were women, whereas in the regional Clandestine Revolutionary Indigenous Committees (CCRI), which are part of the politico-military structure, women had a 33% share. Not nearly enough, the Sup opined, insisting on parity.

Moreover, the contradictions between the politico-military side of the EZLN—the Zapatista Army of National Liberation vs. civil Zapatismo as expressed in the autonomous municipalities and the Caracoles—remained a gnawing problem. "When we conceived of the Juntas, the idea was to accompany the bases in building autonomy, but too often the comandantes would issue orders and give directions" (Marcos).

Another problem that had caused grief for the NGO community was not really a problem, the Sup asserted. The quick rotation of JBG members made continuity difficult, the nongovs complained. They would bring in a project and present it to the Junta, and three weeks later when they returned for a decision, there was a new JBG and they had to start all over again. Aha, Marcos pointed out, "this is our school of government." Besides, if some black soul wanted to corrupt the Juntas, it wouldn't work, because the next time the corruptor tried his schemes, the JBG would have changed and the malefactor would have to start all over again.

Although the Caracoles were linked together in a unified whole, the administration of each was distinct. The Caracol Mother of Caracoles—Sea of Our Dreams, AKA La Realidad, encompassed the autonomous municipality of Tierra y Libertad, a narrow strip that followed the Guatemalan border out to the Pacific Ocean, passing over the Sierra Madre that bisects Chiapas down into the hotlands. Now non-Zapatistas from these distant climes were availing themselves of the JBG—a group of neighbors from Las Canoas Street in the flood-ravaged Sierra municipality of Motozintla grew impatient with the mal gobierno and affiliated themselves with the Junta.

A union of tricycle drivers (a low-rent mode of public transportation in southern Mexico) from Huixtla had been denied licenses by a PRI municipal president and petitioned to become Zapatistas. A fishing co-op denied access by the environmental ministry (SEMARNAT) to traditional fishing grounds at Laguna Panzacola on the coast asked the Junta for guidance. The autonomías grouped together in the Mother of Caracoles—Sea of Our Dreams had unique powers of *denuncia*, and what happened in the far-off towns within Tierra y Libertad could be news the next morning in Barcelona.

Since the mid-1990s, the autonomous municipality of Tierra y Libertad had issued Zapatista marriage licenses and birth and death certificates, a practice now common in all the Caracoles.

The JGB Rainbow of Our Hope (né Ejido Morelia) had long been plagued by timber thieves and polleros coming across the Guatemalan border, and the JBG sought to counter the problem by promulgating "laws" that the community was called upon to enforce. The Law of the Forests obligated any Zapatista base that had permission to cut down a tree to plant two in its stead. If permission had not been obtained, the guilty party had to plant 20 trees. All trucks hauling illegal timber through the ejido would be confiscated and their loads distributed for public works.

The Law of the Migrant instructed community members to detain the pollero and distribute the money he had charged the migrants (usually impoverished Central Americans) equally among them. The community must feed the undocumented workers—one compa caught overcharging for pozol was sternly chastised—and speed them on their way with a warning that the *sueño americano* was not all it was cracked up to be, encouraging the indocumentados to return to their villages and fight together for what they need. Be a Zapatista where you come from.

The jurisdiction of the Caracol Resistance Until the New Dawn, at La Garrucha, extended through the Cañadas all the way to the Montes Azules, but the actual installations in the autonomous municipality of Francisco Gómez is small and tidy with some site-specific features. The Cyber Pozol café was the first of its kind in Zapatista territory, a meeting ground for visiting internationals and compas aspiring to become cyber-nauts. By 2005, all five Caracoles would be Internet accessible, which has tied autonomous structures even more closely together.

Because of the distances between settlements and a relatively flat terrain, bicycles are popular in the Cañadas, and the *taller* (workshop) in La Garrucha, materially aided by a Critical Mass collective in Ithaca, New York, both repairs and rents bikes to the villagers and the visitors.

By 2004, Oventik, Resistance and Rebellion for Humanity, was fast being urbanized. In addition to the Junta's offices, each of the autonomías that sat on the JBG Center of the Zapatista Heart Before the World had its own private offices, as did Mut Vitz and Yaxil, the coffee collectives, the seed collective "Mother Seeds in Resistance from the Lands of Chiapas," and the artisan women's co-op. The Guadalupana clinic now had an ambulance donated by the Italians. The Che Guevara general store was stuffed to the gunnels with Zapatista paraphernalia. Two schools and an Indigenous Language Center were going full blast at the bottom of the hill. The language center, a Schools for Chiapas concept, taught both Spanish and rudimentary Tzotzil to internationals who coughed up a small tuition that was dedicated to feeding and housing secondary school students who often came from far-off villages.

Of the five Caracoles, Roberto Barrios, the Caracol That Speaks for All, seemed the most vulnerable. Dug in out in the savannahs near the royal Mayan city of Palenque, the Caracol was surrounded by PRIistas—many of them affiliated with Peace and Justice, whose pistoleros continued to make life hell for the eight tentative autonomías in the north of Chiapas. Cataláns, who themselves had created a Caracol in Barcelona, operated the clinic (therapeutic massage was offered), and the education program Seeds of the Sun taught a rebel curriculum that revolved around the EZLN's 13 basic demands. But the incessant intrusions of Peace and Justice types, annoying visits from the military, and Big Ecotourism's designs on the scenic Bascán cascades just downriver made the Caracol That Speaks for All a fragile haven from the neoliberal storm.

This Is What Autonomy Looks Like

Eyes. Many many eyes. Dark x-ray eyes framed by black ski masks. Eyes on the walls of the schools, the stores, the chapels, the clinics, the meetinghouses, the tortilla factory. Everywhere a wall, every wall brimful of eyes. The penetrating stare of Votan Zapata, of Francisco Villa and Ricardo Flores Magón. Zapatista eyes, ancient eyes, baby eyes, staring out from the walls at you staring into their eyes. A Caracol of Eyes. The Zapatista Vision.

This is what autonomy looks like.

Iñaki García, whose Barcelona collective published a calendar of EZLN murals, says there are 400 of these heroic, brightly hued wall paintings in the Zapatista zone. The most common motifs are Votan Zapata, the Guadalupana, and corn, great golden ears of maize. Now there are many Caracoles. In one tableau, a ski-masked Zapatista astronaut reaches for the stars. There is a Zapatista Spiderman at La Garrucha and another wall filled with Zapatista animal crackers.

Some of the murals have been painted by brigadistas in collaboration with the community, and some have been painted by the communities alone without outside artists to guide their brushes. Other walls have been painted by world-class throw-up artists—the stellar London street artist Banksy journeyed to La Realidad and played futbol with the compas. Now he stencils ski-masked Zapatistas kicking soccer balls around on the walls of England. Both Banksy and Gustavo Chávez, a leader of a new generation of Mexican muralists who has covered many Zapatista walls, have taken on the Israeli Separation Wall, vowing to muralize all 600 kilometers of the odious barrier.

The most celebrated of the Zapatista murals, "The Life and Dreams of the Perlas River Valley," was a highly bucolic vision of Zapatista autonomy that featured waddling ducks, spectral butterflies, a tranquil equine or two, a bespectacled Flores Magón, and the most benign Zapata you have ever seen. On April 10, 1998—Votan Zapata's annual death day and also the inauguration of the autonomous municipality that took the name of the murdered Oaxaca-born anarchist Ricardo Flores Magón—Croquetas's state cops along with Zedillo's army troops fell upon the new autonomía, looting and burning the public buildings, arresting scores of villagers, laying waste to "The Life and Dreams of the Perlas River Valley," hog-tying its creator, Sergio "Checo" Valdez, an art professor at the Metropolitan University in Mexico City (Marcos also taught there), and dragging the artist off to Cerro Hueco, where he would spend a full year, the first Mexican muralist since David Alfaro Siqueiros to have been so crucified for his art.

Fortunately, transparencies of the original had been taken and were projected onto other walls and painted in. Some had just drawn the mural from memory, and now the Dream lived on from Nogales, Arizona, to Berlin, Germany—El Checo counts 34 different versions of his tranquil mural. Jeff Conant, who was collared by the Mexican migra during the raid at Flores Magón and deported, went home to San Francisco and convinced Lawrence Ferlinghetti to let him resurrect "The Life and Dreams of the Perlas River Valley" on the façade of City Lights Bookstore facing Jack Kerouac Alley.

The Dream finally came home to Flores Magón in early August, although Hermann thought the new version a little too cubistic. The occasion was yet another inauguration, that of the Compañero Manuel Teacher Training Center in La Culebra, on the edge of the Montes Azules, where the autonomous council now sat. El Checo was a cherished guest.

The Compañero Manuel Teacher Training Center, named for a miliciano who fell in Ocosingo on January 1, 1994, is what autonomy looks like. The complex was built quiet as a whisper over several years by a Greek NGO working side by side with the village. The project had originally been cooked up by two Athens architectural students, who submitted the plans as part of their senior thesis. But Stavros and Yannis insisted that this was not just an academic exercise—they really wanted to build it. A magazine called *Smoke Dreams* helped them out. A Danish NGO was generous with seed money. The Zapatistas agreed.

The construction took many months, years. Now the classrooms and the dormitory were finished—the structure would be topped by a large "beehive" with space enough for public assemblies. Hermann pegged the architectural style as "Hellenic-Tzeltal." The Greeks printed up large-type posters of their popular poets and hung them in the still-empty library.

"I didn't even know there was a place called Greece or where it was," El Rubio, who organized the local work crews, told Gloria Muñoz. "When I first saw the Greeks, they frightened me. They were tall and white with blue eyes; I am not used to talking to people who are not of our race. But then I met the one they call Panayotis, and I could see he was a farmer because he wore sandals like us and his feet were hard."

Although the Tzeltales barely spoke *Castilla*, language proved a surmountable barrier. "I didn't know the names of the tools in Spanish, so I learned them in Greek. A 'spiri' is a hammer."

The Greeks and the Tzeltales invited their neighbors to the big blowout, and 1,000 Zapatista bases from nearby communities showed up on the first weekend in August to dedicate the Compañero Manuel center. The Greeks said the party would be an "anti-Olympics, a reference to the Anti-Terror Summer Olympic Games about to get under way back home in a locked-down Athens. The Cataláns came from Roberto Barrios, and the Danes who had helped underwrite more than 70 schools in the zone. The Madres of the Plaza de Mayo, who never seem to miss a Zapatista party, hobnobbed with the recently graduated education promoters.

Education is at the core of rebel consciousness and the training center had already turned out two generations of promoters, 150 in all, mostly young men and women ages 15 to 25 whose home villages sponsored them while they studied.

"We were *chiquitas* when the rebellion began, just babies. The struggle is what we have always known," Hortensia, a teenaged educator, explained to Muñoz. "The education that we think about is not just to teach reading and writing but so our *lucha* will be dignified by ideas and that we may speak better from the heart."

"All our graduates have the responsibility to share with their community what they have learned here. If not, this preparation makes no sense," considered Josue, a member of the Flores Magón education commission.

That night, they danced under the stars—and an occasional cloudburst—the teachers and the students, the Tzeltales and the Greeks, Franceses and Americanos, Catalanes and Choles, all the worlds the world needs to really be the world. This too is what autonomy looks like.

This Too Is What Autonomy Looks Like

Subcomandante Marcos arrived dog tired in La Realidad after an all-day ride over the top of the Sierra of Corralchén and strung up his hammock in the *champa* (hut) he keeps in town. He was still sawing wood early the next morning when the sanitation commission rapped loudly on the door. "Compañero Marcos, you have not covered your latrine with *ceniza* (ashes) and *cal* (quicklime)," the commissioners reminded him. The Sup sputtered an excuse or two—I'm sorry, I was too busy fighting for the people, or something like that. When informed that the sanitation commission would return that afternoon to check on his progress, the Sup sheepishly slunk off to clean out the outhouse. "You don't really want to cross these guys," he wrote. That too is what autonomy smells like.

Six flatbed trucks as big as battleships groan up the switchbacks toward San Cristóbal. They are carrying enormous anti-aircraft cannons to be delivered to the 31st military region at Rancho Nuevo. No one can quite figure out what they are for. After all, the Zapatista air force is made out of paper.

Meanwhile, up in Mexico City, under the chandeliers at the extravagant Casa Lamm, *La Jornada* convokes a roundtable of sympathetic intellectuals to try to define Zapatista autonomy. "Autonomy is body armor against neoliberalism," postulates Gilberto López y Rivas, the former EZLN adviser. "Autonomy is a nation model" ripostes the UNAM's Luis Villoro. The salon is jammed to the rafters and everyone in it has a distinct definition of what Zapatista autonomy looks like. This too is what autonomy looks like.

"For this it is very important / that the mal gobierno knows / the Zapatistas, we are rebels / and have our own government now." The *músicos* pumped up "The Cumbia of the Juntas de Buen Gobierno of Oventik," the Yamaha brayed and shrieked. And suddenly went stone dead. "*¡Pinche gobiernos!*" the keyboard player cursed at the dead electric lines. Oventik is still on the government's power grid, although the compas have not paid the electric bill since 1994 in defiance of the mal gobierno. *Ni modo*. This had happened before. The compas rolled out the marimbas.

On such evenings, when the Federal Electricity Commission's thrombosis spreads throughout vast swatches of the Altos and the jungle of southeastern Chiapas throwing the region into pitch darkness, there is only one point of light shining for all the world like Christmas Eve—La Realidad, where the turbines the Italians trucked in and the electrical workers union installed have gotten this rebel outpost off the government grid. This too is what autonomy looks like.

Fiesta De Los Caracoles

No one quite guzzles posh in the quantities that the Chamulas do. The Tzotziles of San Juan Chamula imbibe this high-octane moonshine morning, noon, and night, when a baby is born and a grandfather dies, at weddings and graduations, to worship the saints and to seal the sale of a cow. Posh permeates electoral activism in Chamula, and with municipal elections on tap in October, the white lightning was flowing like the mighty Orinoco in August.

Posh tends to incite mob rule. Now the Chamulans had taken the outgoing municipal president and five henchmen prisoner for failing to deliver on promised public works, and a drunken throng surrounded the jail and threatened to burn it down and roast the politicos locked up inside alive. When Public Security was summoned to quell the lynching, the police took one look at the sloshed crowd and shrugged. What can you do with such a *"bola of indios bolos"*?

Two mountains removed from the *bronca* at Chamula, the Zapatistas of Oventik were celebrating the first anniversary of the Caracol Resistance and Rebellion for Humanity and the Junta de Buen Gobierno Center of the Zapatista Heart Before the World. They were having the usual fun, playing basketball, dancing cumbias, and wolfing down tamales, but what distinguished the fun the rebels were having from the Chamula kind of fun was the absence of the *trago* that so enlivened and eventually immobilized their Indian brothers just over the hill.

The Zapatista Army of National Liberation had long ago liberated itself from the curse of strong drink. Indeed, if the EZLN had not early on barred alcohol from the base communities, it is doubtful that January 1, 1994, would have ever turned out the way it did. The trago was a weapon of the counterinsurgency just as much as Paz y Justicia and Luis H. Alvarez's corrugated roofing, and some had succumbed and defected to the other side.

The EZLN remained vigilant in keeping the beer trucks out of its bailiwick, but after Zedillo's February 1995 treachery, the bolos proliferated. You could see them sleeping it off face down in the dirt track between San Miguel and Garrucha in the Cañadas or staggering down the two-lane blacktop skirting Oventik, objects of derision and stern warnings to Zapatista youth to keep on the straight and narrow. Abstinence had been good for the communities. Domestic violence had dropped precipitously, and the zone now recorded the lowest level of reported incidents in Chiapas. Without having to deal with drunk and abusive husbands, the women were more mobile, and although participation in the autonomous structure was still hit or miss, the warp and woof of community life was more settled and together.

But the rebels had their own drug of choice—Coca-Cola. The Zapatista penchant for "the Real Thing" always seems like collective cognitive dissonance. Had not the Fox been the president of Coca-Cola Mexico before he became president of Mexico? Nonetheless, the red cans filled the shelves of Zapatista dispensaries in the highlands and jungle of southeastern Chiapas. The EZLN drank Coke in the vast tropical expanse of the Montes Azules and up in the cold climes of Los Altos. Trailers pulling double loads of this noxious beverage plied the highway between San Andrés and Chenalhó. You could turn in 25 tab tops of the stuff and redeem a kilo of beans. Coca-Cola, like the trago, was a weapon of the counterinsurgency, but on the first anniversary of the Caracoles, the compas toasted their future with cans of warm Coke.

I hung with the hoopsters on party day, a 50-team tournament in progress down on the cancha, a concrete island in a sea of mud.

Before the Israelis wrecked my back, I had played my share of b-ball in the zone, particularly down in Garrucha, where the scrimmaging was strenuous. When you went up for a shot, two guys tackled you down below and a third hacked you hard on the wrist. Passing the ball was an unknown art, and wild flings that sometimes miraculously clanked in (there were no nets) was the way the game was played.

Now, 10 and 20 years later, the Zapatista game had far more finesse, players moved the ball with an eye out for the open man or woman or worked it around for the best shot. Zap *basketboleros* now played B without maiming their opponents. In fact, Zapatista hoops were a lot like the rebellion itself, more controlled and assured, mature, with style.

The Anarchy of Chenalhó prevailed on the men's side that day. The women's tournament was still in progress when I had to go.

We stood on line to offer our solidarity and salutations to the Junta de Buen Gobierno Center of the Zapatista Heart Before the World. Inside the hobbit-like blockhouse with ears of corn gleaming on its walls, the members of the Oventik JBG were weary. The Juntas, sort of like rebel Seven-Elevens, were open 24 hours a day for business, and Dos Moisés was catching some zzzs tilted back from the desk. When the one woman member of the JBG woke him, he almost fell off his chair.

The room was snug. Christmas lights blinked on and off, and one wall was covered with an Italian antiglobalization banner. I didn't notice the Virgin of Guadalupe but I know her image was in there somewhere. A portrait of a supremely cross-eyed Sub Marcos hung over the junta table lending an *antisolemne* (anti-solemness) cast to the proceedings.

How was it going, this job of making autonomy, I asked Dos Moisés? "*Ay va*," he breathed, "we are learning to walk alone without the mal gobierno. We make many mistakes but we are learning how to serve the communities by *mandar obedeciendo*."

The most difficult task had been the coordination of the autonomous municipalities. "Each community had different ways of governing, and we had to learn to make them work together. The work of the juntas is different from the way the mal gobierno works. Here we are rescuing the traditions and the culture and keeping them alive in the way we govern."

Dos Moisés seemed most gratified that the rebels' old rivals, the PRIistas, now came to them for counsel. "They are Indians just like us and the mal gobierno treats them just as badly as they do us. We are grateful to help."

A New York Minute

Dos Moisés was absolutely right; the Zapatistas had a very different way of doing politics than in the so-called civilized world outside the Caracoles. The otherness really grabbed me a few days later when a half million of us gringos marched up Manhattan's Seventh Avenue in a collective urge to stain the nomination of George Bush for a second term as U.S. president.

The EZLN does not look kindly on such electoral spectacle. Elections are bought and sold, the votes stolen, voters are manipulated and become disappointed and cynical, the parties poison the communities with their bribes. Another world must be possible.

We moved uptown carrying multiple images of Bush as Satan, with horns, with bloody hands, as a skunk, a snake, a turd, with a stake through his vampire heart. "Whose streets? Our streets!" Someone said the New York Zapatistas were gathering on the corner of 23rd and Sixth, but who could find them in this mob? The great march paused before Madison Square Garden, where the Republican National Convention would begin tomorrow to give Bush the universal finger. "*¡Chinga tu pinche madre Boosh!*" "*¡Asesino!*"

Inside the Garden, in real life the unhallowed home of the New York Knicks, Dubya was playing the fear card hard, pushing the buttons of patriotic Amurikkkans, still swearing revenge for 9/11 (whose third anniversary would be marked in a few days).

Outside, New York's Finest were busy batoning, tear-gassing, entrapping protesters in weird orange plastic netting, and hauling them off to a toxic bus barn on the docks, 1,800 of them. Black helicopters lurched over the city. The smell of Chicago '68 was in the air.

An extra press credential got me inside for the final act of this grotesquely orchestrated death carnival. Bush strutted around the runway below, preening, pumping up the lynch mob while Code Pink women were manhandled by plainclothes police. Four More Years, the multitudes yowled! Four more wars, I hollered back, and a Republican male wearing a cardboard elephant hat tried to punch me out. "You're going to get us kicked out of here," my coconspirator Norm Stockwell warned. "I don't know, Norm," I marveled, "the Zapatistas just don't do politics like this."

The Voice of Those Without a Voice

"*Ya se mira el horizonte, combatiente Zapatista. . . .*" The stirring strains of the insurgent anthem mingled with the early morning banshee cries of randy roosters. "*Buenos días compañeros y compañeras.* I hope you have woken well this morning," the young insurgenta's voice chimed. It was still dark out. The slapping sound of tortillas being fashioned emanated from every kitchen in La Realidad. "We have many good programs for you today, so here's a reminder to get your music requests in early."

Radio Insurgente was back on the air.

The voice of "La Voz de Los Sin Voz" today was Toñita's. Years ago, when the Sup had written of how Zedillo's soldiers had ransacked her house and broken her toy teacup, the civil society had sent her many teacups. As a little girl growing up in the rebellion, Toñita had received national attention for refusing to kiss Marcos because his beard was too scratchy. Now she was a 16-year-old member of the Zapatista Army who had her own morning show on rebel radio.

Today, the women had prepared a radio skit titled "What Do Zapatista Women Want?" What do you think women want, Tonita asks "the First Lieutenant," who gets very flustered and keeps repeating the question over and over again: "What do Zapatista women want?" Toñita finally cuts him off in exasperation and sentences the "Teniente" to follow "that rat Bush" around and translate all his dumb words into Tzeltal.

The answer, stupid, to what Zapatista women want is R-E-S-P-E-C-T—but instead of spinning Aretha, Toñita picks Paquita la del Barrio, Mexico's most petulant torch singer. Radio Insurgente's musical palette is like that. At any moment, Pedro Infante and/or the Almanac Singers' version of "We Shall Not Be Moved" might occupy its airwaves. Only the Sup plays jazz.

Other highlights of today's programming include a report from the San Pedro de Michoacán health promotion team, an announcement from the Junta de Buen Gobierno that seeds (not transgenic) are still available to the compas at a discount, a recital of Pablo Neruda's poetry (2004 was the Chilean Nobelist's centennial and the Zapatistas intended to read all of the Canto General poem by poem), and in prime time, as usual, the one and only Sub Marcos reading his children's story not just for children, "Pánfila the Witch" (she could be beautiful in the day and ugly at night or vice versa, but her lovers had to choose which).

In between, there will be news stories culled from the Internet—Radio Insurgente opens a window on the world that brings place names like Baghdad and Gaza and Chechnya into Zapatista homes. The daily chatter from the autonomías fill in the community on who was born, who died, whose birthday it is today, always accompanied by "*Las Mañanitas.*"

Radio Insurgente broadcasts daily on the FM dial from sunup to sundown with an hourlong short-wave program (6.0 megahertz on the 49-meter band) Friday afternoons at 3 p.m. Zapatista Time for the rest of the world. Launched in February 2002, The Voice of Those Without Voice has had its ups and downs, mostly downs—techno-glitches are redundant. Radio Insurgente forms part of the EZLN's politico-military structure and is operated by insurgents for insurgents—the station's roots are in the rebels' pre-1994 communication systems, a kind of homegrown grandbaby of the Salvadoran revolution's Radio Venceremos.

The Mexican military tries to sabotage the Zapatista signal, so the insurgents move the transmitters every day. Radio Insurgente is entirely portable—the compas haul it up the mountain in the morning and take it back down at night. Despite the military's not-very-successful attempts to jam its signal, the soldiers themselves are avid listeners, maybe because Radio Insurgente's musical menu is the liveliest in southeastern Chiapas, or maybe just because its down-home flavor reminds them of, well, home. Bored troops out at the checkpoints or lolling around their bunks at San Quintín are often plugged in, and Zapatista radio carries a special message for them: "Soldier, you are like us. Do not fight against your own people. Open your eyes and join the Zapatista Army of National Liberation!"

Radio Insurgente audiences include the military and the paramilitaries, the police and the mal gobierno, truck drivers, road crews, internationalists, and any other visitor to the zone (the station has many listeners on the south side of the border) in addition to 1,111 (or 2,222) villages grouped in 29 autonomías in five distinct regions of southeastern Chiapas. Actually, there are three Radio Insurgentes, one for each language zone (Chol and Tzeltal are grouped together), and about half the programming day is in *lengua*.

The EZLN's radio component has a television side: the Zapatista Intergalactic Television System (SITZ), which periodically distributes "videos you can read"—"we're a unique television system," Marcos explains, "Our kind of television has no visuals and no audio."

In the fall of 2004, the SITZ produced four videos that had wide distribution—at least on the pages of *La Jornada*. "The Broken Pocket" is a treatise on neoliberal economics as seen through the eyes of a small Zapatista boy trying to buy candy in La Realidad. "The Velocity of Dreams" speaks to the brutish nature of the Fourth World War and curses Bush's occupation of Iraq. "But dreams move faster than nightmares," the Sup concludes. The video you can read is a shout against despair as Bush's reelection loomed.

"The Boot" takes its inspiration from a photograph of a solitary weather-beaten boot caught by the camera eye somewhere in the desert of Iraq and asks, Susan Sontag–like, its history. Is it the boot of an invader or of a resistance fighter? Was the foot that once filled the boot now dead or still alive? Whatever the details, the boot is a grim, graphic representation of Bush's New World Order.

The Zapatistas wear boots too, Marcos reminded his viewers, they even make and export them now. But the Zapatistas' relationship to their boots is very other. Sometimes the young women will walk barefoot for miles to play football, and only when they get to the match do they put their boots on.

"In the Defense of Giraffes" was produced for the "Recovery Channel—dedicated to recovering the memory of Giraffes," and speaks to how very otro giraffes are. The pelt of each giraffe describes unique patterns. Giraffes have excellent hearing, a keen sense of smell, acute vision, and very long legs. "Giraffes are about as other as an animal can get and still be in the animal kingdom." The Indians are a lot like giraffes—only the Indians are not a protected species. After the video's release, blue giraffes began to appear on the walls of the Zapatista zone.

Despite their electronic media pretensions, the rebels still have a lot of faith in the printed word. By late 2004, *Rebeldía* magazine had published 25 issues, was autonomous, and paid for itself.

What's black and white and read all over? The EZLN did not yet have its own daily newspaper, but *La Jornada* published most every communiqué they had ever emitted, had published the first interview with Sub-comandante Marcos and the CCRI, flogged rebel fortunes in editorials and special supplements, and kept Hermann Bellinghausen and his jeep in the conflict zone full time.

La Jornada was born on September 19, 1984, during an era when inves-tigative reporters made the *mal gobierno*'s kill lists. *Plata o Plomo*—silver or lead—was the government's operating strategy to curtail truth-telling back then. And many of the paper's new reporters had jumped ship from *Uno Más Uno* when its editor was bought out by the PRI government.

On *La Jornada's* first anniversary, September 19, 1985, Mexico City was savaged by a killer earthquake, and the paper gained new enemies by exposing widespread corruption in building construction.

La Jornada has been permanently attached to covering social upheaval in Mexico, and its back issues (which have been invaluable to the writing of this *Crónica*) tell you the full story of a generation of the struggle for a democratic Mexico.

September 19, 2004, was *La Jornada's* 20th birthday, and the EZLN, along with big-time brains like Noam Chomsky and Saramago, sent its best wishes. Marcos was worried about the future of the industry though. "There will come a time when newspapers are only read by those who write them," he predicted darkly. Those of us who have labored long in these once fertile fields share the Subcomandante's preoccupation.

The Day of the Dead of the American Left

November 1 and 2 are the Mexican Days of the Dead—the first is for the *angelitos*, the children unblemished by sin who go straight to Paradise, and the second is for the rest of us poor sinners. Los Días de los Muertos are rooted deep in Aztec (Mexica) tradition—autumn was the season of the dead, when those who had gone on to Mictlán (the west, the direc-tion of the dead) were remembered but not necessarily mourned.

Today's Mexicans keep the old ways alive by building altars to their dead ancestors filled with *cempaxutl* flowers (a kind of marigold), *pan de los muertos* (sweet bread of the dead), turkey mole, copal incense, candles, tequila, and the *difunto*'s favorite cigarettes and songs so the *calacas* (skeletons) can get up and dance once more. Mexicans do not blink at death. Born-in-the-bone fatalists, they expect it—but they also mock La Muerte as a way of keeping it at bay. Suffice to say the most enduring icons of the Días de los Muertos were drawn by Jose Guadalupe Posada as political cartoons lampooning the rich during the early days of the Mexican Revolution.

November 2, 2004, the final Mexican Day of the Dead, coincided with election day in El Norte: Bush vs. a devious onetime Vietnam Vet Against the War, a period in his life he chose to white out in his official bio. But despite John Kerry's omissions, Bush's gung-ho Swift Boat Veterans hung him in effigy as a traitor every night in prime-time TV hit pieces.

Iraq was at the core of the debate between these two bozos. Kerry bragged that he could do a better job of annihilating the Iraqis than the draft dodger Bush—"I will hunt down and kill the enemy without mercy." Those who stood against the war deliberately didn't hear what the Democratic Party's candidate was telling them. They believed he was lying or maybe it was just a slip of the tongue. He didn't really mean it in his heart of hearts—presuming that he had one. Theirs was a faith-based vote every bit as much as those Christian soldiers who cast their ballot for Bushwa. The sad truth was that whoever won the White House, the war would go on and on.

As Argentina's piqueteros and the Zapatista Army of National Liberation never fail to remind us, our dreams are not in the ballot box.

What the Bushites had to avoid at all costs was losing the popular vote all over again, and, in ballyhooing same-sex weddings, San Francisco's Ivory Tower mayor, Gavin Newsom, handed Karl Rove a wedge issue that ran up his boss's vote in the 11 states where he was able to place an anti-gay marriage initiative. This god-fearing groundswell would nullify the Michael Moore *Fahrenheit 9/11* factor and put Bush on top.

The clincher was Osama Bin Laden's election eve address to the nation. Draped in a golden prayer shawl and radiating Koranic karma, his beard fulminating like Jehovah on Jihad, the Al Qaeda boss of all bosses put the fear of god and the god of fear in every Caucasian voter's heart. Al Qaeda made no qualms about endorsing Bush—"His stupidity and his religious crusade will be beneficial to Muslims."

As polls closed in California, ABC-Disney was calling Florida for Dubya. The annual Día de los Muertos procession snaked its way through the darkened alleyways of La Mission. I wore a crown of skulls and a noose around my neck, and I was exactly where I needed to be. While the nation divided itself into states of red and blueness, our communities in resistance provided the best defense against the fascist insect that would prowl the White House for four more years.

One could say that November 2 was the Day of the Dead of the American Left if, in fact, the Left had not been long dead. Perhaps *The Night of the Living Dead* was a more fitting movie title. We were all that poor black guy trapped in the flimsy house in the middle of the cemetery with George Romero's zombies crashing through the walls, about to devour us.

Booshwa

Every Tuesday afternoon, they had gathered in the back room of a politically hip café to quaff cappuccinos, write political manifestos, paint banners, and brainstorm on how to beat Bush in November. They were a rainbow bunch—students, feminists, gay activists, well-meaning matrons, old lefties united in their intentions to dump the U.S. president. But what was wrong with this picture was that it wasn't being framed in San Francisco's Mission district or Boston's Jamaica Plains, but in downtown Mexico City, and those who huddled each week at the Café de la Red were Mexican citizens, who had no vote on November 2.

Baby Bush was not a popular politician south of the border down Mexico way, and the natives had a tough time swallowing the results of the Day of the Dead election. Had not the peoples of the world risen as one to demand that this cancer be extirpated from the corpus delecti of a planet Boosh had so wounded in his first four years of tyranny?

But what the Mexicans did not understand is that the people of the United States of North America had little in common with the world's peoples—they lived in their own delusionary world, hermetically sealed off from the rest of humanity. Such separation caused mass psychosis—40% of all "Hispanic" voters living inside the bubble had cast their vote for this killer.

The grateful president rewarded his Hispanics with attorney general Alberto Gonzales, who as Bush's clemency officer when he was governor of Texas had signed off on more than 100 death warrants of mostly black and brown prisoners, some of them Mexican citizens. Gonzales is believed to be the first attorney general of Mexican ancestry to consider the Geneva Convention quaint.

Was the U.S. 2004 election on the up and up? Global Exchange, which after the 2000 Florida fiasco vowed never again to send a team of observers to Mexico to evaluate the legitimacy of the election process there, invited a select posse of Mexican observers to pass judgment on the U.S. balloting, among them Sergio Aguayo, a founder of Alianza Cívica (Civic Alliance), which had been instrumental in ritualizing foreign observation on this side of the border. Don Sergio observed November 2 from inner-city precincts in Cleveland, Ohio. State election officials (the state election secretary also headed up the Bush campaign) had allocated few polling stations to what is essentially an African American district, and once people had found the precinct they were forced to stand on line for long hours under a hard rain. In Mexico, this technique is called the *ratón loco*, the "crazy mouse," in which voters scamper from place to place looking for a voting booth. Don Sergio did not know how many voters had given up and gone home, but in the observation team's final report, the credibility of the U.S. election was judged to be on a par with recent voting in Kazakhstan.

In 2000, Mexicans—indeed, the much cited world's peoples—had let the U.S. electorate off the hook because they too had had one election after another stolen from them. But on the Mexican Day of the Dead 2004, the gavachos had unquestionably given the bloody Bush four more years in which to torment and torture them. Bush's reelection was a declaration of war on the world and its people, and every single gringo was guilty now.

George Bush did not waste much time in making his murderous intentions manifest. Five days after his triumphal reelection, the U.S. president launched a genocidal assault on Fallujah. Mosques and hospitals were blown to dust and 6,000 civilians slaughtered, many burnt beyond recognition by napalm and white phosphorous ("Whiskey Pete"), which goes right through the victim's clothes and burns to the bone.

Montes Azules: The Endgame

The endgame was on pace in the Montes Azules. All throughout 2004, the environmental colonialists of Conservation International and their Lacandón enforcers had pushed and prodded settler communities into forsaking the rain forest. Way back in January, 25 families had been removed from Ignacio Allende by the Mexican navy and their homes burnt behind them. Just to add to the bitter draught of surrender, the villagers were obliged to apologize to the Lacandones for having "usurped" their lands. The Fox government described the eviction and incineration of Ignacio Allende as "a peaceful relocation."

Emboldened by this successful aggression, CI and the SEMARNAT petitioned the military to destroy the landing strip at Nuevo San Gregorio at the heart of the Montes Azules. Established in the 1970s by Tzotziles who trekked in from Huixtan, Nuevo San Gregorio—an ARIC-Independiente beachhead—was the longest-lived legal settlement in the reserve.

Seeking to put a pillow on its *mano duro* (hard hand) dealings with settler communities, the Foxistas and their ecotourist allies began buying out settler communities so that the Indians' forced removals from the Indian forest would appear to be "voluntary."

Some of the first evacuees to receive this royal treatment were 190 former residents of the small settlement San Francisco Caracol (not a Zapatista Caracol, but so named for the snails in the nearby river), political affiliation unknown, who were removed from their Montes Azules homes on July 4 and airlifted in a convoy of 18 helicopters to their spanking-new "model village" in Marqués de Comillas just east and south of the reserve. Once part of the rain forest, until big timber took away most of the trees, the municipality of Marqués de Comillas is still dotted with islands of jungle that remain under environmental protection—in one of which the recently uprooted villagers were about to be resettled on a tract named with deadpan irony for Absalón Castellanos Domínguez, the butcher of the Mayans. "It is not logical," mused Miguel Angel García, director of Maderas del Pueblo (Wood of the People). "They have moved these people from one reserve, where they were cutting down trees to plant corn, to a smaller reserve, where they will cut down a greater percentage of the trees to clear land for their corn."

Governor Pablo, environmental secretary Alfredo Cárdenas, representatives of the Lacandón community, and a Conservation Internationalist or two were lurking in the trees to greet the new arrivals. Televisa and TV Azteca had been enlisted to communicate this historic "relocation." The terror in the eyes of those who had just been helicoptered out of the only home many had ever known (most had never flown before) was as startling as it must have been when the indígenas saw their first white man. Once the visuals had been shot, the government men wouldn't let the press near the Indians.

Santa Martha would be the name of their new village, they were told. Whether this "model village" (what the Guatemalan Kaibiles called Vietnam-style "strategic hamlets" during the genocide just across the border in the late 1970s and early '80s) had been blessed with the name of a little-known saint or that of President Fox's wife remains speculation—another thesis is that Santa Martha was named for the very active Agrarian Reform agent in the region, Martha Cecilia Díaz. Each family would receive a new home equipped with a 75,000-peso environmental toilet and a small stipend to tide them over until they had cut down enough trees to plant a crop.

Fate is a twisted branch in this neck of the woods. According to the writings of Jan de Vos, the ex-Jesuit historian of the Lacandón, Santa Martha and the Absalón Castellanos Domínguez Environmental Reserve, in which it is located, had been installed atop the ruins of Sac

Balhan, where the first Lacandones (the present ones were interlopers) had held off the Conquistadores between 1586 and 1687.

Other Indians pushed out of Montes Azules that year would be resettled in a model village called simply "New Montes Azules."

While the villages were being "peacefully" pieced off and relocated one by one, the Eco-Conquerors were moving in. A second safari of 50 Japanese ecotourists sponsored by the Dunlop Tire Company was spotted tooling around Chajul in the spring. Infrastructure projects were stripping the fragile environment that Conservation International had sworn to keep pristine. A road about as close to a freeway as you could build through this environmentally sensitive reserve would connect up Lake Miramar, the Montes Azules' top tourist attraction, with the four-lane thoroughfare that now straddles the Guatemalan border and would eventually hook up with the Pan-American Highway.

Governor Pablo boasted of 52 ecotourist projects under construction, including ecotourist inns along the Jataté River. State moneys had been allocated to train the Lacandones of Nueva Palestina in "kayaking, rappelling, and trekking" so they could function as "adventure tourism guides."

The most significant hunk of new infrastructure in the reserve was a heavy-duty bridge over the Jataté where it pours into the Lacantún—when completed the bridge at Amatitlán would be the largest man-made structure in the Montes Azules.

The phantom of "B. Traven" (the alias of a German anarchist named Ret Marut), a much loved author in Mexico, whose 40 novels and collections of short stories often turn on social conflict in this wild corner of Chiapas, hung indelibly over this crossing. Traven's ashes had been scattered here on the banks of the Jataté after his death in the 1960s. Hermann remembered that Traven had once written a story, "A Bridge in the Jungle," in which a bridge much like this one, designed to bring progress to the Indians, precipitates tragedy.

The *Jornada* reporter pulled himself up onto the construction platform and found the chief engineer. His job was to build bridges but he wasn't so sure about this one, he told Bellinghausen. What was it really for? To open the forest to tourists and timber companies? To sell the Indians Coca-Cola?

By late 2004, at best count 12 Zapatista-affiliated settlements remained in the reserve—five in the north of the Montes Azules and seven tiny outposts in the ticklish geography around Chajul in the south. All were effectively autonomous and on their own because of the great distances between themselves and the nearest Caracol.

Under the reorganization of autonomy that had created the Caracoles and the JBGs, the Mother of Caracoles–Sea of Our Dreams meeting at La Realidad was responsible for the communities in the south of the reserve; the northern settlements, which were not, at least for now, in the line of Fox's fire, pertained to La Garrucha/Francisco Gómez.

Faced with the forced eviction of their comrades—or worse, co-optation by the bad government—the Junta at La Realidad announced its own relocation plan, "not because we are afraid of the mal gobierno but because it will be better for our compañeros. Right now, anyone could come for them—Bush, Bin Laden, the Fox, or anyone who dedicates themselves to the slaughter of the innocents. We have a responsibility for their safety." For now, four of the seven settlements would be consolidated to better provide for their defense. The others would receive land in the autonomías Libertad De Las Mayas and San Pedro de Michoacán upon which to reestablish their village.

In the end, the reasoning behind the Zapatistas' relocation plan was not all that distinct from Conservation International's—to preserve what was left of the Lacandón rain forest. The difference was whom they wanted it preserved for. Behind its green rhetoric, CI had opened the door to the transnational tourist trade. On the other hand, the EZLN wanted to preserve the Montes Azules because it was their home.

The Mother of Caracoles–Sea of Our Dreams dispatched its beloved heavy-duty truck, *Chómpiras,* into the still-muddy jungle to bring the compañeros out—the first load counted 50 comrades from six families, carrying with them their sacks of corn, cooking pots, *coas* (planting sticks) and machetes, a few skeletal dogs, their chickens and their babies and the clothes on their backs. By December, they had settled into their new homes outside of the official boundaries of the valuable real estate of which they had been dispossessed but still very much in the resistance.

Amado (Much Loved)

The Christmas season in San Cristóbal was packed with *posadas* and piñatas, *ponche* and paisanos recently returned from El Norte with fists full of pesos and ready to party. The cobbled colonial streets around the plaza swarmed with international tourists, and the carrying capacity of the narrow sidewalks was overrun by the sheer press of humanity. But in all this sea of faces, there was one that was missing. My dear colleague Amado Avendaño had passed on in early May. I read about his death in an Internet café in Cerro de Pasco, Peru, 15,000 feet up in the Andes. The woman who minded the machines handed me a tissue to dry my tears.

Amado ("much loved") Avendaño, a native of tropical Pacific Coast Chiapas, came to San Cristóbal in the 1960s and began a family with Conchita Villafuerte, a daughter of an old Coleto dynasty—Conchita was always the battery behind Amado's blissful smile. An attorney by profession and a journalist by *oficio* (a position of responsibility), Amado defended the *jodidos* of San Cristóbal from the burghers' justice. Sometimes, Bishop Samuel Ruiz would have to lend him money to bail his mostly indigenous clients out of jail. For a brief period, Amado was chosen by the PRI (there were no other parties then) to serve as municipal president, but he soon returned to journalism with a vengeance.

For 30 years, Amado and Conchita published *El Tiempo*—sometimes it was a weekly and sometimes a monthly—and later, the single-sheet *La Foja*, both of which relentlessly unmasked the foibles of the wealthy Coleto caste and defended the Indians from their depredations. For their efforts, their home in the San Diego barrio where they both raised a family (three daughters and a son-in-law became journalists) and published their subversive newspapers was shot at and broken into and there were always death threats on the telephone. An honest reporter could ask for nothing less.

"Amado Avendaño had a house in his heart, and long ago he opened it to the people who are the color of the earth," Marcos mourned upon hearing of his death.

Soon after midnight on January 1, 1994, photographer Antonio Turok rang up Amado with the news. "Maestro, you won't believe this but rebels have taken San Cristóbal. They are wearing ski masks and palia-cates but you can tell they are Indians." Amado wondered how drunk Turok was, but at first light he went downtown to see for himself.

City hall and the streets around it were occupied by masked Indian fighters. One in particular greeted him by name. "We knew Don Amado by his word, and we knew he had an attentive and respectful ear for the pain of the indígenas long before the war against oblivion came to San Cristóbal that morning," the Sup reminisced in an obit in *La Jornada*.

"We saw him that morning with his glasses and that little English hat he always wore. He had on a scarf and a kind of overcoat and he hardly spoke. But we could see that he had many questions in his eyes." Several days later, Marcos wrote Amado and inquired if *El Tiempo* might want to publish the EZLN's first communiqués: "The compañeros have given me the task to find a place to publish our words, and your newspaper would be the right place. We don't ask that you agree with us, just to give us a place to be heard."

In the summer of 1994, the EZLN suggested that Amado run for governor of Chiapas, the only time the rebels have ever endorsed anyone for public office, and he accepted as a candidate of the civil society. The PRD offered him its registration (times were different back then).

With less than a month to go in late July, Amado was beating the bushes for votes out on the Pacific coast, when he was summoned by interim governor Javier López Moreno up to Tuxtla for a candidates' breakfast. Early the next morning, he and his team were on the road when their rental car was hit head on by a licenseless 18-wheeler deadheading down the coast highway toward Tapachula. The driver fled upon impact and the truck's registration was traced to a phony address in Nezahual-cóyotl just outside Mexico City. Amado's nephew was killed outright as was his campaign manager, Agustín Rubio, who back in 1985 had taken a day off from hectic farmworker organizing to show me the underbelly of Chiapas. Amado's body was shattered. He was flown up to Mexico City in a coma—Salinas, perhaps worried that he would be tied to the caper, even visited him in hospital but, mercifully, Amado was still in a coma. It was four months before Amado could speak again, and he lost his left eye.

Nonetheless, on August 21, having just emerged from a coma, Amado Avendaño, his stature swollen by the *coraje* (outrage plus courage) of the people, was elected governor of Chiapas, a victory of which he was immediately despoiled by the usual PRI fraud.

Several years later, ace investigative reporter Pepe Reveles uncovered undeniable evidence that Amado had been set up that terrible July morning by an old confederate, Jorge Enrique Hernández, once a polit-ical prisoner and embattled journalist who had defected to the PRI— under Croquetas, Hernández would become state attorney general and later director of public security, the post he held when the massacre at Acteal came down.

In the face of the election swindle, the EZLN prevailed upon Amado to become the governor in rebellion, and he was installed that December in a ceremony full of copal and feathers, dancers and drummers, and the staffs of government. The government in rebellion set up offices out in the abandoned National Indigenous Institute (INI) compound adjacent to San Cris's Indian market. There was no phone and Amado had to borrow coins to make important calls. We turned on the lights by stealing juice from a close-by private line.

In his threadbare suit with his indefatigable good humor and now-dead eye, Amado set sail to conquer the world, and soon the government in rebellion had a branch office in Barcelona and some modest funding. Amado would always argue that his was a government in transition— that is, it would be the last government. After he was done, the people would decide for themselves.

Six years later, in December of 2000, Amado's stint as rebel governor was finally up and he turned the reins over to no one. The EZLN praised him to the heavens for having disseminated their Word in the world. Despite having dissolved his office, Amado Avendaño would always be the governor to those who shared the Zapatistas' reality.

We saw each other at the stations of the Zapatista year up in Oventik or down in San Cristóbal, embraced and caught up on where our lives had led us. During the first days of the rebellion, I had shown up on his doorstep with Ramsey Clark in tow, and he had given us the run of the place, fed us, let us use his phone and fax, and even provided a guide to take us into Zapatista territory. I dedicated my first book to Amado Avendaño.

Amado was always optimistic that change was going to come, but when he spoke about the assassination attempt that had nearly cost him everything, he sounded bitter and hurt.

Marcos had heard about Amado's passing on the radio, but reception was bad and he wasn't really sure that he had heard it right. Maybe they wouldn't see Don Amado anymore this year, he wrote, but the Sup planted a branch just outside his hut up in the mountain so that in case he did return, he would know where to find him.

The summer after Amado passed, I ran into Conchita up at the Caracol party in Oventik and confessed how much I missed my old friend. But he is still here, she told me pointing to her heart. Conchita has integrated Amado, Ofelia Medina explained.

I didn't go up to Oventik that New Year's Eve for the first time in years. It didn't feel right without Amado and, besides, I didn't have a ride. Instead, I walked San Cristóbal's crowded streets and rapped with Amado's ghost.

There was a smallish crowd at the Caracol Rebellion and Resistance for Humanity, Hermann reported, but I wondered about how dense it was. The Zapatistas are increasingly together, compacted; they, like Conchita, have integrated their *muertos*. There may have been only 3,000 at Oventik, but you can be sure they carried around many more inside.

11. Winter/Spring 2005

The Literary Life

Guadalajara's International Book Fair (FIL) is the premiere event of Mexico's literary year and industry. Each autumn, planeloads of Nobelists and near Nobelists, particularly those who write in the Spanish and Portuguese languages, are flown in to present weighty *ponencias* (papers), read from their latest opuses, and sign tons of books to the delight of their publishers—Saramago, García Márquez, Vargas Llosa, Peru's Bryce Echenique, Spain's Arturo Pérez-Reverte, the Mexican warhorses Carlos Fuentes, Monsiváis, Poniatowska, and Paco Taibo are among the marquee *luminarios* on the FIL bill each year.

One high point of FIL 2005 was a tribute to the late Manuel Vázquez Montalbán, the corpulent Catalán detective writer who had keeled over at the Bangkok airport a few months earlier. Vázquez Montalbán's publisher, Sealtiel Alatriste, read encomiums from several well-known Mexican writers, among them Subcomandante Insurgent Marcos. In the late 1990s, the creator of the Barcelona-based gumshoe Pepe Carvalho had traveled to Chiapas, and his book-length interview with the Sup, *El Señor de los Espejos* ("The Lord of the Mirrors"), had resonance with the rebels.

"He was a bridge for our words," Marcos wrote from the mountains of the southeast.

Actually, Marcos wrote a lot more, but Alatriste had seen fit to excise certain offending text, which he considered not germane to the *obra* of Vázquez Montalbán. Indeed, most of the comunicado targeted not just the fair but also Guadalajara itself, where in May 2004, 100-plus global-phobes had been beaten, tortured, and jailed during a Latin America–European Union summit—11 were still imprisoned. Despite pleas from the National Human Rights Commission for their release, the archly PANista governor Francisco Ramírez Acuña was determined to keep these troublemakers locked up indefinitely.

The outspoken Saramago labeled Alatriste's censorship of the Sup a disgrace and walked out of the FIL. When a dozen globalphobes—now rechristened *altermundistas,* or "other worlders"—burst into the salon demanding freedom for their comrades, the other invited literary lights quickly gathered their papers and glided off toward their next presentations.

Paco Ignacio Taibo II has a generous œuvre. Every book on the high shelves behind his desk in the capital's Condesa colony is written either by Paco Ignacio Taibo I or Paco Ignacio Taibo II—the elder Taibo fled Franco when the republic fell. Taibo II is a keen historian of the Mexican left but is particularly enamored of "black" or detective fiction, a genre known here as the *policiaca*. Taibo II's shamus is a softhearted, sad-eyed Mexican Basque Irisher, Héctor Belascoarán Shayne, whom he has already killed off at least once.

Soon after the ruckus at the FIL, Paco was visited by the Sup's *correo* (courier), probably a diminutive nun who had faithfully served Tatic for years even while distributing Marcos's comunicados. The courier pre-sented a letter from Sub Marcos in which the guerrillero littérateur recalled how Vázquez Montalbán had once suggested that Pepe Carvalho join hands with a Zapatista detective in a co-authored policiaca. Now that the Catalán was gone, might Taibo II be interested in picking up the project as an homage to the burly Barcelonan? If so, the correo had a second letter for Paco Taibo II. The second letter contained the first chapter of *Muertos Incómodos* (Incommodious Dead Guys).

"The insanity of the offer had an enormous attraction for me," Taibo II told the *New York Times*. Paco put aside a Pancho Villa bio for which he was on deadline and went to work. The writing of *Incommodious Dead Guys* was a kind of rapid-fire literary ping-pong match. Taibo II would never meet or even speak with Marcos about the text. "We communicated like Chinese spies."

Muertos Incómodos—Falta Lo Que Falta (missing that which it is missing), "a novel of four hands and 20 fingers," began running in *La Jornada* on the last Sunday in November—11 more chapters would appear from December to February. The writer—be it Marcos or Paco—had five days in which to pen the chapter, and there was no room for revision. Marcos wrote from "the mountains of the southeast" and Taibo from the center of power in the capital, and the center-periphery dichotomy is present on every page.

Although the EZLN had quietly been building autonomy in southern Mexico for several years, they got little ink for their endeavors. On the other hand, the Taibo-Marcos collaboration piqued the jaded taste buds of the international press. "What to do when the revolution stalls? Write a novel!" the *New York Times* snidely headlined, dismissing the work as "thinly veiled propaganda."

The Sup's detective is not even a real detective. Elías Contreras carries a business card that identifies him as a member of "the Zapatista Investigation Commission, Mountains of the Mexican Southeast, corner with Guatemala." Nor was Elías even alive—he had been killed January 1, 1994, during the taking of Las Margaritas alongside Subcomandante Pedro. In fact, a lot of the characters in *Incommodious Dead Guys* were already dead—Belascoarán Shayne had been resuscitated after Taibo had him killed off in *No Habrá Final Feliz* (literally, "This Is Not Going to Have a Happy Ending"). Belascoarán's phone machine rang off the hook with messages from a dead guerrillero who called every day inquiring about a certain Morales with whom he shared a cell in the black palace of Lecumberri prison after the 1968 student uprising.

As it turns out, Morales is precisely whom Elías is tracking. Morales, AKA "El Mal y El Malo" ("the Evil and the Evildoer"), is a kind of Zelig of Mexican intelligence agencies who had been an actor at Tlatelolco, infiltrated the student movement, was undercover with the White Brigade during the Dirty War, and had his fingers in every other political crime against the left on the books (including Digna Ochoa and Acteal). For both the Sup and Taibo II, Morales acquires the aura that Moriarty had for Sherlock Holmes.

Actually, the character was rooted in a very real ne'er-do-well: Salvador Morales Garibay, "Comandante Daniel," who had come out of the Metropolitan University with the Sup and deserted the EZLN in 1993, later spilling the beans about Marcos's true identity to Military Intelligence, for which he was commissioned a captain in the Second Section, the inner sanctum of Mexican spookdom. Morales Garabay is believed to be living in Los Angeles under witness protection.

It takes about seven chapters for Elías Contreras to catch up with Belascoarán on the esplanade of Mexico City's Monument to the Revolution, where they exchange files in re El Mal y El Malo. The indigenous investigator is lost and confused in "El Monstruo" (the monster city), shaken by the hustle and bustle. A taxi ride frightens him to death— "Well, I am dead, but the driver didn't know that."

In his travels, Elías picks up Morales's scent with the help of El Chino, a Chinese-Mexican Trotskyite, and El Ruso, a Purépecha Indian Maoist who runs a Guadalajara torta stand—significant clues are provided by an informant at the Bin Laden Taquería in Ciudad Juárez. Elías is taken in and falls in love with La Magdalena, a transvestite *sexoservidora*.

Eventually, the Zapatista investigator learns that Morales is in Chiapas scheming to steal the riches of the Montes Azules, and he and La Magdalena return to the scene of the crime, where Marcos creates a super-secret team code-named NADIE (No One) and, in a cartoon climax, NADIE corners Morales in an Ocosingo cantina, and he is sentenced to 10 years at hard labor in a Zapatista autonomía. Tragically, La Magdalena is shot in the fracas trying to defend Elías. El Fin.

Well, not quite. You see, Taibo II got stuck with chapter 12, so he had to kill off El Mal y El Malo in his own way, which was to have Belascoarán kick Morales down 41 flights of stairs at the Latin American Tower, a skyscraper that spires over the Centro Histórico. El Fin II.

Most of the action in *Incommodious Dead Guys* is crammed into the final few paragraphs. The narrative—particularly the chapters written by the Sup, which are sometimes twice as long as Paco's—is filled with deviations, parenthesis, ruminations, and downright preaching to the chorus. Subcomandante Marcos is a superb epistemologist, but his style is a bit over the top for a buttoned-down genre like detective fiction, which needs to be controlled, laconic, hard-boiled, and full of false clues.

Whatever the critics discerned, *Muertos Incómodos* was being translated into English, Greek, Turkish, and at least two Romance languages before it was even finished. Proceeds from the sales would be donated to Enlace Civil, the NGO that serves as the link-up between NGOs and the EZLN, whose bank accounts were about to be frozen by Bancomer, now owned by the Spanish Banco Bilbao-Vizcaya. But that was another mystery.

Science Fiction

On March 3, Elio Henríquez, the *Jornada* correspondent in San Cristóbal de las Casas and Amado's son-in-law, reported that the Coleto mayor of that old colonial city, a PRIista whose Christian name was Sergio Lobato, would host a banquet for Bishop Emeritus Samuel Ruiz García at which Tatic would be presented with a diploma for his contributions to the construction of social peace in Chiapas and the world.

"I feel like I am living a moment of science fiction," Tatic side-mouthed to Elio at the ceremony.

Las Muertas

On the frigid morning of January 5 in Ciudad Juárez, a stone's throw away from the U.S. border, the battered, still-breathing body of an unidentified woman was pulled from a back alley garbage container in that border city's tawdry downtown. The victim, who died on the way to hospital, was approximately 25 years old, measured 154 centimeters, and had long black hair and a scar from a recent Cesarean across her abdomen. She carried no identification and had no name. She was the first Muerta (dead girl) found in Juárez in 2005 and joined a macabre roster of 417 women murdered in the city since 1993.

The victims had been beaten with bottles and fists, butchered with kitchen knives, shot and pistol-whipped, raped and throttled, burnt, tortured, stomped on, sliced up, or else drugged and kidnapped for Satanic rituals and snuff movies, trussed up and shot full of heroin or hacked down to torsos with handsaws and dumped out in the desert at the edge of this hardscrabble border town.

Others never showed up anywhere. More than 4,100 disappearances of women had been reported in Juárez in the past 12 years, according to the Madres of las Muertas.

Former federal prosecutor María López Urbina says only 35 are still missing.

Down the years, Ciudad Juárez has achieved a dubious reputation for world-class misogyny. Jane Fonda, Sally Fields, and Eve Ensler (*The Vagina Monologues*) marched through Juárez along with tens of thousands of feminists and human rights activists on the 10th anniversary of the first femicide in 2003. The total number of dead girls back then was 370. Two years later, it was 417.

Juárez is a sprawling, gritty slice of border where the maquiladora industry has been grinding out consumer goods sold exclusively in the U.S. for 40 years. But a lot of stuff that isn't made in the maqs comes and goes across the border bridges—drugs, people, guns. A lot of dead bodies turn up on Juárez streets and not all of them are women. Life, like the wage scale, is really cheap here.

Work in the maquiladoras draws women from all over Mexico, many escaping from domestic abuse back home, and their dreams too often go bust in this city of "opportunities," where women workers are always replaceable by the next wave of internal migrants to wash up at the maquiladora doors.

A very large number of Las Muertas (no one knows how many—53 dead girls have never even been identified) worked at one time or another in the maquiladoras, throwaway women in the corporate rush to the bottom line. At least a dozen were murdered still wearing their *batas*, the coverall that is mandatory in the maqs. Others were purportedly slain by bus drivers hired by the maquiladoras—the fares were deducted from the workers' paychecks—to drive them "safely" home after evening shifts to their ill-lit *colonias*, where their corpses were later found discarded in barren lots like "the cotton field" and "the hill of the black Christ." Whodunnit?

An Egyptian chemist is in jail for a few of the murders, as is a gang called "The Rebels," whose members say they were hired by the Egyptian to kill the dead girls. The first victims were young, slim, with long black hair. There are a series of murders in which the victims' breasts were mutilated. An FBI agent who was consulted by Juárez authorities thought at least two serial murderers were at work, perhaps U.S. psychopaths who made frequent trips to the border.

Three Mexican presidents, three Chihuahua governors, and a carload of special prosecutors have failed to stem the killings. Evidence is lost, names mixed up. Many femicides are never investigated. Women disappear from bars and discos, and the PAN authorities that have governed Juárez while corpses pile up dismiss them as *putas* whose unspeakable end was their own fault.

Two thousand maquiladoras strung along 3,000 kilometers of border demand a pool of fresh human flesh to function. The border is a kill zone for women workers—more than 200 women have met with violent deaths in Sonora, next door to Chihuahua, in the past five years, and dozens of Muertas are turning up in Chihuahua city, a few hundred kliks south of Juárez.

But femicide is epidemic in all of macho Mexico, where two-thirds of the women interviewed by the federal Integral Family Direction (DIF) report they are physically abused by their partners—one in five say they are beaten daily. Four women die each day in Mexico at the hands of their mates or former partners. Mexico state, the nation's most populous, reported 497 violent deaths of women in 2004 alone—more than a whole decade of Muertas in Juárez. Whodunnit? Men.

Mexico's women are not the only victims of this slaughter. Guatemala counted 527 Muertas in 2004, an average year. In Salvador, the dead girls number into the hundreds annually—Mexico, Guatemala, and Salvador are maquiladora countries where throwaway women abound. "It's like the son of Jack the Ripper is loose in the Americas," writes novelist Sergio Ramírez—45 women were murdered in Nicaragua in the first months of 2004.

To be sure, the bloodletting north of the border in the U.S., where there are more firearms in circulation than citizens, is even more acute. In the U.S. 4,000 women die violent deaths every year, 11 a day.

Chiapas has not escaped this scourge. Here 350 women have been murdered since the new millennium dawned; 13 were murdered in San Cristóbal de las Casas between January and October 2004, the equivalent of 130 Muertas in Juárez, given the population disparity, and rapes and harassment were skyrocketing, according to Coleto women's organizations. "It seems the more violent a man is to the woman, the more of a man he thinks he is," one battered Tzotzil woman told *La Jornada*.

On March 8, International Women's Day, a thousand indigenous women gathered at Acteal to give voice to their pain. In Mexico City, 50 sexoservidoras donned ski masks and marched to Bellas Artes. At the other end of the country in Ciudad Juárez, the mothers of Las Muertas stood on street corners like black-clad birds, passing out photos of their daughters and asking passersby if anyone had seen them.

The Plots Against El Peje

"Pejelagarto: (1) a gar-like fish found in the swamps of Tabasco state, considered a local delicacy when roasted whole." (2) Andrés Manuel

López Obrador, the mayor of Mexico City, whom President Vicente Fox would love to roast whole.

Ever since the 2003 midterms, El Peje had been in the gunsights of the PRI and the PAN (López Obrador grouped them together as the "PRIAN"), who had made it their patriotic duty to prevent a López Obrador presidency by any means necessary. The projected election of López Obrador in July 2006 stood to be the first presidential victory for Mexican progressives since Lázaro Cárdenas back in the Depression and the latest triumph for the anti-neoliberal Latin American left.

Although he has been pumped up to hero status, Andrés Manuel López Obrador is actually quite a nebbishy-looking guy with a tropical tongue and temperament that lights up the air around him. Like most PRD hotshots, he is an ex-PRIista; he once ran the National Indigenous Institute in his home state and forged important ties with Tabasco's indigenous farmers.

In 1988, El Peje threw in with Cuauhtémoc Cárdenas's crusade and nearly became governor of Tabasco in elections held just a month after the great fraud in the presidential balloting, but was beaten back by the usual PRI mojo. Tabasco politics are a lot like those in Louisiana just up the Gulf. The kingfish down here was Roberto Madrazo, the son of a PRI reformer killed in a strange 1969 plane crash, and the godson of the late Carlos Hank González, the *capo di tutti capi* of the PRI, whose motto was "The only bad politician is a poor politician."

Madrazo and López Obrador went at it again in the '94 governor's race—the unctuous kingfish was bankrolled by accused drug-dealing billionaire Carlos Cabal Peniche, who had fleeced two banks gifted him by his *cuate* (pal) Carlos Salinas before hotfooting it off to Monte Carlo to escape prosecution—the croupier state apparently was beyond the reach of Mexican law enforcement. When Madrazo stole the election, El Peje marched a ragtag army of poor farmers 1,300 kilometers up to Mexico City and encamped for a month in the Zócalo.

In 1996, AMLO mobilized Indian farmers seeking reparations from PEMEX for acid rain damage to their crops and shut down 60 oil platforms in Tabasco during a time when Mexico was being forced to deposit all its export oil revenues in the U.S. Federal Reserve as collateral for the Clinton bail-out. For the first time, the Yanqui embassy noticed El Peje and sent a political officer to Tabasco to take his measure and find out what he wanted.

In his spare time, El Pejelagarto organized a national referendum against the FOBAPROA swindle by which Zedillo had dumped $80,000,000,000 USD in outstanding bank debt on the backs of the Mexican taxpayers to bail out the newly privatized banking system. Two million angry Mexicans voted against this scam.

López Obrador's combativeness earned him the PRD party presidency, from which vantage point he engineered Cárdenas's 1997 victory as Mexico City chief of government. López Obrador himself became mayor in 2000 on the same day that Vicente Fox was voted in as Mexico's first opposition president.

El Peje was a wildly popular mayor. In contrast to the dour, patrician Cárdenas, AMLO seemed a scrappy, honest Everyman who eschewed ostentation and lived in a tiny apartment down by the university with his three teenage sons and a pejelagarto in a large fish tank—Rocio Beltrán, López Obrador's partner, died in the first years of his term as Mexico City mayor. The masses appreciated AMLO's peppery style, and El Peje had a heart about as big as a politician's is allowed to get—"¡Primero los Pobres!" (The Poor First!) was his battle cry, and under his administration, old people who are often pensionless in this cockeyed social structure were soon receiving 600 pesos a month and free medical attention. He provided free milk for young mothers, found shelters for the homeless, and built pharaonic public works projects that provided employment for tens of thousands. When he erected a second level on the ring road (*periférico*), Gabriel García Márquez attended the inauguration. While he was a mayor for the poor, the middle class appreciated his efforts to keep their killer cars moving on the city's freeways at the expense of Chilango (Mexico City–ites') lungpower.

And while AMLO governed for the poor of the city, he also struck an early alliance with Carlos Slim, the third richest man in the world, who funded the reconstruction of the Centro Histórico (Slim was born in the neighborhood) and brought in Rudolph Giuliani to straighten out urban crime, an initiative that flopped badly. But for the Fox and Marta, El Peje was the demon in disguise, a demagogue and dreaded populist. A danger, in short, for Mexico.

The first plot against El Peje was disclosed by a green-haired, bulb-nosed clown named Brozo whom Televisa had hired to read the morning news. One February morning in 2004, a PAN deputy with the un-Mex-ican name of Federico Döring, and a lapdog of La Señora Marta, put a videotape in Brozo's paw purportedly depicting prominent PRD politicos accepting large piles of pesos from a fixer whose face is dis-torted on camera. So many bills were being passed across the table that René Bejarano, the leader of the Mexico City legislative assembly and once AMLO's personal secretary, could no longer pack them into his attaché case and began stuffing them into his suit pockets like he was on *Saturday Night Live*. Another PRD honcho, Carlos Imaz, weighs the money rather than counting it out.

Brozo slapped in the cart, and for the next three months, this orgy of PRD greed and venality was exhibited ad nauseam in Mexican households.

The perpetrator of the incriminating tapes, the fixer, Carlos Ahumada, was a pissed-off Argentinean construction tycoon whom the Peje had cut out of city contracts. In retaliation, Ahumada had taped PRD runners picking up money for his lover, former Mexico City interim mayor Rosario Robles, who was campaigning for the party presidency. Although the filmed exchanges appear to be venal bribe-taking, they were actually quite legal under Mexico's feeble campaign financing laws, which exempt pre-campaign funding from scrutiny.

Ahumada had turned the tapes over to the PAN at a secret meeting in the lounge of a five-star Polanco hotel attended by the CISEN, the attorney general's office, and El Jefe Diego before fleeing to Cuba in a pri-vate plane. The black hand of AMLO's all-time nemesis Carlos Salinas was all over this caper—Ahumada's chauffeur testified to driving his boss to Salinas's Tlalpan mansion on at least five occasions, and Cuba had always been the reviled ex-president's getaway. Ahumada was tracked down after Robles, who had fallen head over heels in love with the cad, was trailed to Varadero for a weekend tryst. Ahumada, who had 50 more tapes that he had not yet released, told Cuban authorities that the Fox had concocted the sting.

The tycoon had also corrupted AMLO's secretary of finances, Gustavo Ponce, a man with a penchant for Las Vegas blackjack tables. When Ponce was captured on a U.S. Treasury Department tape apparently high-rolling it with the people's tax money and the tape displayed relentlessly on Televisa, López Obrador questioned how such classified footage had found its way onto Mexico's screens. The chagrined Bush government later suspended the information flow to Mexican law enforcement because of the leak, and Interior Secretary Creel, then a probable presidential rival, accused López Obrador of thwarting anti-terror operations.

Although the Fox video operation ran out of steam without ever touching López Obrador, the plots against El Peje thickened in the spring of 2004 when the right wing of the right-wing PAN—the *Yunque* (or plow team)—organized a massive march of *perfumados* (perfumed ones) to protest "insecurity" in AMLO's city. A horrific series of kidnappings and homicides, mostly committed outside López Obrador's jurisdiction, was heavily publicized by Televisa and TV Azteca to terrify the middle class into marching, and the month-long blitz turned out hundreds of thousands of white-clad, god-fearing souls, mostly of the Caucasian persuasion. Many carried anti-AMLO banners as well as signs calling for the reinstatement of capital punishment. Along the route, AMLO supporters joined the march en masse and neutralized its anti–López Obrador content by turning the chants against Fox for failing to stop the massacre of Las Muertas up in Juárez.

The Desafuero

El Peje seemed to be coated with Teflon. Everything thrown at him bounced back and sullied those who hurled it and only strengthened the left candidate's ratings. The PRIAN's desperation to criminalize AMLO had hit a wall. Reactivating 10-year-old charges of terrorism and sabotage for leading the Indians against the Tabasco oil fields was an option—the Mexican government commonly jails activists on long-dormant warrants when they threaten the PRI-PAN plan. But El Peje's profile was by now so high that this trick just wasn't going to fly. Then the Fox gang blundered into El Encino.

El Encino ("the Oak Tree") is a valuable chunk of real estate out in the Santa Fe district of upscale western Mexico City where transnationals like Hewlett Packard are building corporate headquarters. Every inch is worth its weight in gelt, and a company called Promotora Internacional Santa Fe owned either 83,000 or 110,000 square meters of it, depending upon whose measurements you swallowed. When AMLO decided to build an access road to the American British Hospital, an elite institution that also offers free care to the poor, he tried to expropriate a narrow strip of right-of-way from El Encino, but a Mexico City court found the takeaway to be unkosher and threatened contempt-of-court proceedings. Although AMLO immediately called off the project and the road was never built, heavy machinery lurked around the property for days and Promotra Internacional Santa Fe prevailed upon the judge to issue a contempt citation. Now the PAN and its PRI colleagues had settled on the four-year-old citation to bring down El Peje.

During Christmas week 2004, the president summoned Supreme Court Justice Mariano Azuela to Los Pinos to probe the plot's legal legs, and when Hizzoner gave the thumbs-up, the project was turned over to Interior Minister Creel, Fox's handpicked successor, to organize the judicial persecution of López Obrador and to fine-tune political support for it in the lower house of Congress. Attorney General (and General) Rafael Macedo de la Concha and his special prosecutor, Carlos Vega Memije, most recently the tormentor of poor Digna's environmental farmers, were to prepare the case for *desafuero*, literally the taking away of AMLO's *fuero*, the immunity from prosecution that every Mexican politician enjoys while in office. The charges would then be presented to a five-member congressional commission on which the PRD had only one vote. If the charges were approved by the commission, a majority vote of the whole Chamber of Deputies would strip El Peje of his immunity from prosecution, at which point he would be immediately clapped into prison under Mexico's strict Napoleonic Code, in which one is guilty until proven innocent. Imprisoning AMLO would automatically bar him from the presidential ballot.

"No one is above the law," Fox and his surly spokesman, Rubén Aguilar, an ex-Jesuit who fought for the FMLN in Salvador, never tired of harping. Aguilar always referred to the Mexico City mayor simply as Señor López. "There is only thing worse than a lawbreaker and that's someone who breaks the law and thinks he has a right to do so," admonished Creel. Carlos Monsiváis objected vehemently in print to this legal lynching, likening Macedo and Vega Memije to Inspector Javert and his obsession with punishing Jean Valjean for stealing a loaf of bread.

The penalty for the heinous crime of seeking to build an access road to a hospital was one to eight years, and the Foxistas rubbed their hands in anticipation of seeing El Peje behind bars—suggested venues included the Super Maxi in Matamoros or Mexico's Alcatraz at La Palma, where AMLO would rub elbows with the nation's narco-lords and Mario Aburto, Colosio's supposed assassin. "This is like a preventive coup d'état," the Sup gasped from the jungle.

By February, López Obrador was telling bursting-at-the-seams 6 a.m. city hall press conferences that he was prepared for prison, would even welcome it as soon as possible—the strategy was to force the dropping of charges before the January 15, 2006, cutoff date for registering his candidacy. But if not, he would campaign from behind bars much as Francisco Madero had done after Porfirio Díaz had cast him into a San Luis Potosí prison to knock him off the 1910 ballot. Madero had, of course, escaped, fled to El Paso, declared the Mexican Revolution, and became the nation's first democratically elected president, AMLO reminded his persecutors.

This history lesson had some gaps in it, Sub Marcos noted. After Madero, a hacienda owner and outspoken defender of private property, became president in 1911, he denied Emiliano Zapata's demand for the return of his village's land in Anenecuilco, Morelos, and the revolution kicked into high gear.

Francisco Madero was later assassinated in a plot orchestrated by U.S. ambassador Henry Lane Wilson and the bloodthirsty general Victoriano Huerta installed in power. Financial support for Huerta's coup was underwritten by one Luis Creel, whose Chihuahua holdings were bigger than the kingdom of Belgium. Luis Creel, as the reader has already guessed, was interior minister Santiago Creel's paternal grandfather. The history of power in Mexico is a closed tape loop.

El Peje's People

Mexico's would-be Mandela has always had awesome powers of convocation. I remember one Sunday in the 1994 Tabasco campaign when the PRI shut down all public transportation in the state to prevent AMLO from amassing a crowd and people walked or got on their bikes or hopped on their donkeys to arrive at the fairgrounds outside Villahermosa. The low-end police estimate was 50,000.

But drawing 300,000-plus to the Zócalo on the morning of April 7, 2005, the first day of official mourning for a dead pope in a nation that professes to be 93% Catholic, was a real stunner.

April 7 was the date Congress had set aside to vote up the desafuero, and the mob that was shoehorned into the Zócalo that morning was AMLO's answer. These were El Peje's people, the people the color of the earth, the jodidos in their worn huaraches and broken shoes, those who spend all day on public transportation trying to reach the lost colonias buried at the limits of the megalopolis, hobbling on canes and crutches, clutching squirming babies to their breasts. The shared fury at the railroading of their Peje rose in waves: *"¡No estás sólo! ¡No estás sólo!"*—the same cry as when the comandantes had filled this plaza four years earlier, only today the EZLN was missing in action.

The bad gas that misery and frustration brews always seeps just under the surface in this city, and the PRD piped in pop music and festooned the Zócalo with yellow ribbons in an effort to contain the savage beast the downtrodden can sometimes turn into given the right conditions of repression. El Peje would march off alone to face the music before the congress of his country just a few blocks east of the plaza: "A politician can risk his own life but not those of his people."

"¡No estás sólo! ¡No estás sólo!"

"What the Peje doesn't understand, John," the 24-hour-a-day activist Nuria Fernández counseled, "is that this movement no longer belongs to him."

López Obrador's words to the congress that evening were less dramatic than Fidel Castro's 1954 "History Will Absolve Me" speech to the Santiago court or Marcos's classic "What Gives You the Right to Pardon Us?" some 40 years later, but they pulsed in the same vein: "Today, you will judge me, but just remember that all of us will be judged by history," El Peje warned the 500-seat Chamber of Deputies, which then proceeded to strip him of immunity by a four-to-one margin. When PRDistas in the lower house rushed to the tribune to disrupt the Star Chamber proceedings, PANistas launched loogies, an accurate measure of the level to which political debate had degenerated.

What might happen next was anyone's guess. No presidential candidate had been tossed in the pokey since Madero 100 years ago. General Macedo and his Javert, Vega Memije, reviewed the roster of available judges who could be counted upon to issue an arrest warrant for AMLO and delivered a truckful of case files—the *expediente*—to the courtroom of Lic. Juan José Olvera at the southern penitentiary (Mexican courtrooms are built into jails).

The desafuero constituted "a new paradigm of legality that will be the envy of the rest of the world," the Fox prognosticated from Rome, where he and la Señora Marta, along with other faith-based political poltroons like Tom DeLay and Robert Mugabe were attending Karol Wojtyla's long-anticipated funeral.

Meanwhile, a pair of PAN fresas in the lower house took it upon themselves to post bail for El Peje when the apprehension order was handed

down, a not-so-subtle ploy to blunt AMLO's martyrdom and cancel out
the obligatory photo op of the candidate behind bars. A court later ruled
that the fresas had no standing. If López Obrador wanted to go to jail,
that was his constitutional right.

The White House was quick to back up Fox. The desafuero was "proof
of Mexico's maturing democracy," Ambassador Garza informed the
American Chamber of Commerce at a Polanco séance—the AmCham
represents about 85% of all foreign investment in Mexico. But the business class was antsy about the "social decomposition" that the jailing of
AMLO could trigger. The bad gas kept seeping down below.

The international press advised caution. López Obrador was a "mes-
sianic leftist who threatened free market reforms," editorialized the *New
York Times*, "a demogogue with a history of leading violent demonstrations"—but still, he had a right to run for president. By the third week in
April, unidentified CIA sources (aren't they all?) were warning about
"instability," even using that dread seven-syllable word "ungovernability."
During a secret Mexico City huddle with Fox that same month, Richard
Myers, the chairman of Bush's Joint Chiefs of Staff, reportedly used the
same word.

When the civil society comes out of its house here and fills the boule-
vards from gutter to gutter, fusing into one fat fist of defiance, it is truly
an awe-inspiring spectacle. Such moments are rare—1968 during the
watershed UNAM strike, 1988 when Cárdenas was denied the presidency, the Zapatista convocations of the 1990s, the March of the People
the Color of the Earth in 2001—but April 24, 2005, dwarfed those mammoth moments. The desafuero had touched a deep and visceral nerve for
the jodidos and not-quite-jodidos of this country. El Peje had become, as
the expression goes, the *costal*, or sack, in which the people deposited
their many grievances.

The huge throng had been assembled from every corner of the city,
every colony and barrio and block and building and apartment and
room on the Horton Hears a Who principle of organizing—each one
tells the next one. According to Mexico City police estimates, 1.2 million

residents of Whoville marched to back up their Peje that day, the largest political demonstration in the history of the republic.

The marchers moved in silence, many with their mouths taped up, to remember the first great eruption of Mexican civil society on September 13, 1968, just three weeks before President Gustavo Díaz Ordaz ordered the massacre of hundreds of striking students at the Tlatelolco housing complex in downtown Mexico City. In fact, the route was the same—from the monolithic anthropology museum in Chapultepec Park in whose vaults the treasures of the Indians are hoarded, along the elegant Paseo de Reforma into the narrow old quarter, and finally bursting into the sun-scorched Zócalo at the political heart of Mexico.

As the silent tumult snaked like a great plumed serpent along the nine-kilometer route through the city, the marchers' shoes and signs spoke for them. "This is not a nightmare, Fox—we are real!" "They won't listen to our voices—now they must listen to our silence!" "We are no longer invisible citizens!" "1810: Revolution—1910: Revolution—2010: ????" "¡Todos Somos Señor López!" And inevitably: J-LO with AMLO!"

No banner that I could locate made any reference whatsoever to the Zapatista Army of National Liberation. Although Subcomandante Marcos had minced no words in condemning the desafuero and encouraged his minions to march against it, the compas were just not present at this critical moment in the political life of the country.

"I have traveled to every district and state in our country and I have seen the hunger and poverty of our fellow citizens, and together we are going to change this rotten economic system and save Mexico," El Peje pledged, sounding not just a little like the Sup. Like Marcos four years previous, AMLO spoke from a stage that had been constructed up against the National Palace from which, in less than 15 months, he could be ruling the nation—if they didn't shoot him first. Just to maximize this breaking reality, as had long been anticipated, López Obrador made it official by announcing his candidacy for the presidency of the United States of Mexico in the July 2, 2006, elections.

"¡No estás sólo! ¡No estás sólo!"

The mob was so dense that it took an hour just to separate oneself from it. Although the Fox would hide behind cooked Federal Preventive Police estimates that AMLO's snake had not amounted to more than 110,000 misguided marchers, the enormity of his miscalculation must have already dawned upon the president. In just two weeks' time, AMLO had tripled the size of the Desafuero Day meeting, and his popularity was snowballing out of control.

Emboldened by the enormous turnout, AMLO strode confidently into city hall early Monday morning—for a week he had refrained from dispatching from the mayor's office, temporarily turning over the reins of government to his bulbous Sancho Panza, Alejandro Encinas, for fear that his legal entanglements might lead to charges of "usurpation of powers" that could only complicate his situation. But now he was going back to work. The Supreme Court would have to sort out if El Peje was or was not still mayor of Mexico City.

Waiting for him as he climbed the marble stairway to deliver his daily 6 a.m. press briefing were hundreds, nay thousands, of representatives of the national and international press. The Peje vs. the Fox had long legs.

That Tuesday, President Fox sailed out for his weekly photo op and public *abrazo* (hug) with the people, today in the little towns just outside Oaxaca city. In one of them, Raúl Alberto Sánchez, a 17-year-old pre-law student at the Benito Juárez autonomous university, holding a hand-lettered sign that read "Fox—Traitor to Democracy," spoke truth to power.

"Who is a traitor?" the shirtsleeved president boomed. "You are, sir," Raúl mumbled back. "But why do you think this?" "López Obrador," the boy responded, just two words, his voice gaining strength. "But do I control the congress? Can I tell it how to act?" "Yes, you can—you and others." "Do I tell the judges what to decide?" "Well, yes, you appoint them." By now, Fox's handlers were tugging on his elbow, trying to steer him back to the motorcade.

When the president flew back up to Mexico City that night, more bad news awaited him. Inexplicably, the young judge whom Macedo de la Concha had handpicked to issue the arrest warrant had returned the expediente and all the paperwork to the attorney general's office, because he had been unable to determine whether or not AMLO had actually committed a crime and thus declared himself "incompetent" to proceed.

Vicente Fox is, above all, a businessman and he knew when it was time to cut his losses. Twenty-four hours later, the president fired General Macedo as attorney general, which did not much please the military, and ordered the case against Andrés Manuel López Obrador shelved, a limbo from which he could always retrieve it if he had no other option to thwart an AMLO presidency. Then the Fox went on national television to inform his fellow citizens that anyone was free to run for president, even Señor López.

Under the Trees

"We did not rise up in rebellion so that the PRD could be elected to public office," Subcomandante Marcos had written then-president of the PRD Porfirio Muñoz Ledo in October 1995 after the EZLN had dismantled a number of polling stations in the mountains and jungle of southeastern Chiapas, thereby demolishing the Party of the Aztec Sun's electoral ambitions in the region.

The dispute went back to the beginning. The PRD and the EZeta had gotten off on a bad footing in the first days of the rebellion, when Cuauhtémoc Cárdenas, the son of an army general, had encouraged the military to snuff the rebels. But Cárdenas, "the moral leader of the Mexican Left" who was about to launch a second failed bid for the presidency, rectified quickly and arm in arm with the civil society, he led the grand march that had forced Salinas to call a cease-fire.

That May, stalking the outback for votes, Cárdenas and his entourage showed up in Guadalupe Tepeyac to ask the rebels' unlikely support in his crusade for electoral democracy and received a tongue-lashing from the Sup—in all fairness, Marcos directed his fire at the party and Muñoz Ledo and, although he mistrusted Cuauhtémoc's failure to lead protests after the 1988 fraud, seemed quite respectful of the son of Tata Lázaro. In fact, in 1995, the EZLN proposed Cárdenas to lead the very short-lived (one afternoon) Movement of National Liberation.

López Obrador had been an infrequent visitor to Marcos's jungle hide-away prior to Zedillo's 1995 invasion of Guadalupe Tepeyac and had met with Amado as governor in rebellion. During the Forum on Democracy and Justice in San Cristóbal in 1996, in preparation for the never-realized second table of negotiation, the Subcomandante huddled publicly with both Cárdenas and AMLO.

But Cárdenas's victory in Mexico City the following year, the most significant electoral victory the left had achieved in many moons, set off warning sirens in the EZLN's war room, and the comandantes marched 1,111 insurgents up to the capital to advise the PRD that there was more than one Mexican Left. One afternoon during the rebels' stay, at the EZLN's founding convention, held in a Guerrero colony dance hall, the recently elected Cárdenas, along with his 80-year-old mother, Doña Amalia, Lázaro's bride, waited five hours to welcome the EZLN to the city he now governed and finally left in disgust. Five minutes later, 1,111 Zapatistas marched into the salon.

The tipping point was, of course, the PRD's Senate vote for Indian Wrongs in 2001—contrary to what Marcos continues to assert, the PRD delegation in the lower house walked out rather than endorse Indian Wrongs. Meanwhile, back home, Pablo's victory had co-opted struggle organizations with whom the EZLN had recouped land after the rebellion. Now the ORCAO, ARIC-Independiente, and CIOAC, all aligned with the PRD, confronted the rebels in every corner of their geography. The zipizapi at Zinacantán had only been the last straw.

Despite the *mala leche* (bad milk) between the PRD and the EZLN, Subcomandante Marcos had signed off on a March 2 communiqué that instructed "all honest men and women to oppose the injustice" of the desafuero. Congress and the Fox were staging "a preventive *golpe de estado*" by barring AMLO from the ballot and "destroying the only way by which free men and women could come peacefully to power." Such manufactured malfeasance would return Mexico to the dark age of 1910.

The Subcomandante urged all those who sympathized with the EZLN to join the mobilizations to stop this legal lynching.

Marcos's appeal was directed not at the electoral left but at "the real left, whose power is in the street." The Sup did not want to leave the impression that the EZLN supported AMLO or the PRD by participating in the struggle against the desafuero. The demonstrations would demonstrate who was for AMLO and who was against the desafuero. But Marcos warned that AMLO and his crowd of "Salinistas" would try to channel the people's rage into "the straitjacket of legal protest," adding ominously, "The clock of *los de abajo* ticks to a different time." Even in far-off Chiapas, the EZLN could smell the bad gas seeping from down below.

Despite Subcomandante Marcos's impassioned plea for participation, no one showed up for the marches. In San Cristóbal, protests against the desafuero were led by evangelicals and university students. Up in Make Sicko City (Carlos Fuentes dixit), the EZLN plunged into protracted debate about whether or not to march alongside the forces of El Mal y El Malo and never emerged. Although AMLO actually muttered thank-yous to Marcos for this backhanded endorsement, the eclipse of EZLN visibility during these frenzied moments in Mexico's political life vastly diminished the rebels' voice in the national tumult over the desafuero.

The March 2 communiqué, "Down with the Left," made it abundantly plain that at least in Marcos's jaundiced eye, AMLO and the PRD were the maximum mal. The now familiar litany of PRD crimes against the compas was repeated. The Sup had long accused AMLO of covering up the murder of Digna Ochoa. Since the New Year, Subcomandante Marcos had waged a letter-writing campaign charging El Peje and his district attorney, Bernardo Bátiz, with complicity in the deaths of both Digna Ochoa and 24-year-old UNAM altermundista Pavel González, who had been found hanged naked from a cross at the top of the highest peak in the Ajusco south of Mexico City—both deaths had been ruled suicides. "You can say you are a good person and on the left but your words stink of hypocrisy," the Sup scorned Bátiz, whom he had once asked to serve as an EZLN adviser during preparations for negotiations with Zedillo's reps. Bátiz was not alone on the list of advisers who had gone wrong—intellectuals like Luis Villoro and Monsiváis were on the diss list, largely because they didn't come up on the Sup's side during the UNAM strike.

In Marcos's rarefied vision, AMLO's greatest sin and treachery to the left was that he had surrounded himself with "Salinistas"—a reference to Manuel Camacho Solís and his flunky Marcelo Ebrard (AMLO's successor as Mexico City mayor). While Camacho had been a member of the Salinas crowd during the The Bald One's "Maoist" university days, he had publicly broken with the president after Colosio ("Salinas with hair") was designated the heir to the throne. Camacho had, of course, been Salinas's "peace negotiator" in Chiapas, a job designed to finish off his political career for good and from which he was ultimately forced to resign.

The concept that AMLO was some kind of closet creature of Salinas was a little hard to swallow even for die-hard Zapsymps like this writer. Salinas was AMLO's own El Mal y El Malo, his personal Moriarty upon whom the Peje pinned every plot and perversion, so pernicious that he could not even be named. Whereas López Obrador referred to Salinas in Beckettian terms, as "The Unnameable," Marcos named AMLO by that same unnameable name, *El Innombrable*.

It was not AMLO alone who was spreading all this evil. The PRD was "the left hand of the right hand." It had made "being on the left into a business." Every six years, the PRD came to the people and asked them to forget how they had been betrayed by the party, "a campaign of dismemory." Now as the nation shifted into presidential gear, it was happening all over again.

From afar, the Zapatistas can look like one of those huge paintings of tropical landscapes that Central American miniaturists are so fond of, leafy jungles in which they embed whole villages under the trees, with people pushing wheelbarrows, plowing the fields, throwing up a wall, baking bread, or gathered around the washing hole.

Mexico City is not accustomed to thinking so small, so it missed all this. Obsessed with the desafuero, the Indians' day-to-day construction of their autonomy seemed trivial and unimportant. Nonetheless, this was the rebels' real work during the season of the desafuero, and the fact that they took time out to notice and object to the desafuero was a sign they were not separatists at all, that they had not quite given up on the national reality no matter how ugly it was. Although the EZLN took no part in the great mobilizations in the spring of 2005, the marches and meetings would probably never have happened without them.

Solidarity

While diminished in the U.S. under the great weight of the war in Iraq and a pause in overt repression in Chiapas (North Americans seem to demand victimization to raise material aid), solidarity with the EZLN remained rock solid in Europe, where I was invited to declaim at universities, left-wing bookstores, cultural cafés, and anarchist squats in the spring of 2005.

In the Luddite north of England, Zapatista solidarity was strongest in Leeds, which has adopted 16 de Febrero, the EZLN's newest autonomía in Simijovel, named for the day the San Andrés Accords were signed. I spoke in Nottingham, where anarchists were preparing to head for Chiapas and sit at the feet of the five JBGs. Veiled Muslim women attended the presentation in Edinburgh, where the Anarchist Golfing Association was playing daily foursomes at the nearby Gleneagles course, searching out possible breaches in the perimeter to use when G-8 came to town three weeks hence.

Spain is the spine of EZLN solidarity in Europe. Brigadistas and material aid are forever in transit between Barcelona and País Vasco, Andalucía and the Rebel Zone. Iñaki García at the Barcelona Colectivo set up enthusiastically attended events at the Casa de Solidaridad and the local Caracol, "*La Lucha Sigue*." Presentations in Granada, Amsterdam, and Istanbul were packed with *solidarios*.

Euro aficionados were really fired up by the prospect of future futbol matches between Inter Milan and the EZLN. Representatives of Inter's owner, Massimo Moratti, were in La Realidad in early spring to express their solidarity and inspect the site for a new futbol field in Guadalupe Tepeyac. Pupi Zanetti had sent along a team shirt for the Sup.

The Zapatistas are short but stocky and play futbol just as energetically as they do *basket*. In 1999, during the consulta, the EZLN selection had faced off against a squad of "old glories" of the Mexican soccer world and lost by only 5 to 3. ("We didn't lose—we just ran out of time to win," Marcos argued.) Now the Sup challenged Inter to a seven-game match of *cascarita* (kicking the ball around) for the just-created "Pozol de Barrio" Cup.

Three games would be played in Mexico; two at the 160,000-seat Azteca Stadium in the capital, where fans had taken to chanting "*¡Osama! ¡Osama!*" anytime a U.S. team took the field. Receipts would benefit indigenous projects. A third match, in Guadalajara, would raise funds for the Otherworlders still languishing in Jalisco's maximum-security prison. Three matches would be played in Europe, at least one in Euskal Herria. Marcos wanted to site the seventh game in Los Angeles as a benefit for the indocumentados, but if the Zapatista terroristas could not get visas, they would fly off to Cuba and scrimmage on the lawn outside Gitmo.

The ace striker "Marigol" Domínguez, barred from the Mexican men's professional league, had already agreed to a Zapatista contract. Diego Maradona and the great Brazilian midfielder Socrates would be the referees. To combat the ugly head of machismo that always pops up at such sporting functions, all the cheerleaders would be transvestites and transgendered.

What was Marcos puffing upon in his curved Sherlock Holmes pipe?

But all was not sunshine and puppies in the European solidarity league. The BBVA Bancomer cancellation of six Enlace Civil accounts, with over 2 million pesos destined for the JBGs to finance projects in the autonomías, threatened to disrupt the aid pipeline. In Barcelona, weekly demonstrations at the bank sought to call public attention to this swindle. Bancomer had informed Enlace that suspected terrorist money laundering was the reason for the suspension—part of the money came from the autonomous regional government of País Vasco (where the bank was based), and everyone knows that terrorists wear berets.

HSBC would soon follow suit and cut off Enlace accounts.

Another problem was coffee. There wasn't any, and the European solidarity movement thrives on the jitter beans, selling Zap java in bulk and in progressive cafés and restaurants. Hamburg fair traders, who had been importing 15 containers a year, had not received coffee that should have been shipped in March. It was now May.

The catastrophic Christmastime tsunami had wiped out the South Asian crop, and coffee prices, which had been quietly climbing out of the doldrums after touching bottom in 2002, were zooming—although fair traders suspected that finagling by New York and European commodity brokers had more to do with the price rise than the tsunami. Now the *coyotes* (freelance coffee brokers) who had been dormant when the price of a pound of coffee was in the four-peso range knocked on every campesino's door in Los Altos offering up to 22.5, about what the co-op was getting from the NGOs but minus the transportation costs, and the hungry farmers had gone for it.

The fair traders made a beeline to Oventik and presented their case to the Junta de Buen Gobierno Center of the Zapatista Heart Before the World. The contracts they had signed with Mut Vitz and Yaxil were not being filled. On the other hand, the price boom had made the contracts they signed with the co-ops obsolete. But the Junta deferred intervention. Something else was brewing on the Zapatista stove.

Red Alert

I flew into Istanbul for the final session of the World Tribunal on Iraqi war crimes, an international effort to rekindle the Bertrand Russell Vietnam tribunals and hold the warmongers responsible for their crimes—20 previous sessions had been held in Europe and North America, and independent tribunals had met in Japan and South Korea. I had come to deliver testimony on Mexican deaths in Iraq—the so-called green card Marines, who now totaled nearly 100 and spread the Word of the Zapatistas in Turkish cafés.

The all-star jury was headed by the iconic Arundhati Roy and included the "Zapatista lawyer" Miguel Angel de los Santos, who had taken a week off from trekking the jungles and mountains of southeastern Chiapas coordinating the work of the Network of Community Defenders to sit in judgment on the U.S. genocidal war in Iraq. Others on the panel included the always solidarias Madres de la Plaza de Mayo; Eve Ensler; Barbara Olshansky, the lead lawyer on Guantanamo; and a gentleman who listed himself as "a miner." In the end, the jury got hung up about whom to indict for these horrific crimes—Bush, Blair, Aznar, Berlusconi, the U.N., Judith Miller. "Add your favorite war criminal—it's like graffiti," Roy laughed.

The sessions were held in an ancient, gloomy auditorium on the Topkapi Palace grounds. The testimony was terrifying and exhausting. Witness after witness decried the unspeakable cruelties of this imperialist war. It felt like one had stumbled into a black hole, an Abu Ghraib of the mind. Weighing upon the tribunal were 100,000 dead Iraqis, and it was difficult to breathe. Each day I would escape into the sunlight and the cyber cafés in the surrounding neighborhood to read the news from back home.

On June 21, my screen lit up right away. In large letters, it announced that the Zapatista Army of National Liberation had called a Red Alert. On the EZLN danger scale, a Red Alert indicates the highest level of threat. In the 12-year saga of the rebellion, there had been only four previous Red Alerts, the last immediately after Acteal in 1997.

The communiqué issued by the CCRI under Subcomandante Insurgent Marcos's name the previous day closed down the Caracoles, ordered the JBG delegates back to their communities, asked all NGOs to stop all projects in the autonomías and leave, and sent internationalists still inside packing. Radio Insurgente was taken off the air. Wow, I fretted, there must be some serious *mal y malo* afoot.

What could have trip-wired the Red Alert? Mexican army troops poking around Rayón in the way north of the state had taken down 44 marijuana fields a few days before and, although the area is heavily Zoque with little EZLN influence, had tried to pin the bust on the rebels—which was bosh and everyone knew it. CAPISE had reported unusual military movements around Rancho Nuevo, but the army claimed it was normal troop rotation. Fray Bart recorded an uptick in paramilitary operations in the north of Chiapas. The bank cutoff might have signaled an international anti-terrorism sweep. But none of these ever-present threats and harassment added up to a Red Alert.

Marcos's penultimate eruption prior to the alert had been one more brutal swipe at the parties and their candidates. "The Impossible Geometry of Power" harped on AMLO as if he were Satan incarnate: "The desafuero was a comic reality show" but also a measure of the discontent below. AMLO, the Sup scoffed, had called a silent march and then could not stop talking about power. *La Jornada* columnist Jaime Avilés, an AMLO booster, detected Hitlerian connotations in the text.

Had the EZLN opted to make its final break with the political class? Did this imply a new military initiative? Miguel Angel worried that as the political-military structure became diminished in the autonomías, the military side might be considering new armed action to reassert its supremacy, definitely a worst-case scenario. "Maybe they are going to form a political party," my Turkish comrade Tolga Temuge mused, an equally calamitous turn of events.

Back in San Cris, Elio Henríquez had taken it upon himself to drive up to Oventik to investigate the lay of the land and found the gate to the Caracol Rebellion and Resistance for Humanity wide open, the slats flapping in the mountain breeze. The Che Guevara General Store was padlocked. In fact, Oventik was deserted, a ghost town, even the dogs were gone. A painstakingly hand-lettered sign tacked to the door of the Junta de Buen Gobierno read "Closed up because of the Red Alert." Where was everyone? Why had they left? A few internationals emerged from a hut. They didn't know whether to just leave or wait for the military to attack so they could submit an observation report.

My screen filled up with urgent messages from everywhere from Vietnam to Vermont. What did it all mean, the comrades wanted to know, what could they do? Wait, I counseled, this will play itself out soon. . . .

On June 23, *La Jornada* published a follow-up communiqué. If anything, it sounded more dire, a farewell note although it began by insisting, "This is not a farewell note." "The EZLN can survive without its leaders," the note underscored. All Zapatistas were free to leave the EZLN. They had "the moral liberty to decide whether they wanted to continue being Zapatistas." Much gratitude is expressed to a long list of supporters for their solidarity over the past dozen years. "This may be the last time you ever hear from us." Thank you and good night.

My gulp was audible enough for the person at the next machine to ask if I was ill.

But two days later, on the 26th, the crisis seemed to be lifting. The Red Alert did not mean a new military initiative. Rather, it had been "precautionary" and "defensive." The EZLN was in consultations, the Sup reported, and Zedillo had once attacked the communities when they were in this mode. "We have been preparing our people for this next stage for four years now." The next stage? *Falta lo que falta*. What was missing?

Book Three

The Time to Move On

12. Summer/Fall 2005

The Sexta

Nine days had elapsed between publication of the Red Alert and the Sixth Declaration of the Lacandón Jungle (the Sexta), enough time for the bases to have met and chewed over its dense content but hardly enough in which to reach consensus. Had the Red Alert been more a clever work of cybernetic political theater than a danger warning, a test message designed to see who was listening? If so, the stunt had accomplished its purpose. Zapatista antennas had shot up, and all over the world the fan base was tuned in to *lo que sigue* (that which came next).

I began reading the Sexta in a low-rent pension on the Turkish coast and rode it all the way back through Amsterdam and London and New York and eventually Mexico. The Sexta actually ran for three days in *La Jornada*, beginning June 29, and spelled out the Zapatistas' future for a long time to come.

The document declared an eventual break between the political-military structure and the more democratic autonomous one. A new generation "who are better Zapatistas than we are" was now in charge, and the

EZLN, the CCRI, and the Comandancia were free to do other things. What other things? *La Otra Cosa.* . . .

The Sexta was the first Declaration of the Lacandón Jungle to be issued since July 1998, when the CCRI broke a protracted silence with Speedy González's immortal battle cry of *"¡Yepa, Yepa!"* These declarations are always a thrusting outward beyond the physical limits of Zapatista boundaries, and the Fifth Declaration had called for the building of a national alliance and the holding of a *consulta* that turned out 2,000,000 votes in favor of San Andrés. The First Declaration had contained such a thrust—the EZLN "would march on the capital of the country, defeating the federal army on the way."

The Second Declaration, issued in the summer of 2004, was an invitation for the outside to come in, summoning the civil society to the National Democratic Convention to figure out how to deal with coming presidential elections. The Third, promulgated in February 1995 just before Zedillo's invasion, called for the building of a Movement of National Liberation, a cross-class coalition to save the nation as the economy plunged into freefall. The Fourth, in December 1995, as negotiations between the EZLN and the mal gobierno got real, affirmed the primacy of the Word over the Fire, advertised that the rebels really did not want state power, and called for the 1996 Intergaláctica and the formation of the EZLN. The Sexta contained a similar thrusting outside. For four years, the compas had been building autonomy, getting off the grid under the trees, seemingly having turned their backs on the rest of Mexico. Now they were turning back.

The Sexta is divided into seven sections. "Where We Are Coming From" tells the Zapatistas' story in their own words and blood—part of that testimony opens this book. The text is unique—this is the part of the Sexta that seems to be written by the collective voice of the People Who Are the Color of the Earth, uncoached by Sub Marcos.

"Who We Are Now" asks the question, What has changed in all the years and seasons of the rebellion? "Our hearts are not the same now— they are bigger and more lacerated." The comandantes had watched a whole generation grow up in rebellion. "Those who were young men and women when the rebellion began are men and women with families now, and those who were babies back then are young men and women now." Now the Comandancia had decided it was time to turn it all over to these new generations. They had come to the conclusion, they explained, that the Indians could not go forward without aligning themselves with the farmers and the students and "those who work in the cities." "We see that we have advanced as far as we can under this schema, but we have to keep advancing." This would be their job from now on. To reach out. "The hour has come to risk everything again."

Sections four and five plumbed "How We See Mexico" ("in the countryside it is like when Porfirio Díaz ruled . . . in the cities, the men and women sell Chiclets and phone cards in the street . . . hypercapitalism has left Mexico a shell . . . globalization has been a reconquest—but it is not easy for them, because there is always resistance") and "How We See the World" ("before, the rich could only exploit people in their own country and now there are no borders . . . capitalism is the enemy . . . it turns people into merchandise").

"What We Want for the World" is an anthem to solidarity. The smallest of the small would fill up *Chómpiras* with eight tons of corn and 200 *tambos* of gasoline (at 200 liters per tambo) and drive it all the way to Cuba, because the Zapatistas were part of Cuba too. Last year's harvest had been good, and this year's should be ample too if the military did not interfere. So don't worry, the compas had plenty to eat. In fact, there was enough left over for the People of the Corn to send corn to their indigenous brothers and sisters in Ecuador and Bolivia and to the piqueteros in Argentina too. "We are so proud to be a small part of you."

What the Zapatistas also wanted for the world was a new Intergaláctica, which gladdened the hearts of Zapsymps throughout the galaxy, "but not one of those meetings where a few people speak and the everyone else listens."

Finally, "What We Want For Mexico" and "How We Will Go About It" formed the Sexta's action plan. "In Mexico, we want to make a plan and go to visit with the Mexicans where there are simple and humble people. We are going to go and listen to them because they are like us and together we will build a common anticapitalist, anti-neoliberal movement with them. This is our simple word."

What had been missing—*la otra cosa*—was the rest of Mexico. It wasn't enough to build autonomy in the mountains and jungles of the southeast while the rest of Mexico and the world were crumbling all around them. Maybe they had been slow to acknowledge this, but first they had to ensure that their autonomous communities could survive without them and that they would always have a place to return to. "We may be jailed or killed. We may never return," Marcos had prophesied.

The new idea was to build a grand alliance of jodidos and Indians, *otros y otras* and the "real left" from the ground up, that would stand outside the parties and the electoral system and work toward the calling of a new constitutional convention and the writing of a new anti-neoliberal constitution that protected the wealth and resources of the nation and, at long last, made Indian Rights the law of the land.

The political class from Vicente Fox down to the doorman at the PRD were prompt to congratulate the EZLN for laying down its weapons and joining the political process. Luis H. Alvarez winged off to Chiapas to await a meeting with Marcos. This was a dangerously inaccurate reading of the Sexta. Where in the Sixth Declaration of the Lacandón Jungle did it say the Zaps would join the political process? In fact, it says precisely the reverse: The EZLN will continue to oppose and resist the political process.

And where did it indicate that the Zapatistas were disarming? Words were useful but fire was still a part of the equation.

The EZLN had tried to build a handful of mass organizations during their life on earth with minimal success. The National Democratic Convention (CND) was supposed to weld the left to the civil society, but the left, as it always does, got the upper hand and then splintered into smithereens. The Movement of National Liberation lasted less than an afternoon up in Querétaro when the ultras stomped the proposal of a cross-class alliance into the auditorium floor. The National Indigenous Conference (CNI) had high hopes of crystallizing a pan-Indian movement under the banner of "Never Again a Mexico Without Us," but while it still had its power spots, indigenous struggle is so rooted in place that a national alliance was doomed to failure. There had been a network of communities in correspondence following the 1999 consulta that seemed a valuable asset, but it had frittered away in the 2000 election of 15-Minute Man Fox. The EZLN had veered desperately left in the UNAM strike and nowdays scared off all but the hard core.

So why would this new plan work any better? Because this time the Zapatistas would go straight to "the simple and humble people who are like us"—there would be no middleman, no self-serving left or wishy-washy civil society in between. They would deliver the news directly to El Pueblo.

The vehicle for this thrust outside, this leap of faith into the darkness, would be the Other Campaign. La Otra would run parallel to the 2006 presidential election campaigns, but it would be an anti-electoral, anti-campaign campaign. The Sexta Commission would be in charge of direction and logistics. "First we will send someone as a test, and if he (she?) does not disappear or isn't killed or taken prisoner, we will send more." La Otra would be a thrust up and out from the bottom, and what the hell all of this meant was to be hashed out at six meetings in the middle of the jungle—well, at least in the Cañadas—in August and September. Bring rain ponchos and rubber boots.

Penguin Days

Subcomandante Insurgent Marcos had not been seen in the flesh for four and a half years when he walked out of the woods on August 6, 2005, near Francisco Gómez–La Garrucha in the Cañadas surrounded by an all-woman bevy of ski-masked *milicianas*. In the flesh was an appropriate descriptive—the Sup had put on some kilos, and a middle-age paunch (Marcos was nearing 50) spilled over his military belt buckle now. Just an illusion, Marcos argued; it was all in the camera angles. Besides, fat is beautiful.

The Sup clutched in his arms what he said was a penguin. The bird certainly walked like a penguin, lurching from side to side like a drunken sailor. It awked like a penguin. It was black and white, penguin colorations. But maybe it was just a *muy otra* chicken, a jungle mutation. Penguins were very popular that summer. *The March of the Penguins* was on the silver screen up in San Cris.

Over the next seven weeks, thousands of Mexicans would defy drenching rains, neck-high mud, venomous vipers, clouds of insects, tropical diseases, and uncertain transportation to travel to the Cañadas and deposit their *grano de arena* (grain of sand) at prolonged gabfests gathered under the trees in the Lacandón jungle. For the first time since 1999 after the consulta, the EZLN had invited in the outside world to figure out how best the rebels could travel outward. It was all very Caracolish.

Six meetings would be held each weekend beginning in August, with a plenary set for the weekend of September 16. Marcos urged all organizations to send delegations and not to descend on the Cañadas en masse, or else "they will finish off the country before we are done."

Each weekend, a distinct constituency would parade before the mic to offer their endorsement of the Sexta—"adherence" was the word, as if the document was some sort of social epoxy—and their suggestions on how the Other Campaign should navigate. Organizations and individuals who "adhered" to the Sexta were encouraged to hold discussions of the document in private homes and public cafés before they headed for the jungle.

The first weekend, August 5-7, was dedicated to the views of what Marcos called "the real left" as opposed to the electoral variety, "the left of the *torta* stands," the left down at the bottom, "the left that never got close to power." But the "real left" came with the baggage of the old left, the left of the flags and the factions and the isms. Despite an appeal to leave all *dogmatismos* at home, there was plenty of dogma to go around. The newly minted Mexican Communist Party (ML) showed up waving brilliant red flags inscribed with gilded hammers and sickles.

Despite prohibitions on the participation of the electoral left, comrades who still entertained such pretensions slipped in under the ideological radar screen, and soon the inevitable questions were resounding from the mic. By promoting electoral abstention, wasn't the Other Campaign handing the election to the PAN and the PRI? "We're not telling anyone how to vote," Marcos riposted irritably. For anyone who still thought the PRD was on the left, he would introduce him or her to Zapatistas shot by the ORCAO.

The debate resonated far beyond the Lacandón. The letters to the editor page in *La Jornada*, a PRD paper, was filled with calumnies. The Zapatistas were sick sectarians. The Zapatistas believed that worse was better. Oh, the Zapatistas were so ideologically pure! La Poniatowska, who had thrown in with AMLO, denounced the Zapatistas for "dividing the left." The PRD columnist Miguel Angel Granados Chapa gnashed his teeth because "the left was eating the left" all over again. "We invite you to come down here and convince us of López Obrador's charms," Marcos challenged Don Benito Rosas, an elderly *Jornada* reader. Marcos grew irate with *La Jornada* after the newspaper, which had nourished a dozen years of Zapatista struggle, falsely claimed that he had emitted a Bush-like ultimatum: "You are either with me or with López Obrador."

The critics really didn't get it. The Other Campaign was a battle for the hearts and minds of the Mexican Left, and El Peje was just a convenient target. But the Zapatistas were not challenging his persona so much as they were taking on the electoral process itself. Say No to the Lesser of Two Evils! Another *Política* Is Possible!

A ragtag bag of lefties attended the initial session, 32 organizations and about 200 participants (it was the smallest of all the conclaves), which led former Zapatista adviser Magdalena Gómez to question if this was an appropriately representational constituency to write a new constitution and save the nation.

The second session to which indigenous organizations and peoples had been invited was convened from August 12 to 15 in Javier Hernández (also named for a combatant who had fallen in Ocosingo on January 1, 1994), about two hours out of Ocosingo, in the Cañada of San Manuel.

Wixaritari (Huicholes) and Rarámuri (Tarahuma) activists, tall men from the north in elaborately beaded clothing, dazzled the Tzeltal kids. The meeting began with a moment of silence for the old Purépecha warrior Efraín Capiz, who had passed away in the spring. *¡La lucha sigue y sigue y sigue y sigue y sigue y sigue! ¡Don Efraín Capiz! ¡Presente!*

Then the Sup startled his guests—51 indigenous organizations were in attendance—by declaring that the Zapatistas were on the left before they were Indians, but no one walked out. Meeting with the Indians here in Indian country had a certain symmetry, and the convergence was perhaps the least polemical of the seven sessions. The Indians would be vital building blocks for the Other Campaign. They would host and feed and house the compas while they were on the road.

Labor, NGOs, and other social organizations convened August 22–25 deep in the canyons at Dolores Hidalgo. The Sup rode out of the forest still clutching his penguin—he was once again encamped in the Cañadas, where he had maintained his headquarters on the Prado ejido since the 1980s.

About 400 delegates huddled under a tarpaulin—dissidents in the teachers' union, Mexico City subway workers, militant feminists, democratic lawyers, and Catholic liberationists prepared to discuss how to construct a nonhierarchal, nonsexist, nonelectoral, anticapitalist left when Marcos stomped in, itching for a fight, and opened up on AMLO with both barrels. Among other evidence of the perfidy of the electoral left was a long list of PRIistas who had converted to PRDistas to earn the Party of the Aztec Sun's nomination for some *hueso* (bone.) With that off his chest, the Sup pulled out his notebook, lit up his pipe, and took copious notes on what the speakers had to say for the rest of the day. Meanwhile, the miliciana Erika had tied around the penguin's neck a napkin embroidered with a red star, and the bird lurched up and down the comandantes' table kind of looking like he was coming for dinner.

"Maybe we are all chickens who aspire to be penguins," ideologue Pablo González Casanova, ex-rector of the National University, proposed.

Curiously, other than Sub Marcos, the comandantes did not speak up at these sessions except to offer formal words of welcome, and one wonders what they thought of the oft garishly coiffed crowd that had come to visit them.

Hairstyles and piercings were a particular feature of the fourth session, August 29–31 at Juan Diego (not the newly anointed saint but two fallen milicianos named Juan and Diego), at the foot of the Corralchén sierra, when co-ops, collectives, communes, communities, committees, commissions, cliques, circles, cells, blocs, brigades, focos, and anti-groups converged, the most autonomous and diverse part of the Zapatista support movement, the ones who sell the coffee and block the avenues, make the videos and man and woman the community radio stations.

All the little worlds that fit into the Zapatista world took the mic all day and all night—urban agitators and organic farmers, gays, lesbians, the transgendered, antiwar activists, antivivisectionists, punks, *darketos*, Goths. Floridly dressed Tzeltal girls marveled at the mix. The rap was rich, if self-indulgent, and some overstayed their time at the mic. When a tall anarchist woman from the ¡Ay Carmela! Brigade in San Luis Potosí blabbed on so interminably the comrades tried to hoot her off, Sub Marcos intervened: "Let her say what she has come to say—she has come from the other end of the country to say it, and we have been waiting for 500 years here to hear her say it—we can wait a little longer."

Cultural workers expressed their adherance to the Sexta in songs and poems and "performance." One chubby homeboy from Chilangolandia said that he felt useless, that he didn't know anything except how to dance hip-hop, but it had always been his dream to dance hip-hop for the Sup and now he was going to do it.

The fifth session, during the first week in September, began with the National Anthem and the Mexican flag—September is the patriotic month and the Zapatistas never forget that they are Mexicans too. Individuals and families were the focus group on hand for the weekend, and the testimony was highly confessional, often bordering on psychodrama. "This is an encounter of all our lonelinesses," one distraught woman moaned. The AMLO thing was a well of angst. "I confess that I am a bigamist—I love both Marcos and Andrés Manuel," one man anguished. Marcos seemed impatient with the frustrations of the speakers and insinuated that the PRD has infiltrated the session.

The final gabathon, September 7–9, was advertised as being for everyone else—all for those who did not fit into a previous convoked category and/or those who just hadn't been able to adhere until now. Hermann thought it the most businesslike and political of the six gatherings. The eternal Madres of the Plaza de Mayo were on the guest list, as were the *Hijos*, the sons and daughters of the Argentinean and Chilean diaspora, and the mother of Carlo Giuliani. A lot of nuts and bolts had to be nailed down, and the sixth gathering was dress rehearsal for the plenary session set for the JGB Road to the Future at La Garrucha on September 16, Mexican Independence Day, where the final shape of La Otra Campana would be determined. Be There or Be Square and oh yah, it was raining like Katrina had come south, so better hire a canoe.

The Shape of Things to Come

Throughout 2005, in public pronouncements from Madrid to the Montes Azules (a catered lunch with evacuees), the Fox relegated the Zapatistas to the past—"They are things of the past," he would tell European potentates and visiting dignitaries. Although the lame duck Fox was himself about to become "a thing of the past," the president had a point. The EZLN could have never survived the neoliberal onslaught without the bedrock of their Mayan past, which so colored their present. But now it was time to talk about the Zapatista future.

The Zapatista future was the sole item on the agenda at the long-awaited plenary, September 16–18, in La Garrucha-Francisco Gómez, the most significant gathering of outsiders in EZLN territory since the 1996 Intergaláctica nearly a decade earlier—2,069 non-Zapatista delegates registered for the event. Moreover, amid whispers of strains and splits in the CCRI, all 23 senior comandantes were present—Esther, David, Tacho, Susana, Zebedeo, et al., plus Comandanta Ramona, the smallest of the small, who had not been seen in public since she returned from

Mexico City with a new kidney in 1997. Although rumors of her death still circulated in the zone, Ramona looked quite alive, reportedly joking with Marcos about AMLO El Malo and the Sup's pitiful penguin.

The penguin continued to lurch up and down the table reserved for the ski-masked Comandancia, a congruent emblem of the very otherness of this army.

The first order of business was to turn La Otra over to the adherents to do what they would with it—they would be responsible for plotting the logistics and raising the gas money. Control remained in the hands of the Sexta Commission, which ultimately took its direction from the CCRI. Debate focused on the shape of the Other Campaign—would it be diffuse and amorphous, a coalition mutually motored by anarchism and diversity, or a structured, centrally controlled action able to respond to threats and political necessities rapidly? Lives, after all, were at stake.

The debate was tightly monitored: Five minutes and you got the hook. Facilitators held up one-minute-warning signs to nudge the speakers to wrap up. The debate was carried live worldwide on the Internet by Chiapas Indymedia, thanks to Timo and Luz. You could sit in in Mexico City or Malaga or, for that matter, Inner Mongolia and be a part of it, except that sometimes the rain drummed down so hard on the auditorium roof that the speakers were drowned out.

Away from the mic, an argument broke out when the Mexican Communist Party (ML) ("the Neanderthal left," as *La Jomada*'s Luis Hernández Navarro described them) displayed enormous full-color portraits of Joe Stalin, not a very appropriate icon for a gathering devoted to building a nonhierarchal left from the bottom up, and many anarchists demanded that the commies (ML) remove the offending portraiture. The Comandancia took note, and Marcos ruled that the anarchists were being divisive and Stalin would stay.

So the debate continued under old Joe's steely squint, and in the end, the Zapatista Army of National Liberation, the CCRI, and the Sexta Commission determined how the Other Campaign was going to look.

La Otra would proceed in a profound spirit of accompaniment. It would be civil, peaceful, national (but not nationalist), anticapitalist, anti-electoral, left-wing but with another way of doing politics, of listening; "the privilege of the ear" would be respected. "We recognize the limit of individual action and the necessity to unite with other struggles."

The Other Campaign would kick off on January 1, the 12th anniversary of the EZLN's War Against Oblivion, and would travel to all 31 states and the federal district to "listen to the simple and humble Mexicans like ourselves." La Otra Campaña would extend to the northern border meeting with the Other Campaign on the Other Side in Ciudad Juárez and Tijuana in mid-June.

Although the Other Campaign would transit the country during the Mexican presidential election season, it would be anti-electoral. Its goal was not to elect a candidate or a party but to piece together an alliance of the exploited to achieve a new constitution, so it would continue long after the July 2 election, at least through March 2007, when La Otra's effectiveness would be reevaluated.

The first anticampaign campaign team would be compact: Sub Marcos, now doing business as Delegate Zero, would travel the nation's highways and byways, "walking and questioning" among the Mexicans. The choice was a logical one—the Sup ehhh Zero certainly had the gift of gab—the EZetas' sexiest symbol would lure the curious into the tent. The downside would be an upsurge in the already formidable cult of personality that had sprung up around Marcos. Another obvious drawback: While Marcos was bi- and tri-lingual, he was not an Indian, and although he professed to speak for the Indian people, no Indian voice would speak for the Zapatistas on the Other Campaign. Moreover, the voice of Zapatista women who have so enriched this struggle would not be heard as the Otra worked its way through the Mexican landscape.

The Other Booby Traps

In the August Parametría survey of 1,000 carefully culled citizens, Marcos registered 36% unpopularity (he boasted about it), while 23%

saw the Sup in a favorable light. A full 78% knew who he was—up 10% from a similar poll taken two years earlier. On the other hand, the EZLN was less popular (21%) than Marcos and less well known—44% considered the EZLN to be an armed guerrilla band, 26% thought it was a political organization that inclined to the PRD(!), and less than 20% of respondents identified the Zapatistas as an indigenous group.

There was, however, consensus that the Other Campaign began on the far side. "Are you a *malcriado* (creep)? Do you eat with your elbows on the table? Drop ashes all over the rug? Don't wash your hands after you use the bathroom? Are you a transgressor of good manners? Then the Other Campaign is for you!" the Sup recruited.

The Other Campaign would not be just another way of doing politics but literally, a campaign of others—a campaign of all the *otras y otros*, the most marginalized Mexicans, the Indians and the lesbians and the gays and the transgendered, the disabled, the prisoners, the useless, the simple and humble people of Mexico, and by the end of October, 1,000 organizations and 2,000 individuals had adhered to the Sexta and its very otro offspring.

The EZLN had a checkered history when it came to presidential elections. In 1994, the Zapatistas refused to endorse Cuauhtémoc Cárdenas but were keen to lead post-electoral struggle if he was once again cheated out of victory—Cárdenas, the rebels figured, would be reluctant to go beyond the bounds of legal protest. In 2000, while Mexico voted the PRI out of power and installed the Fox, the EZLN had simply sat on its hands, silently observing the electoral fallout. In 2006, the comandantes would utilize the electoral calendar to promote their own anti-electoral, anti-party, anti-candidate anti-campaign.

Such a strategy was fraught with frightening scenarios: PRD mobs would burn Delegate Zero alive in small-town plazas. Roadside assassinations, preventive detention. What if the Other Campaign was really successful and no one voted for AMLO? The PRI's reconquest of power would animate elements in the military that still wanted to crush the Zapatistas and excite the paramilitaries' thirst for blood.

Another six years of PAN rule would be no more palatable to the future of Zapatista autonomy.

Another booby-trap planted in the electoral underbrush was that the Other Campaign could become so identified with the official campaigns that it would come to behave like that which it detested. This was already happening. When a reporter at the plenary session shouted out to Marcos, "What do you have to say to López Obrador?" Delegate Zero cast a fat finger into the heavens. "Read my *dedo*," he shouted back.

The misconception that the Zapatistas had embraced the political process was the kiss of death, but by campaigning against it while the electoral calendar ticked down, they had, in a sense, joined up. Given the votes they would steal from AMLO, the Other Campaigners risked becoming the Ralph Naders of the Lacandón jungle. No matter who won, they would be attacked. But there was no turning back.

What the Zapatista Army of National Liberation was about to do— challenging the electoral option at high noon on its own turf—was an audacious if ultimately lonely gesture, but one had to start somewhere. Besides, there were 12 critical presidential and parliamentary elections in Latin America scheduled from December 2005 through December 2006, and the Voice of the Other would be heard a long way off. It was time to move on.

Stan

When Katrina finally got to Chiapas, she had changed sex and was known as Stan ("Stanley" seems kind of a wimp handle for a hurricane). Stan hovered between a hurricane and a tropical storm over the Pacific coastal plain of the state during the first week of October, dumping tons of incessant rain on the already saturated ground (*"llueve sobre mojado"*). A hundred rivers burst their banks, wrecked 600 wretched villages encamped upon the flood plain, blew 90 bridges, buckled the highways, and wiped out 70% of the coffee crop—500,000 to 700,000 sacks of primer Soconusco coffee, the lifeblood of the region. Meanwhile, fair traders who had salvaged what they could after the coyotes picked Los

Altos clean, lost their entire stash in a New Orleans warehouse under Katrina's waters.

But what Stan did to western Chiapas played second fiddle to the havoc that Wilma wrought upon Cancún's infrastructure a few days later, blowing away the beaches and the luxury resorts and the gringo turistas, shutting down the hotels and the airlines that move them in and out, not to mention its effect on the low-rent workers out there in the swamps by the airport, whom, of course, no one ever mentioned. And, of course, because Cancún is under the thumb of the transnational travel and hotel barons, the Fox government directed its relief efforts to getting that "nest of snakes" (its Mayan name) back on its feet before the holiday package tour season kicked in.

Despite Boosh getting caught with his *pantalones* down on Katrina, presidents love these natural disasters. Even Dubya was strutting around in his hard hat just a couple of weeks after disaster struck, directing relief efforts, a "hands-on" president. Similarly the Fox and Señora Marta flew into Chiapas once a week, the president promising aid that was already on its way to Cancún, the first lady patting wrists and mopping brows like some pinche Clara Barton. The only material aid (bottled water, out-of-date medicines, shovels, roofing materials, canned foods) was being parceled out by the political parties in exchange for votes—but the presidenciales were a long way off, so there wasn't even much of that to go around.

The tragicomedy of the disaster named Stan was that all this had happened before almost to the month and date back in 1998 when Mitch had creamed Central America and this end of Chiapas. The same rivers had overrun their banks and flattened the same homes on the same flood plains, and the poor had fled to the same makeshift shelters until the waters receded and then had gone back and picked up the pieces. The parties moved in and handed out the same bottled water and roofing materials in exchange for the *damnificados'* (flood victims') votes. In the sierra, the same threadbare colonies were buried under the same mud, and the same refugees from the same blasted villages blocked the same roads begging the few motorists for coins.

But the difference this time around was that the Zapatista influence was spreading in the once again devastated region. In October 2005, fewer communities waited for the mal gobierno to bail them out. Many now turned to the Caracol Mother of Caracoles–Sea of Our Dreams and the Junta de Buen Gobierno Toward the Hope and the autonomous municipality of Tierra y Libertad to give them a hand—Colonos in Tapachula, Motozintla, and Huixtán, taxistas, street vendors, fisher-people, *triciclistas*—and the EZLN mobilization in the weeks following Stan was an indicator of their spreading influence in the Sierra, along the border, and out to the coast.

Martín, living in a downtrodden colony above the flooded-out Coatán River in Tapachula, didn't have a roof—he had taken refuge up there when the waters rose and then it had fallen in. But he wasn't asking the mal gobierno to fix it for him. "Here there is no government. Our government now is in La Realidad," he explained to Hermann and to Gloria Muñoz. Martín's taco wagon was, in fact, licensed by the JBG at La Realidad.

Other rebel outposts wrestled with the temptation to take government handouts. The damnificados in the Che Guevara popular colony in Motozintla were perplexed, so they agreed that all those who wanted to accept the sacks of concrete and roofing materials would have to divide it equally with those who had refused to take the aid from the mal gobierno's hand.

Meanwhile, *Chómpiras* and its mate, *El Catalán*, were driving corn to the waterlogged compas. Marcos had made a personal Internet appeal for direct aid to the victims of La Otra Tormenta (The Other Storm), and NGO supplies and corn—good Indian corn from Oaxaca—poured into the region. Up in Huixtán, Zapatista brigadistas had established a small clinic to deal with the health care overload caused by Stan.

The EZLN was really just doing its job: *mandar obedeciendo*, governing by serving, obeying the will of the people. There were no TV crews such as trailed Fox and Bush and their wives around while they ministered to the victims, no telethons, no obsequious ceremonies of gratitude, no notice really except by those who took the EZLN to be their government now.

Out of the Chute

In an extravagance unmatched by all the frivolities of the Fox years and an abject insult to those 70 million Mexicans who live in and around the poverty line, the IFE (Federal Electoral Institute), Mexico's maximum electoral authority, allocated 66 billion pesos ($6.6 billion USD) for the upcoming 2006 presidential election, more than the sum total of all the budgets of the nation's antipoverty programs. Of this, $22 billion pesos would be divided up among the parties in accordance with midterm vote tallies—the PRI would walk off with the lion's share. Much of this enormous boodle would accrue to Televisa and its junior partner, TV Azteca, for libelous spots unanimously directed at Andrés Manuel López Obrador. The IFE bone was a big one, and the parties circled the pile like a pack of snarling pariah dogs preparing for a fight that would put *Amores Perros* to shame.

Let's switch to horse-race metaphors. By autumn 2005, the candidates and the parties were jockeying fiercely to hold their positions in the starting gate for the July 2, 2006, run for the roses. Only AMLO, who had no competition for the PRD nomination, was already out of the chute.

After months of stubborn resistance to ceding the PRD nomination to AMLO uncontested, a bitter Cuauhtémoc Cárdenas had collected his cards and gone home, still fully convinced that a fourth run would finally have carried him to the presidency, the destiny his father had decreed for him, as it had for his good friend Lula.

El Peje's plan was to stump-speech through all 300 electoral districts, introducing himself to voters in the far-flung corners of the land—although AMLO had the capital sewed up, Mexico City represents only a fifth of the voters in the union, and he needed to sell himself to electors out in the provinces if he really wanted to win this election.

One potential cornucopia of votes was just across the border in El Norte. Mexicans living in the U.S. had petitioned their government for expatriate balloting since 1929, but since the paisanos were economic and political refugees who inevitably favored the opposition, the PRI had fended off their demands for a vote year after year, decade after decade. Now, for the first time, the Mexican congress had authorized a vote beyond the republic's borders—albeit with so many restrictions that only 1% of those eligible were eventually allowed to vote.

When AMLO was invited to Los Angeles to deliver the traditional Independence Day *grito* of "¡*Viva Mexico!* (Let's Go Kill Some *Gachupines*!)," alongside that city's first mayor of Mexican descent since 1842, he eagerly accepted. But the IFE, citing the fine print in the new electoral law, warned El Peje he would be in violation of campaign regulations and could be barred from the ballot all over again if he accepted Antonio Villaraigosa's invite. Having just narrowly averted desafuero, El Peje reluctantly cancelled the trip. A PAN delegation was subsequently greenlighted by the IFE to canvass California for funds. The electoral institute's arbitrary behavior was a depressing reminder that the IFE was committed to preventing a Peje presidency in 2006.

Otros Caballos

The PRI's Madrazo was slow to find his way into the paddock. He had many skeletons in the closet to attend to first. One of these *calacas* was Elba Esther Gordillo, the tiny, miniskirted Jimmy Hoffa of the National Education Workers Union—the largest labor organization in Latin America—and the secretary general of the PRI. The two despised each other, and Madrazo knew that the moment he abandoned the party presidency to declare his candidacy, the Maestra would take his place and cripple his campaign from the opening gun. She had to be eliminated.

The sinister, ruthless Madrazo had her removed as secretary general with an assist from fate—Elba Esther had just undergone chemotherapy for a life-threatening cancer, and a few twists of his scalpel extirpated this tumor from the party's corpse.

Now Madrazo would square off against the dark horse shady governor of Mexico State, Arturo Montiel, in the PRI's sham primary. Montiel, a party hack with a trophy French wife who seemed to suffer from a serious speech impediment, was being pushed by the "Everyone United Against Madrazo" clique that in 2000 had gravitated to the loser Francisco Labastida. On the eve of the party vote, a sheaf of illegally obtained bank documents fell into the hands of none other than Víctor Trujillo, also known as Brozo the Scary Clown, but this time around Trujillo wasn't wearing his green fright wig when he gave Montiel the AMLO treatment. The high priests of the PRI yanked out Montiel's smoking heart for all Mexico to see on national TV, after which, running unopposed, Roberto Madrazo became the PRI's candidate to take back the presidency of the United States of Mexico.

The PAN is a small, exclusive party—a knot of hard-core reactionary poobahs who call the shots corporate-style. The conventional wisdom had interior secretary Santiago Creel—Fox's handpicked successor selected in the style of pure PRI *dedazo* (literally the "big finger-point," or personal selection of a successor by the outgoing president)—as a shoo-in for the nomination, but such prognostication did not take into account how very much the party fathers (there were no mothers) resented Vicente Fox and, most of all, his grabbingly ambitious Mrs.

Besides, Creel proved early on to be a piss-poor campaigner who took to wearing ill-fitting charro suits as he bumbled from state to state. Also in the running was an environmental secretary who had privatized the environment to big business's delight, and Felipe Calderón, a short, balding, shrill politico who had spent some months as Fox's energy secretary but whose best card was his lineage—Calderón was a descendent of a founding PAN family back in the days when the party's bête noire was the "Bolshevik" Lázaro Cárdenas. After six years of a president whose real party was Coca-Cola and the Virgin of Guadalupe, the money that moved National Action wanted a real PANista in Los Pinos.

Once he had been sworn in (Televisa carried the event live), Felipe Calderón borrowed a page from the Fox's book and called in the slimy Washington insider Dick Morris to poison the waters once again.

Even before the smoke had cleared, it was evident that Calderón was

Washington's gallo. Appearing before the American Chamber of Commerce at a séance presided over by former ambassador Jeffrey Davidow, El Peje was greeted with stony silence when he told the suits he wasn't interested in privatizing PEMEX. Felipe Calderón was applauded wildly when he warmly welcomed private investment in the oil giant.

In addition to the big dogs, there were other bozos on the campaign bus. The Mexican Green Environmental Party (PVEM), whose only interest in green is the color of the money, threw in with the PRI to preserve its electoral registration and the handsome subsidies that come with it. The PVEM is a wholly owned enterprise of the González Torres family, but sibling rivalry between Jorge and Víctor, the proprietor of a chain of generic pharmacies, pushed Víctor to seek the nomination of the Alternative Social Democrat Farmers' Party (*sic*), and he had taken to barnstorming the country in an inflatable doctor's suit in the persona of his pharmacy chain's cartoon logo, Doctor Simi. Somehow, Rigoberta Menchú wound up in his entourage.

Then there was poor Jorge G. Castañeda, whom no party would touch (he had joined and burned many) and who had decided to run as an independent without party affiliation—the Supreme Court quashed poor Jorge's dream.

No matter what the Other Campaign did or did not accomplish, it would smell like a rose in the company of these clowns. *¡Qué Se Vayan Todos!*

During the first week in December, the messianic, populist, left-wing, Chavista, Salinista and declared danger to the republic Andrés Manuel López Obrador came to Chiapas on the final leg of his 300-district run from the Río Bravo to the Río Suchiate. In Tapachula, he spoke to a few thousand steamed-up damnificados still waiting for the relief that would never come.

Up in San Cris, AMLO put on the *chuj*—a short Tzotzil serape—and the beribboned sombrero and received the usual *bastones de mando* as has every presidencial who has ever visited the old colonial city, including Carlos Salinas. AMLO knew he was in treacherous territory and tried hard to be conciliatory. "We desire that Marcos has luck on his journey around Mexico." Godspeed. Yes, El Peje would have preferred that there was no Other Campaign, he told Elio, "but there is. Democracy means everyone gets to criticize. *Ni modo*."

Who is in the left, you or Marcos? "We both are, but we have taken different roads. I have taken the electoral way and the Zapatistas another path. The left never agrees on anything. Zapata argued with the Flores Magón." López Obrador would say no more.

For two days and two nights, AMLO barnstormed deep into the Zapatista zone. Everywhere—in Comitán before several thousand Tojolabales drummed out by the Zapatista-hating CIOAC, and in Ocosingo, where the ORCAO and the ARIC-Independiente filled the plaza—López Obrador pledged to make the San Andrés Accords the law of the land. He would not be like the Fox. He would forcefully lobby Congress for passage of the same Indian Rights law his own party's senators had voted down.

The EZLN stayed out of sight during AMLO's perambulations through the zone. No sign at any rally questioned López Obrador's candidacy or suggested that the compas were even aware that El Peje had encroached. AMLO had taken the initiative and dared to spread his manure right under the EZLN's nose, and Delegate Zero had refused to take a whiff.

THE BAD GAS

No se puede vivir
con una muerte dentro:
hay que elegir
entre arrojarla lejos
como fruta podrida,
o al contagio
dejarse morir.

(You cannot live
with a death inside you

You have to choose:
throw it far away
like rotten fruit,
or let it infect you
and die.)

—*Alaíde Foppa, murdered soon after crossing into Guatemala from Chiapas in 1982*

In the eight years since 49 Abejas (including four unborn babies) had been massacred at Acteal, December 22 had become a sort of national day against impunity. The Indians' grief by now was quietly reflective, their martyrs ritualized, but their outrage at the injustices committed against them by the mal gobierno was never quite contained.

The list of those responsible for the killings who had never been called to account started with Doctor Zedillo of Yale. The Chiapas governor at the time, Julio César Ruiz Ferro, had been promoted to the Mexican embassy in Washington and was now a Fox functionary. The interior secretary, Emilio Chuayffet, who did nothing to halt the killing, was the leader of the PRI delegation in the lower house and would soon be a senator again. General Mario Renán Castillo, who implemented the counterinsurgency plan that led to the Abejas' deaths, slept each night in soft beds, as did Jorge Enrique Hernández, the head of Chiapas public security, who had tried to burn the bodies, and the secretary of government, Uriel Jarquín, who had sought unsuccessfully to cover it all up.

Eighty-seven Indians the color of the earth were in jail for the killings at Acteal. Eight years after the massacre, most remained unsentenced. Six had been absolved and 27 arrest orders were outstanding, including two for the white police commanders who had fled into the night. Two other white police officers had served their time and gone home. Many of the prisoners had been rousted and railroaded into prison, scapegoats for a crime that was hatched in the highest halls of power.

Vicente Fox had come to the presidency promising change, accountability, an end to such impunity. He had proposed to fix Chiapas in 15 minutes and it still leaked blood. The whole country reeked just as strongly of impunity as when the PRI ran the show. Monstrous crimes were committed against the people and no one was ever to blame.

Some of the names of these crimes were Tlatelolco and Thursday of Corpus and the Dirty War. Fox had pledged to establish a Truth Commission to get at the bottom of these state crimes, but instead appointed a special prosecutor who was unable or unwilling to tell the truth about the hundreds sacrificed at Tlatelolco or the massacre of students on Corpus Christi in 1971 ordered by then-president Luis Echeverria, or about a *guerra sucia* that had left 600 dead and disappeared.

When Ignacio Carillo Prieto, the cousin of an FLN combatant killed by the White Brigade at Nepantla long before there was an EZLN, subpoenaed military records of the disappeared, the records themselves disappeared. Rooms of incriminating documents in the National Archives at the former Lecumberri prison, where so many of these crimes took place, were declared off limits. Files vanished, witnesses were gunned down. When Carrillo Prieto finally brought Echeverría before a court on charges of genocide, the case was thrown out because the statute of limitations on genocide had expired. In six futile years, the special prosecutor was able to capture one midlevel gorilla. The prosecutor's final report avoids fixing any responsibility at all for these deaths. Thirty-seven years after Tlatelolco, no one was to blame. Case closed.

While Fox dazzled the globalizers with his Coca-Cola smile, a fiesta of rapine reigned down below. In the first month of his presidency, the Fox had overseen the brazen escape of narco-lord Número Uno, "El Chapo" Guzmán, from a maximum-security Jalisco prison. Now Shorty's cartel and its rivals had turned Mexican cities into shooting galleries and the fountains spouted blood. Hundreds had been mowed down in Nuevo Laredo, there were more decapitations in Acapulco than in Baghdad, the Suchiate ran red at Tapachula, and dozens were sacrificed each week in Culiacán, the cradle of all this narco-mayhem. Under Fox, the cartels had built their own private armies, like the Zetas, trained as drug fighters by the U.S. at Fort Bragg before they defected.

The Fox's policy had been to let the slime wipe out the slime, but many innocent citizens had gotten plugged in the process. Meanwhile, El Chapo had his own office at Los Pinos. Nahum Acosta, Fox's travel manager, was accused by the attorney general of conspiring with a Chapo lieutenant. A few weeks later, Acosta was quietly released from custody. No one was ever held accountable. No one ever paid—except, of course, *el pueblo.*

As the Fox neared the end of his term, none of the crimes of the past he had sworn to resolve had been laid to rest. There were 400 Muertas and mounting in Juárez, mutilated torsos tossed out in the maquiladora desert and no one ever knew anything. Who was responsible for the political scandals—PEMEXgate, Amigogate, the videos? Why was no one ever prosecuted? Who orchestrated the plots against El Peje? Raul Salinas is released from prison for stealing the nation blind, and Carlos never ever saw the inside of a jail cell except when he visited his brother. The massacres at Aguas Blancas, El Charco, San Juan de la Libertad? Who ordered the '88 election stolen from Cárdenas? And the 500 PRDistas blown away after the PRI stole the election? Was there even an investigation? Who killed Colosio? What killed Digna Ochoa? Who was to blame for this shame? What were their names? These were the questions that still remained after six years of Fox's strange reign as the nation set sail once again on uncertain seas toward July 2, 2006.

Great crimes were lodged in the intestines of the nation, and until this shit was unstopped, the bad gas from down below would never let Mexico sleep easy

13. Winter/Spring 2006

Revving Up

At roughly 11:28 a.m., Zapatista standard time on the first morning of 2006, the 12th anniversary of the Zapatista rebellion, Delegate Zero, encased in a shiny black-visored crash helmet, mounted a silver and black Yamaha à la Che Guevara and roared out of the Caracol Road to Hope down in the Cañadas to initiate the first leg of the Other Campaign.

A thousand revelers had journeyed down to La Garrucha to see the Sup off. The Che gambit attracted the cameras—even Al Jazeera covered the send-off. But, nearing 50 with a modest paunch, the Sup was no match for the svelte heartthrob Gael García Bernal, who starred in *The Motorcycle Diaries*. Besides, Che's favorite chopper had been an old Norton 500 named *La Poderosa*. Marcos had christened his machine more poetically—*Shadowlight*.

The Yamaha's luggage box carried a handmade bumper sticker: "Caution! Penguin On Board!" But there is confusion about the veracity of this affirmation. Marcos had been seen in La Garrucha with the bird, but whether it was actually on board remains unconfirmed. Hermann insists he saw the Sup plop the penguin in the luggage box. Others claim that the poor animal was served up in a farewell "Sopa de Pinguino" back in La Garrucha.

Both Marcos and Hermann, leaving La Garrucha that first morning must have had mixed emotions. They and the Otra were both moving on. Would they ever be back?

Delegate Zero was awaited by 15,000 compas from Los Altos at the usual gathering place in San Cristóbal down by the Coca-Cola plant, less than on this same day back in 2003, but really only representing one part of the EZLN's base, the Highlands.

The march into the city at dusk featured no flaming torches as it had three years before. In fact, there was precious little illumination along the route—the PRI mayor of San Cristóbal had maliciously doused all the streetlamps. The marchers surged toward the Cathedral Plaza, but the street was blocked and the line of march piled up on those in front, turning the center of the city into a mosh pit. When I protested after going down for the third time under the shoes of the UNAM students behind me, they taunted, "¡Fuera, pinche Viejo!" (Get out of here, you fucking old man.) The scent of youthful intolerance wafted on the evening zephyrs.

That part of the Comandancia that was on hand to formally bid adieu to the Sup was gathered on the speakers' platform beneath a great swirling mandala of a mural. Red flags unfurled in the crowd below, a portrait of Joe Stalin or two. The Mexican Communist Party (ML) had tried to drape a hammer-and-sickle banner at the front of the march, but the compas made them remove it. The MLers were becoming a regular feature of the Other Campaign.

Tacho delivered a prototypical rant in defense of the campesinos of Mexico against the NAFTA killing machine and encouraged farmers everywhere to sign on to La Otra. Comandante Kelly invited the women to join the campaign—Mexico needed to take them into account: Women were not just *cosas* (things) of the *cama* (bed) and the *cocina* (kitchen). Zebedeo spoke to the young people of the land Marcos would soon be visiting and urged their participation in La Otra. David was grave: Delegate Zero would encounter great dangers as he rode out to visit with the simple and humble people of Mexico. The mal gobierno would make the passage a difficult one.

Delegado Zero acknowledged his companeros' concerns: "If something bad does happen, you should know that I am proud to have fought alongside you." But the Sup was revving up for the road, championing the Other as the antithesis of "The Pact of Chapultepec," the pet project of multibillionaire Carlos Slim, AMLO's moneybags, to put a happy face on the pain that neoliberalism has inflicted upon the poor. Proposed at Chapultepec Castle, where the Emperor Maximilian once held forth, and inked at the Palace of Bellas Artes by 4,000 impresarios, intellectuals, and politicos, la crème de la crème of Mexican high society, the Chapultepec Pact would lock Mexico's great divide between rich and poor into place for all eternity. Embraced by Calderón and less energetically by AMLO, the Pacto de Chapultepec was designed to make neoliberalism more palatable to the pobres. Now Delegate Zero would sally forth to do battle with this dragon.

The next morning the Sexta Coleta (non-Indian San Cristóbalites who adhered to the Sixth Declaration) met out at the experimental "University of the Earth" in a wooded corner of San Cristóbal's periphery. The all-day session set the style for how the Otra Campaña would operate. Adherents took the mic to express their dissatisfaction with the conditions of their lives. Zero took copious notes, occasionally emitting words of wisdom. When I kvetched to the Sexta Coleta about being moshed in the plaza the night before and asked for a place in the Other Campaign for the "veterans," every grayhead in the house raised their fist in solidarity. Marcos puffed his pipe and said nothing. La Otra was already the property of the young.

Chiapas was arguably the most dangerous of the 32 entities La Otra would visit in the next months. Pockets of resentment at the EZLN and the Other Campaign smoldered in distinct corners of the state. The ranchers and now the PRD would be lying in wait.

The test drive was the January 3rd trip to Palenque in the north of

Chiapas. If trouble came, it would happen out here on the curvy two-lane blacktop, an "accident" such as wrecked Amado's life, a sniper's bullet. There were few supporters waiting by the side of the highway but many levels of police assigned to "protect" Delegate Zero, although the EZLN had adamantly protested their presence. It was in the Fox's best interests to "protect" the Sup, wrote Guillermo Almeyra, an AMLO unconditional, so that the Other Campaign could be unleashed against López Obrador. Almeyra likened such protection to the steel rail car the Kaiser had provided for Lenin enabling him to sneak back into Russia unnoticed to start a revolution and force the czar to move his troops off Germany's eastern flank.

Five thousand members of base communities in the north of Chiapas awaited Delegate Zero at the gates of that tropical city adjacent to the great Mayan ruins at Palenque. As we marched toward the plaza, I committed the sin of looking up (Marcos counsels adherents to "look down"). A ragged "López Obrador, Our Next President" banner flapped in the sultry breeze.

Although the ride over had been a benign one (the Sup was now being conveyed in a white van), Marcos insisted that dozens of armed ranchers were waiting for him outside of town. Nonetheless, La Otra returned to San Cristóbal without incident, and Delegate Zero spent the next afternoon navigating the steep allies of the Hormiga colony, where so many of the evangelicals expelled from Chamula now lived. The Hormiga figured prominently in the Zapatistas' prehistory, having provided weapons and transportation for the rebels back on that fateful first of January, and the Sup warmly greeted the Imán Domingo López Angel like an old comrade in arms.

Now the expedition began in earnest. The Other caravaned cautiously downhill past Zinacantán to meet with adherents in Chapa de Corzo and the state capital, Tuxtla Gutiérrez, then swerved west to Cintalapa, pausing to salute political prisoners at El Amate, the high-security lockup with which Governor Pablo had replaced the crumbling Cerro Hueco, and turned south on the Pacific coast highway to gather the damnificados of Stan.

The first days of La Otra were exuberant ones, "like a great burst of hope, a breath of air" from the dull plod of politics as usual, wrote Luis Hernández. The Other "aspired to make visible the invisible," to build a great alliance of "simple and humble people" that could stop the mal gobierno in its tracks. *¡Ojalá que sí!*

COMANDANTA RAMONA, THE SMALLEST OF THE SMALL

Those who die for life are not dead! Not one minute of silence but a life of struggle! ¡Viva Comandanta Ramona!
—Sign on the wall of the Cine Paraíso in Tonalá, Chiapas

Sub Zero was playing a dilapidated movie palace in Tonalá when word reached him that Comandanta Ramona had passed as she was being rushed to hospital in San Cristóbal. There was a hurried huddle in the lobby, and Marcos announced to the handful in attendance that the Other Campaign was suspending its activities and would return to Oventik to accompany Comandanta Ramona, *la mas pequeña* (the smallest of the small), back to the earth of her beloved San Andrés.

Ramona had been an early member of the Clandestine Revolutionary Indigenous Committee, the organizer of the Zapatista Army of National Liberations in the highlands around Sakamch'én. In 1993, Ramona and Comandante Susana were commissioned to take the Revolutionary Law of Women to the communities for discussion and confronted much hostility from their male comrades. But Ramona stood her ground. Just over four feet in her muddy boots, Ramona carried a 12-gauge shotgun almost as long as herself down to San Cristóbal that January 1st under the command of another Zapatista woman, Major Ana María. Due in part to Ramona's diligence, a third of the Zapatista fighting force were women.

Perhaps Ramona's most iconic moment came during the conversations with the mal gobierno in Don Samuel's Cathedral of Peace just six weeks after the rebellion. Seated next to Tatic, her tiny feet not even touching the floor, she suddenly whipped a neatly folded Mexican flag out of her shoulder bag and tried to hand one end to Sub Marcos, but she could not reach him. Gallantly, Manuel Camacho Solís, Salinas's peace negotiator, stepped in, and a thousand flashbulbs popped. The rest was herstory.

Ramona fell ill during her stay in the cathedral, and a doctor from a local peace group diagnosed her with kidney failure. But there seemed no way to move her to Mexico City for treatment. That summer, when the women chanted for her at the National Democratic Convention in Guadalupe Tepeyac, Tacho explained that she was too ill to attend. Later, *Reforma* reported that she had died. I attended a memorial service for her in Querétaro just hours before Zedillo invaded Chiapas in February 1995.

But then weeks later, with soldiers occupying Zapatista communities in the jungle and the highlands, the EZLN issued a video in which Ramona seemed quite alive, telling Zedillo's sardos to go home to their mamas.

The most memorable frames I have stored in my scrapbook of a mind come from October 1996. The Zaps and Zedillo were nose to nose. The National Indigenous Congress had invited the EZLN to its founding convention in Mexico City and the CCRI had accepted. "We're going!" But the mal gobierno claimed that the rebels were under house arrest in Chiapas and would be arrested for sedition the moment they crossed the state line. "We're going!" Marcos repeated. "They're Coming!" the Mexico City dailies reported in big black headlines.

On October 9, reporters were summoned down to La Realidad for the Zapatistas' defiant departure. Marcos met us at the ejido house. "We have decided to send our most belligerent warrior and our greatest symbol of war," the Sup deadpanned and walked over to a nearby hut from which emerged Comandanta Ramona. The reporters were flabbergasted. Was that all there was after all this woofing?

In her brilliant Tzotzil blouse and long skirt, Ramona was a dead ringer for the dolls the Chamula women sell to the tourists in San

Cristóbal. But she was sick, her kidneys were failing and the Indian congress, which would be held in a medical center auditorium, seemed the best way to get to a hospital.

Ramona returned from the capital with a new kidney in early 1997 and was not heard from for eight years. She became, in effect, her doll. "This is Marcos," the Chamula women would point at the Marcos doll, "and this is Ramona," thrusting her proudly at the buyer. But then in September 2005, at the plenary in La Garrucha, suddenly there was Ramona. There had been rumors of schism in the Comandancia, and all of the members of the CCRI were compelled to attend. She looked healthy, reported Hermann, who is a medical doctor in his spare time, as she sat at the head table joking with the Sup.

In the first interview ever granted by members of the CCRI, Ramona told Blanche Petrich how hard the lives of the women were—sometimes if there was not enough food the women would feed their husbands and children and go hungry themselves. But in fact Ramona had neither husband nor children—she had never married. Or rather she was married to the EZLN.

Ramona lived all her short life in one of the 46 parajes clustered around Sakamch'én. Her *oficio* (her place in the community) was as a *bordadera*, a master embroiderer, stitching the brilliant red threads into magnificent huipiles that sometimes took three years to complete. In public, her little fingers were always moving, sewing invisible threads. Ramona and her sister bordaderas of Los Altos literally turned apartheid into art—the Conquistadores had ordered that each village wear a distinct pattern so that troublemakers could be easily weeded out, and the Tzotzil women had fought back by creating stupendously beautiful huipiles.

Comandanta Ramona was laid to rest on a bright blue winter Sunday under a cloud of white flowers with a cortege of a thousand women softly singing hymns in Tzotzil behind her—hundreds came from Chamula to honor the little rebel who had made them a good living.

President Fox sent condolences (via Luis H.). So did Bishop Arizmendi and Oliver Stone. The *New York Times* ran an obit. Televisa revealed that her real name was María Santiz, 49. But to the Zapatista rebels in the mountains and jungle of southeastern Mexico—and to many more around the world—she will always be Comandanta Ramona, *la mas pequeña,* the smallest of the small.

EVO PRESIDENTE!

On January 22, Evo Morales, the Aymara Indian leader of Bolivia's coca farmers, became the first indigenous president of that majority indigenous country (60-80%) to the dismay and disdain of Washington.

Evo was hardly the first Indian president of a Latin American nation, as some claimed. That honor fell to the self-hating Zapotec Benito Juárez, who was president of Mexico in the mid-nineteenth century. Right next door in Peru, Alejandro Toledo was a Quechua from Ancash who had been shanghaied by the Peace Corps and brainwashed by the World Bank before he was returned to country to run for the presidency. But Evo was a *red Indian*—his party was the Movement Toward Socialism (MAS), and he favored the nationalization of Bolivia's immense natural gas deposits and the commercialization of the sacred Inca plant, coca. The Aymara's ascendancy to the presidential throne so spooked the Bush that a garrison of Yanqui Special Forces was stationed in Paraguay just across Bolivia's eastern border.

Evo's inauguration was a high note on the Latin Left's nascent 2006 social calendar. Filled with Aymara ritual and the burning of bushels of coca leaf to the Pachamama, the affair drew dozens of Latin luminaries to La Paz with Comandante Chávez in the lead. The five-star hotels were packed with the retinues of Lula, Néstor Kirchner, Tabaré Vázquez, even Ricardo Lagos, the outgoing president of Chile, with which Bolivia entertained a hundred-year-long beef over access to Pacific ports.

Vicente Fox, who had already squabbled with the new Bolivian president over his intended nationalization of privately owned gas fields, snubbed the coronation. Fox had openly scuffled with every left leader in Latin America during his five-plus years in Los Pinos, breaking off diplomatic relations with Cuba even before Castañeda had cleaned out his desk at the foreign ministry.

Fox had also gone up against Kirchner and Hugo Chávez (and even futbol idol Diego Maradona) at the Summit of the Americas in Mar de Plata, Argentina, the previous November. Chávez had blasted Fox as "a puppy of Imperialism," and the two Latin oil titans had withdrawn ambassadors.

Subcomandante Marcos was a no-show. Early on, Evo had extended Marcos a special invitation, not because he shared the EZLN's eccentric ideology (he had termed eschewing state power "absurd" when we spoke in Cochabamba in 2004) but because the Zapatistas were such a potent symbol of the indigenous awakening in Latin America.

But as might be expected, Marcos did not RSVP and his bad manners were sharply criticized by adversaries like Almeyra: "[Marcos] won't go to Evo's inauguration, because it is a successful example of the people taking power through the ballot." Other detractors saw Delegate Zero's failure to fly off to La Paz as evidence that he had abandoned the Indian struggle.

The EZLN distrusts those who take power from above—although arguably Evo had done so with the collective power of those down below—and it was the direction not the man that guided them now. The Other looked down. La Paz is 12,000 feet up in the clouds.

The truth was that Sub Zero didn't have any time to pay social calls that January as he crisscrossed the three states of the Yucatán Peninsula hearing out the poor and pissed-off, preaching "peaceful" class war and the overthrow of the government, "swimming against the electoral current" (Hermann) as he caravaned from one downtrodden ejido and popular colony to the next.

Marcos's modus operandi was to arrive early, sometimes with the roosters, hold bilateral huddles with local struggle organizations, and do a public meeting in the town plaza in the early evening. Sometimes there were 50 "adherents" to receive him, sometimes several hundred. The Sup drew 4,000 in Cancún (Hermann's count) and 2,000 in Mérida, just about what the real candidates were pulling in during the early weeks of their presidential campaigns. The crowds were swollen by the curious and police in plainclothes. Lots of police.

"Death to Marcos!" was painted on the pastel walls of Mérida, a PANista stronghold. Danger was always just ahead on the road map and security was tight. Each state Otra Campaign took charge of keeping the Sup safe and sound. Sometimes there were disputes over who owned his time.

A few days after Evo Morales had been inaugurated president of Bolivia, a position with little job security (187 presidents in the Andean nation's 200-year history), Delegate Zero pulled into the Hopelchén ejido in the middle of Campeche's Calakmul jungle and took a moment to finally RSVP La Paz. "Our idea is not to turn above but to look belowm" the Delegate reiterated to a handful of Mayan farmers at the ejido assembly. "It is not the Zapatistas' way to meet with great leaders. We think a whole people must come to power, not just one person. That is why we have come here today to listen to you—because no one else ever does."

But despite their failure to show up at his big party, Evo really must have been listening. When sworn in as his country's first indigenous president, he pledged, "as Subcomandante Marcos says," to "*mandar obedeciendo*," to govern by obeying the will of the Bolivian people.

POSTCARDS FROM THE OTHER MEXICO

Marcos is in Mérida. Everywhere he perambulates on the Yucatán Peninsula, people ask him why he wears that stupid mask. "*¡Quita la capucha!*" (Take off that hood!) the Yucatecos yell at him in traffic. So now before a few thousand aficionados in the park, he is going to do a striptease. The adherents gasp as he doffs his crumpled Mao hat and headset and grabs his scalp. "Oops, I think I dropped my wig," he mutters and then pulls off the ski mask—to reveal a second mask, the black cotton ones the Zapatistas wear in hot weather. It is really hot in Mérida.

The muddy white van pulls up to the state prison in Tacotalpa, Tabasco.

Delegate Zero is determined to visit two political prisoners the Fox once promised to set free. Don Pancho Pérez and Don Angel Concepción are both adherents of the Sexta. The Tabasco Other Campaign has made arrangements with prison authorities, and Marcos plus two local representatives will be allowed to enter. But as they disappear behind the big barred prison gate, a palpable shudder runs through the hundred or so supporters gathered outside, and as the minutes tick by, the nervousness builds. Was it a trap? Have they taken Marcos? But an hour later, the Sup is sprung. He is carrying a sheet of school notebook paper, testimony from Don Pancho and Don Angel that the authorities had tried to bargain their release for a photo op of Marcos with Luis H. Alvarez.

Marcos does the prison tour of the Other Mexico. On the Oaxaca isthmus, he disappears inside the Tehuantepec CERESO (social rehabilitation center) to gab with adherents, and up in Oaxaca City he is allowed in the dread Santa María Ixcotel lockup to hear out 16 new adherents, Zapotecs from the Loxichas accused of being members of the EPR and now in their tenth year behind bars. The Sup will visit Tepic prison in Nayarit, the scene of bloody prison riots, and try to enter the CERESO in Guanajuato, city of mummies, but will be refused because he won't remove his mask. Furious, Delegate Zero calls for an international tourist boycott of Guanajuato. No other candidate or anti-candidate will campaign in the prisons of Mexico. But then Marcos isn't looking for votes.

Iberdrola is a Spanish-based global energy conglom that is "turning the wind into money" (Delegate Zero) at La Venta, Oaxaca, where the aeolian blasts are already fierce enough to tip over trailers. The blades of the giant wind farm decapitate migratory birds that fall to the earth headless by the hundreds. The weight of the mills is so great it is pressing into the water source. El Zero assumes the appropriate stance, a new Quixote tilting his lance at the global windmills. Up the hill, an irate rancher annoyed by the Sup's visit releases a herd of unruly bulls and they come charging down, all red-eyed and snorting steam. Los Otros y Las Otras dash for the vehicles and beat it out of there. Out on the highway, the convoy is stoned by PRD supporters.

Marcos is in a hotel room in Puebla. Suddenly, a tiny suitcase is thrust under the door, followed by none other than, ahem, Don Durito of the Lacandon. He has caught up with the Other to be Delegate Zero's *escudero* (lance holder.) The beetle advises that he has permission from the MAREZ of Charlie Parker. "Charlie Parker?" the Sup asks himself—there was no MAREZ named for Charlie Parker when he left.

Delegate Zero tells this tale and others to a crazy-quilt gathering of "alternative" media in Tlaxcala in mid-February. Indeed, there was no other media but the "alternative" kind, save for Hermann and an intermittent stringer for *Milenio* covering La Otra. The Tlaxcala encounter results in the founding of the Other Journalism, which resolves to look down. Since most alternative journalists are already down, the injunction is to just look around.

Marcos plunges through a rose-colored door in Apizaco, Tlaxcala, a truck drivers' town. The interior walls are painted a whorehouse pink. The Sup has come to this "Casa de Citas" at the invitation of a dozen or so sexoservidoras who adhere to the Sexta and the Other. They are serious women "with a wounded look," Hermann notes. Most are single mothers. They sit at the living room table and chew out the police and the health authorities and the hypocrisy of small town morals. Marcos is not a candidate. He can't do anything about their grievances. Only they can change all this by aligning themselves with the simple and humble people all over the Other Mexico. The group draws up a call for the formation of a national sexoservidoras union.

Delegate Zero has not visited much Indian territory on this sojourn. Mostly, he connects with them on the ejidos and in the popular colonies, but he is traveling through mestizo turf now, and often the only Indian motif at the rallies are the Mohawks of the punks. On March 18, he enters Huichol (Wixarika) lands in the Altos of Jalisco and meets with the autonomous council of elders in a clearing in the forest. The elders speak slowly, reflecting upon their spiritual connection to these mountains. The encounter lasts for nine hours. Delegate Zero seems impatient to get his message across. He does the usual number on the political class and calls for the overthrow of the government. Hermann describes the meeting as "cordial but reserved." As Marcos has moved farther and farther away from the Zapatista communities in Chiapas, his connection to the compas who confer upon him both authority and authenticity has frayed. Delegate Zero has another agenda now.

Sub Zero is invited to speak with Nahua Indian adherents in Huayacocotla in the Hidalgo Huasteca, a mountain range that spans five central Mexican states. His audiences are all women—the men have been driven to El Norte by *desgraciada pobreza* (disgraceful poverty—a popular corrido.) The Sup talks to the women about Zapatista women, about *nuestra jefa* Comandanta Ramona—he wears a black mourning patch. But the women have some nuts-and-bolts questions: How do the Zapatista women handle drunken husbands? They really need to talk with the Zapatista women themselves, but there are no Zapatista women and Marcos is neither a woman nor an Indian. Indeed, the voices of both the Indians and the women were not heard on the Other Campaign. This was a one-man show.

SEPARATION

Uncle Sam drew first blood in the border Intifada of 2006. Twenty-two-year-old Guillermo Martínez was shot in the back with an expanding bullet fired by a migra agent named Faustino Campos as the young migrant's brother tried to pull Guillermo back through the triple fence up at the Zapata canyon in Tijuana's Colonia Libertad. Todd Fraser, spokesperson for the San Diego sector of what is now called Immigration Customs Enforcement (ICE), a wholly owned division of the Department of Homeland Security, explained that Guillermo had been throwing rocks and hurling insults at agent Campos—there had been 218 such stonings in fiscal 2004-05, he pointed out. Fisher underscored that agents were now encouraged to use deadly force if they considered their lives endangered. The Israeli Defense Force uses an identical rationale for gunning down Palestinians.

Guillermo Martínez died on New Year's Eve at the Tijuana Red Cross clinic, one more muerto on the list of 450 Mexicans and Central Americans who die each year trying to get across the line to take a job no gavacho would touch. QDEP.

During March and April, La Otra Campaña convoyed through the dusty outback of central Mexico—Hidalgo, Querétaro, Aguascalientes, Guanajuato, Jalisco, Nayarit, Colima, Michoacán, Guerrero, feeder states that send their men up to El Otro Lado generation after generation. Many never come back. At pit stops along the dry country roads, there were only the very young and the very old to receive the caravan, the young men, and increasingly the women, having gone north. Separation ran like a seam of pain through the meetings.

Mexican immigration became a hot-button issue north of the Río Bravo in the spring of 2006. Between March 25 and May 1, an estimated 5 million mostly Mexican and Mexican-descent marchers took to the streets of major and not so major U.S. cities to protest a repressive bill passed by the House the previous November that made it a felony crime to be inside the U.S. without proper papers. HB 4437, popularly known as the "Ley Sensenbrenner" for Wisconsin Republican James Sensenbrenner, the Kimberly Clark heir who sponsored the measure, also provided five-year penalties for any U.S. citizen who so much as offered an undocumented worker a glass of water.

A half-million marched in Chicago and a half-million in Los Angeles, not once but twice. Dallas turned out hundreds of thousands, and Salt Lake City, not a popular destination for Mexicans, 50,000. A hundred thousand gathered before the Washington Monument, invoking Martin Luther King's dream. "¡Si Se Puede!," César Chávez's battle cry (it was the 15th anniversary of his passing), rang out all across the land. The marches represented the largest outpouring of public protest in Gringolandia since the Vietnam War, outdoing massive protests against Bush's mad war in Iraq. How did all this happen?

The mega-marches were organized by a very ad hoc coalition—old-line Latino organizations like the Council of La Raza, the League of United Latin American Citizens (LULAC), the Chicano student organization MECHA, even the Mexican Brotherhood, the late Bert Corona's legacy, joined forces with the Mexican service clubs of migrant workers from feeder states such as Zacatecas, Michoacán, and Oaxaca, whose members send billions back to their home states annually and who have considerable credibility and clout in the Mexican migrant community. The Catholic Church—Los Angeles Cardinal Roger Mahoney was pivotal—blessed the marches and encouraged the participation of the faithful. The unions, particularly the Service Employees (SEIU) and the Hotel and Restaurant Workers, which had been organizing undocumented workers for a decade, signed on. So did Big Business—the National Chamber of Commerce endorsed a guest worker program backed by Bush that would permit corporate America a stable supply of undocumented workers who could be legally exploited. Hotshot Mexican DJs in Chicago and Los Angeles got on board—El Mandril, El Cucuy, El Picolín—and the kids heard the news. Mexican teenagers walked out of their classrooms, and the jailbreak spread from high school to middle school right down to kindergarten.

On May 1, the day on which the world honors labor everywhere but in the country where the celebration was born back in 1886 during the struggle of immigrant workers for the eight-hour day in Chicago, a new generation of immigrant workers surged into the streets. Organizers had called for a boycott—no work, no school, no shopping. The action was modeled on a popular flick, *A Day Without a Mexican*, in which all the Mexicans suddenly disappear for 24 hours and the U.S. shudders to a dead stop," and May 1 put a dent in the workforce—Las Vegas casinos, heavily dependent on Mexican labor, went dark and absent workers slowed down the fast food lines at McDonald's and its ilk. "Who will watch your baby when I'm deported," read a handmade sign at the New York march.

EL ROLLO

The Otra traveled through a landscape of desolation, its compass describing the trail of pain that neoliberalism had blazed upon the Other Mexico. Delegate Zero heard the same sad stories night after night—tired farmers gathered in the ejido house wearily told how they had been dispossessed of their land by a new airport or tourist development, exhausted market women displaced by yet another Wal-Mart, workers who went to work one day and found the factory shut down and the bosses gone, mothers whose kids had all migrated north and never returned.

There were too many tragedies and not enough tears to go around. A Nahua elder tells of the 20 years he spent in prison for cutting firewood on government land, an angry youth wasting away from AIDS weeps as he recalls being denied care at hospitals in the PANista state of Yucatán. Repression, oppression, depression, police brutality, false imprisonment, evictions, restrictions, the death of a forest. The simple and humble people brought their grief to Delegate Zero all day and all night as if he were some human mailbox who could deliver their desperation to those who live on top. "I am not a candidate," he kept repeating, "I can't do anything about all this. Only you can change this together with other simple and humble people. . . ."

Not all of the stories were sad. Despite the misery inflicted by the neoliberal scourge, some continued to fight back, to say no to the installation of a gas station that would contaminate groundwater in Cuautla, Morelos, or the Parota Dam in Guerrero that would flood out 26 communities and 17,000 hectares of corn land. The campesinos would never be bought off, never surrender. They would die here under the waters of the government dam.

But such heroic resistance came in short spurts. Colonos would block a highway one day to protest some outrage the mal gobierno had dumped on their persons or properties and then go home the next to their hovels, unsatisfied, with the crumbs. No one was connecting up the dots between these small displays of defiance. That was the job of the Otra Campaña.

So Sub Marcos trekked this trail of tears pleading with the simple and humble people to come together and overthrow the government. "*¡No están sólos!*" he would urge his audiences, you are not alone, exactly what Mexico had said to the Zapatistas on the March of the People the Color of the Earth five years before. *¡No están sólos!*

Frustrations mined this difficult passage, and those who traveled with Delegate Zero would say (off the record) that he seemed impatient and cranky. "This is an activist Marcos we have never seen before," Hermann confided. No candidate worked as hard as the anti-candidate to get his message out, but often it was misunderstood. Chontales in Tabasco asked for bridges and roads as if Marcos was Roberto Madrazo or López Obrador. No matter how often he laid it out, many who came to the meetings mistakenly thought the Sup was running for office. "We don't want your vote. We don't want to be the government. We want to overthrow the government."

El Zero had different pitches for young people, Indians, women, and workers. He talked in a cant Hermann tagged "Castilla de Indio," the way Indians like Elías Contreras spoke Spanish when they went to the big city. Marcos was not an Indian, but this was a way of telling you he had lived a long time with Indians, much as white people who have grown up around African-Americans talk black.

Marcos said different words to different people, but it was the same *rollo* (political rhetoric) every day and every night. "Look down below!" "The system will fall!" "Overthrow the mal gobierno!" "Down with capitalism!" "Our destiny is victory!" Spieling about "new forms of resistance" got old fast. The pace was grueling and like all candidates and anti-candidates, the Sup sometimes spoke on automatic pilot.

In his ceaseless *chorro* (stream of words), Marcos often breached decorum, libeled the president and the parties and the political class and

AMLO, the biggest skunk of them all, always calling for the government's overthrow (albeit "peacefully"). His words tested the limits of free speech in a Mexico where, not so many years ago, the mal gobierno would have cut out his tongue for having uttered such barbarities.

But there were many signs that not all was copacetic in the belly of the Otra. "¡Marcos! ¡Marcos!" chanted young fanáticos. "Bless the mother who gave birth to you," a woman in Cholula waved her sign, trying to get the Sup's eye. The adulation was debilitating. Subcomandante Insurgente Marcos has always danced on the edge of personality cult, and being a one-man band enhanced the danger of stepping over the line. His speeches at public meetings seemed to grow longer and longer, but maybe that was only the way Hermann reported them. Was he still listening to anything more than what his headset told him?

Fears that the largely dormant but still armed guerrilla in Guerrero might object to the Other's arrival in their turf proved false. In fact, the ERPI and the FARP expressed adherence. Only in Atoyac, on Guerrero's Costa Grande, from which Lucio Cabañas had risen in rebellion three decades earlier, was there trouble, when two groups claiming the old guerrillero's mantle started brawling during a wreath-laying at Lucio's statue.

The hammers and sickles, red flags and portraits of Stalin had become campaign paraphernalia as the Other moved toward Mexico City. The Mexican Communist Party (ML) and other revolutionary Communist factions shadowed La Otra every millimeter of the way, selling their literature, handing out leaflets that expressed "critical support" for the Other Campaign, which they opportunistically utilized as a recruiting trough. Marcos was blasé about the infiltration. All of the left was welcome on board, even these Neanderthals. Some people are turned off by the hammer and sickle but that was their business, he declaimed. "We rose up in rebellion. We are not afraid of these things. We respect all of the parties of the Communists."

At a meeting in Bellavista, Nayarit, in an old factory that had been converted into a labor museum, Delegate Zero cleared the air: "We are going to overthrow the government and kick the rich out of the country. We will install a workers' government and replace capitalism with socialism." Down below (the podium), there was pandemonium as hundreds of red flags undulated wildly and the militants of three Communist splinter parties cheered on the new direction of La Otra. What had begun last summer and fall as an anarchist romp to build a nonhierarchal left from the bottom would arrive in Mexico City flying a portrait of the totalitarian Stalin.

Falta lo que falta. What was missing? The Sexta had tried to answer that question: the rest of Mexico. Now out here in the rest of Mexico, what was missing was the heart of the Zapatista rebellion, the Indians.

FEAR AND LOATHING ON THE CAMPAIGN TRAIL (WITH APOLOGIES TO HUNTER T.)

By Holy Week, with less than 90 days until July 2, the campaigns had turned unabashedly ugly. As the candidates took the final turn into the home stretch, it was everybody and anybody—not just the Sup—against AMLO, and El Peje had slipped into a flatfooted tie with Felipe Calderón, at least according to Consulta Mitofsky pollster Roy Campos, whom Televisa had contracted to feign neutrality. The PRIistas' Madrazo was already anchored in deep third.

Televisa and TV Azteca were deeply indebted to the Fox and his PAN for having pushed a "reform" of the national radio and television laws through the senate. Derisively dubbed the "Ley Televisa," the "reform" gave Mexico's two-headed TV monolith 40-year concessions on the entire electromagnetic spectrum, once the property of the nation.

Televisa, which had flagellated AMLO with the videos and the desafuero for years, tilted toward Calderón from the opening day of the electoral season, even carrying his campaign kickoff live—no other presidential hopeful was offered such treatment. While the PANista's rallies went to the top of the news, El Peje was often shown in herky-jerky frames against a soundtrack of spooky music to underscore the danger that he represented for Mexico.

DANGER! That's the way the PAN played it. With the connivance of

Fox News hit man Dick Morris, who had been on the PAN payroll back in 2000 as well as Bill Clinton's in 1996, and Antonio Sola, who had done the same dirty work for Jose María Aznar, the right-wingers plunked down a billion pesos of the taxpayers' money (via IFE subsidies to the parties) for Kill AMLO spots that sometimes ran four to a single commercial break: The Peje's amiable mug intercut with boogeypeople like Hugo Chávez and Subcomandante Marcos, riots, lynchings, the city collapsing into dust. The big red letters were stamped across the screen. ¡PELIGRO! Andrés Manuel López Obrador was a DANGER to Mexico!

AMLO kept his cool and refused to take the PANistas' bait after initially mixing it up with Fox, whose furious attacks on AMLO were unprecedented for a sitting Mexican president. López Obrador had retaliated by calling the president a *chachalaca* (chattering bird) and then went Zen serene. He would even refuse to join the candidates' debate in late April, and his reluctance to hit back gave Calderón the opening to climb on top.

El Peje had initiated his crusade in Metlatónoc, the poorest municipality in the poorest region (La Montaña of Guerrero) in the republic. AMLO's campaign was guided by the same principle with which he had run Mexico City—¡*Los Pobres Primeros!* (First the Poor). He too, much as Delegate Zero, was looking down at the simple and humble people, those who are the color of the earth. Like Marcos, he spoke to *los de abajo*—those at the bottom—and advocated peaceful class war. There were, in fact, three candidates vying for the votes of Mexico's 70 million poor in this election—López Obrador; Roberto Madrazo, for whose PRI the impoverished campesinos and workers of Mexico had always been electoral cannon fodder; and Marcos and the Other Campaign. Calderón was the candidate of Fox and the fat cats. If the presidential elections had been billed as a wresting match, the marquee might read "The People Who Are the Color of the Earth vs. The People Who Are the Color of Money."

As the days dwindled down, the bad gas kept building. On April 21, 800 elite state police, backed up by the PFP, slammed into a strike-bound steel plant in Lázaro Cárdenas, Michoacán, killing two workers, wounding dozens, and arresting 13. But strikers fought back with sling- shots and iron ore pellets and eventually drove the cops off with heavy machinery. The strike had been called by the Mexican miners' union to which the steelworkers pertained, after their corrupt *charro* (literally an ornate cowboy) union boss had been ousted by Fox's labor secretary in retaliation for leading a national wildcat strike after 65 miners were killed in a methane blast in a Coahuila coal pit. The bad gas was rising to critical levels.

The killings came down in a steel mill complex named for Lázaro Cár- denas in the port of Lázaro Cárdenas and were ordered by the governor of Michoacán, also named Lázaro Cárdenas (Batels), Cuauhtémoc's son, the first Lázaro's grandson and a lifelong member of the PRD. The gov- ernment assault came just a few days before the centennial of the mas- sacre at the great Cananea copper mine in Sonora state in 1906, from which the Mexican labor movement drew its first breath, and foretold a combative May 1.

The breach between the Otra Campaña and the PRD had expanded exponentially in the months Delegate Zero had been on the road. AMLO had been sandbagged into appointing Jesús Ortega as his campaign manager—Ortega was, of course, the PRD senator who engineered the legislative mutilation of Indian Rights back in 2001, the embodiment of "El Mal y El Malo" for the Zapatistas. It would get worse. The PRD, mired in venality and opportunism, recruited hated PRI caciques who had been spurned by the former ruling party to fill out its Senate and House lists. Among those drumming up the PRD vote in Chiapas was *ni más ni menos* than Croquetas himself, Roberto Albores Guillén.

There had been woofing along the route of La Otra. In Juchitán, the leftist COCEI coalition of workers, farmers, and students, which had run city hall for decades and was now aligned with the PRD, barred the Other from celebrating a meeting in the town plaza. Although the COCEI had always welcomed the EZLN with brass bands and flowers, there were nasty *chingaderas* (name-calling) this time around.

346 • Zapatistas: Making Another World Possible

Invited by adherents to an assembly of the militant Section 22 of the education workers' union in Oaxaca city, Marcos was reportedly confronted by AMLO supporters and, when he tried to leave, found the doors locked (Section 22 locks its doors during such assemblies). Apparently fearing a political kidnapping, the Sup had picked up a chair and threatened to bust out a window before the door was unbolted and Marcos allowed to escape into the night. And in Tulancingo, Hidalgo, a PRD city, the mayor turned out police dogs and armed the local gendarmes with automatic weapons to welcome the Sup to town.

Now Delegate Zero was about to enter a city where the PRD had held a 60% majority for the past 10 years. He must have known the reception would not be as it was back in the glory days of the EZLN— Ramona's visit, the March of the 1,111, the Consulta, the arrival of the People Who Are the Color of the Earth. Many had gotten off the bus. Elena Poniatowska, the celebrated journalist and novelist, had thrown in with AMLO—for which the PAN shamelessly shredded her in toxic TV spots. And even more cruelly, Doña Rosario Ibarra de Piedra, oft imagined as Marcos's surrogate mom, now headed the list to become a PRD senator.

On the eve of Delegate Zero's foray into Peje City, there was alarming news from Mitofsky: Felipe Calderón had caught AMLO and was now two points on top. By the first week in May, the PAN was claiming a 10-point lead.

EL MONSTRUO

The Masked Wanderer circled El Monstruo (that's what Elías Contreras had called the capital) like a wrestler looking for an opening in his opponent's defenses, surveying the city from distinct angles to ensure the most advantageous approach. Meanwhile, La Otra palavered with the simple and humble people of Mexico state, which surrounds the capital on all sides, listening to the pain of the Mazahuas and the Otomíes and the mestizo underclass of the nation's most populous entity.

In the bowels of Chiconautla prison, Delegate Zero met with new adherent Gloria Arenas, AKA Colonel Aurora, of the ERPI, who along with her companion Jacobo Silva were buried under 52-year terrorism sentences. On April 26, the Sup rode into San Salvador Atenco on horseback, where the Macheteros and 200 adherents were inducted into La Otra Campaña.

The Other Campaign slipped into the great city from the east on April 28. Delegate Zero had been on the road for 119 days and had passed through 20 states. There were now only 65 days until election day.

The Karavana (in the Otra's alphabet the letter *c* was now replaced with *k*) first put into Ixtapalapa, a PRD-governed *delegación* (borough) and the poorest in the capital, where the Francisco Villa Popular Front (Independiente) took the Sup under its wing. The "Panchos," once staunch allies of the EZetas, had split and AMLO had walked off with the leadership. A few days later, Delegate Zero moved into the core of the city, holing up at the Rincón Zapatista, a onetime EZLN hangout on the edge of the old quarter.

Note the "onetime" designation: the Zapatista Front of National Liberation had been liquidated by the fiat of the Comandancia before La Otra hit the road. No explanation was forthcoming, although Marcos did apologize to anyone who had been deceived by the Frente, some of whose movers reportedly had committed the deadliest sin by joining AMLO's team. The general drift was that the Other Campaign would replace the EZLN as the Zapatistas' latest effort to build a mass organization.

Mexico City police stayed discreetly glued to the Sup, ringing the Rincón Zapatista with squad cars and tailing him to every event. Meetings with adherents of the Otra Mexico City were small, in the low hundreds. Public meetings, especially at the CCH popular high schools where students have long been radicalized, drew in the single-digit thousands, but the numbers were a long way from the March of the People Who Are the Color of the Earth, which had put a quarter of a million people in the Zócalo.

The corporate press paid no attention at all. With AMLO trying to pick himself up off the canvas and Mexico City in the grasp of a knock-down drag-out electoral slugfest, Marcos was less than a minor attraction, a sort of kult figure plying the fringes of the megalopolis.

The Other May 1 was the first real test of the Otra's scratch. International Working Men and Women's Day always fills the Zócalo, but most workers attend not for conviction but to have their names inscribed on the check-off list to avoid being fined by their union. This year, though, the Mexican labor movement was in an uproar over the murders of the striking steelworkers, and you could taste the anger of the rank and file in the capital's putrid air as one charro after another took the mic to recall Cananea and fulminate over the deaths of the comrades in Michoacán.

El Zero refused to march with the charros. These labor fakers had sold out the working class and were all PRIistas and PRDistas anyway. Instead, La Otra gathered its forces down Reforma Boulevard in front of the U.S. embassy while waiting for Organized Labor to clear out of the Zócalo. Marcos spoke from atop a battered old van that had accompanied the urban popular movement since the great quake of 1985. He may have been the only speaker at the many meetings and marches that day who remembered the Martyrs of Chicago, the men falsely hanged for heaving the bomb in Haymarket Square during the struggle for the eight-hour day. The Sup lavished unexpected praise on U.S. activists who stand up to their own mal gobierno.

The Other May 1 had been called in solidarity with the millions of paisanos in El Norte who were on the hoof for their rights that day, and Marcos pleaded with them to put away the flag of the oppressor their leaders had forced them to wave and pick up the one emblazoned with an eagle devouring a snake in the boughs of a maguey cactus. Several facsimiles of the Stars and Stripes were ceremonially set ablaze.

The procession up Reforma to the Zócalo was lively but sparse. Hammers and sickles and old José Stalin accompanied the contingents. Although La Otra had become overwhelmingly a young people's movement, Marcos marched with a delegation of braceros who had been cheated out of millions by U.S. banks and the Mexican government back in the 1940s and '50s—he had met them out on the road in Tlaxcala. The

Macheteros of Atenco, their field knives stiffly raised in salute, formed an honor guard around Subcomandante Marcos. Phalanxes of *granaderos* (the SWAT squad) were packed in front of the U.S.–owned hotels and fast-food franchises that now line the route to the Zócalo.

By my count, there were 8,000 on the march, and those waiting in the great plaza may have doubled that number, but the rally came on the heels of a huge outpouring of union members and occupied only a small corner of the immense square. The 15,000 or so who pressed in around the speaker's platform represented less than a tenth of those who had filled the Zócalo to the brim back in 2001. "We are going to overthrow the government," the Sup reiterated, "the Zapatistas always mean what they say!" Delegate Zero's words echoed hollowly in that great empty space.

This overthrow-the-government stuff was a little tricky. Delegate Zero scrupulously applied the qualifier "peacefully," which made it sound a little like he was calling for a Ukraine-like solution. On the other hand, the Sup had proposed the installation of a workers' government and replacing capitalism with socialism. All of this unnerved those who had always believed the EZLN's prevailing ideology to be communalism and autonomy, getting off the mal gobierno's grid, taking charge of your own destiny, and changing the world without taking power. Marcos maintains there is no contradiction between overthrowing the government and rejecting the temptation of taking over. "When together we have forced the mal gobierno to abandon power, we will go home to our mountains like the Great Zapata and become the Guardians of the Night."

ATENCO—THE FLOWER WAR

Rather than slay their enemies on the battlefield, the Aztecs captured and fattened them up for sacrifice. Then the victors would dine on their haunches at a feast held behind a curtain of fresh-picked flowers. Hence these battles were dubbed "flower wars."

The farmers of San Salvador Atenco have grown flowers since those good old days. The Aztec poet-king Nezahualcóyotl, the pre-Conquest ruler of these lands, made the bloom and wilt of flowers the stuff of his best verse. For generations, the flower farmers of Atenco had sold their gladioli, roses, carnations, and chrysanthemums in the neighboring municipality of Texcoco, on the sidewalk alongside the Belisario Domínguez public market.

May is a big month for them. May 3 is Santa Cruz or Holy Cross, always a fine day for floral arrangements. The fifth is Cinco de Mayo, a patriotic holiday, which requires wreaths of honor. And the tenth is Día de los Madres, when sales max out to pay tribute to the *mamacitas*.

But Texcoco, once a PRI stronghold, had a new PRD mayor now, who was determined to sweep the center of town clean of street vendors and relocate them to the periphery. Before dawn on May 3, the flower farmers tried to set up shop outside the market, but they were ordered to move on. Accompanied by leaders of the Popular Front to Defend the Land (FPDT), Nacho del Valle and Felipe Alvarez, the farmers of Atenco did not move on easily and a wild *zafarancho* (battle royal) ensued that lasted much of the morning. When the dust cleared, eight farmers were under arrest, and Nacho and his people were holed up in a house a block from the Texcoco plaza, surrounded by dozens of cops, in what turned into an all-day standoff.

How quickly the incident at the market, a mere blip on the Richter scale of social injustice in Mexico, blew up to national and even international proportions is one more measure of the bad gas that keeps leaking down below.

The word spread quickly. Church bells clanged down the road, and the townspeople of San Salvador Atenco gathered to avenge their comrades. The FPDT and its followers blocked the highway that runs parallel to Atenco, an important trucking artery, tying up traffic for many miles.

Delegate Zero was prowling my neighborhood, the Centro Histórico, that day. Early on, Hermann mentioned that there was a problem in Atenco and the Sup was thinking about driving out there later to fix it. A reduced pack of Otros and Otras plus members of the alternative press (but no major media other than *La Jornada*) accompanied Delegate Zero on his appointed rounds: a meeting with sexoservidoras on the Alameda green strip, which is surrounded by old working-class neighborhoods that are fast being gentrified by Carlos Slim's operators. The father of the Chapultepec Pact and his *palele* (literally, "lollipop") AMLO were the real *putas* (whores), Marcos railed to a slim crowd.

Next stop was legendary La Merced, the oldest public market in the Americas, dating back to before the Conquest, where amid scavengers picking through piles of rotting refuse, darting "Diablo" boys (hand truckers), strong men in leather aprons, and many adoring market women, Delegate Zero spoke from a loading dock redolent with sacks of fresh onions. As usual, the Sup talked the talk: "We-don't-want-your-vote-we-don't-want-to-be-the-government-we-want-to-overthrow-the-government." There was light applause. The market workers looked a little baffled. Doña Magda, 82 or 84, has sold strands of garlic and country herbs in La Merced for 60 years. She told me she was very *feliz* about Delegate Zero's visit. "All the candidates come to the Merced," she grinned proudly. But she herself was going to vote for Andrés Manuel López Obrador. That was her *gallo*.

From La Merced, El Zero motorcycled over to the "*barrio bravo*" (tough neighborhood) of Tepito, a thrumming thieves' kitchen of a kasbah where anything—anything! so long as it was stolen, pirated, or otherwise illegal—was available 25 hours a day. "*¡Tepito Sí! ¡Wal-Mart No!*" the Sup shouted to amazed bystanders. Tepito is also the cradle of Mexico's scrappiest boxers, and Marcos jabbed away at El Peje relentlessly, not such a hot idea in a neighborhood where AMLO has built a formidable machine.

By afternoon, the zafarancho had engulfed Atenco. Hundreds of police charged the town and were repelled three times by the machetes of the farmers and a hard rain of rocks, bottles, and Molotov cocktails fashioned on an impromptu assembly line. Twelve police agents who had infiltrated Atenco were taken hostage. One downed federal cop was repeatedly kicked in the testicles by the enraged mob. Televisa and TV Azteca sent up helicopters and captured an aerial view of this near-lynching. The film ran frame by frame over and over again all afternoon, with the TV channels calling for the military to quell this criminal rebellion. Marcos caught the drift and knew what would happen next. Already there had been one death, 14-year-old Javier Cortez, hit in the chest by a bullet fired by "unarmed" state police.

Around five, Delegate Zero spoke in the Plaza of Three Cultures in Tlatelolco, where the blood of the 300 students massacred by the mal gobierno on October 2, 1968, still pooled up under the stones. As is the tradition, the Sup declaimed from the steps of the Chihuahua Building, from which the strike leaders were addressing a small crowd when the signal for the massacre was sounded. Now, nearly 40 years later, another massacre was in the making.

The situation was grave. The farmers of Atenco were adherents of the Sexta, part of the Otra, "part of us"; Atenco was "Zapatista territory," *¡No están sólos!* In light of the seriousness of the moment, the Sexta Commission had ordered La Otra Campaña suspended and declared a Red Alert, the second in a year. Despite the fact that there was no apparent danger to the Zapatista communities in Chiapas, once again the Caracoles were closed down, the members of the JBGs ordered back to their villages, NGO operations shuttered; once more the internationals packed up and left the zone. Radio Insurgente, "The Voice of Those Without a Voice," once again went silent.

Imposing a Red Alert on the autonomías from Mexico City seemed disproportionate and alarmist, but really this Red Alert, like the one that preceded the Sexta, was promulgated to maximize attention, this time focused on Atenco.

Delegate Zero awaited a formal invitation from the FPDT to head for Atenco. América, Nacho del Valle's hypercombative daughter, arrived from the front lines, and the Sup met with her in a carpenter's shop in the basement of the Chihuahua Building. Although Marcos did not encourage those who heard his words in Tlatelolco that evening to go directly to Atenco, some got that message and went anyway. Many of those who did would be brutally beaten, arrested, raped, and even deported. One young man would be killed.

"The Other Campaign has taken a dramatic and radical turn," warned Hermann the next morning in *La Jornada*.

ATENCO—THE FEAST OF BLOOD

The retaking of Atenco ("Operation Rescue") was plotted from the highest echelons of the Fox regime. The president's security cabinet met hurriedly and designated secretary of public security Eduardo Medina Mora, former chief of the CISEN, to oversee the counterattack. Medina's man on the ground would be Vice Admiral Wilfrido Robledo, ex-commander of the Federal Preventive Police, who now headed the Mexico state security agency. Up until now, the crowning moment of Robledo's career had been the breaking of the 1999–2000 UNAM strike, during which 700 were arrested—the vice admiral was later bounced from the PFP for cooking the agency's books. Robledo was also the cousin of Mario Villanueva, who turned Cancún into a Cali cartel beachhead while governor of the state of Quintana Roo and who now languished in the federal super-maxi at La Palma, also in Mexico state.

The chain of command extends all the way to the top in such acts of state terrorism as Robledo and Medina More planned, observed dirty-war specialist Carlos Montemayor in the pages of *La Jornada.* The commission of such atrocities implies a degree of political damage, so the political class must sign off on the violence either before or after it comes down. The Fox had good reason for revenge against the Macheteros of Atenco who had spoiled his billion-dollar airport, and he could not have not been in the loop.

In the darkest hour before the dawn on the fourth, a crack state-federal police force stormed San Salvador Atenco on three flanks—the fourth fronted the blocked highway—and smashed its way toward the center of town, crushing everything in the way—cars, taco wagons, dogs, unlucky townspeople who were beaten into the pavement like so many Mexican baby harp seals. Taking a page out of the dirty war, masked informers were brought in to identify the homes of the FPDT leaders and their followers. Doors were kicked in, shots fired, the residents clubbed bloody and cuffed, even the furniture reduced to kindling. The idea was total submission.

One unfortunate 53-year-old woman was at the corner grocery store buying a toy for her 10-year-old son when the police smashed up the place and forced her to perform oral sex on three "officers" in exchange for letting her go home. Twenty-two-year-old Ollin Alexis Benhumea, who had been at Tlatelolco with his father and came the night before to Atenco, was hit at point-blank range with a police tear-gas shell and went into convulsions. When Dr. Guillermo Selvas, "El Doc," who had followed La Otra from Chiapas with a van full of free medicine and who had been hiding in the same house as Ollin Alexis, went into the streets to plead for an ambulance, he was badly beaten and arrested.

Although Televisa and Azteca were allowed to overfly the combat zone to record barbaric acts of vandalism attributed to the Macheteros the day previous, on the fourth they were embedded behind the brave police to record their heroic defense of law and order, and almost inadvertently the cameras recorded some of the most stomach-wrenching scenes of police brutality ever displayed on a Mexican television screen.

Two hundred and nine men, women, and children were arrested in Atenco, including two paraplegics, and charged with blocking the highway and other organized crimes. Most had been beaten so badly that they required hospitalization, but only a few received it and they were chained to the beds. Nacho de Valle and Felipe Alvarez, the two key FPDT leaders, had been arrested the evening before and were already in La Palma, the prison where Vice Admiral Robledo's cousin was also a tenant. The two were not charged with any crime incurred in the defense of the flower sellers but rather for a "kidnapping" they had purportedly commited during a school meeting with state officials in Atenco in April. When the officials had gotten up to leave, the farmers locked the door. The "kidnapping" carried 50-year sentences.

Women had been on the front lines of the resistance—both farm women from the communities and those who had come to Atenco in solidarity. Of 40 injured and arrested women packed into a police van for transport to nearby Santiaguito prison, 23 were sexually abused by the police goons, at least seven of them raped. The horrific ride lasted six hours as their tormentors pawed the women, masturbated on them, and like classic serial rapists, ordered their victims not to look at them during the assault.

Lorena is a diminutive university student who has been a Zapatista supporter since she was 12. "First they threw me into the van on top of women who were hurt and bleeding. There was blood all over the floor and I tried not to get any on my face. Then they ordered me to lie flat and one 'officer' ripped off my pants. When he saw that I was menstruating, he yelled that now he would really make me bleed." Later another pig tried to penetrate Lorena anally, but the van was nearing the prison, and when a confederate warned him to stop, he grew furious and smashed Lorena's head against the vehicle's bulkhead.

In addition to the female rape victims, one young man was reportedly sodomized with a police baton. Four non-Mexican women (two Cataláns, a German, and a Chilean) who were sexually abused on the road to Santiaguito were deported under Article 33 before they could denounce the violence committed against their persons.

Delegate Zero arrived in Atenco on the evening of May 5, leading a march from the agrarian university at Chapingo that swelled to 5,000 along the route. Although police helicopters buzzed the marchers, Robledo's cops held their fire. In the small plaza of San Salvador Atenco, its walls still daubed with blood (the governor later sent gallons of whitewash) and appeals to the citizenry to vote July 2, Sub Marcos broadcast to that little bit of the world that was still tuned in that he would not be leaving Mexico City until the prisoners were released from La Palma and Santiaguito. The struggle to free the prisoners would gauge the strength of this new national left movement that Delegate Zero boasted was already a fact. Atenco would be where La Otra would dig in its heels and make its stand.

Obliterated from public notice by the election blitz, Atenco unexpectedly offered the Other Campaign a window of visibility and, at least momentarily, transformed the anti-candidate Marcos into a wild card in the July 2 election.

MEET THE PRESS

Subcomandante Marcos made one other eyebrow-raising decision in Atenco on May 5: After a five-year moratorium, he would once again be available for interviews by the commercial press. There were caveats, of course—everything he said must be printed or broadcast without editorial cuts. *La Jornada* was the first to accept these conditions, but other corporate media, weighing the Sup's plummeting ratings, backed off.

Hermann's interview ran in double-truck installments over three days but revealed little that was not already surmised. The Sexta Commission had had no choice but to suspend La Otra—Atenco was exactly what the Other Campaign was all about. Who the Sexta Commission was, was not probed. Had Atenco been a trap laid by the mal gobierno? HB asked, but the Sup just kept churning out the rollo. "The Other Campaign is the only political movement that can save Mexico!"

Marcos also went into the studio with Carmen Aristegui for CNN en Español, and on May 9 startled the receptionist at Televisa-Chapultepec when he strode into the high-gloss lobby of "El Canal de las Estrellas" (The Channel of the Stars) and sat down with star anchor Carlos Loret de Mola for an amiable chat on the morning news.

For 12 years, Subcomandante Marcos had denounced and lampooned Televisa, sometimes barring the network from covering EZLN events. That very morning, *La Jornada* carried a banner headline culled from Hermann's interviews: "Marcos: Today Big Media Governs." What was even more stunning was that Marcos had committed to the interview just weeks after the senate gave away the dial to Televisa and Azteca, the aforementioned "Ley Televisa." "Doesn't Marcos know that Televisa is a neoliberal enterprise?" asked a puzzled Javier Corral, a maverick PAN senator who had carried the losing fight against the giveaway.

Now here was Subcomandante Insurgente Marcos in the flesh—the pipe, the fatigues, the crushed Mao hat, the headset, the rollo, the real deal. The interview went swimmingly. The Channel of the Stars gives its guests the star treatment, and Loret de Mola probed the Sup's private life—was he married? Did he have kids, as the CISEN had once rumored? No, no, the life of a guerrillero is too difficult for marital bliss. Was he afraid of death? Finally, the two got around to politics. Who would win the July 2 election? "The candidates are all mediocrities," the Sup figured; each was selling their product to a different constituency but AMLO did it best. Besides, there were more poor people to fool than rich. López Obrador would win.

This was Marcos's assessment and not an endorsement, but in the context of the bitter electoral war between the PAN and the PRD, Marcos became a Calderón spot overnight. The Sup was just another PRD militant, Felipillo charged. Rip off his ski mask and you will find AMLO underneath!

Whether the Sup's pronouncements were the kiss of death for López Obrador or just a peck on the cheek, the moment had the same feel as when Osama Bin Laden took to the tube to address the American people on the eve of George Bush's reelection.

WHY IS LA OTRA LIKE A BICYCLE?

The Other Campaign was sort of like a bicycle. If you didn't pedal and if it didn't go forward, it fell over on its side.

Marcos was inflexible. The Other Campaign would not move from Mexico City until all the prisoners were released. Those down the road and up on the border would just have to wait their turn. Even Nacho del Valle, in a note smuggled out of La Palma, urged Delegate Zero to keep the show on the road, but El Sup was not listening. The bottom line was *"Aquí estamos y no nos vamos"* (We are here and we are not leaving), and any discussion of what happens next must begin from that assumption.

Wittingly or no, Subcomandante Marcos had tethered himself to a *guerra de desgaste* (war of attrition). The mal gobierno was not about to release the prisoners—at least not until after the election took place and the next mal gobierno was chosen. "Marcos can declare all the red, blue, white, and green alerts he wants," snorted Fox's self-righteous spokesperson, Rubén Aguilar, "but this government is going to preserve law and order." The so-called Zero could hold his marches and meetings "without any risk to his person," Aguilar snidely added.

Despite Fox's "guarantees," El Jefe Diego was already calling upon the attorney general to rescind the immunity from arrest that Congress had once granted the Zapatista leadership in exchange for entering into long-asphyxiated negotiations. Admiral Robledo was even more vehement: Delegate Zero was "inciting social discontent" and should be locked down in La Palma with Nacho del Valle, the rest of the Atenco trouble-makers, and his own cousin Mario.

The mal gobierno had Marcos right where it wanted him a month before election day: under heavy surveillance (Mexico City's interim mayor, Alejandro Encinas, had put 120 cops and 20 patrol cars on El Zero) but still free to hammer away at AMLO. Meanwhile, the forces of La Otra would dwindle down to a precious few hardcore losers as the mal gobierno stonewalled their demands for the release of the prisoners— already the Sup was reduced to young and very young students and the Neanderthal left.

The Other was pinned down in the capital and could not reach out to similar hot spots as desperately in need of solidarity as Atenco, such as the beleaguered autonomía of San Blas Atempa or the farmers under La Parota Dam. When five young Otros were busted in Guanajuato for painting walls in defense of Atenco, the cops tossed them in the slammer, laughing that Marcos couldn't help them now because he was too busy marching around Mexico City.

How had a brilliant political-military strategist like Subcomandante Insurgente Marcos bumbled into this trap? Although the machinations remain murky, my hunch is that collective decision-making had broken down and the Sup was freelancing.

Much as in the ill-fated 1999-2000 UNAM strike, decisions of the Atenco defense campaign were taken at prolonged sessions in venues like the Che Guevara auditorium at the UNAM, where once the Ultras had strung barbed wire across the stage to prevent opponents from getting to the microphone. In fact, the Ultra rump of the General Strike Council still occupied the Che Guevara, and Adolfo Gilly unsuccessfully pleaded with the Sup to use his influence to return the auditorium to the university.

Decisions taken in the Che Guevara and other meeting sites like the Venustiano Carranza movie theater were not exactly collective ones, although consensus was needed to take action. By virtue of his moral authority, the Sup was able to impose his will upon the assembly. If the Otras and Otros balked at Delegate Zero's plan of struggle, he and the Sexta Commission would just go it alone. "We have done this before," he warned.

Although the Other Campaign had hit a speed bump in Mexico City, the defense of Atenco had resonance in pockets of Zapatista support all over the world. Demonstrations were held in scores of countries, mostly handfuls of Zapaphiles posted in public squares of European cities with hand-lettered banners calling attention to the atrocities. Noted intellectuals signed and published condemnations. When the Fox flew into Vienna for a Latin American–European Union summit, he was greeted by a dozen demonstrators demanding justice for Atenco.

But in a larger world, where cruelty to one's fellow man and woman is measured by the daily industrial-size mayhem in Baghdad, Atenco didn't have much of a chance, and despite the terrifying human rights violations documented there, on May 19, Mexican diplomat Luis Alfonso de Alba was elected president of the newly revamped United Nations Human Rights Commission in Geneva.

On the home front, the multiple rapes had aroused feminist *coraje*, and Ofelia Medina once again stepped forth to organize her sister *telenovela* (soap opera) stars. Mujeres Sin Miedo (Women Without Fear) set up pup tents in the parking lot outside Santiaguito prison, behind whose walls the Atencos were on hunger strike—each night a different movie star fasted in solidarity with the strikers.

By the end of May, the parking lot had become solidarity city. The National Indigenous Congress was now encamped there, as was the Movimiento Mazahua, a group of Mazahua women demanding the release of a compañera who had been caught up in the police riot.

But the longer the Sup stayed stuck, the more the air leaked out of the Otra's tires. The marches peaked around 15,000 on May 28, an international day of solidarity with Atenco, and then began to splinter. Not enough bodies could be mustered up for highway blockades. Daily protests at Los Pinos, the stock exchange, the interior ministry, the embassies of important countries were barely sustained by diminishing numbers of student activists. The wrangles in the Che Guevara got longer and longer.

After a month on life support, Ollin Alexis Benhumea passed on to a better world than this one. A memorial march on June 10 drew maybe 500 to the Zócalo—the date also commemorated the slaughter of 23 students on Corpus Christi Thursday in 1971. América del Valle was on the lam and sent a tape that sounded like it was recorded at the bottom of a bottle. Delegate Zero was eloquent and dramatic, presenting Ollin Alexis's father with a tear-gas shell found in Atenco stamped "Made in the USA." "*¡Qué muera la muerte!*" Marcos cried out—That death should die! Toward the end of the speechifying, one group of students attacked another group of students and expelled them from the meeting. The portrait of Joe Stalin suspended above the stage flapped up and down in the wind like a monkey on a wire.

14. Summer 2006

666

A day before the June 6 presidential debate, in which AMLO would finally face his tormentors, imprisoned blackmailer Carlos Ahumada, he of the famous video "scandal," disclosed through his lawyers that he would release two additional tapes positively incriminating López Obrador in shady finagling, at high noon on 6/6/06. Televisa and Azteca blocked out time slots on the prime-time newscasts for the promised "revelations."

Then, early next morning a little after 6 a.m. (6/6/6/6), an anonymous caller squawked to police emergency that Cecilia Gurza, Ahumada's annoyed-looking wife, her three children, and their rogue-cop chauffeur had come under attack when the family's bullet-proofed beige Suburban was raked by gunfire as it pulled out of the driveway of their palatial San Angel home. Televisa and Azteca sped to the scene to film the perforated vehicle, and the story ran all day accompanied by the usual spooky music.

When Ahumada's lawyers called off the video release, Rubén Aguilar, speaking for the president at the morning press briefing at Los Pinos, intimated that AMLO was trying to muzzle his detractors. But it didn't take long for Mexico City D.A. Bátiz to smell a skunk, and investigators soon debunked the supposed assault as self-inflicted.

The debate that night was a shadow show played out against the background of such dirty tricks. "Now there are bullets in the campaign," whined the unctuous Madrazo, whose candidacy was losing steam fast. AMLO was "a man of violence," Calderón hissed and squealed. Felipe would uphold the law with his *mano dura,* and he thrust his index finger into the eye of the camera to demonstrate how he would squash out the DANGER that López Obrador presented to Mexico.

By contrast, AMLO was calm and presidential, a reasonable man with unshakable principles. He was the candidate of the poor *"¡Primero los Pobres!"*—and Felipe the candidate of the fat cats. "Liar!" snarled the PANista, flapping his flipper-like arms frenetically, and for a while the two parried about who was the bigger liar. Then El Peje produced a fat file folder that, he explained, contained irrefutable evidence that Calderón's brother-in-law, Diego Hildebrando Zavala, a data-processing tycoon, had won lucrative no-bid contracts from the secretary of energy when Felipe filled that post. Moreover, he had paid no taxes for years.

Indeed, Zavala had dozens of contracts with the Fox government, not just with Energy—his portfolio included the social development ministry, whose former chief Josefina Vázquez Mota was now Calderón's right-hand woman, and, not least of all, the Federal Electoral Institute.

The charges smeared the PAN's illusory incorruptibility with high-gloss fecal matter. Calderón had campaigned on the moral high ground of *Manos Limpias* (clean hands), and now he had been caught with his fingers in the masa. Although the TV pundits declared the debate a tie, AMLO had scored a knockout. A week later, Televisa-Mitofsky verified that the scrappy contender had now regained the lead from Calderón by a scant point, 35-34.

MORE BAD GAS

Subcomandante Marcos skipped the debate. He wasn't interested, he told reporters after participating in a roundtable to celebrate the centennial of Bertolt Brecht's birth under the chandeliers at the ritzy Casa Lamm.

But while Delegate Zero plied the Colonia Condesa's literary salons, more bad gas was blasting from down below. This time the scene of the explosion was the historic center of Oaxaca City, a colonial gem designated as the patrimony of man- and womankind by the United Nations, where tens of thousands of striking teachers had been encamped for a month.

With the election looming and the teachers threatening boycott (a quarter of all state polling places were in schools), Governor Ulises Ruiz, a Madrazo clone, wanted to show his own hard hand and run the protesters, who were decimating the tourist trade, out of town. To this end, he sicced a thousand state police on the militant *maestr@s*. More than a hundred strikers were sent to hospital, several with gunshot wounds, and two unconfirmed deaths reported. Police slammed concussion grenades from low-flying helicopters into the swirling masses below and filled the central plaza with tear gas. Automatic weapons were allegedly discovered at teachers' union headquarters.

But like the steelworkers in Michoacán and the Macheteros of Atenco, the teachers resisted the onslaught, regrouped, and three hours later took the plaza back. When Governor Ulises petitioned the president to send in the Federal Preventive Police, the Fox stalled—all this mayhem was helpful to selling Felipe Calderón as the champion of law and order.

CLOSING DOWN THE CAMPAIGNS

The World Cup kicked off on June 9 and would continue for a month, temporarily braking political passions but animating futbolistic ones. Saints were dressed out in Team Mexico jerseys, and archbishops blessed the national selection from the pulpits. Televisa had shamelessly puffed up Mexico's slim chances in this every-four-years free-for-all—the two-headed TV monster stood to reap a bonanza every bit as juicy as the one it was sucking off the presidential campaigns.

Mexico's *Presidenciales* and the *Mundiales* coincide every 12 years, and the candidates have to adjust their campaigns. Calderón temporarily pulled his AMLO hate hits and bought spots in which he ran around in shorts playing *cascarita* (soccer scrimmage)—El Peje's sport was *beisbol*. But although the fanáticos cheered on the national team with mindless chants of ¡Make Sicko! ¡Make Sicko! the impact of these colliding passions was minimized when Make-Sicko got booted out by Argentina early in the second round, and politics took center stage again.

The Zócalo belonged to Andrés Manuel López Obrador—Madrazo and Calderón had to retreat to other gathering sites for the traditional campaign closers so as not to be put to shame by AMLO's usual tumult. Actually, the June 28 throng that filled the great Tiananmen-size plaza was a modest one by El Peje's standards—150,000, just a hint of crowds to come.

The campaigns officially closed down at midnight on June 28, and Televisa-Mitofsky offered its final poll: AMLO up 35-31 and pulling away.

The pre-election tension in my neighborhood was spiky. Mobs stormed the senate building and the cops waded in with truncheons drawn. An armored military vehicle pulled up and trained its cannon on the esplanade. "Cut!" boomed the man in the beret with the bullhorn. Hollywood had rented out the Céntro Histórico to shoot a remake of that old presidential assassination classic *Vantage Point*, but to many of my neighbors it looked a lot like a dress rehearsal for July 2. At La Blanca, Carlos Díaz stared out the window at the fake squad cars crowding the street. "I hope it's only a movie," he pondered.

With the due date spiraling down to July 2, the Other Campaign held a two-day plenary at an abandoned movie theater not far from the Sonora witchcraft market. Marcos had plans to "interrupt" the electoral process and entice voters to think about Atenco. About 2,000 young diehards dominated by the radicalized Chilango delegation packed the loges. No one inside the theater opposed the "interruption"—which boiled down to the usual march from the Angel of Independence statue to the Zócalo on election morning—but longtime Marcos supporters like Adolfo Gilly grumbled that it was not a good idea. A motion to kick out of the line of march anyone who showed up with a purple thumb (proof of having voted) was vetoed by Delegate Zero.

And so the stage was set for perhaps the most consequential—and uncertain—election in modern Mexican history. This was Madero vs. Díaz and Cárdenas vs. Salinas all rolled into one, the poor against the fat cats, brown against white, the people the color of the earth against the people the color of money, and a referendum on the pain the neoliberal curse had inflicted upon the land.

The Mexican presidential election of July 2, 2006, had great geopolitical significance as well. Would Mexico break the chains of servility that had so bound the nation to the north since NAFTA had blown in, or reach out south to the left-leaning democracies of Latin America that offended the Bushites?

The White House had its eye glued on this one. The populists were at the border, the *New York Times*' David Rieff gulped in a hit piece aimed at AMLO. Dick Cheney had taken to confusing "populists" (of the Chávez variety) with "terrorists"—and now the *terroristas-populistas* were in voting distance of San Diego! Washington could not afford to lose this one.

¡FRAUDE ELECTORAL!

Mexican elections are stolen before, during, and after the ballots are cast.

Late on Wednesday night, June 28, as the campaign deadline drew nigh, a crack team of investigators from the attorney general's Organized Crime Unit descended on La Palma prison in a last-ditch push to pressure ex-Mexico City finance secretary Gustavo Ponce into giving up his ex-boss for embezzling city moneys to finance his presidential bid. But Ponce was a stand-up guy and wouldn't talk. The visit wasn't the first time Fox had tried to use his attorney general to bag AMLO and failed—but the dénouement was a bitter disappointment for Televisa and Azteca, which already had stationed crews in the La Palma parking lot to transmit the thwarted confession live, and the news anchors had to scramble to fill the block set aside at the top of the news.

That was Wednesday. On Thursday morning, June 29, AMLO's people awoke to find his campaign page hacked for the umpteenth time. A phony note signed by a phony López Obrador urging his supporters to go into the streets "if the results do not favor us" had been posted, and although the PRD immediately decried it as a hoax, the anti-AMLO media ran the story for hours, browbeating party president Leonel Cota into pledging that the faithful would refrain from street protest and that López Obrador would abide by the results the IFE was already cooking.

That was Thursday. On Friday, June 29, after five years of blunders and false starts, Fox's special prosecutor for political crimes finally issued a house arrest order for former president Luis Echeverría, 86, for his role in the genocide of student protesters at Tlatelolco on October 2, 1968. Of course, right after the election, once the dirty trick had had its desired media effect, the arrest order was rescinded. The intention had been to put the hoary mug of the old despot, a pseudo lefty to whom Calderón had repeatedly compared López Obrador, back on the front page.

That was Friday. On Saturday, July 1, a severed head was found on the steps of the PRD-run Acapulco City Hall and two AMLO poll watchers were gunned down elsewhere in Guerrero state, invoking the shadow of 1988 when hundreds of Cárdenas supporters were slain in political violence after Salinas had stripped Cuauhtémoc of victory. By July 2, the memory of '88 had descended over the election like a crepe curtain. "All we need now is for the system to collapse," Luis C., a *veterano* like myself of that terrible time, joked bitterly.

The heebie-jeebies were jumping on election morn. Ironically, one of the few islands of calm was the Otra as it gathered around the Angel. The batucada bammed and several thousand stylishly dressed young people danced off down Reforma for the Zócalo. Even Joe Stalin was smiling.

Stranded in the midst of the vast plaza, Marcos MC'd the reading of an interminable manifesto lecturing the electorate on the uselessness of voting. Meanwhile, under the porticos on the western flank of the Zócalo, thousands of frustrated citizens trying to vote at the special *casilla* (polling station) for Mexicans in transit (it was vacation time) were informed that the ballots had run out. *"¡Queremos votar!"* the would-be voters yelled testily, "We want to vote!" It was an odd counterpoint to what the Otr@s were spieling just a few hundred yards away.

The special casillas are always a flashpoint. By law, only 750 ballots are allotted to each one, purportedly to prevent ballot-box stuffing, and they are never enough. When AMLO supporters caravaned down to Tijuana from Los Angeles to cast their ballots for López Obrador, they were told that all the ballots had already been used—by the police and military, who had lined up early. On line at another Mexico City special casilla, AMLO's favorite writer, Elena Poniatowska, and her children were displaced by hundreds of presumably Calderón-voting nuns.

The *mapaches* (literally "raccoons") on all sides were up to their usual tricks on July 2—stuffed ballot boxes *(urnas embarazadas),* voters erased from the lists *(rasurados),* multiple voting ("the carousel"), *el ratón loco* ("the crazy mouse," in which polling places are moved around), and *el fraude de la hormiga* ("ant fraud," in which two or three votes are stolen from every ballot box) were just as popular on July 2, 2006, as they were back in the days when the PRI ran the circus. But the big fraud was being perpetrated on the UNICOM terminals down at the Federal Electoral Institute bunker in the far south of the city.

The whiff of cybernetic chicanery had been in the wind for weeks. *Jornada* columnist Julio Hernández opened an IFE Web page to check out the number of bajas or *rasurados,* registered voters who did not appear on the voter lists, and found two columns, one considerably longer than the other, for every electoral district in the country. In the time it took him to call the IFE for an explanation, the second list vanished from the screen.

Ace reporter Carmen Aristegui was tipped that if she punched in the password "Hildebrando 117" at the appropriate slot on one of Calderón's Web pages, she would discover some interesting data. When she did, up came the voter registration rolls crossed with a list of recipients of Josefina Vázquez Mota's social development programs. The page was shut down while she was still on the air. Ah, the magic of Hildebrando!

AMLO awaited the results at a glitzy hotel on Reforma. At 8 p.m., both heads of the TV dragon were to announce their exit poll results but cancelled out at the last second because, they lied, the election was "too close to call"— *Proceso* magazine later reported that interior ministry officials had prevailed upon the outlets to release no numbers.

At 11 p.m., the IFE's Fox-appointed director, a gray-faced bureaucrat named Luis Carlos Ugalde, appeared on the national screens to present the results of the preliminary count. The PREP had confirmed winners in the past two Mexican presidential elections, and this was the moment the nation had been waiting for. Mexico held its breath.

But Ugalde offered no results either. There was no clear tendency, he mumbled and walked away from the mics. The 1 a.m. cut was abruptly cancelled. There would be no official results until the 300 electoral districts finished tallying their votes between Wednesday and Sunday. Under PRI rule, the period between election night and the finalization of the tallies in the districts was the time to fix the final results.

López Obrador knew they were stalling for time, trying to figure out what to do now. His own exit pollers had him a half-million votes ahead when the nation's 130,000 casillas closed down at 6 p.m. At midnight, AMLO went to the Zócalo, where thousands had gathered awaiting word of a victory that would never be called. AMLO tried to calm tempers. "Smile! We have already won!" he chirped, repeating a campaign slogan. "*¡Fraude Electoral!*" his people howled back with one throat out there in the rain-soaked darkness, "*¡Fraude Electoral!*" The chickens of 1988 had come home to roost.

"VOTO POR VOTO"

The PREP ran all day Monday and AMLO could never get closer than two points to Calderón—which is where the two stood when the PREP was shut down with 98% of the count in, and the Big Press, both national and international, ran to the phone booths to crow the PANista's victory to their editors. But there was one big fly in the IFE's ointment. Forty-two million Mexicans had voted but only 39 million were in the PREP.

What had happened to 3,000,000 voters? AMLO demanded to know. Oh those, Luis Carlos Ugalde suddenly remembered during an interview on the same Televisa morning news Marcos had appeared on—they had been set aside because of "inconsistencies." Embarrassed IFE officials quickly dumped 11,000 casillas back into the PREP totals (13,000 had been removed). Most had been for AMLO, reducing Calderón's suspect edge to 0.6%. Nonetheless, big guns of the U.S. poodle press—the *Washington Post, Los Angeles Times,* and *Chicago Tribune*—were already coronating Calderón.

On Wednesday morning, the 300 electoral districts convened to tally the *actas,* the results that were attached to each ballot box. These would be the "valid" results, as opposed to the PREP, which was only a guesstimate. AMLO's people had detected startling differences between the actas and what had been entered in the PREP. One Mexico state casilla registered 188 votes for AMLO, but only 88 appeared in the preliminary count. Another Mexico state casilla that had been awarded to the PAN appeared 20 times. Many more ballots had been judged null and void than the margin of Calderón's alleged victory. In the 16 southern states that López Obrador had won, more ballots had been cast for senators and congressional representatives than for president—in Tabasco the difference was 100,000 votes, despite the fact that both AMLO and Roberto Madrazo are native sons. In the 16 northern industrial states Calderón had won, the reverse was true.

AMLO's team demanded that the ballot boxes be opened and the votes recounted as guaranteed by law. Ugalde responded by ordering the strictest legal interpretation and ordered the IFE *vocals* (regional heads) in each district to proceed at breakneck speed despite having until Sunday to complete the count. Here's what *New York Times* reporter James McKinley, covering his rookie Mexican election, saw in Guadalajara (a PAN citadel) District 13: "Rodolfo Ponce Sánchez (the IFE Vocal) was rattling off results as fast as an auctioneer, barely giving the representatives of the parties time to contest the numbers before declaring them valid." The one box that was opened while McKinley was around yielded more votes for AMLO than listed in the acta. Nationally, only 2,800 out of 130,000 ballot boxes were opened and recounted, and in virtually every instance, the recounts added votes to AMLO's totals.

By 2:30 Wednesday afternoon, López Obrador had a solid 2.6-point lead over Calderón. Then suddenly, inexplicably, his numbers began to sink incrementally with each new cut released by the IFE, even as the PANista's increased. Supporters stood transfixed before the screens, not believing what they were seeing. By 8 p.m., López Obrador's lead was down to a single digit, and by 4:05 Thursday morning Calderón went up for good, eventually peaking at 0.58 in time for comida corrida.

No one had slept a wink all night when at 8:30 a.m. AMLO, looking haggard, addressed the press and declared in his hesitating, Peter Falk–like diction that he could not accept these results. "I have won the election," he insisted, demanding that the ballots be recounted one by one, and summoned supporters to the Zócalo on Saturday to begin the defense of the vote.

Later that afternoon, George Bush, an electoral pickpocket who has stolen the White House not once but twice, rang up Felipe Calderón from Air Force One to congratulate him for "winning" the presidency of Mexico, albeit by the thinnest margin ever recorded here (actually a bit bigger than Bushwa's 537 vote "victory" in Florida in 2000).

A half million people the color of the earth jammed into the Zócalo and the surrounding streets of the Centro Histórico that Saturday afternoon. I don't know if Marcos was there in mufti (he would have been strung up on the nearest lamppost if he had shown up masked), but if he was, it must have been a humbling experience. On the part of Radio Insurgente that he reserved for his weekly broadcast, the Sup claimed to have inside info that the PAN had dumped 1.5 million premarked ballots into the totals, but in the cyclone of charges of Fraude Electoral that had swirled over Mexico since July 2, the revelation raised few eyebrows.

Fraude Electoral was the motif of the great meeting. Large "Wanted" posters for Ugalde were slapped up on central city walls, and the throng sometimes drowned AMLO out with thunderous chants of "¡Fraude

Electoral!" López Obrador looked like he was on the verge of tears at the outpouring of support as the people the color of the earth pushed in around the speakers' platform. *"¡No estás sólo! ¡No estás sólo!"*

Andrés Manuel wanted the ballot boxes reopened and the contents counted *voto por voto,* and his lawyers would go into court to demand that the seven-judge panel that sits as the TRIFE, the supreme electoral tribunal that is the court of last resort, order a recount. But he also called his people into the street for a second election, convoking a national exodus for democracy from each of the 300 electoral districts in Mexico to converge on the capital on Sunday, July 16.

TO BE CONTINUED

On the Saturday before the July 16 second "informative assembly," I walked the highway down from Morelos state with a callused handful of campesinos who tilled plots on the ejido of Anenecuilco, Votan Zapata's home turf, the land for which this incorruptible revolutionary was martyred. "We have an obligation to fix this fraud—the general would not forgive us if we did not try," a weather-beaten farmer named Saúl Franco avowed. "If Zapata was still alive, he would be with us today," Saúl suggested, echoing the hand-lettered cardboard sign he carried.

The ejidatarios of Anenecuilco were enthused by AMLO's combative posture. You could feel it in the way they strode along the shoulder of the road. Andrés Manuel would never double-cross them *(doblegar)* or sell them out *(vender).* He was *muy decidido* (very committed), declared Saúl. But the farmers did not at all trust his party, the PRD. They had suffered a PRD municipal president and "things went badly," explained Saúl's cousin, Pedro Luis—just as things had gone badly in Texcoco, where a PRD mayor had sicced his police on the flower vendors of Atenco; and out in Michoacán, where young Cárdenas sent in crack troops to gun down striking steelworkers; or down in Chiapas, where the assassin Croquetas was now campaigning for AMLO.

But despite the PRD's penchant for treachery, the men from Zapata country drew the line when it came to El Peje. He was different. He would never betray them, as had so many who had risen from the ranks of the Mexican Left.

The toxic indignation of *los de abajo,* those who had seen lucha after lucha co-opted or corrupted, contaminated, bought and sold, pissed away, or just savagely crushed by the Mexican murder machine, was tempered that Sunday afternoon by the slim beam of hope that maybe this time around, the muy decidido AMLO would really battle on until the *últimas consequencias,* that he was not just mouthing those magic words like so many vacuous politicos who inevitably compromise and surrender. And it was this narrow shaft of hope that AMLO would not sell them out that once again filled the Zócalo to bursting, filled all the streets of the Centro Histórico, filled the Alameda and the Paseo de la Reforma and Chapultepec Park all the way to the Periférico ring road, a 13-kilometer chorro of humanity that never stopped moving for six hours. The Mexico City police called it at 1.1 million, the PRD at 1.5—perhaps the largest in the history of this distant neighbor nation, but who really knows?

Indeed, El Peje held the previous mark—the April 24, 2005, march against the desafuero. But what was more pertinent to understanding this numbers game was the fact that they were growing exponentially. Back on April 7, 2005, López Obrador had drawn 300,000 to the Zócalo and two weeks later tripled the participation, forcing the Fox to back down from the desafuero. Now, six days after the Great Fraud of July 2, AMLO had put a half million in that same plaza and a week later doubled or tripled the turnout, depending on whose numbers one swallowed.

Speaking once again from a stage set up against the National Palace, El Peje summoned his people to massive peaceful civil resistance and a third magna "informative assembly" two weeks hence that would settle once and for all which of these humongous outpourings really was history's largest.

But no matter how many millions marched that Sunday, some could not or would not count them. Ginger Thompson, the Condoleezza Rice of the *New York Times,* misplaced a million marchers, the journalistic equivalent of the IFE's evisceration of the PREP. The PAN and Felipe Calderón labeled the history-making gathering "irrelevant," a kind of defining moment in the post-electoral struggle of 2006. In the eyes of these odious elites, the most gargantuan outpouring of righteous indignation in the annals of the republic was just "irrelevant."

Where all of this is heading as I dance on the blade of deadline is uncertain. Should the TRIFE ignore hard evidence of computer manipulation and the myriad electoral crimes committed in more than 50,000 casillas that AMLO's legal team has submitted to the judges, and refuse to order a recount *voto por voto,* thus upholding the IFE's fraudulent awarding of the election to Calderón, things are bound to get downright nasty. The bad gas is rising even as I dot the final *I*'s and cross the last *T*'s.

It is difficult to conceptualize how Felipe Calderón could govern Mexico with the majority of its citizens permanently pissed off and refusing to recognize his legitimacy. After Salinas stole the presidency from Cárdenas in '88, he had to call out the military to beat down the Cardenistas, and hundreds were killed in the patriotic slaughter to redeem his larceny. Salinas's dark reign remains indelibly stamped on the Mexican psyche, but it is not the only one. The stealing of the 1910 election from Francisco Madero triggered the Mexican Revolution.

On the other hand, should AMLO prevail, and the ballot boxes be reopened and the votes counted out one by one and El Peje prove the winner as he insists, it will be a watershed day for electoral democracy here, even more dramatic then the moment when the PRI was finally toppled from power back in 2000, where this volume began.

But such an outcome is hardly guaranteed. Even if López Obrador is finally deemed the winner, the PRD is mortally flawed, venomously venial and vulnerable to splintering into brittle battle over scraps of power. AMLO's option for the poor will be blunted at every turn by his many enemies—the bankers, the neoliberals, the avaricious business class, the PRIAN, the Church, Washington. A worst-case scenario? Think Salvador Allende.

So we come to the end of this part of the story, always with the caution that it is to be continued. At the base of the Mexican pyramid, the bad gas is billowing, but those at the pinnacle do not seem to sniff the danger. Should it all fall apart, should los de abajo be driven back into their cages, the rage of the people will pulse slowly for a while, brooding and plotting revenge until suddenly, without much warning really, their frustration will explode in a geyser of bloodletting. It is the Mexican way, the historians and scholars will pontificate and bolt their doors. And it may very well be that should this come to pass, the much maligned gaggle of Otr@s—or something like them—and the Zapatista Army of National Liberation—or something like it—will be the only players left standing on the battlefield to pick up the pieces.

The metabolism of revolution in Mexico is precisely timed. It seems to burst from the subterranean chambers every hundred years or so—1810; 1910; 2010? To be continued.

Epilogue

The Milpa

I have come back to Chiapas—this narrative demanded such closure. It is raining torrentially, the scowling, freighted sky collapsing upon the valley of Jovel, submerging the ancient cobblestone streets of San Cristóbal and chilling my old bones more than in any other rainy season I can remember.

Chiapas seems the same, only different, quieter, as a reporter friend tells me, without Marcos. El Peje won the state big and the PRD is going to get fat. Next month, a PRD governor will be elected, although like all PRD candidates these days, he really is an ex-PRIista, the son of a former governor famous for massacring the Indians and the nephew of Mexico's most romantic poet, both lifelong members of the PRI. The ascension of the PRD to state power here is not a harbinger of better times to come for the Zapatista Army of National Liberation, although with all the "ex"-PRIistas in its fold, the mal gobierno will not look much different from the way it has always looked to those down at the bottom.

The hullabaloo up in Mexico City, far away at the center of power, looks different from the periphery. Everyone is curious—even the few

Zapatistas I spoke with—about the contours of the Fraude Electoral. What will happen next? Will AMLO really fight until *las últimas consecuencias?* But for now, the decisions will be taken as they always have been—far away, in the capital of the country—and there are urgent matters of place to attend to closer to home. The corn for one.

On a Saturday morning under glowering, pregnant clouds, I hop the combi destined for Bochil and hop off at the Oventik gate. A big black slab of painted pine wood is staked out by the roadside: CLOSED FOR RED ALERT. The driver grumbles that he is losing passengers because of the pinche Alerta Roja. You hear a lot of grumbling like that down in San Cris.

The Caracol Resistance and Rebellion for Humanity ("where the people govern and the government obeys") is locked down tight as a drum. Looking down the steep main street from the bolted gate, the place resembles a stage set for a Western movie ghost town. The side gate, too, is padlocked, as are all the offices of the co-ops and the JBG. The basketball court is abandoned. Where thousands partied each January 1 to celebrate the advent of this unique rebellion from the roots, the only moving thing is a mangy gray *chucho* (mongrel) scavenging for food in what's left of the garbage.

A young girl appears from somewhere, hauling a bucket of water to someone unseen in one of the outbuildings. The only audible sound is the hum of the refrigerators in the Che Guevara General Store up by the road. The corn grows silently on the hillside across the two-lane highway.

But of course the Zapatistas don't really live at Oventik—it is only where the structures of their autonomous government sit. The Zapatistas of Oventik really reside just down the two-lane blacktop a few hundred meters, alongside the road and up on the mountainside and down in the hollows, tending to their cornfields. Behind their ski masks, the Zapatistas are always farmers.

Two young men squat on a ledge facing out on the valley, scanning it for intruders and keeping tabs on police and military movement on the roads, informal sentinels keeping an eye out for danger. Isn't that what the Red Alert is all about? Neither wears a ski mask but both are milicianos. I slide down on the muddy ground next to them. Beneath us, a Tzotzil farmer weeds his milpa. No, there are no elotes yet, one young man replies laconically to my question. There is a lull in the conversation.

"*¿De dónde viene usted?*"—Where do you come from?—one of the milicianos finally thinks to ask. "Day Efe," the federal district, I reply. "Day Efe," they repeat. There is another lull. I ask them when the Red Alert will end. "*¿Quién sabe?*" they breathe back—Who knows?

They change the subject. To my surprise, they are curious about the election. Did López Obrador really win? How was it with this fraud? I explain a little, give examples. "They screwed us again." They feign nonchalance. "That is what we thought, *un gran fraude.*"

The milicianos grow more animated when I tell them the Sup is staying near my neighborhood up in Mexico City. They want to know what he is doing. They ask about Atenco. Where exactly is it? What happened there? I am sure that they already know and are only testing my veracity. Would they go up to the Monstruo to save the Sup if they were summoned? We are waiting for the order, they tell me.

We shake hands in that soft Indian way, and I catch a ride over to San Andrés Sakamch'én with a Christian who is blasting catchy hymns from the car radio. The offices of the autonomous municipality in San Andrés are similarly shut tight. CLOSED FOR RED ALERT, reads a scrawled piece of notebook paper taped to the window.

I hike out to the edge of town to see if I can find Ramona. The municipal cemetery is a tangled field dotted with small crosses and a lonely mausoleum. "Do Not Tether Animals," warns a sign posted by the autonomous authorities. "300-peso fine for sheep. 500 for horses and other animals."

Some of the graves are just mounds of red earth, vines and stickers and summer flowers poking from them. Ramona's place is easily found—two decaying wreathes placed there by La Otra mark the spot. "María Díaz Santiz, January 6, 2006" is written on the small black cross. No birth date is given. Ramona lies alongside Andrés Díaz Santiz, who went underground four years earlier. I do not know how they were related. The low-hanging clouds grow even heavier and darker, threatening drenching rain. I pick an orange daisy-like flower from the Comandanta's grave and later give it to Luz down in the city. Here, this is Ramona, I tell her.

The path leading back to the center of Sakamch'én is lined with milpa, the broad-leaved deeply green stalks spindly, some topping seven feet. The ears have only begun to sprout, thrusting out their beards in anticipation of sweet elotes to come. As always with us old guys, nature urges me off the path to answer the call of my kidneys. While I stand there dribbling, I slip back a tassel to inspect the new cob, its tiny teeth just forming, and each kernel seems to be shaded with the image of a ski-masked Zapatista—but then I am a poet and metaphor sometimes clouds my vision. I zip and make my way back down the mountain.

So this story ends where it began, in the milpa, as it always must and always will if the Terminator seed doesn't get us first. The Zapatistas are Mayans and the Mayans are the People of Maize, not just because it is the center of their universe but because they are actually made from it. And like the maize in this resilient season of rain and growth and greenness, despite all the pain that those the color of money inflict upon this land, the people the color of the earth return, renew themselves, are reborn and flourish. So, as Old Antonio tells us, the first gods, the ones who shaped the world, have ordered

Acknowledgments

AGRADECIMIENTOS: Hermann Bellinghausen, the *cronista* of the Zapatista rebellion who wrote this story; my editor, Carl Bromley, who had blind faith in what the Blindman came up with; Elizabeth Bell, who, as always, polished up these words and shaped them into an intelligible text; Sasha Crow for her warm friendship and support; Joe Blum for his acute camera eye; Celia Cruz and the Hotel Isabel for providing shelter, and Carlos Díaz and the Café La Blanca for the best coffee in the Centro Histórico; also *La Jornada,* the morning bible of the Mexican Left, Café de la Red, Roger Stoll, Rocio G., Mark D., Sid Dominitz, Carol Moné, RedTap, John Gibler, Timo y Luz, Iñaki García, Sigfrido, Ernesto Ledesma, Gaspar Morquecho, Tomás Johnson, Beatriz Aurora, and Helen Gilliland for their logistical support on this long strange journey. *Agradecimientos* to you all.

Index

Salazar Mendiguchia, Pablo, 27–28, 29, 150, 195–196, 234
Salinas de Gortari, Carlos, 10, 11, 13, 22, 31, 132
San Andrés Accords, 3, 38, 53, 73–74. *See also* Indian Rights Law
Sánchez, Samuel, 28, 35
September 11, 2001. *See* World Trade Center attacks
Sexta, 301–302, 302–304, 318–319
Sharon, Ariel, 99–100
Sinclair, Upton, *The Jungle*, 219
Sixth Declaration of the Lacandón Jungle, 1–4
Spain, 158–161, 292, 293–294
Starbucks, 154, 155
sweatshops. *See maquiladoras*

T
Tahuantinsuyo, 220–221
Televisa, 70, 343, 354
tourism, 177–183, 200–201, 263
Traven (Ret Marut), 263

U
United Nations, 6–7, 168–169, 170–171, 359
United States government, 20, 33, 60, 344
    Department of Homeland Security, 337–338
    foreign policy, 109, 115–116, 117, 200, 204, 332
    immigration laws. *See* immigration laws
    intelligence, 227–228
    Iraq War. *See* Iraq War
    presidential elections, 30–31, 252–253, 258–261

W
Wall Street Journal, 51, 169
WalMart, 216
War Against Oblivion (Ross), 12, 116

War in Defense of the Gas, 223–224
War in Defense of the Water, 221–222
Washington Post, 369
Weiner, Tim, 73, 179
White Guards, 9
White Overalls, 53, 54, 69
wind farm, 335–336
women
    liberation of, 9–10, 80–81, 82
    violence against, 274–276, 324, 354, 354–355
    Zapatistas, 59, 329–332
World Bank, 14, 152, 332
World Economic Forum, 51–52
World Trade Center attacks, 106–119, 168
World Trade Organization (WTO), 200, 201–204

Y
Yale University, 22
Yañez, Fernando (Germán), 61–62, 75, 157

Z
Zapata, Emiliano, 10–11, 68–69, 86, 222
Zapatistas
    coalition building. *See* La Otra campaign
    communiques, 301–304
    headquarters, 131–132
    history of, 185–186, 209–212
    media outlets, 253–257
    outside Chiapas, 53–56, 57–59
    as terrorists, 114
Zedillo, Ernesto, 3, 13–14, 14, 15, 22, 87–88, 322

About the Author

John Ross has been chronicling the underbelly of Mexican life for the better part of four decades. A veteran correspondent (for *Noticias Ali- adas-Lima, San Francisco Bay Guardian, Texas Observer,* and *Counter- punch,* among other screwball publications) and author of eight books of fiction and nonfiction, Ross is the recipient of both the American Book award (*Rebellion From the Roots,* 1995) and the Upton Sinclair ("Uppie") award (*Murdered By Capitalism,* 2004). Ross's three volumes on the Zap- atista rebellion and his dedicated touring on their behalf have earned him the sobriquet of the "Willie Loman of the Zapatista Army of National Liberation." One of the few surviving Beat poets still standing, Ross has nine chapbooks of poetry in and out of print, the latest of which, "Bomba!" is due soon from Calaca de Pelon Press. Ross, a Human Shield in Iraq and Palestine, has lived in a cluttered hotel room in Mexico City's crumbling Centro Historico for 21 years from which he issues a weekly online jeremiad "Blindman's Buff," a mordant collation of polit- ical outrages south (and east and west and north) of the border.

MY HUSBAND
MY MAKER

SHARON RIES

HARVEST HOUSE PUBLISHERS
Eugene, Oregon 97402

Except where otherwise indicated, all Scripture quotations in this book are taken from the King James Version of the Bible.

Verses marked NIV are taken from the Holy Bible, New International Version, Copyright © 1973, 1978, 1984 by the International Bible Society. Used by permission of Zondervan Bible Publishers.

MY HUSBAND, MY MAKER

Copyright © 1989 by Harvest House Publishers
Eugene, Oregon 97402

Library of Congress Cataloging-in-Publication Data

Ries, Sharon, 1948-
    My husband, my maker.

    1. Ries, Sharon, 1948-   . 2. Missionaries—Chile—
Biography.   Missionaries—United States—Biography.
I. Title.
BV2853.C6R547   1989   266'.0092'4 [B]   87-81661
ISBN 0-89081-603-4

Printed in the United States of America.

To Chile,
Colombia . . .
and to the Uttermost Parts of the Earth.

Contents

Acknowledgements

A "smooch" to Raul and my boys without whom there would be no story.

Thanks to the expert guidance from Al Janssen who meticulously organized my thoughts.

Thanks to Caesar Guzman for joyfully reading my blunders and instructing me accordingly.

To Elvira Reymond, for constructive criticism.

My appreciation to all the staff and to Lucy, the cook at the mission house in Chile who listened unexhaustedly, offered comments, encouraged, and took care of my needs while I wrote.

Thanks to sweet Lisa for typing up the mess.

Love to my ladies from our women's ministry who continued without me.

Sincere gratitude to Chief Editor Eileen Mason for her sensitivity to our Lord which demonstrates itself in kindness and patience. Also for being confident that I could write despite difficult circumstances and crowded schedules.

And finally I thank Lela Gilbert who came to the rescue at the end to brush on the final strokes my story needed to be fit for publishing.

To God be the glory and the honor throughout eternity!

Introduction

As usual I was scared, but this time it seemed worse.

According to the last registration count, there would be 400 women staring at me as I made my way to the podium to speak. This was the seventh Calvary Chapel Pastors' Wives Conference at which I had spoken, and by now I should have felt well-poised and relaxed. I wasn't. Pastors' wives are very special women. It is an honor to address them, but at the same time, doing so represents an awesome responsibility.

Just days before, Kay Smith had outdone herself inspiring and encouraging the nine of us Calvary Chapel pastors' wives who make up the planning board. "Remember," she had said, intense in thought, "pastors' wives usually have no one to confide in. Who can they trust if they're hurting or having marital problems? People expect them to have it all together, when in reality some of them lack a sense of their own identity. Many pastors' wives feel hopelessly inadequate."

Every word Kay said was true. We all knew it because we'd experienced some of these heartaches ourselves.

Kay paused thoughtfully. "It's difficult. It really is. But I know from my own experience," her eyes lit up as she concluded confidently, "that once we focus on Jesus and develop a deep, personal relationship with Him, we are free to be all that God has created us to be. I think we've all learned that He is the only One who can bring fulfillment to our lives!"

We could do nothing but listen attentively. Kay knew what she was talking about. She and her husband, Pastor Chuck Smith, had been in the ministry for nearly 40 years.

Pastor Chuck is the man God chose to teach the Bible "line by line, from cover to cover" to southern Californians from all walks of life in the early sixties. His congregation continues to grow even today, and his radio and TV teaching programs are still increasing in popularity around the world.

Kay is a tall, black-haired beauty. Her attractive, well-groomed appearance distinguishes her as an elegant lady, and her vibrant personality radiates through her every gesture. Kay's heart is knit to the heart of women in general. She hurts when they hurt and laughs joyfully with them. I know—I was one of the many who sat under her teaching, and I loved it. Her presentation is always simple and sincere, funny and yet deep. She exemplifies true inner beauty. Her quest for God always leaves me hungry for Him.

"Pastors' wives are really just like other women," Kay said. "All women are complex in their desires and needs. . . ."

Kay then reminded us of the main purpose of this annual conference. "We must seek for God's guidance through His Word and through prayer that we may be able to comfort, instruct, and exhort them to develop an intimate friendship with Him."

At last the time came for me to deliver my message. Women were crowded into the half-moon shaped auditorium, the mothers with babies were in the back. Behind them, outside, the trees were showing off their brightest array of colors, as they always do in autumn.

Kay sat up front on my right, along with a couple of the other pastors' wives who would be teaching. Each of them was so much better at public speaking than I was. It frightened me! Just as I was reviewing the opening comments on my topic, "Heart Entwined With His" [your husband's], a sudden thought struck me: "Do these women think I have it all together?"

"Don't worry," I encouraged myself. "They're only women, just like me: simple and complicated, sensitive and uncaring, emotional and calm, gentle and angry, jealous and satisfied, hard-working and slothful, energetic and weary, joyful and resentful, giving and taking, inadequate and capable." Like women in different parts of the world whom I had addressed at Bible studies, luncheons, retreats, and conferences, these women desired love and tenderness. Above all, they longed for deep spiritual fulfillment.

The clock was ticking. I rushed through my introduction: "How can a woman's heart be entwined with her husband's? I'd like to give you my definition of the word 'entwined.' It describes two individual vines growing independently, with separate root systems, and yet becoming gracefully interwoven with each other. As time passes, a steady, healthy growth process will combine their boughs and branches into an inseparable, beautiful masterpiece."

I looked around the room, into the women's eyes. In spite of the lovely picture I had just painted with words, I could hear the questions they sometimes ask:

How can I love him when I'm so filled with hate?

How can I keep forgiving? When will I have suffered enough?

Where can I go to run away?

In a group this size, there had to be some women who were really hurting. I wanted to help them the way I had been helped, but was there time? It had taken me 40 years to learn what I wanted to express!

I tried to organize my thoughts, but I couldn't. I could tell that the women were silently praying for me, and I was strengthened enough to tell a few stories with a couple of Bible verses mixed in between my tears and laughter. That's the way public speaking is for me. And, as usual, I learned that a number of the women shared my former hopeless feelings. Afterward, anonymous notes acknowledged many hidden sorrows. I wished that I'd had more time, that I hadn't forgotten some key points.

On this particular occasion, however, it didn't matter so much. Soon they could read the rest—I had been writing my story for the last year. At first I had hesitated to do so. A book about my personal world would violate my sense of privacy. But one day I read these words right out of my Bible:

> My heart is stirred by a noble theme as I recite my verses for the king; my tongue is the pen of a skillful writer (Psalm 45:1 NIV).

"Yes!" I decided. "I should do it. I'll do it because I want others to know my Maker, the King who calls me His beloved and His bride. I want them to meet the Captain of my ship, my Friend and Lover. He's the only one who really understands me, who brings order to my confusion and gives meaning to my life. Why shouldn't I talk about Him?"

My story actually began long before I can remember, the day He thought of me, before He made the world. Even then He was mapping the journey I would take, thoroughly equipping me and numbering my days.

But let's start at a place and time I do remember—in a foreign port city, when I was a girl of just 13. Up to that moment, life had offered me only smooth sailing. Now there was a change in the wind. The plans I had made for my life were abruptly interrupted. Circumstances had turned against me. I no longer wanted to continue my journey.

My Maker would have to carry me through. Board my ship, and I'll show you how He did it. Join me on the docks in the beautiful city of Valparaiso, Chile.

The Harbor Lights

1

It was a muggy, windless summer day—a miserable day for traveling. Despite the steamy weather, Valparaiso—Chile's main port—was bustling with activity. All morning, dock workers had been hard at work loading our ship with cargo. Cranes with big hooks effortlessly swung crates, barrels, and boxes skyward, then lowered them through a large square opening on the main deck. During our voyage, that same deck area would be used for sunbathing.

The gray concrete shipyard with its drab, tin-roofed warehouses was brightened by throngs of people dressed in colorful clothing. My sister, Shirley, and I quietly studied the scene from the ship's deck, exchanging whispered comments about the rich women who promenaded below us, their fine jewelry gleaming in the sunlight. We pretended we were rich, too. This wasn't especially difficult because Mother always dressed us elegantly. That day we wore cheerful yellow eyelet dresses made for us by our family seamstress in Santiago.

Mother was a happily married, tall, green-eyed blonde who always looked beautiful and behaved likewise.

Shirley and I giggled, watching various sailors and male passengers staring at her. We were proud to be her daughters.

Our ship was called *La Reina del Mar*, one of the many British ocean liners that sailed the waterways of the world. In the early 1960s, this particular liner made its way through the Panama Canal between England and Chile, stopping at major ports along the Caribbean Sea and the Pacific Ocean.

The liner was an extravagant mini-city, complete with dress shops, hair salons, and a glittering ballroom. Shirley and I explored every corner, feeling as if we were in a fantasy world. This environment was dramatically different from the simple, unpretentious missionary life we normally led.

On the passenger list were names of the rich and famous as well as the working class. Most of the wealthy were in the midst of extensive, worldwide journeys. They occupied the upper part of the liner, enjoying the most opulent quarters. Passengers going to specific destinations, such as tourists and international commuters like us, traveled second class. We were lodged in the middle section of the liner with only a few less comforts. Third class was located in the lowest sections of the ship. Students, military personnel, and passengers on the most limited budgets traveled there.

Mother said second class was a good place for us, but I felt differently. First class attracted me with its sparkling pool, glamorous dining area, and fine clothing. Shirley and I agreed to spend most of our time there.

As we continued to investigate our new surroundings, a woman with an English accent interrupted us. "Come to dinner, girls," she instructed, guiding us through long hallways, up the stairs, and into a very formal dining area. The lavish red carpet and spotless white tablecloths were a little intimidating. Long-stemmed red roses formed the centerpieces on tables which were finely arrayed with silver and crystal. "You will sit here with the children and your parents will dine later on this evening," our guide primly explained.

Ever the impulsive one, I nudged my sister. "I don't like this. Why can't we sit with Mother?"

"It's probably because you're only 13 and look so young," responded Shirley, who had just turned 15. It was evident that she had matured a lot faster than I.

Fortunately, Mother quickly came to our rescue. "You two got captured by the first-class child attendant," she smiled. "But don't worry, in second class, we all eat together."

Mother hurriedly led the way back through the hallways, down the stairs, and onto the main deck. "Our friends are on the docks waiting to see us off. Daddy is looking for you, too," she spoke a little breathlessly. It would be a few months before our father would catch up with us in the United States. He planned to stay behind in order to turn our ministry over to new missionaries.

I didn't want to be reminded of the realities this trip represented. For me it was a nightmare, and I wanted to wake up soon. My parents had been missionaries in Chile since I was just four years old. Although I had spent my first four years in Colombia, Chile was all I knew. Nevertheless, Mother and Daddy had decided to take us to the United States to learn the English language and to receive an American education. But the length of our stay was unclear, and my heart was breaking. Chile was home—the home of my friends, the mission, my neighborhood . . . and the boy I loved.

Besides, why couldn't Daddy come with us? It never seemed possible for him to travel with us because of the overwhelming amount of work he always had to do. I yearned to see him have fun and relax, to watch him spend time with Mother. Would we ever have time to talk? If we did, would I be really open and frank with him—open enough to pour out my hurts about leaving Chile? Surely he was sorry about leaving too.

Deep inside, however, I knew that I would never say a word. Kids in Chile didn't question their parents. They just obeyed and suffered silently.

I would miss Daddy. I continuously missed him because he spent so little time with us. His work involved teaching Bible school every night as well as overseeing all our denomination's Chilean churches. His responsibilities required a lot of traveling. But Daddy loved people, especially the poor, lonely, and rejected. His life was devoted to them.

Although the pressures of life sometimes triggered an explosive temper, Daddy had a fun-loving, jovial character overall. He always brought us wonderful gifts from his journeys. It was fun to wait for his return, trying to guess what he would bring us next. He would provide items like gum, candy bars, and jars of peanut butter. We made the peanut butter last for months. Shirley would spread it on thin so it would last longer. I hated it thin, so I would spread it on thick and eat one slice of bread to every two of hers. One time he had made a trip to the United States and brought us some pure nylon dresses. I lost an entire sleeve of one to a very hot iron. Daddy hid the gum and candy in a trunk with three locks which he kept in a little storage room in our house. The room also had two padlocks on its door. Chileans were especially attracted to our American cargo. Daddy would open the locks every so often and let us pick out a stick of gum and a candy bar.

These memories were scrambled in my mind as we finally found ourselves on the overcrowded deck. "There you are, girls!" Dad exclaimed, handsomely dressed in a neatly pressed beige suit.

He took us both in his arms and kissed us. We both automatically rubbed our lips, because his pencil-thin, red mustache left a tingling sensation. "Now remember, don't wear your new watches when you get off at the ports. Otherwise you might have them stolen."

I noticed tears gathering in his green eyes, although he tried to hide them. I couldn't cry even though I wanted to. Everything hurt too badly. My heart beat fast. My throat was dry.

Daddy was the last to get off the ship, just before the stairs were removed. I waved goodbye to our Chilean friends, who disappeared into the background as my eyes focused on Daddy. All too soon the distance erased him and the whole traumatic scene from my sight.

I wanted to run, but there was nowhere to go except down to our living quarters. There I could be alone. I climbed onto the bunk with a porthole facing the docks. I watched, my young heart aching, as the land I loved slipped away. I couldn't hold on no matter how hard I tried.

Memories carried me back to another farewell. I remembered being just four years old, leaving the United States. As I'd clung to one end of some crepe paper streamers, our relatives on the docks had grasped the other end. At last the distance had forced the colorful streamers to break. This time I made a vow. "Distance will never break my ties with you," I spoke softly into the porthole. Realizing that I was talking to myself, I directed my conversation toward God.

I had always talked to God, but never with such intensity as now. "God, do You know what I am feeling? Do you care that I am being stripped away from the beautiful country I dearly love?" He didn't answer. I hoped He had heard, even though He couldn't possibly be concerned with every heartache of every single person in the whole world.

But then, He is God, I thought. *Maybe He does answer every single request. Maybe He does give each person everything he longs for.* "Please, God, let me come back home soon," I earnestly pleaded with Him.

I couldn't imagine life in another country. Would I be greeted at dawn by a sight as majestic as the snowcapped Andes Mountains? Would the beaches have tide pools, swarming with shellfish, reflecting beautiful sunsets? Would the cities pulsate with life? Would there be a place where the kids meet while the hand-organ man plays and his little monkey sways for a peso or two? Would the streets be lined with vendors displaying their snacks from ship-shaped carts, smoke curling out of their smoke stacks? Would there be vast sand dunes to roll on and lush campsites, complete with waterfalls?

I would sorely miss the sprawling mission house with its magnificent garden, and the succulent snacks we enjoyed from its trees. And as for my Monopoly partners, the Bible school students, and the cook—when would I see them again? I couldn't imagine life without Chile. And even less could I imagine living without Fernando.

Fernando Leighton and I had met when I was 12. Although he had recently moved, he remained a part of a very special neighborhood gang from the double dead-end street where we lived. We gathered together every evening beside a white wrought-iron fence to share good times and laughter.

Sometimes we all played hide-and-seek and some of us would disappear between the houses to hold hands and kiss. Panchy, a little red-haired, freckle-nosed friend, was invariably selected to count. "98 . . . 99 . . . 100!" she would yell, and then proceed to find us. It wasn't long before she tired of our romantic little game and went home to bed.

Now the events of the night before lingered sadly in my thoughts. I had walked with Fernando to the bus stop, unable to think of anything to say to him. We hadn't spoken a word—just held hands and stared at each other. Young as we were, I always knew what Fernando was thinking by the look in his eyes.

There were so many things I wished I had said. Yet somehow, the night before, it had taken all the courage I had just to utter one question. "Do you have a picture I can take with me to remember you by?" Fernando had reached into his pocket and had given me his I.D. picture. "I have more than that to remember you by," he said quietly.

He then said goodbye with a soft, gentle kiss. And now he was gone.

I closed my eyes and concentrated on him—his hazel eyes, his fair skin, his wavy, black hair. I never wanted to forget his face. For me, Fernando was the epitome of beauty and genuine gentleness. There was a sadness in his countenance that I never understood or asked about. No matter—he only had eyes for me and I knew it. And someday I would come back to him.

My thoughts faded as I realized that the land was now almost completely out of sight. Some words from a popular melody played softly in my hurting heart:

> I saw the harbor lights
> They only told me we were parting,
> The same old harbor lights
> That once brought you to me....

The land was gone. Just a couple of faraway lights twinkled somewhere near the now-darkened horizon. I felt lost at sea. I had no home, no friends, no Chile—only emptiness and pain. One unbearable thought sent rippling chills along my spine: "What if I can never come back?"

Looking for a City

2

"Wake up!" The airline stewardess gently shook my arm. "We're coming into Los Angeles!" I'd slept all the way from Panama City, where we had transferred from our ship to an airplane. Past experience had taught me that flying had a bad effect on my stomach, so I had decided to sleep the hours away.

The aerial view of southern California's nightlife was the most incredible sight I could have possibly imagined. It looked as if God had spilled a handful of luminous glitter over the land. Rain had washed the air clean, and as the plane slowly dropped in altitude, I could see streetlights mirrored on the wet pavements.

Los Angeles throbbed with activity. Broad highway arteries, larger than any I had ever seen, pumped thousands of tiny vehicles in and out of the heart of the city. I felt a surprising exhilaration that interrupted the sorrow I had experienced since leaving Chile two weeks earlier.

"I'll enjoy myself while I'm here," I decided, "and I'll learn to speak English." After all, didn't most of my friends dream of coming to the United States? "Then, when my visit is over, I'll go home." This final thought lingered until it was interrupted by the sound of our

27

plane's wheels hitting the runway.

We passed through customs and eventually emerged into the airport reception area. Several long and lanky relatives, some with vaguely familiar faces, greeted us with tears of joy and "welcome home!" phrases I scarcely understood.

"Chile's food must have made the girls short," I heard mother laugh. But height wasn't the only thing that set us apart. Shirley and I could immediately see that, having lived all our lives in South America, we were thoroughly foreign, not only in language but in culture.

During the next few hectic days, mother wasted no time moving us into a tiny one-bedroom, one-bath guest house behind the residence of my grandpa, Reverend Lee Roy M. Kopp. We were amazed to watch mother transform that little, abandoned place into a sunny, yellow dollhouse which we called "home" for the next 12 months.

"When Daddy comes from Chile, we'll get our own place," she assured us. "Then you'll have a bedroom of your own."

Soon Christmas was just around the corner. Grandma Kopp enthusiastically introduced Shirley and me to her much-too-small-for-baking kitchen. "Why I've had my cookie cutters since I was a young woman."

"They look like it too!" Shirley giggled.

"And those big jars of rainbow-colored sugar are from Knott's Berry Farm!" She wanted us to enjoy her kitchen, and we did. We had never seen anything like it.

Every year she made a basket of homemade cookies and candies for each of her six children and their families. The 11 grandchildren would each receive a real silver dollar wrapped in bright-colored cellophane, trimmed with a neatly curled ribbon. Shirley and I were thrilled to help Grandma make the 1001 cookies for her yearly presentation. "Now, each cookie must be individually cut, baked, and decorated," she instructed, demonstrating her technique on a gingerbread man. "Then we'll distribute them into the six baskets."

I was deeply impressed by Grandma's ability to love each individual in the family equally. She'd barely become acquainted with Shirley and me, and yet we were just as close to her heart as the other grandchildren she knew so well.

Christmas arrived, and with it came our relatives. At that time, everyone we met was from Mother's family. My father's mother lived in South Sioux City, Nebraska, and the rest of his family was scattered in different cities throughout the United States. We later visited with them.

Mother had given us some family background before we left Chile. "A lot of my relations are pastors, Bible teachers, and musicians," she had explained. Somehow, my preconceived notion of this "priesthood family" had been of drab men, and of women wearing long black skirts, no makeup, and having tightly rolled buns on the back of their heads. What a relief it was to discover that they were not at all the way I had pictured them!

As a matter of fact, Shirley and I were amazed by the sight of our aunts, uncles, and cousins. One by one they arrived, wearing a broad variety of clothing which included everything from the ultraconservative to the most stylish, multi-colored fashion items.

"I like them," I thought to myself, feeling proud to be part of such a handsome group of men and women.

That first North American Christmas brought an all-new meaning to the season. It was more than being in a Chilean Christmas play, forgetting my lines, with Daddy taking far too many pictures. It was more than sharing Christmas dinner with friends and a few misplaced, lonely people who we invited to our home on Christmas Eve. It was more than receiving a beautiful homemade doll, while being reminded by my parents to give last year's doll away to a child who didn't have one.

That Christmas taught me a new dimension in giving. I listened, transfixed, as Grandpa Kopp shared his missionary journeys to the Holy Land, practicing his Hebrew on us. Meanwhile Uncle Paul described in great detail his own journeys to Israel, and the miracles that God had done there. I noticed how his wife, my Aunt Betty, lovingly admired him. I heard my cousin Janet calling me "my cuz," which gave me a warm sense of belonging. Cousin Connie said, "I love you." Up until then, that tender phrase had only been expressed to me by my parents.

After the very last piece of pumpkin pie had been devoured, Grandma called us together, and her fingers began to skillfully move across the piano keys. "Okay, everybody. Let's all gather around the piano and thank God for His wonderful love!"

Singing with that family was like being in a church choir. We all knew our parts. Even though Shirley and I didn't recognize all the songs, we harmonized anyway.

Finally, to everyone's delight, Grandma sang one of her own melodies. She had written it to express the deepest longing of her heart—being with Jesus in His heavenly city. It reflected the hopes and dreams of nearly everyone there. Young and old alike, these people knew Jesus Christ in a personal, intimate way. They sincerely looked forward to spending eternity with Him.

Tears ran down Grandma Kopp's cheeks as she sang with all her might:

> Some Golden Daybreak, Some happy day!
> Some Golden Daybreak, We shall see Christ!
> Break through the heavens, With power
> and glory!
> Some Golden Daybreak . . .

Glancing around the room, I noticed that everyone was communicating some form of tenderness toward the person next to him. Some were holding hands, others stood arm in arm. Tears were running down our cheeks. Then unexpectedly, nostalgia waylaid my thoughts.

Suddenly my own longings caused me to envision a different kind of "golden daybreak." Much as I appreciated the spiritual yearnings of my relatives, heaven was not a priority for me at that time. Some golden daybreak would find me returning to the earthly city I longed for—Santiago, Chile.

I imagined myself gracefully disembarking from a white ocean liner wearing a slim, white suit. My long, red hair was flowing in the wind, burnished by the sun's rays. The dock was swarming with people, but one person stood out above them all: Fernando. He was taller, more handsome, and had grown remarkably mature.

Our eyes locked, and I fell into his arms.

I loved Christmas. I had greatly enjoyed my new fellowship with our long-separated family. But nothing brought me more joy than the thought of loving and being loved. It was my favorite dream.

No promise of some faraway heaven was about to take it away from me.

A
Shooting Star

3

After my arrival in America, I received and answered dozens of letters from Fernando. In time I became weary of our relationship, realizing that distance would never permit it to mature.

Correspondence during the three years of our separation revealed dramatic changes in our lives. Fernando was becoming an extremely literate and productive young man. Although in some ways our friendship had richly deepened, I was saddened by the fact that life was taking us in different directions. Inevitable changes develop during long separations, but along with those, Fernando had acquired some beliefs at the university that diametrically opposed mine. There was no end to the agony of our being apart, and I found my interest in writing letters slowly diminishing. Regretfully, I tucked Fernando's warm memory away in my heart.

By then I was 16 years old, beginning my junior year in high school. The first time I noticed Raul, it was fall—a season that I loved. The school's lawns were scattered with an infinite variety of the Creator's individually designed leaves. As I gazed out the classroom window at this delightful scene, the lunch bell rang.

I dashed out of class and rushed across campus, hoping to beat most of the student body to the front of the lunch line. All at once I noticed someone carelessly approaching me in a loose-fitting white T-shirt and a pair of very faded blue jeans. I slowed down, hoping to get a better look.

Yes—just as I thought, he was gorgeously built, handsomely designed, and wonderfully beautiful. True, he was young, and I liked older guys. But his greenish-brown eyes; his tanned, fine-featured face; and his black, wavy hair made him very acceptable. My first impression was that he summed up the ultimate dashing Spanish conqueror, and at that moment I definitely wanted to be conquered. Fortunately we made immediate eye contact.

"Hi ya," he said, eyeing me from head to toe.

"Hi," I answered breathlessly.

It seemed like a good beginning. But much to my dismay, our future encounters remained identical to our first. At this pace, I would never be conquered! Well, that was just fine. I didn't have time to worry about him because, after all, he seemed a bit immature. Besides, I had plenty of other interests to keep me busy.

By now our family had moved to a comfortable home. Daddy had a good job and was pursuing some opportunities for higher education. Our new lives in the United States required continuous adjustment, and carried responsibilities I had never known before.

Some of my spare time was spent designing and sewing clothes for Mother, Shirley, and me. In Chile, it was a job either Mother or our seamstress had always done. I was glad to have inherited it, because I loved fashion. I even sewed for other people, earning extra money in order to keep my closet jammed with all the latest fads.

Going to church with the family also absorbed a lot of my time. Participation in plays, musicals, and social events was a source of genuine pleasure for me. I especially admired our pastor, Carl Green. This man loved young people. He said caring, important things that caused me to make meaningful decisions that would impact my life forever.

One Sunday, as tears rolled down his cheeks, he said, "God has a special plan for each one of you young people. To discover that plan, you must get to know Him. . . . You must talk to Him, read His words, meditate upon them, and then do what He says. If you give your life entirely to Jesus, He will guide you and you will find life, for He is the life."

And so I turned my life over to Him—again and again and again. "God, I want to know You," I would plead. "Who are You? What do You want from me? How can I know Your will? God, please forgive my sins. Forgive the things I do that are not pleasing to You, and make me the way You want me to be."

I made spiritual promises to myself that I could not possibly keep. My hectic life prevented me from really concentrating on God's Word. I didn't have much time to meditate or to obey. But I did talk to Him about my problems every night.

I was very involved in high school. Since the first day that I arrived onto an American school campus, I was accepted by my peers. However I harbored fears of not fitting in, and in some areas could not relate at all to the "American way." After spending a couple of weeks hiding in the school halls during lunchtime with my sister, I was invited to join a group of girls who were involved in all kinds of school activities. Leadership had always been a natural aspect of my life, so by the time I became a junior, I had been involved in the Pep Club, German Club, Drill Team, Student Class Council, and several other activities. When I became a senior I was elected as one of the Drill Team heads and as Director of Finance for the Associated Student Body.

Each year the athletes at our school hosted an all-sports dance for which they chose a court of princesses. I had always shied away from these very "popular" fellows. Although I seldom missed a sports event and cheered fanatically for the participants, unlike the boys I had been raised around, they seemed too aggressive and forward for me. However, my junior year I was chosen by the tennis team, which at the time was made up of the studious guys on campus. Some of them were my classmates, hence I was deeply honored to represent them.

It was spring, and my relationship with Raul still had not grown past the "Hi ya, you look great" stage. Since the princesses were responsible for getting their own escorts, I saw this as a great opportunity to invite Raul to the dance. This was a particularly radical step for me, because asking a boy to go out was impermissible in my traditional Chilean upbringing.

I stayed up half the night before I asked him, finishing the new dress I planned to wear the next day. I got up extra early so I could brush my freshly-washed, long hair at least 100 times. Mascara and eyeliner went on neater and thicker than ever. Having taken great care with every possible detail of my appearance, I made my way to school and waited by Raul's locker until he came by.

"Hi, Raul."

"Hi, how are you doing, Sharon?"

"Can I talk to you?" I asked shyly.

"Sure." A mischievous smile played around his lips, and he eyed me intensely.

"Well, I've been chosen to be Tennis Princess at the All-Sports Dance. I was wondering if you could escort me." I went on to explain why I wasn't inviting my regular boyfriend. "Mike is out of school, so he can't go with me."

"Sure," he answered coolly.

Since my disillusionment with Fernando, I had been dating Mike. He was both fun and good-looking. I'd been crazy about him until I met Raul. Mike regularly attended church with me, but neither of us ever had really matured spiritually.

Although I enjoyed and respected Mike, I couldn't get Raul off my mind. I had heard somewhere that Raul admired Mike's "street fighting" techniques. Apparently they were very similar to his. Eventually the night of the All-Sports Dance arrived. I zipped myself into the white organdy dress I had designed. It was lined and trimmed in yellow taffeta, and was gorgeous enough to hold its own among the array of dresses that would grace the princesses' court. After stacking my hair on top of my head in a cascade of curls, I waited nervously for Raul.

"So who's Raul?" asked Mother, admiring me in my finished dress project.

"Just a friend from school," I responded.

"Is he a Christian?"

"I don't know, Mother. He's just my escort tonight. I don't plan on marrying him."

"Boys" was the only topic I avoided discussing with my parents. Daddy's repeated counsel was continuously hammered into our minds. "Get an education, follow a career, and don't think about boys till you're 26. About that time God will bring you together with the man of His choice, just like He did with your Mother and me."

Mother's concern was that we date boys who loved God. "If he loves Jesus, he will want to do His will. And he will always want to love you, too."

It always sounded so simple when they were saying it, but in reality their instructions created great conflict within me. I enjoyed dating much more than running around with a bunch of silly girls. But most of all, I craved being cared for, and thrived on conversation and companionship. As for waiting for that elusive "Christian boy," I was already 17 years old, had spent all my life in church, and had never yet come across one that appealed to me.

My compromise, therefore, would be to take my boyfriends to church. There I would see that they were introduced to God, and the "Christian boy" problem would be solved for all of us.

"Well, you look beautiful," Mother smiled. "I have to keep an eye out for my girl, you know."

"Thanks, Mom. I love you."

The doorbell rang. I introduced a very well-behaved Raul to my parents, and we left. The hours that followed soon became one of the most fun-filled nights of my life. We laughed, we danced, but mostly we simply looked at each other. I couldn't think of anything to say. What I was feeling seemed too deep to discuss on a first date. I stored the thoughts away in my heart along with the rest of my treasured memories.

Raul took me home without even a hint about seeing me again. Our relationship soon slowed back down to its normal "hi ya" pace. But my desire to be with him grew steadily, and continued into my senior year.

Throughout that year, the main theme around campus was the Vietnam war. Which senior boys would get drafted? Some would escape by pursuing education, others would have to go, and many would probably volunteer. No one would admit to being afraid. Personally, I couldn't imagine anyone going to war when education was such an easy out.

I started making my own plans for the future. I loved attending school, and determined that I would get a good education. I wanted to major in Social Science and minor in Spanish. This would be the logical course to prepare me for my return to Chile.

At our school, homecoming was the biggest event of the year. Senior princesses were chosen by the entire student body and were honored during halftime at a hard-hitting football game. Being the over-involved senior that I was made me one of the eligible candidates. My classmates voted for me, and once again I found myself needing an escort to a very important dance.

As before, Raul accepted my invitation. What a thrill it would be to spend one of the year's memorable events with him. As far as I was concerned, he was the most fabulous, fun-loving guy in all the world.

Two days before the event, he telephoned.

"Hello, Sharon. This is Raul."

"Hi, Raul! Are you ready for Friday night?"

"Yeah. Well, that's what I called about. I'm really sorry, Sharon, but I won't be able to take you. See, I got in a little fight last weekend at a party and now the school won't let me go to homecoming."

"Just because of a little rumble?" I was devastated.

"Well, you know how they are."

Heartsick, I hung up the phone. Everything had gone wrong. Not only had I lost my long-awaited date with Raul, but my reproduction of one of Jacqueline Kennedy's ball gowns had turned out to be a total flop. Surrounded by rumpled white satin and my sewing gear, I sat on the floor and wept. I felt like Cinderella, except I would never make it to the ball.

"Oh God," I prayed, "why do my plans always fall apart? Why can't I ever have the boy I want?" I always talked to God more when things went wrong.

Mother invariably brought order to my chaos. She calmly walked into my room, picked up "Jackie's" dress, examined it thoughtfully, then laid it down without comment. She proceeded to rummage around in my overstuffed closet and triumphantly pulled out a beautiful coral chiffon dress I had worn in my cousin Janet's wedding. She ripped the veil off the pearl-beaded headpiece and quietly said, "This is what a princess should wear!"

A male friend escorted me during the halftime ceremony. Although I was deeply honored to participate in the gala event, I fought an overwhelming sense of disappointment. One very important missing person could have made that night a dream-come-true.

One of Mother's many proverbs struggled to penetrate my preoccupied mind. I could almost hear her voice saying, "Jesus is the only Prince you'll ever need." But at that moment, someone else was on my mind.

After the dance began, led by the princesses and their escorts, my friend had to leave. I was left alone in my coral dress, pearl-beaded crown and all. I decided to be depressed, and proceeded to do so.

Barely a moment had passed when, all of a sudden, I noticed some mischievous eyes watching me behind the stage curtain. I ran backstage, and there was Raul. He had sneaked in. His lawlessness scared me, but not enough to make me run away.

"How's my princess doing tonight?" he grinned.

"Miserable without you!" The words found their way out of my mouth before I had time to catch them.

"How 'bout a dance?" he asked, impulsively taking me into his arms. We laughed, acted crazy, and gazed into each other's eyes till the clock struck 12.

After homecoming, our relationship slowly began to grow and continued to do so until graduation. I never greeted Raul that he didn't tell me how beautiful I looked, and how much he wanted to date me. It would have seemed obvious that he was in love with me, but for some reason he never asked me out. I silently hoped, and once again, I waited.

"And I'll wait forever," I determined in my heart.

Graduation was near. Some of my friends were investing in fabulous dresses at expensive stores. This time I designed mine early so it wouldn't end up in the ragbag. It was a total-white-eyelet success.

Everybody wanted a special date for graduation evening, and I was no exception. I knew very well whom I wanted to be with, but this time it wasn't my place to ask. I didn't.

After receiving the congratulations of family, friends, and loved ones, the senior class exuberantly crowded into several buses. They would take us to Long Beach Harbor where we would embark on an all-night cruise to Catalina Island. Our destination was one last occasion of shared laughter, friendship, and fun.

I squeezed into a seat at the front of the bus. It wasn't long before I was overwhelmed by an invasion of fearful thoughts. Emotionally, I was a mess. Fernando was a dream that had refused to come true. Mike was no more than a sweet memory. And Raul? He was like a mirage that would never become reality. There I sat, alone again.

Our commencement ceremony had caused other questions to crowd my mind as well. Would I be able to achieve the high goals I had set for myself? College seemed like such a complicated prospect. Various ambitions would soon scatter my classmates to the four corners of the world. Would I ever see them again? What would take the place of cheering at football games? Of cruising local burger hangouts in a '57 Chevy stuffed with screaming, giggling girls? Of staying after school for student council meetings?

Was there life after high school?

Would I ever get to go back to Chile?

When we got off the buses, we scrambled for the ship like a bunch of lifelong prisoners being set free. I was herded right through the door and immediately found myself on the wide dance floor. Only a second could have passed before my eyes focused on Raul's, all the way across the room. This time something different gleamed in their brown-green depths. They seemed to say that the long-awaited conquest of my heart was about to begin.

It did. We spent the night walking around the deck, holding hands, staring at each other. Words were unnecessary. Memories of Chile, Fernando, and Mike stood as still as the constellations on a moonless night. A shooting star had flashed across the sky, interrupting my life. I was destined to follow it.

That night, Raul and I set sail into a new tomorrow. My head resting on his shoulder, I couldn't quite understand my emotions. I could only feel that the sea was calm, and all was well.

What would tomorrow bring?

Navigating On My Own

4

A warm, breezy June afternoon found Raul and me sitting on my front porch. I wasn't allowed to entertain boys in the house when no one else was home, so we were enjoying each other's company along with the outdoor scenery. Daddy had surrounded our house with a lush carpet of grass, bordering it with a variety of seasonal flowers and tree roses.

Under my window he had planted a white camellia just for me.

"You've enlisted in the Marine Corps?" Horrified, I repeated Raul's statement to be sure I'd understood.

"Don't worry, Sharon. . . . I'll write to you every day!" He tried to pacify me by kissing my cheek repeatedly.

I'll write to you. . . . A familiar pain threatened. I remembered the many letters Fernando and I had exchanged. Some of their memorized lines slowly tiptoed across my mind.

"But you don't understand . . ." I wanted to explain, but couldn't.

"Don't worry . . . everything is going to be just fine," Raul interrupted.

"So where will you go?" I asked.

"To boot camp in San Diego for eight weeks, and then . . . somewhere in the world!" he continued, kissing me between words.

His exhilaration bothered me. The fact that we would be separated didn't seem to concern him in the least. And besides, what if he ended up in Vietnam? What if he got killed? Loneliness once more stood at the door of my life trying to push itself inside. But Raul's persistent teasing, laughter, and intermittent kisses distracted my thoughts. All was well—for the moment.

He left for boot camp vowing that I would hear from him and, to my surprise, I did. In every letter he begged me to wait for him, and he continuously promised that he would "change." Waiting had become a painful way of life for me. But I couldn't understand why he needed to change. I loved him just the way he was . . . fun, visionary, and most of all, affectionate. His zest for life sparkled like a fountain, and I wanted to splash in it!

Raul had enlisted for a four-year tour of duty with the Marines, so I proceeded with my intentions to get an education and to fulfill some of my dreams. My plans invariably included my sister. Shirley and I had always been best friends. It's unbelievable but, as far back as I can remember, the number of fights we've had can be counted on one hand.

I wanted to work full-time during the day and go to night school. Shirley felt that it made perfect sense for me to get a job at the electronics factory where she worked. She made a strong case for my taking a job there.

"You'll make good money. And you can study while you work, because the job doesn't require you to use your brain. Besides, we can ride to work together."

Shirley and I never imagined that we would be apart. At night, after the lights were out, we planned our entire lives together as we always had. After our nightly bedtime chats with Mother, like typical Chileans we stayed up late and talked, often past midnight. Shirley was the one with all the ideas.

"First, we'll go to Europe. We'll visit Paris, Rome, Venice, London, and Madrid. Then we'll go back to Chile and you can see Fernando!"

"What's it like in London?" I listened, spellbound, while she described the faraway places she loved so much to envision.

Shirley seemed to know everything. She read to me while I sewed for her. She devoured travel books and magazines, studied maps, and memorized tour pamphlets. She calculated that we could go to Europe on five dollars per day. "And that includes lodging, food, and transportation!"

We prayed for God's blessing on our decisions and went to sleep dreaming of adventures.

Meanwhile, the environment of my full-time factory job brought society's hopelessness into full view. People at work seemed to be going nowhere. Their personal goals amounted to getting a raise and taking weekends off. Foolish, dirty talk dominated almost every conversation. The whole scene posed a grave threat to either intellectual or spiritual growth.

Shirley and I contented ourselves with plans for better tomorrows. She would become an international airline stewardess, satisfying her wanderlust. I, too, expected to do something daring and unique.

At the end of eight weeks, Raul's boot camp was over and I received a phone call from his mother. "Sharon? This is Josie. Raul called and he wants us to take you with us to his graduation from basic training."

"Thanks for asking," I answered respectfully, "but I'm already planning to go with a girlfriend." A new worry entered my heart: Would his parents, brother, and sisters like me?

The day came. A brilliant blue sky stretched all the

way from the Los Angeles suburbs to San Diego. When I arrived there, I met a delightful family.

First, petite Josie ran over to meet us. My Latin American upbringing enabled me to recognize the pure Spanish blood that ran thick in her veins. She was a handsome, fine-featured lady. Papi, Raul's dad, reflected the well-built sturdiness of his half-German, half-Mexican breeding. Josie was loud and bubbly; Papi was amusing, but more reserved.

Raul had a younger brother, Xavier. He also had two sisters, Sonia, a 12-year-old beauty, and little Chrissy, with whom I fell in love at first sight.

The Ries family made it quite clear that they were extremely pleased with Raul's choice of a girlfriend. Papi seemed especially impressed at my ability to rattle off Spanish fluently. He tested me with countless questions and smiled approvingly at my answers.

Our chatter was stilled as we walked across the Marine base together, and our attention was drawn from each other and toward hundreds of perfectly regimented, meticulously uniformed Marines. They marched up and down the spotless parade grounds chanting their marching cadences.

Once Raul came on the scene, I saw no one but him. I was amazed by his appearance. A little bit of strenuous exercise could certainly make an already beautiful human specimen even more spectacular! It also pleased me to learn that this young man was not only fascinating to look at, but a top achiever. He graduated with high honors. The family was proud. He was perfect. I silently hoped that he was mine.

"Yes, I will wait for him," I resolved. What else could I do? I felt somehow as if I had found a missing puzzle piece that completed the picture of my life. I welcomed him into my world, even though I knew it would mean being alone.

That September, Raul received his infantry training at Camp Pendleton near San Diego. After a couple of letters, he stopped writing. I couldn't believe how obsessed with him I had become. Once more I found myself waiting endlessly for the mailman to appear.

Thinking of Raul made my schoolwork far more difficult. How could I have let this happen to me again? The days became endless. An empty feeling haunted me.

Around the first of December, on an unusually chilly day, I unexpectedly met Raul face-to-face at a neighborhood market.

He looked startled. "Hi, Sharon. How are you doing?"

"What are you doing home?" My voice must have given evidence of my dismay.

"Oh, I've been on leave. Tomorrow I'm being shipped out to Vietnam."

I wanted to ask him why he hadn't written or called, but I couldn't. I didn't want to hear him say it was over. But he anticipated my question. And he answered it with a lie.

"Sorry I haven't been in touch, Sharon. They wouldn't let us write to anybody. And since I've been home, I've been too busy getting ready to leave." Later I learned that he'd been home nearly a month and had spent the whole time with his school buddies.

"Well, I gotta go. It was nice seeing you." I walked toward my car, shivering and humiliated.

Raul followed me out, "Sharon . . . I'm sorry. I mean it. I really do want you to be my only girl—honest. Do you think there's any possibility? Do you think a guy like me can have a girl like you?"

Right then I knew, with all my heart, that this was my cue to run away from him—to run with all of my strength. Whatever love I felt for him was of a different dimension than any I had known before, but I sensed danger. My thoughts were scrambled. Past experience warned me to stop the relationship. My upbringing screamed at me to turn and go. Then, as usual, my will yielded. Raul had convinced me to try again.

From that decision onward, I drifted with a tide of events that cost me unimaginable sorrow.

As I drove home, Mother's soft, instructive voice rose above my confused thoughts: "A relationship with a person whose life is not centered on God can only bring heartache."

I was well-acquainted with the misery caused by separation, but the pain I was feeling now was different. Raul's silence, his lies, and then his unexplainable desire for me to be his girl generated distrust and insecurities I had never dealt with before. I rationalized that all my relationships had been hurtful in one way or another. And I still hadn't located that ideal Christian boyfriend.

When Raul left for Vietnam, he didn't want me to see him off. But before he left, he called. There was an unusual tone of desperation in his voice, although he attempted to sound jovial as ever.

"Promise you'll write?" he asked repeatedly.

"I promise. I'm a master at it!" I assured him.

"Do you think we're going to make it?" He sounded genuinely worried.

"I don't know Raul. We will if it's God's will."

"I love you, Sharon. Honest. I'm going to miss you."

"I'll miss you too," I answered, beginning to believe him. As we said goodbye, tears drenched my face.

This time Raul kept his word. He wrote from the U.S.S. *Gaffi*, his departure ship. He wrote from Da Nang, his arrival city. He wrote from camp, from the bush, from the U.S.S. *Sanctuary* after being wounded. He even wrote from Japan.

As I read his letters, I sometimes wondered if he was dead. I cried a lot, and studied his pictures under the microscopes at work. Each new letter brought the assurance of his ongoing life and hope for the future. By now he was making lots of plans for us.

"Please wait for me. I'm coming home. I promise. When I do, will you marry me?"

I always responded that I couldn't marry him because he wasn't a Christian. But, besides that, I didn't fully trust him. I tried to tell him about the plans I had for my own life. "I want to serve God the way my parents always have. I want to discover the plans that God has for me. . . ."

Deep inside I firmly believed that one day I would be a missionary in some distant land.

"I *am* a Christian!" Raul would write, trying to convince me. "Didn't I go to church with you? Besides, I could never hurt you, because you're the only girl I've ever loved. I'm going to spend all my time with you— you'll see!"

His correspondence also revealed his need to be loved, and I wanted to love him. There was an emptiness in his nature that would be filled once he met Jesus. He was simple and uncomplicated, and in some ways childlike. But most of all he loved me, and I wanted to be loved by him. I was bent on waiting this one out.

One year passed. Daddy had been going to college classes with me at night. They were complex and exhausting, but his encouragement made it possible for me to persevere. My father never criticized me or said a single discouraging word. His enthusiasm convinced me to quit my boring job and to tackle an overloaded, daytime college schedule.

On the first day of school, I woke up before the alarm went off. I had wrestled all night with nightmares of lockers not opening, "F's" on my papers, vanished classrooms and, worst of all, being unable to understand wordy, philosophical lectures.

Undaunted, I jumped out of bed, threw on my prearranged-the-night-before outfit, and ran out the door, my schedule in one hand and a piece of toast in the other. I arrived an hour early so I could find my classes and the cafeteria, as well as places to study.

My interests had changed since high school. I was no longer fascinated by clothes or school events. I no longer strove to maintain friendships where I had nothing in common except school events. And because of Raul, boys were off-limits. My intellect, after 19 years, seemed to be awakening from a lifelong nap. A desire for academic achievement stirred within me. Meanwhile my spirit demanded answers to some serious questions. I wanted to settle, once and for all, my place in God's plan, and my reason for being alive.

Students and teachers alike disputed the existence of God. This was news to me. I was born believing in God, and couldn't recall a single day that I had not believed in Him. There were many matters beyond my understanding, and some of them puzzled me. But to disbelieve in God was out of the question.

One day a professor pridefully challenged, "I dare you to open your cluttered minds to discover the truth . . . the truth that there really is no God!"

I took his challenge without any reservations. I was convinced that if Jesus really was the only-begotten Son of the transcendent God, no man's lie could change that fact. I also concluded that if God was the Creator of all things as the Bible attests, then He would be revealed at the heart of any subject I studied. I went to my classes with an open mind, determined to learn all that I could.

After listening to more than a dozen professors, all with differing opinions concerning God and creation, I learned a very important truth: There might be as many opinions about God as there are people on this planet. But how could anyone determine who was telling the truth? Only God could speak for Himself!

As I faithfully sat in my classes day after day, I found that even scientists, knowledgeable as they were, had limited ability to understand anything fully. There were appalling blanks in their theories, and many of their so-called scientific facts were sadly lacking in scientific evidence. It became clear to me that, just as the Scripture says, all human knowledge is incomplete apart from God. We only gain true wisdom as He reveals Himself and His plans to us through creation, the Scriptures, and through His Son, Jesus Christ.

One day my astronomy professor said, "Today we're going to look into some of the marvelous discoveries man has made during the last few decades." He went on to describe facts, not visible to the naked eye, concerning our universe. To my surprise, I had already read about these things in my Bible. The biblical statements I had read had been written with perfect accuracy thousands of years prior to this class, before the telescope or the microscope had even been invented.

I could see that neither students nor instructors were necessarily interested in finding "truth." Instead, each person was choosing to believe whatever would resolve his own moral or intellectual dilemma without interference from a sovereign Lord. How hard they worked at finding evidence to prove their ever-changing perceptions rather than to build solid theories on established evidence. In every class I took, the Bible was absolutely ignored. This was done in spite of the fact that it remains the oldest and most reliable document ever written.

No one seemed impressed that, although the Bible was written by 40 different authors over a period of 1600 years, it is unmatched in its uniformity and unchallenged in its truth. Instead, hours of class time were spent discussing the differing opinions of "thinkers" throughout history—men who went to their graves without ever discovering the truth.

During those months I contemplated the universe with its infinite wonders, radiant splendor, and perfect order. Its complexity declared the existence of an omniscient, omnipotent Creator. "It's as if there had been a master planner," admitted a professor one day as he explained how our entire solar system works together to produce the crop-growing season.

I learned that man, who is made in the image of his Creator and therefore is so like Him in his abilities to reason, discover, and create, often willfully chooses to remain ignorant of God. And this he knowingly does, even though evidence concerning His existence can be clearly seen in all that He has made. But, by His grace (unmerited favor), I had not made this foolish choice. I began to feel wonderful! Not only had I always believed in God, but now I had begun to grasp the evidence concerning Him. The eternally existing God was my Maker!

In the meantime, I was doing well in school. My savings account was steadily growing, promising a summer of travel. And, to top it all, Raul came home unexpectedly.

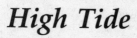

High Tide

5

Raul limped toward me, tired and bruised. He wore battered battle fatigues and beat-up jungle boots. He moved stiffly, favoring the booby-trap wounds on his back and the shrapnel which remained embedded in his left leg. Dark circles ringed his eyes, bearing witness to his constant sleeplessness. He had had to remain ever-alert to an enemy attack. I gently caressed his face. He seemed so fragile . . .

"Sharon! Sharon, wake up, we're almost there!" Chrissy's enthusiastic young voice abruptly ended my favorite fantasy.

"You gonna give him a great big kiss?" Xavier was a tease. I laughed to cover my embarrassment.

"What'll you say to my brother?" Chrissy was possessive of Raul and was enjoying this spontaneous interrogation. "Are you going to marry him? What are you going to wear? I want to be in the wedding!"

"I don't know, Chrissy. What are you going to wear?" I laughed, trying to divert the questions back to her.

I certainly didn't have any answers for the Ries family's inquiries. The truth was, I had plenty of questions of my own.

We were all crowded into their Volkswagen van, making the eight-hour trip to Oakland Naval Hospital in northern California. Raul had called his parents early that morning, asking them to come to see him, and to bring me along. After 11 months of the most unbearable jungle warfare imaginable, he was extremely battle fatigued. He had been flown home from Vietnam two months before his expected return date. His family was overjoyed.

As for me, crammed into a vehicle with five people I didn't know very well, I was a nervous wreck. A chronic case of infatuation, ever-present uncertainty about the future, and the excitement of seeing Raul again had rendered me almost speechless. I stared out the window hoping to avoid any further conversations.

The fertile land which spans the distance between Los Angeles and San Francisco was ready for harvest, about to provide the abundant farm produce that makes California such a fruitful state. Fluffy clouds floated across the broad sky without a care in the world, obeying the course of nature as God designed them to do. Memories of another automobile journey carried me back to my tenth year.

During a visit to America, Daddy had packed Mother, Shirley and me, and our belongings into a new 1958 pink Rambler station wagon. We had barely enough room to sit. He had driven us mercilessly from one state to another in the midst of the most appallingly hot summer I had ever experienced.

Friends who had supported my parents on the mission field had invited us to visit their homes and churches, and to share our missionary adventures with them. Daddy was impressively skillful at bringing the people right into our world. His slide presentation boarded the viewers on an ocean liner and carried them to faraway lands where they encountered the joys and perils of our lives. The crowd laughed and cried and many men and women made new life-commitments to God.

Daddy had a passion for people which radiated from his entire being. "The harvest truly is great, but the laborers are few; pray ye therefore to the Lord of the harvest, that he would send forth laborers into his harvest." Daddy echoed the words of Jesus, and those words were burned into my own young heart.

"I'll go! I'll go! Send me!" I inwardly shouted. As far as I was concerned, the mission field was the only place to be.

Mother had heard the call in her heart to go "South of the Great River," as a young girl of 13. By the time she was 18, she was the director of the Interdenominational Youth Rallies in the greater Los Angeles area. Daddy, a bachelor of 26 just out of Bible college, visited one of these meetings on his way to the mission field. The moment he saw her walk in confidently "like an angel, dressed in white," he knew in his heart that God had brought her to him. They were married in eight months and on the mission field one year later.

Throughout our lives, Mother's love for God was expressed by her faithful support of Daddy in all that he did. During that trip, as always, Shirley and I made our own youthful contribution. We joined Mother, singing her favorite Spanish songs of adoration and thanksgiving to the Lord.

After church, pastors and their families would usually treat us to an all-American chicken, mashed potato, and gravy dinner. They would then kindly thank us and send us off, with a gift of money which enabled us to pay for our gas. Sometimes we stopped at drive-in restaurants along the highways. There we consumed our first hamburgers, Coke floats, and French fries. To our astonishment, they were served by teenage girls who roller-skated out to serve us through the windows of our car.

During the long, hot stretches of driving, Daddy taught us short history lessons and provided interesting facts about each state. Mother entertained us, singing both American folk songs and melodies of inspiration and faith. The setting sun prompted her to tell us one Bible story or another, lessons which buried priceless values in our hearts. She could never have imagined to what extent those informal teachings would guide me through times of doubt and darkness.

I missed Mother now. I needed Shirley to help me understand what was happening to me. I closed my eyes as I often did when I needed to sort things out.

"You're never alone," Mother had said many times.

My heart responded, "God is here, He's always here for me to talk to."

"What am I going to do?" I asked my Eternal Companion.

Raul had written that he wanted to get married once he got home. I wasn't ready for that at all. I still had two years of college to complete, and I knew that I could never marry until I returned to Chile.

I wonder what Fernando is doing? Painful recollections drifted into my thoughts. It had been such a long time since we had written to each other. I needed to return to Chile, to see about Fernando, before I could make any major decisions about the future.

I need time. Lots of time, I thought. *I need time to spend with Raul, to get to know him, to tell him about me, my plans, and my God. We'll go to church together,* I decided. *He'll get to know God and then it'll be alright with God for us to be together! I'll travel during the summer and finish college while he does his remaining two years in the Marines.*

It was a perfect plan. After all, I was only 19. Daddy always said 26 was a good age to get married. Satisfied with this decision, I concluded it would all work out.

A lively wind began to blow as we drove through San Francisco, clearing the city's pollution from the skies.

We had traveled all night and were hot, wrinkled, and uncombed. "Can't we go to the hotel first to get cleaned up?" My question was silently answered as I looked out the car window and saw the Oakland Naval Hospital.

Raul's dad gave us ten minutes to go to the ladies' restroom for toothbrushing and freshening up. There was no sense in arguing with him—we only had one hour to see Raul.

"Lance Corporal Ries will be out in a few minutes. Just have a seat out there," instructed a military police officer, pointing out a picnic table on the grass. As we waited, I looked around, surprised at the enormity of the naval hospital complex.

I tuned out Raul's chattering family and allowed my imagination to carry me away again. I relived my dream once more, picturing Raul in his weatherworn fatigues, emerging from his barracks, making his way straight for me, embracing me gently . . .

Just then I saw him. A chill started in my brain and crawled slowly down my spine. This was real life, and there was the Marine of my dreams, the one I had been waiting for. He was walking toward us wearing impeccable dress greens.

My fantasies had deceived me. He looked healthy and strong. As far as battle wounds were concerned, a very slight limp was the only noticeable change. Eleven months of warfare had matured him. He had become more handsome, very serious, and extremely masculine. The boyhood spark in his eyes had been replaced by a sharp, piercing look.

Something exploded inside me. All the long months of mixed emotions—fear and desire, mistrust and loyalty, longing and independence—combined into a feeling I had never known before. At that fateful moment, I didn't care whether Raul was a Christian or not. I didn't care what Raul was really like inside. I simply liked the Raul I saw, and I wanted him.

I sat quietly while his family hugged and kissed him. They must have asked him a hundred and one questions. Our eyes communicated frustration and the desire to be alone, but there was no time. There never was. The hour was gone with a kiss on the cheek and we were separated once again. How long would it be this time?

During the next six months, Raul was given a few weekend passes. The eight-hour trip from Oakland to Los Angeles and back left us with only a handful of hours to enjoy one another's company. This was made even more difficult by the fact that these were our first opportunities to be together in three years. Hours ticked by like seconds when I was with Raul. When he was gone, even minutes seemed to linger forever.

On the two Sundays he was home, he religiously accompanied me to church. He took communion and went to the altar to pray when the minister suggested it. Good Catholic that he was, he was trying to understand what my God was all about by going through the motions. Nevertheless, I was convinced that he was sincere in his religious gestures. Some day he would surely meet God for himself and would come to know Him personally.

After spending six months of mandatory therapy at Oakland Naval Hospital, Raul was transferred to Camp Pendleton, the Marine base two hours from our hometown where he had taken his infantry training. Not long after he relocated there, Easter rolled around. Raul asked some of his friends and his family to camp at a beach site near the marine base so he could spend a weekend with us.

"Sharon, why don't you and Raul go down early on Friday morning and reserve us a good campsite?" Josie suggested. "Papi and I will go over the border to Mexico, pick up some supplies, and meet you there Friday night."

Raul and I were ecstatic. At last we would be able to spend a few hours alone together before everyone arrived. We met as planned. An entire day with him seemed like only a few minutes. No sunset had ever been so lovely. While we waited, the twilight became evening and the evening, dawn. Our kisses led to the kind of passion that demands satisfaction.

Obviously, no one showed up—not even Raul's parents. We found out later that everyone had had a last-minute change of plans.

We had met at the campsite on Good Friday. Now Saturday's first brilliant rays broke across the horizon. I had not slept all night. The beach was quiet and serene. I wasn't.

The ocean's waves had pounded the shore all night, washing away footprints and sand castles, leaving the beach smooth and clean. How I wished the events that had occurred there in the seaside darkness could have been as easily washed out of my memory.

I had broken my vow with God.

All my life I had made promises to the Lord, believing that in doing so I would somehow prevent myself from disobeying Him. How could anyone break a promise to God? The fact was, I had managed to do it more often than I cared to recall. This time it was serious. I knew it was.

"Why?" I asked myself. "Why couldn't I live up to God's laws?"

While driving home, Raul seemed incapable of understanding my plight. "Why are you so upset?" he asked, puzzled. "You know that I love you."

"I know, Raul, but this isn't the way I wanted our relationship to be!" I tried to explain, but my words failed to express the immensity of my despair.

"Why can't we get married?" he asked again.

"Because God says!" I shot back. "Don't you understand? I've disobeyed God too much already. Now I want to do things His way. I want the very best He has for me! Don't you see?"

I knew very well that I had arrived at this moment because my heart and soul had belonged to Raul, and not to the One who rightfully owned me. Raul Ries had distracted my attention from God and His Word.

"No, I don't understand, Sharon. If you love me and I love you, what more is there?"

"There's God's will. And His will is printed on the pages of the Book that I haven't been reading or obeying! His will is everything. It is life! Actually, I shouldn't even be dating you!"

By now I was crying. In spite of everything I was saying, I was quite sure that I would never leave Raul. And I think I knew, even then, that I would suffer grave consequences for it.

Raul pulled the car over and stopped on the side of the freeway.

"Sharon, come here. Let me hold you. Now listen. I love you. I promise . . . I'm going to be a Christian just like you want me to be. But please, just give me some time. I have to learn how, that's all. Honest, I promise. I'll do it for us."

"Raul, what if I'm pregnant? What am I going to do? I've ruined everything and I'm afraid God is going to punish me really bad!" I could hardly talk for weeping.

"Sharon, you're not going to be pregnant. And anyway, if you are, then you'll *have* to marry me!"

In one sense he was joking with me. But the love in his words made me feel secure. He persuaded me that he loved me and that his intentions were right. He convinced me that he would see me through, no matter what.

It wasn't long before his words were put to the test.

The Captain
and Me

6

The second we arrived at my house, I jumped out of Raul's red Karman Ghia and ran to the mailbox. Setting my worries aside for the moment, I couldn't wait to see if I had any letters from my mother and sister. They had gone on a missionary journey to Colombia.

Not long before, Shirley had made a serious commitment to God, giving Him her life and her future. Now she had taken a break from school, returning to the country of her birth. The call in her heart had carried her beyond contemporary civilization, to a place where modern conveniences are unknown, where rivers are used for bathing, and where God's lights in the sky and the warm glow of fires are all that illuminate the world.

One year after their wedding, my parents had gone to El Secreto, a missionary vision burning in their heart. There, with the help of some native ranchers, they had hand-carved a mission station at the top of a hill, in the depths of the jungle. All their supplies were carried in by mule train.

I have no memory of the place itself. I do, however, recall our breakneck departure during the religious revolution that occurred there between 1948 and 1958. This uprising was intended to curb Protestant penetration throughout Colombia, and left a trail of atrocities and mass murders in its bloody wake. Mother, Shirley, and I had fled our beloved mission at the point of a rebel's machine gun. Trembling, we climbed into a small D-C3 cargo-passenger airplane whose floor was covered with blood, testifying to the cruelty of the revolutionaries.

Daddy had refused to leave, and so a fanatical military commander temporarily had imprisoned him in a concentration camp. During this violent time, the lives of our schoolchildren were threatened, and then the mission was raided and burned. When they were finished, nothing was left but the 14-inch brick-and-concrete walls. That stark, blackened monument remains to this day. It is a mute reminder of the only steps toward progress ever taken in that primitive region.

It is no secret in our family that Mother left her heart in Colombia. Sometimes she talked about "the place out on the plains where two rivers meet and defy the terrain, where palm trees grow tall and straight, and the wildlife is free, where up on a high hill, a mission sits and waits."

"Someday I will go too," I had silently promised myself.

"A letter! I got a letter from Shirley!" Enraptured, I read it to myself and then aloud to Raul.

March 7, 1968

Dear Sharon,

How are you? Remember all the weight I lost for the airline interviews? Well, I've gained it all back!

All we eat is bread, cooked bananas, and rice. If we're lucky, we get a treat—fishhead soup! Yes, you guessed it—with the eyeballs staring at us.

My legs are all swollen up with mosquito bites. Now that I don't have malaria, they love me. Now I understand how itchy and swollen you used to get when you were a child.

Don't let anyone use my rabbit-hair coat. PLEASE.

Mother says she appreciates you taking care of Daddy and the house and that she'll write a long letter soon with all the details.

Don't study too hard!

Love ya,

Shirley

"Poor sis, she must be a mess! And who would want to use her fur coat in this heat?" I had to laugh.

I kissed Raul goodbye, walked into the house, threw myself across my bed, and sobbed. My heart burned with a desire to be with Shirley, out in the jungle, gaining weight so I could be some mosquito's lunch! I wanted to go to the mission and hang in a hammock while the bats flew around the ceiling and the rats ran across the rafters.

"Oh God," I cried, "forgive me . . . please . . . give me another chance . . . I want to be a missionary!"

That night before I went to sleep, a picture that Mother had hung in my room encouraged me. It depicted a young man carefully steering a ship through the midst of a fierce storm. Beside him stood Jesus pointing the way.

A prayer spilled out of my troubled spirit: "Be my Captain, Jesus. Point the way . . . please!"

I opened my Bible to the Psalms. Mother always said the Psalms would encourage me. I read every one, from the beginning. Then Psalm 34, verse 19, stopped me short. Its words penetrated my heart like a sword: "Many are the afflictions of the righteous, but the Lord delivereth him out of them all."

I went to sleep thinking about that Scripture, but I found it hard to digest. First of all, I did not feel a bit righteous. Second of all, I did not like the idea that man has many afflictions. I never wanted to suffer again.

Wrestling with the Word of God, I cried myself to sleep.

During the next few weeks, I busied myself with school, cleaning house, and cooking for Daddy and me. I had but one prayer on my lips: "Please God, don't let me be pregnant."

The endless month finally passed. Raul came knocking at my front door early one Saturday morning.

"How's my love?" Raul grabbed me roughly and began to kiss me.

"Raul, come into the kitchen, I have to tell you something." I pushed him away and walked ahead of him. I sat on the stool.

"Raul, I'm pregnant!"

"You're kidding! How do you know?"

"I know, Raul. Believe me, I know!"

Raul impetuously took me in his arms and started swinging me all around the kitchen. "We're going to have a baby. . . . I can't believe it! I'm going to be a daddy! Now you have to marry me!" He said all this in one breath.

I was absolutely shocked. How could he be so happy? My life had all but ended. I was scared to have a baby. I had never included a baby in any of my plans. I didn't even know how to give birth to a baby, much less how to take care of one. Now I couldn't finish school or travel. I wasn't going to be a missionary. Worst of all, I had shamed myself and my parents.

"Raul you don't have to marry me," I retorted. "I'll take care of my baby myself."

"Our baby . . ." he interrupted. ". . . it's our baby and you are going to marry me!"

I think I would have died in my shame had he not answered me in that way. I did want to marry Raul. Not only was I madly in love with him, but I wanted to make things right as soon as possible. I had broken God's law by becoming one flesh with a man who wasn't my husband—a man who didn't know my Lord.

But now I was no longer alone. Through this baby I had tied myself to Raul for life. He would always be my child's father.

Suddenly I had become a family—Raul, the baby, and me. If my baby was to be all that God wanted him to be, his daddy had to know God. I would do whatever was necessary to make us a family in right standing with God. I didn't care if it took forever.

My own determination frightened me, but life without Raul scared me more. I sensed that if I could take Raul home with me, if I could remove him from his environment, I could show him the way to God. I had read in the Bible that an unbelieving husband could be led to God by the lifestyle of a believing wife. It would take wholehearted commitment to God. I could allow absolutely nothing to get between God and me.

I had known all along that there would be ill consequences for my sins. Everybody in the Bible suffered them. But by now I had sincerely repented and I also knew from God's Word that obedience to Him would eventually start producing benefits—the special privileges that one receives when he submits to God's ways. I just needed to learn how to obey Him fully. I would pursue Him with all my heart and soul until I did.

It never entered my mind that our life together wouldn't work out. The God I had come to trust had historically restored His people to Himself whenever they turned to Him. The One I believed in had parted the Red Sea to deliver His children from their adversaries, then had swallowed up the wicked. My Deliverer had closed the mouths of hungry lions when a man of God was thrown into their pit. God was on my side and would remain there as long as I stayed close to him.

One day I tried to communicate these thoughts with Raul. I told him that my family and I lived for God and that I was resolved to teach my children the same values. I wanted my husband-to-be to comprehend what he was getting into. As if in a daze, trying very hard to grasp all that I said, he held me tight and said thoughtfully, "Sharon, I've always wanted a happy home. My dream came true when I met you. You're the only woman I have ever loved, and I will love you forever."

I believed that he would.

The following Sunday, Raul went to the altar to pray at the end of our Bible study. Surely we were on our way to restoration.

Much to my surprise, I experienced incredible strength as I faced the following months. I had to confront pregnancy, wedding plans, and the hardest semester of college finals ever. No matter how overwhelming life became, I could feel the constant nearness of the Captain. I found indescribable comfort in my quiet times with Him.

Although my best dreams had been suddenly drowned in the depths of my disobedience, the hand of the Lord seemed to be steadfastly pointing me in the direction I should take. I felt a peace that passed all my understanding.

I soon realized that I could no longer be in control of my life. Only God could bring order to this disaster. With Him in control I didn't feel it was necessary to hurt my parents, so I didn't tell them or anyone else (except Shirley, once she returned from South America) about my pregnancy. I felt safe with my secret in His confidence.

Raul agreed to secrecy, too. He did tell his mother, however, and she reacted very lovingly, accompanying me to a medical examination. Raul immediately took control and made himself responsible for me. It felt so good. One evening, over dinner at my house, he valiantly asked Daddy for my hand in marriage. Daddy, being a man of few words, said "No," then briefly explained that I needed to finish school, offered Raul some more vegetables, and calmly finished his dinner.

Needless to say, we decided we'd better get married anyway.

I wept over the letter that should have been the happiest I had ever written. It informed Mother and Shirley of our wedding date and plans.

"... we're going to have a small wedding. We chose your wedding date, Mother, the sixth of July. Come home soon, I need you. I love you, Sharon."

Mother read between the lines. Knowing I was not one to rush into anything, especially marriage, she perceived my dilemma. She and my sister were on their way home anyway, and I was relieved that I hadn't shortened their trip. On their arrival they immediately set about to minimize my pain.

My family never pried into my secret. Raul and I were treated as kindly and affectionately as always. Not one negative word was ever spoken. Mother and Daddy had instructed me explicitly in the ways of God. All that would ever be said concerning the fact that we were spiritually mismatched had already been said. For this I will be eternally indebted to them. During that extremely difficult time, I would not have been able to bear another wound in my already-broken heart.

I owe the same praise to the Ries family. Never have they provoked Raul or me over our unplanned pregnancy.

One night my parents, Raul and I were discussing where we should live once we were married. Mother said, "You must always live alone even if you have to live in one room. Work out all your problems together. Don't involve your families.

"Sharon, don't run home when you and Raul have a disagreement. Put God first in everything you do.

"Raul, the Bible can provide all the guidance you will ever need. Everything is in there. Read it faithfully and you will learn to overcome anything that comes your way."

"Yes, Mrs. Farrel, thank you," Raul nodded very seriously.

Mother's words impressed me deeply, although at that moment I didn't quite realize the importance of their meaning.

"By the way," interrupted Daddy, trying to somehow get a word in, "Mother and I have decided to give you a big wedding. It is a once-in-a-lifetime affair, you know. Sharon, make yourself a beautiful dress because we're inviting the whole world to this wedding!"

I was astounded. I knew my parents could in no way afford to finance a big wedding. It would mean a great sacrifice on their part, and I surely did not deserve it. Their love was like a healing salve on an open wound.

That night before I went to sleep, I prayed, "Dear God, I know that You're disappointed in me. So am I. Please help me make wise decisions. Will You fix the mess I've made out of my life? I promise . . . no I don't want to make any more promises. Can't You just make me do what's right? Yes, that's it. Just cause me to understand Your ways and to do them. And please . . . can I still be a missionary someday?"

Candlelight was the only illumination for the 400 guests who crowded into our church sanctuary. White baskets of green ferns and bouquets of pastel flowers adorned the chapel, filling it with the sweet fragrance of a garden. My bridesmaids wore old-fashioned dresses of rainbow hues.

Sonia glowed in soft mint green. Chrissy, who had demanded a part in the wedding, confidently walked the aisle, lighting the candles. Gowned in pale blue, Shirley never stopped crying till the wedding was through.

Raul's best man, Xavier, stood with Raul's friends who stiffly lined up on the right side of the stage. Most of them, like Raul, were Vietnam veterans, as witnessed by the fierce, angry looks on their faces. I was hoping that something would happen to make them smile. It never did. I have the pictures to prove it.

As soon as my cousin Janet finished singing "O Promise Me," the processional music began. On my head a cluster of orange blossoms held a long, pure silk veil in place. It softly draped over my face and entirely covered my organdy dress. A real cameo set in 14-carat gold accented the high, lace-trimmed neckline. The dress was all that I had imagined it could be. I was not.

I'd never felt so safe walking with Daddy as I did at that special moment. Though I was weak, arm in arm with him, his strength held me up. I fully understood why fathers have to give their daughters away. If they didn't, no bride would ever make it down the aisle.

Daddy struggled to say just the right words. He squeezed my hand. "You will be all that God wants you to be. Don't worry." From the back of the church, I could see Mother's tear-filled eyes. Once more they instructed me. No words were needed. I could read her thoughts.

"Sharon, I've tried to do my best. God gave you to me. I gave you God's Word. I know you're going to make it. Your life was endangered at birth, and I promised God I would name you Sharon Faith if He would save your life. I also asked Him not to give me any children who would not serve Him. So, Sharon Faith, follow Him and serve Him. Be married to Christ. I give you to Him. I won't interfere."

A tearful smile tried to form on my lips as I watched her. She was so gentle, so controlled. I knew that her strength came from God. She trusted only in Him.

By now I could see Raul clearly. His eyes were seeking mine. He was more splendid than all the princes in every storybook I had ever read. He was the fulfillment of every desire I'd ever had. I was his bride and he was my groom forever.

Radiant with confidence, he stood and waited, so very unaware of what he was getting into. The first two rows of seats right in front of him contained my family. I knew they would be praying, that day and every day that followed.

"Who gives this woman to be married to this man?" I heard the voice of Pastor Green.

Daddy gave me away, then moved to the altar to say the marriage vows with us.

I was vaguely troubled to see that Raul was paying very little attention to the ceremony. Instead, he spent those sacred minutes whispering to me, telling me how beautiful I looked. During the ring exchange, under his breath, I even heard him compliment my nails!

Despite his lack of interest, I managed to seriously and devotedly struggle through the vows. Raul's distractions invoked an unexpected urging deep within my being. I found myself saying my vows to Jesus rather than to Raul.

"Whither Thou goest I will go," I whispered to the Lord. "Whither Thou lodgest I will lodge. Your people shall be my people and You God shall be my God. . . . I promise to love, cherish, and obey You."

All at once I could scarcely repeat the words. I became enveloped in a warmth that started from the top of my head and wrapped itself lovingly around me. It was a sensation unlike any I had ever experienced.

"I present to you Mr. and Mrs. Raul Andrew Ries." Pastor Green ended the ceremony by introducing us to the congregation. As we walked down the aisle, a soft voice that I had never heard before whispered to my heart, "I will never leave you."

I don't know how, but I recognized the Captain's voice. I had the unexpected perception that I was glowing. I felt virgin and pure. I was forgiven.

No matter what lay ahead, my future would always be warmed by God's presence. I would never leave Him.

And He would never leave me—for better or for worse.

Ship of Dreams

7

My favorite fantasy never foretold the pleasure and satisfaction that Raul initially brought into my life. Childhood hopes and dreams suddenly and painlessly vanished as he became my yesterday, my today, and my tomorrow. My world became wholeheartedly his.

I genuinely respected the way he accepted his manly responsibilities. Raul Ries was determined to succeed in life, and had the natural ability to do so. He worked hard, and was faithful to me both as husband and bread-winner. No doubt remained—he obviously loved me with all his heart. I wanted nothing but to be his, "to have and to hold from this day forward until death do us part."

By the third day of our marriage, Raul had me nestled into a cozy one-bedroom apartment in Anaheim. It was situated halfway between Camp Pendleton and our hometown. We furnished it with a king-size mattress from Raul's folks, a dinette set from mine, and carloads of wedding gifts. All we lacked was a refrigerator. It wasn't long before Daddy appeared on our doorstep with one that was tiny and loud, but served its purpose very well. It was probably one of the first refrigerators ever made, but Raul modernized it by spray painting it bright yellow.

Raul had very little time to spare, but whatever time he had we spent together. Sometimes he bribed the night guard at the base and came home to spend the night with me. His restrictions were puzzling to me since other Marines went home during the week. Raul explained that it was because of tight security at Pendleton. It didn't matter to me, because I thought it was delightfully romantic that he would sneak out to see me.

In August, the heat kept me up late. Many nights I sat under the stars, waiting for Raul. As I gazed into the vastness of the heavens, my thoughts focused on God and His greatness. Who was I that He should take any thought of me? And yet He did.

I contemplated how Jesus, who was part of God Himself, had left His throne in the heavens at the will of His Father. He had made Himself of no reputation, taking the form of a servant, made in the likeness of man. He had humbled Himself, obeying His Father by submitting to a criminal's death—death on a cross.

In doing this, Jesus took the blame for all our past, present, and future sins. He became our sacrifice, so that we would never have to be punished for our transgressions. The King of kings and Lord of lords was beaten for His subjects.

No matter what I had done, my heavenly Father saw me as a righteous child because of Jesus' death and resurrection. In the Bible I had read that those who believe on Jesus and confess their sins, receiving Him as Lord and Savior, are free from mental condemnation as well as eternal damnation. I had heard this teaching all my life, but had never quite understood it until now. "Who will bring any charge against those whom God has chosen?" Paul wrote in Romans 8:33 (NIV). "It is God who justifies [makes pure]." The awesomeness of these thoughts made my heart explode with joy.

On the nights Raul came home, he would rush in shortly after midnight. Invariably, he would snatch my attention away from all else. We'd stay up half the night. I would try to communicate my innermost thoughts toward God. He'd tell me about all his plans.

"I'm a fighter. I'll always be one. I want to become a professional kung fu instructor. I'd like to open up my own studio someday."

My only desire was to be Raul's wife, to help him unfold his vision. I would fall asleep dreaming about how wonderful it was all going to be.

Four months after our wedding, Raul charged through the front door, laughing hilariously. He picked me up in his arms and shouted. "Sharon, my dear, you are looking at a free man! They gave me an honorable discharge! An honorable discharge! Can you believe that?"

"Raul, why are you getting discharged two years early? And why shouldn't it be honorable? You fought in Vietnam, didn't you? You were wounded twice. You almost lost your life!" I was confused.

"I'll tell you why. Because the therapist at the base doesn't like me at all. That's why he never lets me come home." He handed me the doctor's analysis. I read the report and couldn't believe how absurd it was.

"This doctor is nuts!" I agreed. "He doesn't know what he's talking about. He says your outbursts of anger caused you to be released from the Marines. I don't think I've ever seen you angry, Raul. You don't have an angry bone in your body!"

Raul's expression became serious. He looked very guilty.

"So did you get angry?" Fear rippled inside me. I remembered the fight at school that had kept him from being my escort when I was a homecoming princess. How well did I know this man? Besides, I was a little disappointed. I'd been harboring a secret wish that we might be stationed in a foreign country some day.

"Oh, you know." He flippantly waved my concern aside. "I just got a little mad when those guys tried to get me to do dumb stuff like polish my shoes and brass. Nobody cared about polished brass in Nam, I can tell you that!"

Within days of Raul's discharge he was working nights at the bank where his mother was employed. Soon he was going to college full-time during the day. Busy as he was, however, he would find his way home whenever he had a few minutes. I thrived on his love for me.

On my Mother's forty-sixth birthday, December 21, 1968, Raul found himself driving 100 m.p.h. on the San Bernardino Freeway. A call at work had informed him that his wife was about to deliver his first-born child. He drove all the way to Anaheim with his emergency lights flashing. While the new father was sick to his stomach out by the Fairview Hospital trash cans, little Raul Andrew Jr. and I busied ourselves quickly pushing his 9 lb. 14 oz. body through the birth canal. At last he was safe in my arms.

That first birth was a frightening experience for me. I was afraid of the pain I was experiencing. I was concerned with the awesome responsibility of being a mother. And I was wondering what kind of a dad Raul would be. As soon as I was left alone with my newborn son, I held him straight up in the air and gave him back to his Maker.

"God, I give You this child forever. If he's not going to love you, take him back. I don't want the agony of having a child who will not love You." I determined right then that as long as I had breath to breathe I would instruct this child in the ways of God. In this way I would follow the example of my mother and grandmother. They were still giving instruction to me and my sister.

Mother had the flu, so Shirley, who was home from college, was elected to help me take care of my baby.

Before I did anything about mothering the little fellow, I diligently read all the directions in the baby book. Meanwhile, Shirley disinfected the entire house and boiled all the nipples and pacifiers to pieces.

Although we were a sad pair of nurses, Raul Andrew lived up to the meaning of his name: "strong, gentle commander." He survived this life-threatening episode quite happily. Raul Sr. absolutely adored him. "You look like a little priest, buddy." He gently rubbed his baby's fuzzy-brown head.

"Isn't our little boy the most perfect creation of God you've ever seen?

"Yeah . . ." Raul answered, an inquisitive look on his face.

I had never been so content. My husband and son seemed to be the cure for all that had ever ailed me. For that all-too-brief period of time, loving and taking care of them removed the emptiness from my existence. I gladly poured myself into them. As far as I was concerned, nothing else on this earth had any comparable value.

The fog rolled in that first Christmas Eve, and Raul didn't notice the tiny, lighted Christmas tree I had placed in the window to surprise him. We ate by candle-light while Raulie slept next to the manger scene, under the twinkling lights. When he awakened for his feeding, we took our first family picture. I had on a new robe. Raulie wore the too-big red hat my dad had given him "to wear home from the hospital." Raul sat proudly on his new weight-lifting bench, flexing his Marine Corps muscles.

The day after Christmas, against my will, we packed our few belongings and moved to Covina, near our hometown. Raul wanted to be near his friends and family. I just wanted to be with him and visit our families occasionally. In Anaheim, we had been completely alone. No friends had disturbed our privacy, no telephone had interrupted our dialogue. The move to Covina altered our tranquil family atmosphere into a far different environment.

Within hours of our arrival, Raul began to phone his old high school buddies.

Several days later, he was spending most of his free time with them.

Within weeks, his disposition began to change radically.

My happy dream was over. I was alone again. The haunting emptiness had returned.

The one good result of our move was that my parents lived nearby. This gave me the opportunity to go back to school part-time. Mother was fascinated by Raulie, and delighted in spending a few hours with him each week.

But matters with Raul were not so pleasant. It seemed as if he had exchanged his loving, exciting personality for an altogether different one. Although he still cherished Raulie, he was suddenly disinterested in family life. He became slothful around the house, leaving all the work to me—inside and out. Previously we had been going to church together. Now, if I mentioned going, it annoyed him.

His interests were now self-centered. If I intruded on his plans, he spoke to me with disrespect and became angry. When I refused to go partying with him, he started pushing me around. Before long he began to use filthy language. It hurt me deeply to be called such degrading names. I had been raised in a home where words such as "stupid" and "dummy" were considered vulgar. His words were far worse than any I had ever heard. Because of our lives taking such opposite roads, fighting became a regular habit. With each disagreement, his disrespect and his manhandling of me got worse. He always apologized; therefore, we were constantly making up. I loved him so much. Forgiving him came easy, but when I was alone I cried for hours. I was mourning the loss of another dream.

Raul had started taking professional kung fu lessons four nights a week, as well as on Saturdays. Many times he told me about the fights he got into. He revealed to me that he had been in prison in the Marines for fighting. Now I understood why he hadn't been able to come home to me all those nights.

I noticed something very disturbing in all Raul's stories. No matter what happened, it was always the other person's fault. His irresponsible attitude frightened me. I had trouble sleeping.

One night he came in wild-eyed, his shirt bloody and torn. In my view, he was like a little boy who kept getting in neighborhood fights. I sat down with him the way Mother had always done with us when we were bad little girls.

"Raul, we're adults now. We need to change our ways. I've done that, haven't I? God has given a new life to you, Raulie, and me. Let's love each other and have fun together, okay?"

Raul flared immediately. He didn't like being corrected in any way. "Don't you tell me how to live my life! I'll live it my way. If you don't like it, get out!"

The massive lump in my throat forced me to whisper. "Honey, please . . . please don't say that."

"Are you telling me to forget about my friends? Now you know why I didn't want to get involved with you in high school. I didn't want any woman telling me what to do! I had my friends before you came into my life, and you'll never take their place! Just do your housework and take care of my son. That's all women are good for anyway!" He was still shouting as he threw a kitchen chair at me and stormed out the door. I could hear him outside muttering, "Women! They're all alike! Nag, nag nag!"

I wept all night. The next morning I found a long-stemmed yellow rose in a crystal vase beside the kitchen sink. Next to it was a note. "My dearest little redhead that I love so much, I know I have hurt you really bad. Please forgive me. Raul A. Ries." I did.

We had been so much in love, and now we had nothing in common. He had lost interest in our home and in God. After going to a few of his parties, I realized we lived in two different worlds. I thought back to the unexpected encounter at the neighborhood market, years before, when Raul had lied to me. Something deep inside had warned me to run. Now I could quote the Scripture by heart that I should have remembered that day:

> Be ye not unequally yoked together with unbelievers: for what fellowship hath righteousness with unrighteousness? And what communion hath light with darkness? (2 Corinthians 6:14).

Light has nothing in common with darkness. That much I had learned.

Although Raul and I were practicing birth control, I discovered that I was pregnant when Raulie was six months old. I like to think that this baby sang songs of comfort to me during my pregnancy, because the thought of this child helped to turn my eyes off my troubles and onto God and His abundant favor toward me. Raul didn't like the name Shane ("beloved of God") at the time, but he agreed to it anyway. Today Shane is a songwriter whose tunes fill our home daily with peace and joy.

When the nurse first brought Shane to me for feeding, I lifted him up to the heavens and prayed:

"I give him back to You, to mold within Your hands. Take him back from where he came if he's not going to honor You with his life."

After two more difficult semesters in college, I had to drop out. It was a full-time job taking care of my boys.

While we were faced with our own difficulties, Raul's family was also engaged in continuing warfare. This involved in-laws from both sides of their family. According to Raul, it had all begun the day his parents got married. Papi was an alcoholic, Josie the product of a confrontational home life.

Each person in the family fought against another, taking one point of view one day, then changing sides as new circumstances arose. It was nearly impossible to get close to any of the families without being dragged into a quarrel.

Raul's mother and father were very hard workers who really cared about their four children. Unfortunately, they didn't have the love of God controlling their turbulent emotions.

I tried to reach out to them by baking birthday cakes for everyone, sewing, and helping to decorate their house. I thought maybe I could show them how to love each other. I failed, and the war raged on. Before long Raul's family turned against me, too. This occurred because they didn't like the fact that I was teaching Chrissy about God. She wanted to spend more and more time at our house.

Chrissy filled our home with dancing, laughter, and music. The boys and I never tired of her company. When Mother had been silently sorrowing over my premarital pregnancy, the Lord had comforted her with words from Psalm 113:9: "He maketh the barren woman to keep house, and to be a joyful mother of children."

Chrissy and I lived this verse in the midst of the storm that sometimes swirled around us. We did everything together. We went to church, sewed, cleaned, shopped, and cried together. She suffered from her family's abuse, and I suffered from Raul's. She became the first American friend I could really relate to.

During those days, Raul and his dad would come at each other like two raging bulls. Every time we visited his parents, Raul found himself defending my beliefs, even though he didn't accept them for himself. Raul didn't care if he ever saw his mother and father again. To him they represented pain and, as it was, he could hardly handle his own inner torment.

One night I persuaded Raul to attend one of his family's birthday parties. He didn't want to go, and once we were there, I was so sorry I hadn't listened to him. As usual, a fight broke out after Papi and Raul offended each other. Our little family fled, literally running for the car.

Raul began kicking me as he wildly drove down the street. "You filthy witch! Why don't you just stay out of my life? Why don't you leave me alone? You've ruined my life with your religion and your stupid family."

I clutched Raulie and Shane in my arms, petrified as the car swerved from one side of the road to the other.

"Raul, you are my life!" I hysterically screamed back at him. "Our boys are my life. Don't ask me to get out. I won't! Don't you understand? I'm here to stay!"

Shipwrecked

8

"I'm here to stay!"

The words echoed and reechoed in my mind. I was amazed by what I had said. Although my fear of Raul grew with every passing day, I was committed to seeing my family through. I remembered a Bible verse that says, "God hates divorce." I hated it too. The thought of the boys having another father sickened me.

When we got home, drained by his emotional outburst, Raul went straight to bed. After tucking my two little sleepyheads under their blankets, I put my hands on each of their heads and prayed. "Father, please erase this night from their memories. In Jesus' Name, Amen."

I grabbed my robe and a blanket and went into the bathroom to "pray through." "That's when you pray till you get an answer from God," Grandma Kopp had taught us grandchildren.

Decades before, after she received a 14-page letter from Grandpa, asking her hand in marriage, her father had told her to "pray through." She was in a desperate state. She didn't love the young man who wanted to marry her. After her time of prayer, she received her answer, and I could still hear her describing it.

"I became filled with love for your grandpa, and that pure, divine love has never failed me."

That terrible night I needed to receive the same kind of love Grandma had. Mine was running out real fast. As I wept bitter tears, I grabbed my Bible and beat on it with my fist. "I know the answer is in here, Lord! Please, please show me what to do!"

"I fell in love with a man who doesn't know You," I told God. "I disobeyed You. I sinned. You forgave me and gave me peace, but now I'm reaping the results of my sins. I understand! But, how long do I stay with Raul before it starts doing damage to the boys? I have a responsibility to them too. Your Word says to train up a child in the way he should go so when he is old, he won't depart from it. You also said, 'Suffer the little children to come unto me, and forbid them not: for of such is the kingdom of heaven.' Lord, my children are learning ways that are not Yours," I cried to my heavenly Father. "Am I hindering them from coming to You by staying with Raul?"

I opened the Bible, hurriedly flipping the pages from beginning to end. All at once a verse marked in bright red caught my eye: "Many are the afflictions of the righteous, but the Lord delivereth him out of them all."

"Not that one again." I slammed my Bible shut. "I'll just sit here and wait."

The verse kept repeating itself in my brain. I heard it over and over again. I began to understand. I had my answer, and it came to me straight from God's Word.

I thought about what the words meant. God's people suffer afflictions, but the Lord delivers us from all of them. At that moment I understood that I would suffer a lot. Everybody did. The point was, I didn't have to worry. The love of God would get me through! My bitter tears were dried. Joy and love flowed from my heart in a prayer of thanksgiving.

"Thank you, Lord, for giving me Your unfailing love

for Raul. Save him for me, please. I need him to be my lover, friend, and husband."

My parents never knew the extent of my pain. I never told them. Sundays, when they saw me without Raul, they understood that something was wrong. They never meddled in my life, but always offered encouragement and Scriptures that gave me hope. Like everyone else, they had had their own problems. But they had always worked things out privately without involving Shirley and me.

Raul's parents were under the impression that I dominated their son. I decided to let them believe whatever they wanted. Explanations were futile—any conversation could start another conflict. In any case, they always seemed to be mad at us. Raul and I felt forsaken by them. One day I ran across a promise from the Book of Psalms: "When my father and my mother forsake me, then the Lord will take me up" (Psalm 27:10).

And that's exactly what he did! Just when we needed them, God provided an extra Mom and Pop who showed up at all our family events. No one could take the place of Raul's parents, but Uncle Gayle and Aunt Daphyne, unaware of Raul's and my distress, stood in the gap.

Uncle Gayle was one of Daddy's twin brothers, and Auntie Phene was my dad's only sister. Raul really cherished both of them, which was unusual for him. Santa never came to our house on Christmas. It was Uncle Gayle, sent by Jesus, bringing the kinds of gifts children wish for and parents can't afford. He was the first and last person I've ever heard affectionately call my husband "Raulie." Somehow he even got away with filling our garage with yard-sale merchandise. He is still special in our hearts although he has moved back East and we seldom see him.

Auntie Phene admired Raul so much; her face always lit up when she saw him. She came bearing boxes of fabrics that provided our family with much-needed clothing. Besides all that, we received buckets of love, hugs, and an endless stream of snapshots. A few years ago she retired and moved up to Northern California. We communicate by telephone, shed tears, and I always lack the words to express to her how special she is to me.

In spite of occasional moments of gentleness, by the time another year had passed, my relationship with Raul had become unbearable. I was so weary. One Sunday I woke up to a beautiful southern California morning. Rain had cleared the sky, and the mountains and foot-hills were laden with snow. I was on my way out the front door with the boys. Raul, who usually went dirt biking on weekends, had stayed home.

The phone began to ring. I didn't want to answer it. Raul was already in a rage because I'd asked him to accompany us to church and then spend the day with us. When I'd suggested it, he'd given me his usual verbal abuse. "You are boring. Read my lips," Raul had said to me as he grabbed my face and shoved it too close to his and spelled out b-o-r-i-n-g. "Get that? Now get out of here. Go with your church friends. Out! Out! Out!" he screamed as he pushed me out the bedroom door. It was so humiliating to be thrown around like rubbish. His filthy words always hurt—like knives cutting at my insides. Now I was trying to get out of the house before my day was completely ruined.

"Pick up the phone, you big nag!" he yelled from the bedroom. "Maybe then you'll have someone to listen to you!"

The phone kept ringing. "Hello?" I finally answered, fighting back the tears.

"Sharie, aren't you coming to church?" Daddy's voice sounded worried. "I've been waiting outside to help you in with the boys and the diaper bag."

"I don't know, Daddy," my voice quivered.

"What's the matter? What's happening over there anyway?"

Just then, Raul marched into the kitchen, grabbed my face with his hand, and shoved the telephone receiver into it repeatedly, bouncing my head against the wall.

I screamed hysterically into the phone, "Raul's hurting me, Daddy!... Daddy?" The phone went dead.

Raul released me. He blamed me for the entire incident.

"You witch! You like to get tough, but when you can't handle it you cry like a baby. What's your Dad going to think now? You're making him think that I beat you up."

Raul never admitted to himself that he hurt me. Abusive people usually don't.

"You're an idiot," he continued, "and everybody knows it, too. My friends, my family, the people I work with..."

"Raul, the boys are going to hear you... please stop."

He threw me onto the kitchen floor and yelled louder, "I hope they do hear so they know what a nag their mom is. Nag, nag, nag, that's all you do!"

Raul called me a nag whenever I asked him to take out the trash, mow the lawn, or do anything around the house. It hurt so deeply. At the time, I thought it was up to me to remind him of his duties as a husband, and so I did. I hadn't yet learned that it was better to do things for myself than to try to motivate him.

Besides, whether I asked him once or ten times, he always responded the same way. This was particularly true when I so much as mentioned God or church.

I have learned from other people that some women are accused of nagging even if they are silent. Sometimes their godly life speaks more loudly than words.

I got up and ran out of the kitchen to see where the boys were. They had gone out the front door and were happily sitting in a mud puddle wearing their Sunday best. I held them both very tight.

"Mommy loves you two very much."

"Me too, Mommy," said Shane, sweetly pressing his dirty cheek against mine."

"Me too!" echoed Raulie as he leaped out of my arms and did a couple of somersaults on the front lawn.

Neither had seen nor heard anything. I was so thankful to God.

Daddy arrived. Without any display of emotion, he asked if the boys and I wanted to go for a ride. As we drove along, he said to me, "Trust in God; this will all pass. Don't give up! One of these days Raul will surrender to God. He's a good man, Sharon."

The faith in his words pierced my heart. I returned home, hoping to find a way to go on. There I found a red rose laying on my pillow with a note on it that read, "My little freckled nose that I'm so in love with, will you forgive me? Please? Your Lover, Raul A. Ries." I didn't.

I was disgusted with his notes and his roses. They meant nothing to me. I threw the rose in the wastepaper basket in our bedroom so he could see it. I stored the note with all the rest of them in the little green box I kept in my closet.

The jovial spirit that had once drawn me to Raul was now obscured by his anger. Although he was an intelligent, good-looking man, his temper always caused him to act like a fool. The manliness and control that had once strengthened his character withered under the intense heat of his fury. How quickly his emotions could debilitate him! Wherever he went, he stirred up strife.

I could never defend myself against his words by answering back; it only made matters worse. Raul could quickly think of a more degrading thing to say. Then his retort would repeat itself over and over again in my conscience, tearing at the foundations of my self-respect. Naturally, I didn't dare to fight back physically. I had learned that people who have no self-control prey on the weak.

But, hurt as I was, I wanted Raul to hear how he sounded. I wanted him to hurt the way I did. One night, during a terrible argument, I looked straight into his eyes and said words I had never spoken to him before.

"I hate you. I hate the sight of you. I don't know how I ended up with you. It makes me sick when you make love to me!"

He shouted somethiing back, but I saw the hurt. It was deep. I had reopened some past, unhealed wound. Worse yet, my words hadn't even been true. I had lied in order to hurt Raul. I could never do it again. The depth that a person suffers abuse of any form—whether it be physical, verbal, neglect, or rejection—is many times dependent on the treatment that the individual has received throughout his life. If a person has been highly respected, deeply loved, and always encouraged, a seemingly simple phrase such as "you make me sick" has an incredible, disastrous emotional affect on him. Just as I had hurt Raul deeply, even his "light" abuse tortured my mind to the same degree that his most vulgar statements or worst physical treatment did.

How easily I had learned his ways. Wasn't my heart just as wicked as his? I knew from God's Word that a "gentle answer turns away wrath, but a harsh word stirs up anger." I, too, was choosing to war, to inflict pain.

The outside woodwork had needed a coat of paint ever since we had bought the house two years before. After asking Raul several times (nagging as he called it), I decided to do the painting myself. It was very cold outside, but I was enjoying myself immensely. When Raul drove up after work, he commented on what a nice job I was doing. I noticed he was home very early.

"Guess what? I'm going to open a kung fu studio right around the corner."

"That's great!" I jumped off the ladder so he could tell me more.

"How are you going to work it out with your job?" I asked.

"You're going to go to work and help me!"

I was horrified. There wasn't anything on earth—not clothes, furniture, or even vacations—that could have ever enticed me to leave Raulie and Shane. Who would read them their stories? Teach them Spanish? Pray for their hurts? No one understood their individual strengths and weaknesses like I did. Who else would cry with them or laugh at their silly jokes? Only I could love them the way they deserved to be loved.

I carefully explained it all to Raul. He didn't change his mind.

The next day he informed me that his hours had been cut unexpectedly at the market where he was a checker. He had changed jobs when we moved. "Now you'll have to get a job."

He wasn't a very convincing liar.

The day I threw the rose away, I began to harden my heart against my husband. I threw a few more away. Then he stopped giving them to me.

I no longer wanted to forgive Raul. And I decided I didn't want to suffer anymore, either. I was exhausted— emotionally, physically, and spiritually.

Over and over, I flipped through the pages of the Book. I could find no answer that suited me. I prayed, cried, and crawled into my bed. Before I found a job, I started sleeping in the middle of the day, every day. I was trying to forget my anguish, and being awake meant being aware.

I was lost in a sea of desperation with no lighthouse in sight. Hope was gone. I had finally shipwrecked.

The Captain? I don't know. I didn't think about Him much anymore.

Swimming Against the Current

9

I dragged myself out of bed. Emotionally drained, I felt as if I hadn't slept. The boys were already awake, playing in their toy-cluttered bedroom. I stood at their door unnoticed, watching as they energetically participated in full-scale combat, throwing toys back and forth from one bed to the other. Red, white, and blue wooden Civil War knickknacks that were supposed to be decorating their dressers were scattered all over the carpet.

Raul had escaped with his friends for the weekend, leaving me with a house that needed cleaning, bills to be paid, yard work, food shopping, and two never-resting, mess-making little boys who required constant attention. Where had Raul said he was going this time? The prospect of another weekend without his help or companionship crippled me.

In spite of everything, I ached to be with my husband. Yet the faint hope for change in Raul's behavior had all but vanished. All around me the world was beaming with life, but I was only a spectator. I was enclosed in darkness, and I couldn't find my way out.

Mother was on her way to pick up the boys. She would

take them out for a day of fun, and as soon as they were gone, I would go right back to bed until they returned. I did not want to deal with my circumstances anymore. This was my way of escape. Sleep made the lonely weekends pass more quickly.

"Good morning, boys! I love you," I hoped my cheerful tone would cover up my distress.

"Where's Daddy, Mommy?" asked two-year-old Raulie. He was always aware of everything.

"Gone with his friends, love, but you're going to have a fun day with Banna!" I changed the subject rapidly, hoping he wouldn't pursue it. He did.

"I wanna see Daddy, Mommy!" he insisted.

"We'll go to kung fu with him this week, okay?"

The best way for us to see Raul was to follow him wherever he went. Despite his disinterest in home life, he was proud to have his boys around him. He just didn't want them to divert him from the activities he craved.

Mother arrived, her van fully equipped with an assortment of plastic soldiers, little pieces of wood, rubber bands, ice cream sticks, and plastic egg cartons. These would aid in building dams in the mountain streams, and constructing rafts for floating soldiers.

"Sharon, why don't you go with us? You need a break, honey. The fresh air will be good for you."

"Oh, no thanks. I really need to stay home and get some things done."

"Oh, by the way, I left a letter from Chile on your kitchen counter! It came yesterday," she yelled out the window as she and the boys drove away, waving goodbye.

My heart skipped a beat. A letter from Chile?

It had been four years since I had heard from any of my friends there. A longing for my home country seized my heart once more. The envelope lay on the messy counter, next to a sinkful of dirty dishes. I recognized the hand-writing immediately. It hadn't changed much in the last few years. It was from Fernando.

Up in my closet, in the little green box, I still had all of his letters. Tears welled up inside. I realized that I hadn't even told him I was married. How could I explain all that had happened to me? We had promised each other, year after year, that we would someday be together.

All the curtains were drawn, and the house was dark. I walked slowly down the hall and into my bedroom. After crawling into bed, I read the letter several times.

Dear Sharon,

I can't remember why our correspondence stopped. Probably the distance between us made it impossible for our relationship to develop.

There is one thing very clear in my mind. Our ongoing wish was to see each other some-day, somehow. I still cherish that desire and I hope you do too. I believe that the moment has finally arrived, as I have won a scholarship to New York. I know that it is a long way from Los Angeles, but maybe we can meet somewhere in between. How could life be so cruel as to keep us apart once more?

Loving you as always,

Fernando

I began to weep, quietly but deeply. I didn't resort to the Bible as I always had before when I was in distress. I wanted to feel this moment. I wanted to savor what could have been had I not gotten involved with Raul. Had Fernando been the man God had chosen for me? Why else was the past knocking at my heart's door, mocking me?

I held his letter on my chest, next to my heart. The passions that had always steered my life challenged me to follow their urgings once more. I remembered Chile, the mission, and my childhood love. Dreamer that I am, I drifted back into what once had been my favorite fantasy. It had only changed a little.

Instead of disembarking from a ship, I was getting off an airplane in New York. I was wearing a white tailored suit and, as always, my long hair was blowing in the wind. I was meeting Fernando. He was softly kissing my cheek . . .

The dream came to an abrupt end.

I was married and had two children that I adored! Fernando was single, in love with life, pursuing his career. Why would he want me anymore?

Despite the cold realities, I couldn't bear to answer the letter. I wanted too much to be with him, to forget that I had ever met Raul. It was like a dream come true. The prince had reappeared to rescue the princess. She had been locked up in the dungeon of the castle and abused by the wicked sorcerer. Was this my magical entrance to happiness, just like in the fairy tales? Or was it another deception?

My emotions had gotten me into my present mess. I didn't want to be led astray again.

I remembered God. I wanted to make this decision according to what He said, not according to what the urgings of my heart dictated. "It's a dream, that's all!" A tiny thought convinced me. I put the letter under my pillow and went to sleep, hoping to hush my wayward thoughts.

The following days found me opening my Bible frequently, searching for guidance. Unfortunately, my habitual thinking patterns always interfered with my reading. I was desperately trying to fill my emptiness with fantasy—dreams of the future or memories of the past.

The by-product of my daydreams was the most intense self-pity I had ever experienced.

My focus was entirely on myself. It was causing me to lose sight of all that held any value. My home, my sons, their father, and the love that I had once had for him no longer seemed important.

And now I was dealing with the much-dreaded job Raul had imposed upon me. It was another nightmare. Because I was bilingual, I had landed a secretarial position for which I was totally unskilled. I received minimum wage and, due to my inexperience, my boss didn't seem to like me at all.

All that was overshadowed by my agony over not being with my boys. The first time I took them to the babysitter, Raul went along. He wanted to show me how easy it was to leave them.

"No problem, you'll see. It won't be a problem at all," he confidently assured me.

Shane and Raulie were more fluent in Spanish than English, so I gave the sitter a translated list of words they often used so she could understand what they were saying. We prayed, and kissed each other goodbye. Then, to my horror, I stood helplessly as Raul shoved screaming little Shane back from the front door and quickly closed it on his face!

Driving away, I saw two little blond-haired, brown-eyed boys pressing their noses against the sitter's living room windows.

"They'll get used to it after a while." Raul thought he was comforting me.

"I never will," I whispered under my breath.

At first, I went to read Bible stories to them during my lunch hour. But after a few days the babysitter asked me not to. "They won't stop crying after you leave, and it keeps them from taking their naps." After that I spent lunch alone.

I hated Raul. I realized he was a hard worker, but he made me feel like an object, useful only to help him achieve his goals. While he studied and practiced martial arts, enjoying himself thoroughly, I did the unpleasant menial duties seven days a week. Worst of all, I was being denied time with the boys during some of the most important learning years of their lives.

Trying to work out my problems confused me. Some days I felt that our difficulties were all my fault. I deserved what I had. It was during those days that I suffered with severe depression. Other days, I was convinced everything was Raul's fault. I would be flooded with anger and would entertain vindictive ideas. Either way, I was living in a sick state of mind, and I didn't like it.

Instead of pursuing God, I couldn't get my eyes off myself and my troubles. No longer did I see God's guidance. I just kept telling Him I was sorry and asking Him to help me. "Show me the way out!" I prayed, day after day.

One morning I woke up with a very clear awareness, a change in my perspective which quickly led me to a life-changing decision. A Bible verse broke through the smothering cloud of depression. I had listened to it countless times in my childhood. I could almost hear the thundering voices of various South American preachers echoing it:

> Be not deceived; God is not mocked: for whatsoever a man soweth, that shall he also reap. For he that soweth to his flesh shall of the flesh reap corruption; but he that soweth to the Spirit shall of the Spirit reap life everlasting. And let us not be weary in well doing: for in due season we shall reap, if we faint not (Galatians 6:7-9).

I had planted thousands of selfish, self-pitying thoughts in my mind: thoughts about killing myself, finding another man, running away, and living for myself. Those wicked and destructive concepts had corrupted me.

It dawned on me that my dreams were not real. They were nothing more than mini-escapes from reality, encompassing only a fleeting moment in eternity. My dreams were not true, and they should never be brought to pass unless they were part of the Creator's infinite plan for my future.

For me, indifference toward anyone was not normal. Now, through unhealthy thinking, my hatred for Raul was rapidly fading into indifference toward him. The constant quarreling in his family, causing verbal attacks on us, had also made me indifferent toward them.

Emotional detachment is, in some ways, worse than hate, for when you hate you still feel hurt. Indifference produces no feelings. It is like death. My thoughts were bringing death to those around me and to myself.

Love was dying in my heart.

I needed desperately to start planting God's thoughts in my mind. I wanted to cultivate my hardened heart. I longed to experience life in a way I had never known before. Most of all, I could not allow myself to grow weary—no matter what—in doing the right things. True, life was tough. But God had promised a good result—a happy harvest.

It had been a couple of months since I had received Fernando's letter. It was time to answer it. I knew it would be one of the hardest things I had ever done, but I wanted to obey God. And sometimes obedience to Him isn't easy.

I wrote to Fernando, but hid all the passion that was torturing my mind. How I yearned for this diligent young suitor to defiantly come and rescue me! I craved his forgiveness, tenderness, and companionship. In my letter, however, I told him that I was married and had two lovely children. I invited him to come to our home. Couldn't we at least be friends?

I lived on hope while I awaited his answer. I really believed that my letter would be the beginning of something wonderful—an adult friendship, a renewed contact with Chile. He never wrote back.

Disillusionment gradually kidnapped me again. Fernando was gone forever, and forever was a long, long time to be unloved.

After a few days of trying to climb out of my pit alone, I set the alarm extra early one morning, declaring war against my misery. Determined to change my self-pitying thought patterns, I looked up the word "think" and "mind" in a Bible concordance. The first thing I needed to learn was how to stop my sick thinking from interfering with God's thoughts. Here's what I found:

> The weapons of our warfare are not carnal, but mighty through God to the pulling down of strongholds: casting down imaginations, and every high thing that exalteth itself against the knowledge of God, and bringing into captivity every thought to the obedience of Christ (2 Corinthians 10:4,5).

How exciting! With God's help, I could pull down any stronghold in my life. My imagination was a stubborn one, but He was able to help me destroy the thoughts that governed my life and exalted themselves above His. He alone knew how to take those thoughts into captivity, making Himself the rightful monarch of my consciousness.

I meditated upon the verses I was finding. Another one told me how to get started on my new adventure in thinking:

> Be careful [anxious] for nothing: but in everything by prayer and supplication with

> thanksgiving let your requests be made known
> unto God. And the peace of God, which passes
> all understanding, shall keep your hearts and
> minds through Christ Jesus. Finally, brethren,
> whatsoever things are true, whatsoever things
> are honest, whatsoever things are just, what-
> soever things are pure, whatsoever things are
> lovely, whatsoever things are of good report; if
> there be any virtue, and if there be any praise,
> think on these things . . . and the God of peace
> shall be with you (Philippians 4:6-9).

I diligently complied. Instead of fretting about Raul and fantasizing about Fernando, I started making all my requests known to God. Daily I asked Him to come into Raul's heart, to change him, to make me love him, to protect the boys, to get me a raise, to make my boss like me, to help me at my job, and on and on.

Many times I fell asleep on the bathroom floor, my face buried in my Bible. I memorized whole chapters of Scripture, attempting to brainwash myself with concepts that were true, honest, just, pure, lovely, and of good report. Peace embraced me as the words of God caressed my soul.

I learned that His Word was actually called the Sword. The Sword was fighting for me with its two sharp edges. It was causing me to differentiate between my soul and my spirit. My soul was the center of my will, intellect, and emotions. My spirit could be recognized by its intuition, conscience, and communion with God. Skillfully God's Word was cutting between the joints and marrow, discerning my thoughts and the intentions of my heart.

Whenever I could, I listened to worship music or Bible studies on the radio in order to drown out any thoughts of my past or present circumstances. Soon more Scriptures touched me.

"The wicked, through the pride of his countenance, will not seek after God: God is not in all his thoughts."

(Psalm 10:4). Ouch! That one hurt. I had never thought of myself as wicked or proud. Yet, hadn't I behaved as if I didn't need God or His counsel?

"The fool hath said in his heart there is no God" (Psalm 53:1). Not to believe in God was foolish, leading to an unprofitable life. That wasn't for me! I wanted all that God had for me.

"Let the wicked forsake his way, and the unrighteous man his thoughts: and let him return unto the Lord, and he will have mercy upon him . . . for he will abundantly pardon" (Isaiah 55:7). I had already made the choice to turn from my own thoughts and to seek His. I knew that He had pardoned me—Christ's mission to this earth had been solely to wash my sins and guilt with the blood He shed on Mount Calvary. It was essential that I forsake my thoughts and ways for they were the complete opposite of God's.

"For my thoughts are not your thoughts, neither are your ways my ways, saith the Lord. For as the heavens are higher than the earth, so are my ways higher than your ways, and my thoughts than your thoughts" (Isaiah 55:8,9). Oh, how I longed to think the thoughts of God—to have the mind of Christ!

As I sought to do so, I made another glorious discovery, a single verse of Scripture that was destined to transform my world forever. I found words that no human could ever speak to me—neither Raul, nor Fernado, nor any other mortal could offer me such a promise. Today these words continue to lighten my load, to illuminate my darkness, to guide me through every circumstance:

> For I know the thoughts that I think toward you, saith the Lord, thoughts of peace, and not of evil, to give you an expected end [that for which you are longing] (Jeremiah 29:11).

Imagine—God thinking about me! What an incredible truth! Not only is He thinking about me, He is finding a way to give me the desires of my heart, to fulfill the longings that He put there in the first place!

It wasn't long before I had totally redecorated my house. I planted tulips along the sides of the ugly asphalt walkway, and set camellias under every window in the front of the house—just like at Daddy's. A couple of nights each week I took the boys to the kung fu studio to help Raul work. To my delight, he really seemed to love having us there.

My boss even changed his attitude toward me. Instead of throwing papers on my desk and constantly reprimanding me in front of everyone, he gave me a considerable raise. He also entrusted me with greater responsibilities. His wife and family, who worked with me, treated me with care and kindness. They had no idea about the brutality I still suffered at home on a regular basis. Because of God's favor, they had learned to trust me, to depend on me. Their friendship meant more to me than they will ever know.

God is so good! It was evident that He was working out a plan for my life, even though I had no clue what it could be. I just determined that I would trust Him like a child because His promises were now directing my life.

Now that Raul saw me experiencing peace, he became more uneasy. His anger over my loyal church attendance and my dedication to Bible reading intensified dramatically. As far as I was concerned, I wasn't a "religious freak," as he called me. The fact was, I hated the fanaticism that brought shame to the church; the hypocrisy and the ignorance of God's Word in professing believers. A yearning for the truth is what drew me into having a personal relationship with the One who calls Himself the Truth. I worshiped and studied because I needed to, but that's not the way he saw it.

Raul's mistreatment of me intensified and grew more frequent. He'd grab my face, squeezing his fingers against my eyes or throat. He would kick me in bed, sometimes hurling me onto the floor.

One time he even tried to run me over with his car. It was on a Saturday. Raul seemed very tender toward the boys and decided to spend the day with us. We all jumped into the car and the boys started informing Raul excitedly what each wanted to do. Before long, he and the boys were all arguing about how each of them wanted to spend their fun day. Raul then started shoving the boys around, and I quickly jumped out of the car with them. It was then that he tried to run us over. The boys and I walked home examining bugs, clouds, and any other of God's creations we ran into. We made a picnic when we got home and went to the nearby canyon to enjoy it. Raul didn't come home till late. No matter what He did, God always kept me from getting hurt. I was comforted daily through the Psalms. "It is good for me that I have been afflicted; that I might learn thy statutes" (Psalm 119:71). Suffering had driven me to be in love with God's Word, and that was the most wonderful thing that had ever happened to me.

What disturbed me the most was Raul's inability to love me, or to love anyone else, for that matter. Nor was he able to receive love. I grieved, unable to be comforted, because my husband, the one I had chosen to be my lover and partner for life, might never love me. Even though I knew that God had a plan for me, I was heartsick over the incidents that occurred, leaving me frightened and shaken.

After a year of serious consideration, combined with a sincere dependence upon the Scriptures for guidance, I decided to get out of Raul's life. I had a God-given responsibility to teach the boys God's ways. Raul's uncontrollable anger would eventually damage them, since they were witnessing more of his outbursts with every passing day. Eventually they would learn to abuse their own children and wives.

I had received a couple of phone calls from girls who were looking for Raul. One had expressed shock when I told her that I was his wife. There were occasional nights Raul never came home at all.

According to God's Word, he had broken his marriage vows to me, and before God I believed I was free to leave him. By that time, I wasn't interested in finding another man, and was persuaded that I should guard myself against divorce. I simply hoped that if Raul lost everything he had, he might turn to God the way I had.

It was time for me to prepare to leave him. At that time Shirley lived on the forested campus of a Bible college in Santa Cruz. I had decided that the boys and I would join her there as soon as I could work out all the details.

I had discussed leaving with Raul on several occasions. I was convinced that he didn't believe me. I've since learned that he did. To pamper me into staying he bought me a car. I felt guilty, but I took it. Separation was not what I wanted, but was a step I had to take—one last desperate attempt to save our marriage.

What I really wanted was for Raul to love me enough to not hurt me or the boys anymore. I wanted to be passionately in love with him again, and to have him woo me back to himself.

After five painful years of trying to make my marriage work, I realized I was not able to do it. If Raul were on his own, maybe he would turn to the Lord. There were several Bibles throughout the house, and he knew how to reach God if he needed to call on Him.

I had peace in my heart and a little flicker of excitement about what God was going to do. Maybe now I could be a missionary, a vagabond for Jesus, traveling the seas of the world.

I could do it! I had learned to swim against the world's current. I had defeated the personal emptiness that causes men to drift downstream and into oblivion. In my weakness I had been made strong.

A drastic change was about to occur! But to my amazement, this time the transformation happened in Raul's life, not in mine.

Docked

10

Raul was loudly knocking at the front door. I heard his voice, yelling for me to let him in the house. He never carried a house key, a small annoyance I had long since learned to ignore.

Just a few minutes before, I had walked in the door myself after a Sunday evening Bible study. Before the boys and I had left the church, the pastor had invited people to the altar to make a commitment to God. I had caught a glimpse of Raul rushing in from outside, making his way to the altar for prayer.

I had grabbed the boys' hands and run to the car. I didn't even want to know what he was up to. Raul probably wanted me to see him go up and perform some religious act so I would change my mind about leaving him. He had done this sort of thing before on several occasions. He had also been unsuccessfully exploring Oriental religions in his search for inner peace. I wasn't about to be impressed in the least.

What had impressed me was the sermon I had just heard. It had been health to my bones and strength to my flesh. I wanted to rush home to think about it.

The boys, now three and four, snuggled into the back-seat of my car. As I drove toward the house, I pleaded with God to captivate my thoughts, shielding me from Raul and his nonsense. "Seize my mind with this evening's message," I prayed, and then repeated a Scripture that I knew so well. It had been the pastor's closing verse:

> And God shall wipe away tears from their eyes; and there shall be no more death, neither sorrow, nor crying, neither shall there be any more pain: for the former things are passed away (Revelation 21:4).

The message had concerned the imminent Second Coming of Jesus to establish a new heaven and a new earth. As the pastor spoke, I tried to imagine a day without pain and tears. The idea that God would some-day wipe away all my tears was beyond my comprehension.

But then, knowing Jesus, I could imagine Him doing it! He had always been moved with compassion for those who suffered. Jesus always went out of His way to gently restore a person to spiritual, emotional, and physical wholeness. He cared for them no matter what their intellectual capacity, social standing, or knowledge of Him. Yes, Jesus could wipe away my tears. He was big enough to become small—just for me. How I longed for Him!

These thoughts restored my hope, a characteristic that had once been dominant in my personality. Hope is not a wishful feeling about the future, nor adherence to some fantasy. It is a God-given virtue which flows into a man's being, stabilizing him, making him confident and filled with expectancy. The Bible says that hope is the anchor of the soul.

Now my own tears were silent prayers which I offered to God. Only He understood the meaning of each one, and I was sure that He stored my tears in His bottles in heaven, just as He did with King David's.

It was in this frame of mind that I drove home. Once the boys were asleep, I had a few more minutes to treasure these assurances. Then Raul had come knocking at our door.

"Sharon! Sharon I'm not mad. I'm not going to hurt you. Open the door, I have to tell you something really neat!"

Maybe he'd clinched a part on some kung fu TV show. There was always something exciting happening in Raul's life, usually involving his studio or his weekend escapes.

I opened the door slightly, not knowing what to expect, and found myself looking directly into Raul's radiant smile. It stretched from ear to ear.

"I'm born again!" he exclaimed. I slammed the door in his face.

Wasn't it a bit blasphemous to claim a "born-again" experience just to impress me? He knew what it meant—we had talked about it enough. Sometimes when he left the notes with the roses, expressing his regrets, I would explain to him that it was impossible for him to change apart from Jesus Christ.

"Sharon . . . open the door . . . please," he pleaded softly. There was a genuine tenderness in his voice I had never heard before. For some reason, it reminded me of the quality I heard when Jesus spoke to my heart—when He pleaded with me to listen to Him. Cautiously, I opened the door. Raul reached for me gently, and held my face between his hands—those same two hands that he had often used to hurt me. He kissed me repeatedly.

"I love you, Sharon. I'm so sorry for everything I've ever done to hurt you. I just want to be a loving husband. Can't we start over? I'll never hurt you again." His words were full of hope and joy. Was I supposed to believe him this time?

"Start over?" I was thinking of my own plans to start over without him.

"I know you don't believe me," his voice was persuasive, "and I understand that. But you'll see. Just give me some time to show you."

"Raul, I'm sorry if I'm not excited, but we've gone through these promises before. And, to tell you the truth, I've been pretty excited about the future I've been planning for myself and the boys." I was actually feeling rather guilty.

He attempted to grab me excitedly as if nothing had ever happened between us. I pushed him away.

"Please! Don't do that. Don't touch me." My voice sounded hard, and I pushed his hands away coldly. I didn't like them near me; they'd hurt me too often. It would be a long time before I would surrender to his advances. No matter how I reasoned with myself, every time he got near me, my flesh froze.

Instantly our roles had changed—now he was the good guy and I was the bad guy. He pursued me and I backed off. Raul wanted me, and he told me that he'd wait forever until I was ready to receive his love. He was talking like Christ talks to His bride, the church, and he'd never even read the Bible.

We sat down and talked. It took us half the night to discuss how it all had happened. He confessed that he couldn't live with himself, realizing fully what he had been doing to the boys and me. He didn't tell me that night, but years later he confessed that he had come home that Sunday evening with the intention of killing all of us. In his desperation, he'd been flicking through all the television channels to pass the time while we were in church. Suddenly he'd been captivated by a gentle man speaking to a group of teenagers about the love of God.

Raul explained the man's message. "He talked about the love of God . . . about His character. He said that God loved me and was the only One that could wash my slate clean and give me a new life. Can you believe it, Sharon?

I'm a new person! I can tell!" My husband spoke to me as if he had just discovered a mystery; as if he had been blind but now could see.

We found out later that the man on the television had been Chuck Smith. Today we know him as a man who is absolutely fascinated with the character of God and with the in-depth teachings of His Word. Pastor Chuck abhors the fanaticism and emotionalism that's in the church hindering God's truth from being revealed in its original simplicity. Although he is a theologian, he is most of all a marvelous communicator of the unmeasurable love of God and the way He lavishes it on His people.

Well, under the circumstances, what could I do? I decided to stay, at least temporarily, watching Raul closely to determine if his experience was real. If it wasn't, it would certainly be the cruelest lie he had ever told me. On the other hand, a true conversion would open up incredible avenues for me. In time I would be a missionary! It had to happen. Wasn't it God's will to give man the desires of his heart? Hadn't He put them there?

It was immediately evident that Raul was a new person, as evidenced by his new outlook and vision for life, but it took me a couple of years to be thoroughly convinced of his sincerity. In my lifetime I had seen much hypocrisy in people who turned to God during desperate situations.

Raul's anger continued to explode sporadically, plaguing my mind with doubts. Nevertheless, time and again I saw him go for walks where he called on God for help and guidance. This enabled him to extinguish what might otherwise have become a recurrence of his blazing fury.

Raul's life-changing experience demonstrated to me what Christian conversion really is. When a person is truly born again, he receives forgiveness for his sins and senses a deep sprirtual cleansing, which produces inner joy. Aware of the wickedness of his heart, he knows that he did not merit or earn this forgiveness through his own goodness; he accepts by faith that ". . . the blood of Jesus Christ his Son cleanseth us from all [past, present, and future] sin" (1 John 1:7).

A true convert falls in love with Jesus, even though he may know nothing about Him. As he sees his Lord revealed through the Scriptures and in his life, he develops an even greater hunger to become acquainted with His Savior. His gratitude to Christ compels him to tell others about his experience. He yearns for them, too, to receive forgiveness and freedom from their sins.

A new believer grows spiritually as he nails his old nature to the cross with Christ. He no longer chooses to be controlled by his passions, intellect, or will. Instead, through reading and meditating on the Scriptures, he saturates his mind with God's thoughts. In this way he becomes a new man.

As a new Christian encounters life's daily difficulties, his old nature will try to recapture him. His flesh, with its insatiable cravings, will seduce him. The world, with its false hopes, will lure him, and Satan, the deceiver of mankind, will harass him mercilessly in a mighty attempt to possess his soul.

But, because the convert is becoming acquainted with God through His Word and intimate communion with Him, he learns a new way of thinking—God's way. This strengthens him, and makes him able to resist attacks. In time, the believer is able to surrender to Christ daily, and this transforms him into the image of his God. It takes a lifetime. The Scripture says:

> But we all, with open face beholding as in a glass the glory of the Lord, are changed into the same image from glory to glory even as by the Spirit of the Lord (2 Corinthians 3:18).

Raul's conversion was real. He was miraculously transformed. He was a new creature, a new creation, born again. An incredible metamorphosis had taken place. What a privilege it was to be in the midst of the miracle!

Raul called all of his friends. He cried as he talked to them over the phone, explaining to each one what had taken place. He called my sister Shirley, then his parents, then mine, then his kung fu students, and lastly his old high school buddies.

After giving his kung fu lessons, he presented to his students the biblical truths he was devouring every day. It wasn't long before we had a weekly Bible study meeting at our house, and its number included his friends and students whose lives had already been changed by Raul's witness. Sometimes we stayed up all night praying together until the breaking dawn reminded us to have breakfast.

Although I still felt a personal coldness toward Raul, I could see that he was truly walking with God. He had been loved and forgiven by Jesus; the spiritual understanding of this fact generated a gradual change in all his attitudes. His true repentance was evident. He started taking on more responsibilities around the house and spending his days off with us. It was so, so good—I can still savor it. I was convinced that in time Raul's undisciplined character would be Spirit-controlled. It would probably take forever; that's how it is for all of us. He hadn't become perfect. I would soon see that I hadn't, either.

Our weekly home Bible study grew so big that we were forced to move it to the kung fu studio. By now I had quit my job, so the boys and I would rush over to the studio after Raul's classes were over. We ran the sweeper, sprayed with disinfectant, cleaned the bathroom, watered the plants, and did whatever else we could do to prepare for the study. Later, while Raul taught, I told the kids Bible stories and sang songs, we danced, and did whatever else it took to keep them entertained. I knew my role well and I loved it.

On Sundays we attended Sunday school and church together, and sometimes we drove to Costa Mesa where Pastor Chuck Smith held Bible studies under a great big tent. Thousands of teenagers and young adults gathered there, learning to understand and obey God's revelation to man.

Those days fulfilled all that my heart yearned for—to spend time with my husband, to work with him, to listen to Bible studies as a family, to pray together, to share our spiritual experiences.

At long last, I began to be infatuated with Raul again. Soon I was wildly in love with him, and wanted to be beside him constantly. Enjoying Raul became my obsession. I didn't seem to need Christ's fellowship that much when Raul and I were in such a close relationship. To this day that intense desire for his attention and company interferes with my communion with God.

I guess that's why Paul made such a specific observation about women and their relationship with Christ:

> The unmarried woman careth for the things
> of the Lord, that she may be holy both in body
> and in spirit: but she that is married careth for
> the things of the world, how she may please
> her husband (1 Corinthians 7:34).

God's Word tells us that God is jealous of relationships that draw us away from Him. It also teaches that one of God's many names is "Jealous." God's jealousy is not like our vicious attitude that stems from pride and rises up from uncontrolled covetousness. His jealousy does not express itself in envy, malice, and hatred.

God's jealousy is manifested in His zeal to protect His relationship with His bride. It is God's jealousy that will not allow us to wander away from His love. Although He fills our hearts with devotion for our loved ones, He will fight to be the Master Lover, and it is only through Him that we are able to love one another with a pure heart.

The apostle Paul expressed this same jealousy when he was concerned that Satan might beguile the church through his subtleties. Paul knew what Satan had done to Eve, and did not want to see him corrupt our minds:

> I am jealous over you with a godly jealousy:
> for I have espoused you to one husband [Jesus]
> that I may present you as a chaste virgin to
> Christ (2 Corinthians 11:2).

It is for this reason that the Lord has not allowed me to be enveloped in Raul. Instead His will draws Raul away from me, forcing me to seek out the true Lover of my soul. He wants me to love Him as wholeheartedly as Raul does.

Raul's passion for Christ attracted him to the Word as well as to the spiritually dying people of the world. He was not satisfied with the conversion of the 200 or 300 people who now attended our weekly studies. He had and still has—an intense drive to share what God has done for him with the entire world. This totally excited me. I could sniff the mission field right around the corner!

He started visiting our high school campus during the students' lunch hour, and talked to them about Jesus. He did the same at other schools. Sharing Christ at kung fu exhibitions became commonplace. I accompanied him as often as I could.

Raul's thirst for the knowledge of God was never quenched. He devoured study books and Pastor Chuck's teaching tapes by the dozens. He attended a special class for men like himself whose passion for the Word consumed them.

Although Raul was making thousands of dollars in his kung fu business, neither the money nor his evident success could compete with his love for God. After about a year of working closely together, I began to notice that Raul was gone more and more, off to one place or another sharing the Good News about Jesus. It was impossible for me to go with him because I had my home and children to care for. I started feeling very lonely again.

One day I sprained my ankle. I asked Raul to stay home from a friend's prayer meeting so he could help me with the boys. Putting them to bed was a long process of storytelling, talking, snacks, drinks of water, and anything else they could think of to get to stay up an extra five minutes. I was shocked when Raul said, "I'm sorry, dear, but you're just going to have to handle this one by yourself. I can't miss the prayer meeting."

Self-pity immediately gripped me. Yes, I knew that prayer was a priority, but didn't he understand? I had been alone so long. Now that he was a Christian, I expected him to be there for me.

My dad had always been gone when I was a child. I barely knew him when we came to the United States to live. And, hidden in a secret closet of my heart, there is a portrait of my mother which never fails to hurt me. I can still see her sitting on her bed alone, early in the morning and late at night, her Bible on her lap and tears rolling down her cheeks. She never knew I saw her that way.

Mother had always been our companion, teaching, loving, and caring for Shirley and me. She was known for her jovial, free spirit and her air of personal contentment. She sang and played the piano for Bible studies, ran our day school and sometimes taught at our evening Bible classes. She counseled, gave music lessons, and always had extra time for a mountain or beach outing. Yet, in spite of her love of life, I never forgot my mother's moments of hidden loneliness. As a child I had determined that my husband would never leave me. Yet now I realized that I had lost my own groom to his new Lord.

I crawled around the house that evening, crying as I went, my ankle throbbing. After a few hours I felt I couldn't handle the pain anymore. I called Raul. Did he feel any guilt? He didn't. Instead he prayed for me.

I felt depression come on like a torrential flood. But, by now, I knew what to do. I looked up all the Scriptures I could think of that had to do with wives, husbands, and the biblical duties of married couples. If Raul was doing God's will, I would learn to love it. As usual, the word brought me to repentance:

> But this I say, brethren, the time is short: it remaineth, that both they that have wives be as though they had none; and they that weep, as though they wept not . . . (1 Corinthians 7:29,30).

Another verse I read instructed believers to walk circumspectly, not as fools, but wisely, redeeming the time because the days are evil. It said that we should seek to understand the will of the Lord.

I was humiliated. People were dying and going to hell, and I was worried about my ankle! Wasn't it about time for me to stop my pity parties and get involved? If I was ever going to be a missionary, I needed to prepare myself.

When I confessed all this to Raul, he was excited. He agreed that I should organize a meeting for women who were interested in sewing quilts and other necessary articles for the mission field. To my disappointment, however, when the meeting day arrived, no one showed up.

I tried everything. But no matter how I searched for just the right activity, I found it was neither pleasing Raul nor attracting a single living soul.

The only people that wanted me were the little children. I loved them too, but for a while I was the only babysitter. We didn't want to ask the new converts to babysit. During that time I never got to listen to Raul's Bible studies or to mingle with the adults. In utter bewilderment I cried out to God again.

I'll never forget that night. The moon was bright, and stars twinkled in the clear sky. Sitting on Grandma's hand-me-down couch gave me a good view of the trees in our backyard. I usually pray looking out a window. That night I noticed that our apricot tree was full of leaves and new fruit, while the neighbors' shade tree had no leaves at all.

"Raul is the apricot; you're the barren one."

These were the words that came into my mind. And I had a good idea who had put those thoughts there. God! I would have never thought of myself as barren. I kept a clean house, adored my children, and faithfully taught them the Word. Reading the Word was as much a part of my daily routine as brushing my teeth.

"Why am I barren?"

I asked the One who knew the intimate secrets of my heart. And all at once I understood. "You only read the Bible to find answers to your problems and to ask for things. You never study just to know Me. You don't tell anyone about Me. You are content to live a very private life."

Of course it's appropriate to ask God for things. Christ instructed us to ask, and promised to give us anything we request according to His will. What's not pleasing to Him is when all we do is ask, and when we ask only according to our own self-centered will.

It was time for me to discover who God is. It was vital for me to love Him simply for who He is, not for what I could get out of Him. I needed to ask Him what He wanted from me and how to accomplish it.

Then the awful truth dawned on me—the reason I had wanted to get involved in missions wasn't because I wanted to please Jesus. It wasn't even because I wanted to help people find God. I wanted to see my missionary fantasies come true! Now that I thought about it, I had never asked Him what He thought about my plans. I hadn't even asked Him to help me work them out. As I faced the fact that I had nothing of any value to share with anyone, I wept.

No wonder I was docked, stuck at home alone. I remembered a big old ship I once saw in the Valparaiso harbor. It was on a dry dock where seagoing vessels are elevated for repair and reconstruction. This ship had been battered and torn by years of transatlantic voyages. At least ten colors of paint were visible on its severely chipped surfaces. The ship's name was so weatherworn that it could not be read. I remember feeling sorry for it, wondering how many tales it could relate if it could speak. One thing was obvious: It wasn't going anywhere—not now, and not for a long time. Neither was I.

Then another picture came into my mind, one more memory which helped me understand what God was trying to say. Once, when the boys and I built their tree house, I had hammered a bunch of great big nails into the apricot tree. Later on, a gardener told me that the iron would feed the tree, and cause it to produce bigger and better fruit. I wasn't sure if there was any scientific basis for his statement, but it seemed to have been proven true. Once the nails were there, our tree produced multiplied dozens of juicy apricots—more than it had ever yielded before.

Nails—nails to produce fruitfulness . . . Nails had hung Jesus to the rugged Calvary tree. His death had brought forth His resurrection, and had made abundant life available for all who would believe.

Raul had died to his old ways. He had nailed his past to the cross of Jesus, as the Bible instructs us to do. Now he was truly experiencing life! Meanwhile, I wasn't thinking of the One I was supposed to be loving with all my heart, my soul, and my mind. I was thinking of myself.

I wasn't looking forward to heaven, to an eternity shared with my Maker, the Lover of my soul. I was looking forward to having my personal desires fulfilled during my earthly lifetime. By continuing that outlook, I would miss all that God had for me.

I was trying to save my own life, to live it my own way. Now, in order to find true life, I had to die, too. That's all there was to it.

The Master Shipbuilder

11

Like the old steamer in Valparaiso, my ship needed to
be restored for the voyages ahead. Only God could make
it fit to carry me to life's various ports and to battle the
ocean's storms. I would have to die to my ways and
submit to His ways, His will, and the skillfulness of His
hands. I could not repair myself.

I must have heard the words a thousand times: "I am
crucified with Christ, nevertheless I live." Now I was
about to learn their meaning, personally and practically.

We "die to ourselves" when we decide that our human
will can only make us barren, and therefore unhappy.

We "die" when we realize that God's plans and purposes for us are the only viable ones and must be
brought about in His way, in His time.

We "die" to this lifetime when we turn our eyes toward
eternity and cease to live for earthly satisfaction.

"Barren" is a very desolate word. It means unproductive, unfruitful, and sterile. Jesus taught that a vine
which doesn't produce fruit is cut off, withers, and is
then thrown into the fire.

He also said that if a branch is purged and cut back it
will bring forth much fruit. I had been in the church all

my life, growing like a wild weed, doing whatever I pleased. Now creation's Husbandman wanted to purge me. He began to cut off my dead branches so I could produce something useful, even sweet. I wondered what it would be.

I looked up the word "barren" in my Bible concordance. I found a Scripture written to the bride of Christ, the church. This passage, found in the Book of Isaiah, became the foundation upon which I was to build the remaining years of my life:

> Sing, O barren, thou that didst not bear; break forth into singing, and cry aloud, thou that didst not travail with child: for more are the children of the desolate than the children of the married wife, saith the Lord (Isaiah 54:1).

The Lord was calling me to rejoice. He wanted me to realize a great truth: A desolate (or in my case, lonely) woman can be more spiritually fruitful than a woman whose life is absorbed only by her husband and her natural children.

"Enlarge the place of thy tent," the Scripture continued, "and let them stretch forth the curtains of thine habitations: spare not, lengthen thy cords, and strengthen thy stakes." In more simple words, Make room! Open your house and stretch your heart. Be strengthened in the Lord.

"For thou shalt break forth on the right hand and on the left." God made it clear to me that He had a plan for fruitfulness in my life. And, private as I had become since my high school days, the thought of this frightened me a little.

"Fear not; for thou shalt not be ashamed: neither be thou confounded; for thou shalt not be put to shame: for thou shalt forget the shame of thy youth . . . " I had been ashamed of my premarital pregnancy and my sick marriage. I suffered reproach over the horrible things Raul had once said to me. His words had wounded me, leaving scars that refused to be healed. Had God forgiven and forgotten? Then so should I.

"... and shalt not remember the reproach of thy widowhood any more. For thy Maker is thine husband; the Lord of hosts is His name...." The concept was new, revolutionary, and absolutely breathtaking! My Maker, the Lord of all creation, is my Husband! On my wedding day I had verbally said my vows to God. It was time for me to start living them.

Now the picture became even more clear. Even though I was married to Raul, the studio and the ministry occupied from five to six days and evenings a week. I was a widow—a widow chosen by God. He would care for me as my Husband. He was calling me to cleave to Him, to depend upon Him. I was to lean on Him for support and to draw my nourishment from Him alone.

At first I was elated. But then, as always, the glories of God's truth were soon overshadowed by my day-to-day life. Baseball games, loud drums, street hockey, Boy Scouts, unlovable pets, school outings, chauffeuring kids, dentist appointments, complaining neighbors, model building, bug collecting, stream fishing, boxing matches, and other unfeminine distractions made God's concepts seem distant and impractical.

How I missed my sister! And since Raul's conversion, Chrissy was no longer allowed to come to our house, so I missed her too. I only saw Aunt Phene once or twice a year. My South American childhood still affected me in that I felt out of place. It was still hard for me to relate to American people in an intimate way so I remained more or less friendless. I believe I chose not to establish roots in America so I would not be hurt as deeply as I had been when I left Chile. Inspired as I had been by God's Word, it wasn't long before loneliness began to taunt me.

One day a huge ten-year old boy came knocking on my front door.

"Hi, my name is Tony."

"Hi, what can I help you with?" I barely opened the door.

"Can I come in?"

"No, I don't think so. What do you want?"

"Aren't you Raulie and Shane's mom?"

"Yes."

"Well, then why can't I come in?" he questioned insistently and stuck his big foot in my front door so I couldn't close it.

"I think you better go right now!" I said sternly.

"No!" he persisted.

"What on earth do you want?"

He removed his foot, looked down and sadly said, "Oh . . . nothing" as he walked away.

"Suffer [let, allow] little children to come unto me and forbid them not: for of such is the kingdom of God." I could hear Christ's words commanding me, burning in my heart.

"He's not little!" I pointed out to God. There was a moment of deafening silence.

"Hey, Tony!" I ran out to the street. Tony played hard-to-get.

"Whaddaya want?" he yelled in disgust.

"Come back later and I'll tell you some Bible stories."

Tony's face lit up with a smile. He came back 30 minutes later, bringing the entire neighborhood with him. Tony worked energetically to set up a huge classroom in the garage. Later on it was moved into our house.

Raulie, Shane, and I would put on puppet shows and plays. We would dance, sing, and plan contests and exciting outings for all the children. By the time my sons started school, it wasn't unusual to share our breakfast and devotion time with six or eight boys who would stop to pick them up on their way to school. It bothered my boys if their friends didn't know Jesus, so they would tell them about Him as soon as they could. Most of the children gave their lives to Christ and are still in love with Him today.

For years Tony nearly drove me to insanity, insisting that I teach him anything and everything I knew. He squeezed out every ounce of patience I had ever had, and drove me to plead with God for more. Mercilessly, he chipped away at my accumulated layers of old paint.

During the years that I was docked, Tony was my constant companion. Since then dozens of my sons' friends have been welcome in my house, giving me plenty of excuses to repaint, remodel, and redecorate. Just as the Scripture had taught me, with God's help I have "... enlarged ... stretched forth ... spared not ... lengthened and strengthened" not only my tent, and my heart, but also the hearts of my children.

In the meantime, Raul's Bible study was still growing dramatically and was demanding his constant attention. By then we were having double sessions in the kung fu studio and renting buildings for the kids. Raul had a group of faithful men working with him, so there wasn't as much for me to do there. It was at this time that Debbie and Steve entered our lives. Debbie and I soon discovered that God had revealed to each of us His role as our Husband. Some years later Debbie would show me, as no one else could, how our "marriages" with Him only begin on this earth, and soon will lead us all into his wonderful presence forever.

Raul continued to be gone day and night, teaching Bible studies, visiting schools, studying, and doing kung fu exhibitions. We didn't even ride in the same car any more. He left at dawn on Sundays to pray and meditate on the Scriptures. How I missed him.

But God had a message for me even in my yearning for my husband. His absence became another nail, one that gnawed at me every day. Its wound continues to feed my branches.

I still miss Raul on a daily basis. I have never become accustomed to his being gone. And, truthfully, I never want to get used to being without him. I like longing for him. It teaches me self-control. It forces me to die to my desires, and it drives me to Jesus. It's a down-to-earth teaching on how we, the bride of Christ, should yearn for our Lord. Our hearts should be longing painfully for His return.

We live in a day when people are afraid to hurt. We run to and fro, searching for something or someone to relieve the aching inside. Pain cleanses the soul, it adds character to its recipient. If we do not suffer, we cannot receive the depth of God's comfort. If we have not been wounded, we have not felt the tender touch of the Healer. If we have not been alone, we have really not understood the sweetness of His constant companionship. Pain writes the songs and teaches the lessons by which man is comforted. My necessary separation from Raul has birthed in me a longing for heaven, where there is no loneliness or pain.

One evening Raul burst through the door, bringing some totally exciting news. "A couple of the guys and I are going to go to Chile to 'spy out the land.' We want to see about doing some missionary work there." Joshua had done the same thing before the Hebrew children entered the Promised Land to possess it. Was my Promised Land coming into sight, too?

"When are we leaving?"

"I'm sorry, Sharon, but you can't go."

"I can't go? Why?"

"This is ministry, Sharon. Women can't go along."

I had been involved in ministry all my life. Never once had I felt that I was not a part of my dad's ministry. Our family had always been "the Farrels, who are missionaries."

But, much to my amazement, I heard a self-controlled Sharon say, "You'll love Chile. It's wonderful!"

Raul's early experience in the ministry only involved working with men. At that time, he didn't understand a woman's role. Later, as he looked deeper into the Scriptures, he learned that Jesus and the apostles were surrounded with women who ministered to their needs and to the needs of others. Paul called them his co-workers and fellow servants. Jesus honored devout women in an even more significant way. He allowed them to be the last to see Him on the cross, and to be the first to see Him alive again. It was a woman that God chose to proclaim the good news of the resurrection!

Raul left for Bible study and I flopped onto Grandma's couch. "Snip, snip!" I could hear heaven's pruning shears cutting at my dead branches of unbelief, pride, and anxiety.

"Not yet," the Gardener whispered to my heart.

I became angry, with a talking-through-my-teeth kind of anger.

It's okay to question God. Just don't sin against Him or accuse Him falsely while you're blowing off hot air.

"Why can't I go?" I confronted Him. "You know I've always wanted to go to Chile. I've been waiting for 13 long years!" As if He didn't remember.

"Is it fair that I'm home with all the work, the boys, and everything else? Is it fair that I babysit all the kids at church and don't get to do the things I want to do! Raul is gone all the time. I'm sick of doing it all alone." My angry flesh exploded, and then I fell silent.

I decided now that I'd said my piece, I'd best be quiet and listen. I really didn't expect an answer—not after that emotional outburst. I didn't even open my Bible for once. I closed my eyes in silence.

In my mind's eye, I pictured an immensely large, strong ox. Its muscles were bulging with power.

"That's you," said an inner voice.

"Thanks, I always wanted to be an ox."

Then a Scripture came into my mind:

> Take my yoke upon you, and learn of me; for
> I am meek [power under control] and lowly
> [humble] in heart: and ye shall find rest unto
> your souls. For my yoke is easy, and my burden
> is light (Matthew 11:29,30).

I understood that I was to put on Christ's yoke—that was His will for me. I needed to learn the way our Servant God leads us in His service. I was to submit in unquestioning obedience to the One who controls the existence of everything. He would give my anxious heart rest.

I also perceived that the ox is the symbol of servanthood in the Bible. God was calling me to be a willing servant.

I then pictured this ox pulling a very small cart bearing my two rambunctious little boys. The ox's neck was uncomfortably enclosed in an enormous two-oxen yoke which was leaning awkwardly toward one side. One ox was clearly missing, and if he had been there he would have held the yoke in balance. I was trying to bear a yoke made for two oxen by myself.

I knew who the missing party was, of course. It was Raul. My life without him seemed unbalanced—it rubbed, it put too much weight on my shoulders. I had worn myself out complaining about it.

"Is that fair?" I asked God as I visualized the scene.

Then I pictured Him, the Just One who bore the cruelty of the cross. With His nail-scarred hand, He picked up the yoke on the empty side and held it just right, releasing the pressure from the ox. He bore the burden Himself.

"What if I lighten your load?" a soft voice whispered to my heart. I felt a tremendous surge of joy and understanding.

"Anytime, my Lord" was my ardent reply.

Little by little, I was developing a keen sense of hearing.

God was speaking through His Word to my conscience. Chipping away the paint from my landlocked ship was a difficult chore, but it felt so healthy, so wonderful. I was beginning to feel brand-new and ready to sail. All I needed was a destination!

Raul was deeply moved by my newly developing relationship with Christ. He asked me to communicate what God had done for me with the women in our church. Perhaps I might even start a women's study. I was a private person, remember? I didn't like telling people about my past life. It was buried and that was that. Besides, how could I handle a women's study. What would I do with a bunch of American women anyway? I had already failed once when I had tried to get women together to sew items for the mission field. That was enough for me! I turned down the offer without ever asking God.

After a terrible injury suffered during a kung fu exhibition, Raul's brother, Xavier, received the miracle of the indwelling Jesus into his life. When he married a beautiful girl named Trudy, she promptly decided to be my best friend. At first her company bothered me. She came to our home frequently, and I was always busy in my career as a homemaker, mom, neighborhood watchman, and sitter. I really had no time to visit with anyone.

Furthermore, I couldn't relate to her at all. She was young and a very typical American girl. I finally decided that if she was going to hang around, she'd just have to watch me do my stuff.

It didn't bother her a bit. If I sewed, she'd bring her machine over and sew right alongside me. If I cleaned, she would help me. We planted flowers, cooked, shopped; what I did, she did. And, unbelievable as it seems, when I got pregnant, she did too. We have the proof.

Trudy and I became the best of friends. She was a woman that God chose to be my intimate friend. He brought her to the place where I was docked, knowing that she would paint my surfaces bright and sunny colors—all the exotic hues I loved.

Her sense of humor was just what I needed. Because of the adventurous life I had once led, my present life seemed boring. She taught me to joke about the menial duties that chained me. I learned that even imprisonment could be productive.

My thoughts turned toward Joseph, whose story appears in the Book of Genesis. Unjustly sold as a slave by his jealous brothers, Joseph was falsely accused and imprisoned. But he channeled his heartbreaking circumstances into productivity. First, by being a good steward, he received the position of Pharoah's prison warden. Later, when God finally had him released, he was placed second in command to Pharaoh, ruling over the great nation of Egypt.

From his prison cells, the apostle Paul wrote letters of comfort and instruction. His sole transgression was that he was an ardent follower of Jesus Christ and a vagabond missionary of the highest rank. Guilty of following in Jesus' steps, he became an "ambassador in bonds." In his teachings, he relates the Christian walk to prison life, calling himself a "prisoner of the Lord Jesus Christ."

Maybe someday I, too, would write something—a song or a poem that would share how chains of love have held me to His will.

Our church started meeting in a rented theater, holding double sessions of approximately 500 people each. Still it continued to grow. Raul's heart rejoiced with each person that made a decision for Christ. He had only one desire: to declare the love of God to a decaying world.

Although he studied the Word eight hours a day, searching it from cover to cover, his passion for it compelled him to crowd his schedule even more. He enrolled in a Christian university.

I had been taking kung fu lessons so I could spend a little extra time with Raul. I took a beating three nights a week to be with this guy! I would have preferred to be wrapped up in a blanket with him in front of the fireplace, kissing and eating popcorn until Jesus came back and caught us!

Again, God had other plans. I was about to be further refined by the "little things" in life—things which either sharpen your character or shred it to pieces.

Raul was in the kitchen having breakfast: Trudy sat next to him.

"Guess what, my dear?" I couldn't wait to surprise him. "We're going to have another baby!"

"No! It can't be!" He jumped up excitedly. Raul Jr. was seven and Shane was six. I'd had two miscarriages in the past two years, and we'd felt our childbearing days were over. I have never seen Raul so happy!

How an intelligent human being can call his offspring a "product of conception," minimizing his humanity in order to cover his murderous act of abortion, is beyond my comprehension. There is nothing as exhilarating as having a baby, especially when you know that God is the originator of life. The miracle of it, of two becoming one, leaves the greatest minds baffled.

Trudy was happy for me, but I had learned to read her mind. She wanted a baby, too! Within four months, she conceived. We thoroughly enjoyed ourselves getting fat together and reminiscing about all the perils I had survived with Raulie and Shane.

We named our new son Ryan Brent ("little king"). Along with him came the usual little furniture, little clothes, little stories, little hurts, little tears, little friends, little time, little sleep, and mountains of diapers to be changed, washed, folded, and stacked!

One morning I woke up early. Ryan had been up all night. The entire house had been set up to accommodate Raulie and Shane's army battlefield. They had barricaded every door with booby traps that fell on my head, rang bells, or entwined around my legs. Meanwhile, a dozen unfinished boys' outfits were piled on my sewing machine, the kitchen was its usual mess, Grandma's couch was still warped, and a heap of "smelling fresh" diapers that almost reached my waist lay in the middle of my bedroom floor, defying me to fold them.

I hated the diapers—every single last clean one of them. They looked like an altar where something needed to be sacrificed, like the altars in the Old Testament where our forefathers sacrificed lambs to God.

I knew very well that Christ had become "... the Lamb of God, which taketh away the sin of the world." He had offered Himself as the final sacrifice.

There was only one thing that needed to be sacrificed around our house. Me. I had to die—again—to my will. I needed to submit, once and for all, to the life God had called me to live. I lived in America, not on the mission field. I was constantly alone, restricted from Raul's companionship. I was surrounded by children day and night.

"Oh God, help me!" I cried out, as I threw myself on top of the diapers, flat on my back. Then I quoted my dying prayer right out of Romans 12:1, personalizing it to fit my need. I recited it the way Americans pledge the flag.

"I present my body a living sacrifice, holy, and acceptable unto God which is my reasonable service. I will not be conformed to this world but I will be transformed by the renewing of my mind that I may prove what is the good, and acceptable, and perfect will of God. Amen."

That was it. I was totally sick of trying to make God's will happened for me. I needed to kill all my desires for Chile, the Colombian mission on the hill, and everything I had ever dreamed of becoming. I gave the Master Shipbuilder my life completely, to design it, construct it, and finish it as He pleased, ready for the destination of His choice—no questions asked.

"I will be a living sacrifice." (I still thought it would be a bit more exciting to be a martyr out in the jungle somewhere.)

"I will be holy and acceptable." This wasn't because of my good behavior. It was because He'd cleansed me with His blood, and that was sufficient for me!

"Through His renewing of my mind, I will become transformed. I will allow His good, acceptable, and perfect will to bleed through my being."

It wasn't the first time I would have to put my will on an altar. It wouldn't be the last, either. But isn't eternity forever? This life is only the beginning. And, fortunately, that gives the Shipbuilder, my Maker, all the time He needs to prepare me for the voyages of His choosing.

Traveling First-Class

12

The magnificent snowcapped Andes Mountains can be seen from any part of Santiago. As a young girl, I had taken that for granted. Now, at 34, I savored every detail of Chilean life, culture, and scenery. The main walk in the center of the city was lined with vendors. Many displayed the ship-shaped carts I recalled from childhood, black smoke rising from their smokestacks, their "decks" filled with goodies of all sorts. A crowd of people gathered around the organ man as his monkey grasped for pesos, one after another.

Santiago had grown into a modern, dynamic metropolis. I took dozens of pictures of contemporary glass high rises. These contrasted starkly with the older, more ornate buildings and streetlights which stood in European-style splendor, having survived decades of devastating earthquakes and abuse from times of revolution.

It was a warm October evening. The harsh Chilean winter was over, and every citizen of Santiago seemed to be parading in the streets, enjoying the emerging spring. I was outside for my own reasons, absorbing every aspect of the life I had missed for so long. Any moment I expected to wake up out of this exhilarating dream, but I never did. This was real! It was really me walking on the streets of Chile after 21 years of yearning.

A tugging in Raul's heart had first brought us to this country two months before. I had spent much of the two weeks in my hotel room, looking up acquaintances in the telephone book.

I was delighted to locate my little red-haired friend, Francisca (Panchy) Inostrosa—the one who counted while we played hide-and-seek. It took me a while to find her, but I finally did. Jobless and living with her mother, she had also been a victim of life's cruelty. She had lost her nine-year job as an assistant director at the national television station. An actress for six years before that, she was now unemployed and had suffered the blows of two broken marriages. Due to erroneous child-rearing beliefs she had accumulated throughout her life, she and her little son were having a thoroughly miserable time together.

After spending about an hour reminiscing about the old days, laughing hilariously, and taking pictures, she suddenly turned to me and asked the question of a lifetime: "You're different, Sharon. What do I have to do to be happy like you?"

"Be in love with Jesus" was my immediate reply.

I gave her a Bible and told her to start reading in the Book of John. She has since begun to work out life's problems according to God's ways, and she's reaping the benefits.

Today Panchy works with Lindy Mann, one of our church's missionaries in Chile. She answers most of his mail personally, responding to the hundreds of young people who tune in to Lindy's highly popular radio program. Meanwhile, in several orphanages throughout the city, she brings Bible stories alive, teaching young and old alike about the character of God and how He relates to their lives.

After visiting with several other childhood companions on this second trip, at last I found Fernando Leighton, who today is well-known in Chile as a television director, and producer of a very popular talk-show. Like me, he had been deeply wounded by the misfortunes of life. How thankful I was to learn that he was now married to a beautiful woman, the proud father of three gorgeous children. It was so good to see him, to know that he was well and happy.

During our visit, we poured out the past. The moments were intense. I told him about my Husband, my Maker, who had won my heart to Himself. Fernando, too, had been earnestly seeking Him and was convinced that all creation displayed His handiwork.

When I returned two years later, I sensed the peace that only God can give beginning to control his life. By the Lord's grace alone, today we are the kind of dear friends that I always longed for us to be.

This second trip had brought me to Santiago with two of our church staff's personnel. Our intention was to organize a music festival, with the purpose of presenting Jesus to the young Chilean community in a nonreligious format.

Chile, like many countries in the world, is swamped with the kind of artificial religious piety that is not only disgusting in the sight of man, but is an insult to the heart of God. This kind of religiosity oppresses individuals who sincerely seek intellectual understanding of the Creator's works. It also stands in the way of a truly spiritual, intimate relationship with Him.

The city had closed down for the weekend, so there wasn't much we could do about the "Escape Festival" until Monday. I decided to stroll through the crowds by myself while my friends entertained themselves at a nearby arcade. As I rounded a corner, a strange encounter occurred. I was abruptly stopped by the most handsome man I have ever seen.

His skin was very white, completely unblemished. Soft, jet-black curls crowned his head. He was tall, and perfectly built. I can still see the long black eyelashes that fringed his deep blue eyes. He quickly looked me over from head to toe.

"Hello, most beautiful woman," he spoke seductively.

"Hi." I knew instinctively that I should have ignored him, but I answered automatically. I hadn't seen anything like this in years. I'd been home having babies!

"What are you doing in my country?" His piercing look immobilized me. I noticed different shades of blue blending in his eyes.

"We're here to do a Christian concert and . . ." For a second I thought I would tell him about Jesus, but in the middle of my sentence, I realized that something peculiar was going on. I began to tremble with fear, even though I was perfectly safe, surrounded by hundreds of people and within sight of several policemen.

"I want you," he said confidently, with no hesitation whatsoever.

By now I was panic-stricken. My legs grew weak, feeling as if they might actually collapse under me. I didn't know where to go. I had told my companions I would meet them on that same corner in another hour. I spotted a bench in the middle of the walkway, and told the man I had to go and wait for my friends. I turned my back on him and walked away. He followed me, sitting down close beside me.

"Let's go for a walk. I want to show you something," he said trying to coax me.

I wasn't about to go anywhere with this seducer. Yet I found myself fighting a strong urge to look at him, to study him. Such physical perfection is seldom seen in a man. Inwardly I cried out to the most beautiful of all, the

Lord of lords. The man left and I was rescued.

Later on, I thought of the time when the prince of this world, Satan, had taken Jesus to an "exceeding high mountain." He had shown Him all the kingdoms of the world and offered them to Him, if He would fall down and worship him.

I had seen men approach women before, preying on their emptiness. But never in my life have I felt such evil, luring deception as I sensed in that man. I went to bed that night thinking about a verse of warning: ". . . for Satan himself is transformed [fashions himself] into an angel of light."

As I asked God for His wisdom regarding this incident, He showed me that He was alerting me to the temptations of every kind that lay in my path. I had been docked to prepare my ship for battle. I could expect the enemy to launch a full-scale attack against me and my endeavors. I became keenly aware of the presence of spiritual warfare. I think it's probably the same sensation a soldier feels when he's dropped out of a helicopter into the middle of a firefight.

The apostle Paul instructed us in Ephesians 6:12,13:

> We wrestle not against flesh and blood, but against principalities, against powers, against the rulers of the darkness of this world, against spiritual wickedness in high places. Wherefore take unto you the whole armor of God, that ye may be able to withstand in the evil day.

He has acquainted us with methods for fighting these rulers of darkness. We are to put on God's armor, as described in His Word. Paul graphically compared the Christian's attire to that of a soldier of his day to whom the apostle was probably chained during the time he wrote this portion of Scripture. He certainly would have had a good look at his guard's weapons and attire.

I understood that the pure, simple message of Christ was not welcome in Chile, in America, or anywhere else on earth where Satan is successfully beguiling men to himself. Man, through the lusts of his flesh, willingly sinks into corruption, not recognizing his tempter. The devil certainly knows the bait necessary to lure the weak in spirit into a hideous eternity without God.

How easily man's confidence in his acquired knowledge, financial situation, career, or standing in society causes him to loathe the wisdom of God. The Scripture says that the world by its own wisdom cannot know God. It also asserts that God's foolishness is wiser than man's wisdom, and His weakness stronger than man's might. God promises that He will ultimately make the self-reliant man look foolish.

My encounter with the handsome tempter reminded me that within myself I didn't have the intellectual, spiritual, or physical capacity to withstand the enemy's assault. This was big-time stuff. Unlike the situation at home, we weren't trying to share Christ with just a neighborhood. We were exposing Him to an entire country! It was exciting to realize that as different as the circumstances were, however, the biblical principles I had learned at home would serve me well here, too. Power comes from God, through prayer and obedience to His Word.

I knew it worked—it was prayer and obedience that had accomplished one of the greatest victories in our lives.

When God first convicted me about the barrenness of my life, He immediately told me to forgive Raul's family and to reach out to them once again. Even during our estrangement from them, we had continued to pray for them. Now, one by one, the members of the Ries family began to present their hearts to God.

receive manifold more in this present time,
and in the world to come life everlasting.

I thought of my sons, who have followed us onto the mission field. Many times they have given up their vacation months for the promise of greater rewards. Today it is evident that they have not suffered! On the contrary, they have been marvelously enriched. Raul and I are grateful to share the love, joy, and excitement that surrounds them. They are our best friends and we are theirs. Now they, too, have an exciting vision to contribute to the world. Better yet, we plan to spend eternity together.

God has given me countless opportunities to cooperate in music outreaches, pastors' conferences, women's retreats, orphanage visits, and communion with those who, like me, are enthralled with Christ. But no matter how many times I've gone to the mission field, my two-to-four-week journey's have never completely satisfied my yearning to remain in "the regions beyond."

Here in this country where we enjoy the means and the freedom of worship, we have our choice of several dozen radio or TV teachers. We can hear what we want, depending on the mood we're in. In some countries there isn't one Bible-teaching radio program.

"Oh Father," I often prayed after returning home from South America, "why should I stay here where there is such an overabundance of Your truth? In Your Word You said to Your Son, 'Ask of Me, and I shall give thee the heathen for thine inheritance, and the uttermost parts of the earth for thy possession!' That's what I'm asking for, Lord—that you may use me to reach the hearts of the heathen in the uttermost parts of the world for You! Is that too much to ask for? If it is, I am sorry."

Time and again I lifted this secret prayer to God. In one sense, my heart had learned contentment. But it continued to throb with passion for those who are unacquainted with Christ's love.

Raul called me from work one day. "Sharon, you won't believe this!"

I probably would believe it, knowing Raul and knowing God.

"Some movie producers want to make a film of my life."

"Incredible! When?"

"They're coming out next week. They want us to record some information about our lives on tape so they can write the script."

"Raul, I'm not telling anybody about my life. That's private! I've never told anyone about my pregnancy. My parents are missionaries and know thousands of people in South America. I don't want to shame them and . . ." I rattled on.

"Well, you'd better talk to God about it because I know it's His will for us. Stop thinking about yourself. Think about the people it will help. I'm going to do it with or without your approval."

I lay flat on the couch, reasoning with myself. If God had cast my sins as far as the east is from the west, remembering them no more, why did the whole world have to know about them? What was the purpose? God was blessing our ministry in a wonderful way. Thousands of people were being fed from the Scriptures. The missionary vision, which had first captivated Raul and me, was spreading throughout our church.

"Father, only if You command it, I will do it in Jesus' Name. But why do I have to be a spectacle for all to see?"

The answer was simple. It came from the heart of Jesus: "I was made a spectacle before all the world. And I was sinless."

Humbled, I contemplated His Words to me. Two thousand years before, Christ had borne His cross, with angry throngs pressing against Him from all around. In the terrible hours that followed, He allowed Himself to be hung between heaven and earth, suffering the reproach and scorn of mankind. Only His angels and those who loved Him stood in silent adoration while the earth trembled and groaned at the insanity and blasphemy of it all. The Creator had allowed Himself to be crushed and put to shame by His own created beings. This is the way He chose to demonstrate the depth of His love for us.

"Yes, Lord." My heart submitted, knowing that it was Christ's obedience to the Father that had brought new life into the decaying heart of mankind. I would obey, too.

In the days to follow, God's purpose for using my life story became more evident to me. In the Book of Revelation, we can read that Satan, the dragon or accuser of the brethren, is overcome by the blood of the Lamb and by the Word of the saints' testimony. I already knew that the blood of the Lamb could cleanse my sins and defend me from Satan. But I had never realized that my testimony is also an overcoming weapon. I became excited about what God would do with it, and how it would affect the heart of man. Christ had become a spectacle to give life to man. Why shouldn't I, in order to point them to Him?

Keenly aware of the way God uses man's testimony, Satan set out to mentally torture me. As our story was written and the movie was filmed, it became extremely difficult for me to relive my past in such a detailed form. Some days I hated Raul for what he had done to me. I wanted him to pay. I fought the strongest urges to leave him that I have ever felt. How wicked my heart can become at times! Thank God, the cross of Jesus stood tall and reminded me daily that He had already paid the penalty for all of our sins—Raul's and mine.

Unless God brings the past to our remembrance for His own eternal purposes, it is not profitable to wallow in past hurts or to dig out that which has been forgiven and forgotten. He can always be trusted to work all things together for good—past, present, and future.

After the film was released, I went to several churches "under cover" to see people's reactions. One night hundreds of people were flowing into a well-known sanctuary in Los Angeles. In a self-protective daze, I joined them to see Sharon become a spectacle to the world. On my way in, a young man asked me, "Have you seen this movie?"

"Yes, I have," I answered, and not a word more.

"It changed my life!" he exclaimed.

I swallowed the lump that swelled in my throat. I sat down next to a large family which virtually bubbled with joy and laughter. One of the teenage girls sitting next to me politely asked, "Have you seen 'Fury to Freedom'?"

"Yes . . ." I barely answered.

"Well, it led our entire family to Jesus, and all my friends' lives have been changed because of it."

"I've experienced some drastic changes too," I agreed with her. That was enough for me. I had to get up and empty the hidden buckets of tears—tears of joy and shame mingled together. Joy, because of the words I had heard, bearing witness to the life-changing power of God through the film. Shame, because I'd been such a brat, trying to protect myself, as usual. Sometimes I wonder why God never gets sick of me. I do.

After this "soap opera" trauma, I was ready to continue my pursuit of missions. I went back to praying my "heathen, uttermost" prayer. One day while I meditated on this Scripture hoping to glean a profound revelation from it, gentle words crossed my mind.

"I've already given you the heathen and the uttermost parts of the world."

It occurred to me that, through the movie and Raul's book which had also been written, the two of us were about to become missionaries all over the world at the same time! We were going to the far corners of the globe, to small islands as well as vast continents, to prisoners as well as free men. We were in orphanages, churches, on street corners, with government officials, inside police headquarters, in the privacy of living rooms, behind enemy lines, here, there, and everywhere. What a God! He is a Mastermind with a master plan. It was so big I had almost missed it, and yet God had promised it to me all along:

> For I know the thoughts that I think toward you, saith the Lord, thoughts of peace, and not of evil, to give you an expected end [that which you long for] (Jeremiah 29:11).

At about this time, I began to realize that I was passionately in love with Jesus. His love for mankind was my obsession. His words and continuous guidance demonstrated the quality of love He had for me. I had an ardent desire to see Christ as He is, not as man sees Him, but as the Word of God portrays Him. Reading Scripture in this light gives me an even deeper desire to know Jesus as the Lover of my soul, Eternal Companion, and faithful Husband.

And you know what? Raul is never jealous of Him. When my relationship with Christ is thriving, my love for Raul has no bounds. When my fellowship with Jesus is broken, my relationship with Raul suffers, too. Chapter 5 of the Song of Solomon gives a beautiful description of the Christ I long to behold:

> What is thy beloved [Jesus] more than another beloved, O thou fairest among women [the bride]? What is thy beloved [Jesus] more than another beloved [anything or anyone we love more than Christ].... My beloved is white [pure] and ruddy, the chiefest among ten thousand.

Now long ago, my caring Husband led me to Colombia with a group from our church. Our plan was to take the movie there, once it was completed.

Before leaving on our journey, we discussed some recent kidnappings, as well as the various other perils we might well encounter in the course of our travels. We encouraged ourselves as a group to willingly present our bodies as a sacrifice unto God if such a choice were to be made. This was easier said than done, I was soon to find out.

At the beginning or our trip, I went to Colombia's capital city of Bogota, in preparation for our outreach. Ricardo, our Colombian staff representative, was to accompany me to the main TV stations where we hoped to arrange for "Fury to Freedom" to be shown. After spending an entire day fighting traffic and being insulted, rejected, and ignored by television representatives and directors, I decided that we should shake the dust off our feet and leave Bogota.

There was one more station we hadn't tried. It was one of the biggest, so I figured they would surely turn us down. Ricardo, however, talked me into going. I was so disgusted that I actually didn't want them to have the privilege of hearing the gospel! When I went up to the information desk I spoke in English, hoping that no one would understand. The gentleman at the desk got very excited and dialed a number quickly.

"There is a woman here who cannot speak a word of Spanish. I think she's a producer from the U.S.A.!" he explained rapidly. Ricardo, who had studied in the United States and is perfectly bilingual, glanced at me and we both giggled at God's cleverness.

The next thing we knew, we were sitting in the office of one of the major directors of that network. At the other station, I had tried to evade telling them that the movie was about Christ and His changing power in man's life, in order to get their attention. This time, I really didn't care! I blurted out the facts, wanting to finish what I had reluctantly started. I was looking forward to joining our group on the other side of the steep mountains, down in the city of Villavicencio.

"This movie is what our country needs!" the man exclaimed. "Come back next week and we'll discuss the possibility of airing it." He talked as if we lived right around the corner.

Again, I learned that God and His people travel first-class. He won't settle for anything less. "Smooth sailing. . . ." I smiled to myself. And so it was, until we found ourselves on the treacherous road that winds through the mountains, and sometimes slides down the hills and into the Colombian rivers.

Ricardo was to drive, and Alejandro, a recording music artist from our staff, was to serve as copilot. I made my bed in the backseat of the car, deciding to sleep the mountain ordeal out of existence. For some reason, hundreds of trucks decided to escort us that night. Our exhaust and the exhaust from their poorly maintained engines was so dense that it obscured our vision of the dense greenery, wild-growing orchids, hundreds of waterfalls and, thank God, the cliffs around each bend. Then, to my great discomfort, I began to react to the fumes. I didn't want to complain. After all, hadn't we been trained to endure hardship?

I started to black out, but I held my peace.

I opened the window, but it made matters worse. Panic gripped me. I was losing consciousness.

"Ricardo, can you please stop for a little bit? I feel kind of sick." I was still trying to minimize the problem. Ricardo pulled over.

"You look really sick!" He was clearly worried.

Alejandro added, "You look absolutely green, Sharon. What's wrong with you?"

They both began to rub my tingling head and hands, trying to get my blood to circulate. Determined to carry on, I encouraged them to keep driving. They helped me get back in the car. Ricardo inched along, hoping it would help. It didn't. Desperation and sickness washed over me in immense waves. This road in itself was a death threat. If something happened to me, it would be impossible to get any help. Was this it for me?

Then somehow, between the blackouts, a verse I had learned as a little girl glimmered in my mind: "I will lift up mine eyes unto the hills, from whence cometh my help . . ." (Psalm 121:1).

I looked up. A full moon shone back at me in all its splendor and glory.

"God, I'm so sorry, but if I survive this, I don't ever want to travel this road again. I don't really care if the movie gets on TV or not. I don't have the courage to go on. What a flake I am! I'm sorry. Forgive me, please. If there's any other way, show me. But it can't involve this road. I know You understand. You're the only one who knows how I feel." I lay my head against the window and waited to pass out.

All at once my thoughts were stilled. Jesus' Gethsemane prayer came into my mind: "Oh my Father, if this cup [His death on the cross] may not pass away from me, except I drink it, thy will be done" (Matthew 26:42). I could just hear Jesus saying to me, "I know. I didn't want to hang on the cross either." He understood how I felt. What I was going through was nothing compared to what He had suffered.

"Thy will be done," I whispered.

Instantly I was healed. I no longer felt sick, and the fumes were no longer affecting me. I took a quick look in the mirror. My hair looked like a used mop and my makeup was smeared, but my cheeks were regaining their color.

"I'm okay, guys! Speed up! Let's get this show on the road. We have places to go, people to meet, movies to show. . . . I'm well! God's healed me!"

"Are you sure?" asked Alejandro.

"Of course I'm sure! It's my body and I can tell!"

The rest of the trip was trouble-free. And it was well worth the trouble it had caused. *Fury to Freedom* was the feature film on Colombian television the following Christmas Eve. Our missionary commitment was bearing fruit at last.

Not long after this threat upon my life, just as I was about to address a large group of women, I received an emergency call from Raul. "Debbie is dying." I couldn't believe my ears. After speaking, I drove home, weeping all the way.

"Father, please spare her life," I cried out, again and again.

"Why, God?" I asked.

When I got home, a verse from Song of Solomon answered my question: "My beloved [Jesus] spoke and said unto me [His bride], 'Rise up, my love, my fair one, and come away.' " Her eternal Groom was calling her home; her time on earth was over.

Debbie died two weeks later.

The casket was closed. I wouldn't have looked anyway. I wanted to remember her the way she looked the last time I saw her. We had been together on the beach in front of her house. She had stood looking out toward the ocean the whole time, not wanting to miss one glimpse of the sunset. Her wavy, dark-brown hair was blowing freely in the wind. She was a beautiful woman indeed.

There was a wide, white ribbon wrapped around the casket with the inscription "Steve Loves Debbie." Pictures of her and all her children were sitting on top of it. Behind stood a brand-new surfboard her husband and children had been planning to give her for Christmas.

Steve, her husband who had worked with us in the early days of our ministry, was now an assistant pastor at a sister fellowship near the beach. He performed Debbie's funeral himself, his voice trembling with every word: "On her finger she wore a ring with the inscription 'Jesus' on it." He struggled to continue. "You see, she belonged to Him."

I looked down at my hands; I wore one too.

Steve preceded to compare his wife to the virtuous woman who is described in Proverbs 31. I agreed with his description. But no other love, not even a love as deep as Steve's, had kept Debbie from the Master's hold on her life.

And now she was free at last—free from the body that had held her captive, free to spend eternity with her Husband, her Maker.

Debbie's death confirmed in my spirit the importance of placing our eyes on eternal values. Until the day of Jesus' return or my own death, I determined I would "lay up treasure in heaven." The fathers of our faith had their eyes focused on their eternal home. Even though all the desires of their hearts were not fulfilled in their lifetimes, they clung tenaciously to God's promises, confessing that they were strangers and pilgrims on the earth. "For [they] looked for a city which hath foundations, whose builder and maker is God."

I missed Debbie. My heart grieved for her husband, her lovely children, for all of us who remained behind. Although I was helpless to comfort her family, I was confident that God would be a mother to the children, and would meet Steve's emotional needs. I have learned that He is the All-Sufficient One, transforming Himself into whatever we require.

Jesus' words to His disciples comforted me, too:

> Let not your heart be troubled: ye believe in God, believe also in me. In my Father's house are many mansions: if it were not so, I would have told you. I go to prepare a place for you. And if I go . . . I will come again, and receive you unto myself; that where I am, there ye may be also (John 14:1-3).

Debbie looked forward to seeing her Lord, and she is with Him today. Someday my own longing for Him will be fulfilled. Someday He will come for me, too.

———————

Saturday morning arrived, and I hadn't seen Raul for two weeks. He'd promised me the day before that he would take me to the Queen Mary, a luxurious English passenger ocean liner that once proudly traveled the world's seas. Now she regally reigns in splendor over California's Long Beach Harbor, where thousands of international tourists examine her lavish dining halls, cabins, decks, and extravagant interiors.

The alarm rang. I woke up to a freshly cut red rose from my garden and a note lying on my nightstand. "Sorry, Sharon. I forgot I had to speak at a conference today. Be back late. I know you understand. I love you, Raul."

At first I was angry, and pulled the blanket over my head. My thoughts raced. Shall I be depressed today? The old urge came back to throw away the rose. But I no longer had my little green metal box where I had once stored all my love notes.

In yet another "living sacrifice" offering unto the Lord, I had burned its flattering contents in my fireplace. I had told God that I would be content with His love for me fearing that in my lonely hours, I might turn to them instead of Him for comfort.

I had made a wise choice then. Now I would make another. Why should I be depressed? I would visit the Queen Mary anyway. I would go with my Husband, my Maker.

"God, do You date?" I laughed at the silence.

"Of course You do. Let's go!" I jumped out of bed, showered, and dressed. I was determined to look gorgeous—for Him.

I drove with my Lord to the docks, ate lunch, bought myself a gift—and we thoroughly enjoyed the day. On the way out, I confidently walked along the deck, fully conscious of His company. I sensed a special glow about myself.

Now and then someone turned and looked my way. I wondered if they could see Him: my Captain—the One I travel with.

Other Good Harvest House Reading

QUIET MOMENTS FOR WOMEN
by *June Masters Bacher*

Though written for women, this devotional will benefit the entire family. Mrs. Bacher's down-to-earth, often humorous experiences have a daily message of God's love for you!

FROM FURY TO FREEDOM
by *Raul Ries*

Raul Ries was an angry young man bent on destruction—his own and that of his family. In a gripping true story of pain and personal tragedy, Raul reveals his struggle to escape the chains of "religion" and find deep and lasting relationships with God and his family. Foreword by Nicky Cruz.

STORMIE
by *Stormie Omartian*

The childhood of singer/songwriter Stormie Omartian, marred by physical and emotional abuse, led into teen and adult years filled with tragedy. Searching for an end to the inner turmoil which constantly confronted her, Stormie found herself on the verge of suicide. In this poignant story there is help and hope for anyone who doubts the value of his or her own life. It gloriously reveals a God who can bring life out of death if we are willing to surrender to His ways.

MEN OF STRENGTH FOR WOMEN OF GOD
Has the Time Come for Shared Spiritual Leadership?
by *F. LaGarde Smith*

The role of women in the church and home has
become one of the most significant issues facing us
today. At the heart of the matter are questions about
equality, rights, and leadership. How we address
these issues will determine not only the quality of our
relationships and our personal sense of worth, but
also the future well-being of the church.

F. LaGard Smith presents a timely look at the biblical
teachings regarding the role of women and clearly
establishes the evidence for the principle of male
spiritual leadership. With modern culture threatening
traditional biblical perspectives, here's the critical
thinking we need to reflect on God's original design.

OVERCOMING HURTS AND ANGER
by *Dr. Dwight Carlson*

Dr. Carlson shows us how to confront our feelings
and negative emotions in order to experience
liberation and fulfillment. He presents seven practical
steps to help us identify and cope with our feelings of
hurt and anger.

Dear Reader:

We would appreciate hearing from you regarding this Harvest House nonfiction book. It will enable us to continue to give you the best in Christian publishing.

1. What most influenced you to purchase *My Husband, My Maker*?
   - ☐ Author
   - ☐ Subject matter
   - ☐ Backcover copy
   - ☐ Recommendations
   - ☐ Cover/Title
   - ☐ _____

2. Where did you purchase this book?
   - ☐ Christian bookstore
   - ☐ General bookstore
   - ☐ Department store
   - ☐ Grocery store
   - ☐ Other

3. Your overall rating of this book:
   ☐ Excellent ☐ Very good ☐ Good ☐ Fair ☐ Poor

4. How likely would you be to purchase other books by this author?
   - ☐ Very likely
   - ☐ Somewhat likely
   - ☐ Not very likely
   - ☐ Not at all

5. What types of books most interest you?
   (check all that apply)
   - ☐ Women's Books
   - ☐ Marriage Books
   - ☐ Current Issues
   - ☐ Self Help/Psychology
   - ☐ Bible Studies
   - ☐ Fiction
   - ☐ Biographies
   - ☐ Children's Books
   - ☐ Youth Books
   - ☐ Other _____

6. Please check the box next to your age group.
   - ☐ Under 18
   - ☐ 18-24
   - ☐ 25-34
   - ☐ 35-44
   - ☐ 45-54
   - ☐ 55 and over

Mail to: Editorial Director
Harvest House Publishers, Inc.
1075 Arrowsmith
Eugene, OR 97402

Name _____

Address _____

City _____ State _____ Zip _____

Thank you for helping us to help you in future publications!